QBasic Programming
The Peter Norton Programming Series

Who This Book Is For

Introductory for intermediate QBasic programmers who want to develop and extend their programming expertise and add new performance to their programs.

What's Inside

- More than 100 ready-to-run programs that cover business, mathematical, and scientific programming applications

- Expert hints, tips, and ideas designed to increase program speed and power

- A special learn-by-doing task-oriented approach to programming that shows code in action in a direct, highly readable style

About the Peter Norton Microcomputer Libraries from Brady Publishing

All of the volumes in the Peter Norton Libraries, written in collaboration with The Peter Norton Computing Group, provide clear, in-depth discussions of the latest developments in computer hardware, operating systems, and programming. Fully tested and rigorously reviewed, these libraries deserve a special place on your bookshelf. These libraries are comprised of two series:

The Peter Norton Hardware Library gives you an insider's grasp of your computer and the way it works. Included are such best-selling classics as *Inside the IBM PC, Inside the Apple Macintosh,* and *The Hard Disk Companion.*

The Peter Norton Programming Library focuses on creating programs that work right away and offers the best tips and techniques in the industry. It includes *Advanced BASIC, Advanced Assembly Language, C++ Programming, Visual Basic, Advanced DOS,* and more.

QBasic Programming

David I. Schneider with
The Peter Norton Computing Group

Brady Publishing

New York   London   Toronto   Sydney   Singapore   Tokyo

Brady Publishing

A Divison of Simon & Schuster, Inc.
15 Columbus Circle
New York, NY 10023

Manufactured in the United States of America
10 9 8 7 6 5 4 3 2 1

Library of Congress Cataloging-in-Publication Data

Schneider, David I.
    QBasic Programming / David I Schneider and The Peter Norton
Computing Group.
        p. cm.
    Includes index.
    1. BASIC (Computer program language) 2. Microsoft QuickBASIC
(Computer program) I. The Peter Norton Computing Group.
II. Title.
QA76.73.B3S334   1991
005.265–dc20   91-22109
                                                                  CIP

ISBN 0-13-663022-7

Produced by Micro Text Publications

Contents

Limits of Liability and Disclaimer of Warranty

Trademarks

Preface

BASIC is the most popular computer language in the world. A recent survey revealed that 80% of the members of the Boston Computer Society use BASIC. Also, about 500,000 high school and college students enroll in BASIC courses each year. Hobbyists and recreational programmers like BASIC because it is easy to learn and allows the programmer to exercise all of the computer's capabilities. Professional programmers appreciate the speed and efficiency of developing small programs in BASIC.

The last 20 years have witnessed the arrival of many fine programming languages. Languages like C and Pascal have control structures that permit beautifully designed and easily maintained programs. Unfortunately, these control structures are missing from most of the versions of BASIC that have appeared since the language was invented at Dartmouth College in 1964.

QBasic, the version of BASIC packaged with MS-DOS 5.0, provides the best of both worlds. It is as easy to learn and use as the standard versions of BASIC and yet has the essential control structures and power of the "serious" languages like Pascal and C. Some of the features that make QBasic so appealing are:

- Full-featured editor
- Fast and efficient compilation

- Procedures
- Multiline functions
- Parameter passing
- Local, static, and global variables
- True recursion
- IF... THEN... ELSEIF... ELSE blocks
- SELECT CASE blocks
- DO loops
- Optional line numbers
- User-defined record variables

Overview of the Book

The first three chapters are preparatory. Chapter 1 answers some questions that you might have about QBasic; Chapter 2 shows how to create and execute a program; and Chapter 3 gives an in-depth demonstration of the editor. You can skip Chapter 3 if you have used WordStar, QuickPascal, Turbo Basic, or Turbo Pascal.

The fundamental programming structures and statements of QBasic are presented in Chapters 4–6. Although the greatest emphasis is given to those topics that are unique to QBasic, all the necessary concepts from Standard BASIC are reviewed.

Chapters 7 and 8 provide in-depth discussions of files, graphics, and sound. A knowledge of files is essential since most data used or generated by computer programs is stored in files. Graphics has steadily increased in importance as a programming tool due to the excellent graphics capabilities of microcomputers and the current interest in desktop publishing. Although the use of sound does not have the status of files or graphics, it is included because it's fun. Some in-depth applications of graphics and files appear in Chapters 9 and 10.

These last two chapters explore some applications in mathematics, science, and business programming. Some of the longer programs show how piecewise refinement is used to break a programming task into manageable chunks.

Programs

It is our conviction that programming concepts are best explained by illustrating them with careful examples. So, whenever possible, each new statement or structure is accompanied by a program or program segment that clarifies its use.

In addition, we present the following substantial programs that not only demonstrate how large problems can be broken into manageable chunks, but also accomplish useful tasks:

Program 7-21 — Examine and edit any file. This program allows you to see exactly what is in the files created by major spreadsheet and database software, and to alter the contents. Even non-ASCII files such as .EXE files may be examined and revised.

Program 9-7 — Graph a function. This user-friendly graphing program will even draw the graphs of functions with very large or undefined values. No matter what domain you specify for the function, the program guarantees that a pair of coordinate axes will be displayed. The scale range of values appearing as y-coordinates can either be given by the user or determined by the program.

Program 9-11 — Custom design characters. This program allows you to create up to 128 new characters that can be displayed in graphics mode.

Programs 9-12 through 9-14 — Manipulate matrices. These generic procedures, which add, multiply, and invert matrices, can be included into mathematics programs to perform matrix operations.

Program 10-3 — Analyze a loan. This program allows you to determine the amount that you can afford to borrow, the number of months it will take to pay off a loan, or the monthly payment on a load. After the details of the loan are determined, the program displays a complete amortization schedule.

Program 10-4 — Draw a pie chart. This generic program will produce a pie chart displaying up to 10 values. The programmer merely has to place the values and their descriptions into DATA statements. The program will draw the pie chart along with identifying legends.

Program 10-8 — Draw a bar chart. This generic program displays up to 37 user-supplied pieces of data in a vertical bar chart with descriptions below each bar. The program uses the largest data value to automatically determine the vertical scale. Also, procedures provide for fast printing of the chart.

Program 10-22 — Construct and manage a database. This generic, menu-driven program provides the standard tools found in major database management programs. Features include creating new databases by specifying field names and character counts, listing the contents of the database, sorting on an arbitrary field of the database, and appending, inserting, or editing records. One program does it all; there is no need to write a new program for each database that you wish to create and maintain. You can add new features to this general program and have them available for every database you use or create.

Prerequisites

This book assumes no prior knowledge of BASIC. QBasic builds on IBM PC BASIC. Therefore, if you already know IBM PC BASIC (or an equivalent, such as GW-BASIC), you have a head start. Actually, most programs written in IBM PC BASIC can be loaded as-is into QBasic and run successfully.

Introduction to QBasic

——

QBasic is the version of BASIC included with MS-DOS 5.0, the operating system software for IBM PC compatibles. It is the ideal language for beginning and intermediate programmers. Now, most especially if you're a beginner, you may have a number of questions about BASIC, and even about programming in general. This chapter addresses some of the questions you might have about QBasic, and provides other information that you need to know. Those who are familiar with computer programming and languages, and with past versions of BASIC, can safely skip the first part of this chapter, though you may want to skim over it just to refresh your memory. Information of particular interest to experienced BASIC users is included at the chapter's end.

About Computers and Programming Languages

As we stated in the Preface to this book, the original version of BASIC (an acronym that stands for **B**eginner's **A**ll-purpose **S**ymbolic **I**nstruction **C**ode) was developed at Dartmouth College in 1964 as a teaching language. The other computer languages prevalent at the time — including Assembly, Fortran, and COBOL — were much more difficult to learn and use, and were not necessarily suitable for beginning computer science students.

1

What is a computer language? Sometimes we old-timers tend to forget that not everyone in the world knows what we mean when we say "computer language," and that some who think they know are actually mistaken. So, in an effort to make sure we're all on the same wavelength, if nothing else, we'll go over some fundamental computer concepts, including languages, before returning to BASIC proper.

A *computer* is a device that performs numerical calculations and otherwise manipulates symbols according to a specified set of rules. The rules are conveyed to a computer in the form of a *program*, which is just a list of instructions and data that the computer can interpret and act upon. Each line in a program is usually called a *statement*; each statement usually conveys one instruction (example: add two specified quantities and store the result) to the computer's electronic innards.

You may know that modern computers are both *digital* and *binary*. That is, the information stored within them, be it instructions or data, takes the form of discrete, quantitized values (digits) which are stored in base-2, or binary, notation (example: in binary, the number 5 is represented as 101). Thus, in essence, what a computer is capable of understanding consists of long strings of ones and zeroes. A fixed code dictates how these strings of binary digits are interpreted.

That's good for the computer, but not so good for you and me. To tell a computer how to perform a task, which is what programming is all about, we have to feed it all these ones and zeroes, a cumbersome way for us to communicate. So early on, computer scientists came up with easier ways to communicate with computers. Computer *languages* were born.

Now a language — be it a computer language or a human one — is really a set of rules for forming statements, a statement simply being a way to communicate a piece of information. The earliest computer language was called *Assembly*; it associated a two-letter code with each possible computer command, and allowed numeric values to be represented in their conventional, base-10 form. Before the program could be loaded into the computer's memory and then executed (also known as "*run*"); it first had to be translated into a form the computer could understand (ones and zeroes) by a special program called an *assembler*.

Even Assembly proved difficult to use (as anyone who ever took the course in college can testify). Eventually, more complicated languages were developed, in which the two-letter codes were replaced by entire words. As we said earlier, Fortran and COBOL are two early examples.

It should be clear, however, that the tools of a journeyman are not necessarily appropriate for an apprentice. The wizards at Dartmouth came up with the language BASIC as a way of introducing computer programming fundamentals to beginning students. What's more, BASIC operated in a way that made it easier for students to check their results, by eliminating steps that other languages require before a program can be tested. We'll talk more about this later.

In the years after 1964, BASIC underwent many revisions and enhancements. In 1978, a national standard was adopted that gave the minimal requirements of BASIC. We refer to this minimal language as *Standard BASIC.*

The Basics about PC BASIC

BASICA is the enhanced version of BASIC written by the Microsoft Corporation for the IBM Personal Computer and packaged with versions of DOS prior to DOS 5.0. An equivalent form, known as GW-BASIC, is available for use with IBM PC compatibles. BASICA has about 190 commands and goes way beyond the power of most of the other versions of Standard BASIC.

Get Me an Interpreter

A couple of paragraphs back, we said that BASIC eliminated a step or two that other languages required before a program could be executed, or run. Now it's time to explain what we mean by that.

Recall we said that in order for the computer to execute a program directly, the program instructions must be in the ones and zeroes of machine language, a language that is very difficult to write in. If we write a program in any other language, the statements in our program must first be translated into machine language by another, special program. (This is the special step we mentioned above.) In most cases, the entire program is translated before it is run. But not with BASIC. BASIC is *interpreted.* And to interpret something, you need an interpreter, right?

An *interpreter* is a program, with machine language instructions, that has been written to understand and act upon the instructions in another language, such as BASIC. When the computer runs a Standard BASIC program, it actually executes another program that reads, understands, and acts upon each BASIC instruction in the first program, one statement at a time. A language that is executed in this manner is called an *interpreted language.*

One drawback to an interpreted language is that the computer must read and re-translate an instruction each time it is encountered — even if the computer encounters the same statement 1,000 times in a loop! This duplication of the interpretation wastes a lot of time. Such wasted time is not necessarily a problem for students learning about computers, but for professionals trying to develop saleable products, it's murder.

With QBasic, this has been changed. Like Fortran and COBOL (and Pascal and C and PL/I etc.), QBasic is *compiled.* That is, the entire program is translated into machine language once, before it is run by the computer. The program that does the translation is called a *compiler.*

The QBasic compiler is a program — actually a subprogram within QBasic — that reads and understands the instructions of a BASIC program, checks them for certain types of errors, and translates them into machine language. The compiler only needs to read and translate each instruction once, thereby making it much more efficient than an interpreter. The compiler does not carry out the instructions it translates; it just produces a set of machine language instructions that the computer can execute directly and quickly to accomplish the task of the BASIC program. Two of the outstanding features of QBasic are the speed and efficiency with which it compiles programs.

What's in a Name?

Beyond the question of intrepretation versus compilation (which QBasic addresses), BASIC has always had a number of advantages over other computer languages. BASICA added even more. And QBasic? Why, it has even more advantages, to be sure.

Both Standard BASIC and BASICA are easy to learn. Statements in these languages use familiar words. New *variables* (specially named places to store data) can be introduced at any time (most compilers require all variables to be set up, or *declared,* at the beginning of the program), and there are few complicated structures. BASICA has many advanced graphics, sound, and event-trapping capabilities (ways to determine if something special has happened and take action accordingly) that are not found in many other languages.

Since programs are interpreted, they can be debugged (rid of pesky errors) by stopping them at any point to analyze the contents of the variables.

With these advantages, however, come limitations. First, in both earlier versions of BASIC, each statement in a program must be labeled with a unique *line number*. These line numbers are BASIC's way of identifying the order that statements come in, and also serve as addresses should the need arise for the computer to transfer to a specified place in the program.

Unfortunately, line numbers sometimes make programs hard to write and can make *subroutines* (small programs that accomplish a specific task and can be used inside different, larger programs) difficult to keep track of.

Secondly, all BASIC variables are *global*, which means that they maintain their values in all parts of the program. This actually makes it hard to reuse subroutines, as each has to have unique variable names to avoid monkeying around with other subroutines' data. Even within the main program, you must take care to avoid using the same variable in two different contexts.

Thirdly, the control statement IF...THEN, which is how a Standard BASIC or BASICA program determines what to do next, based on some specified condition, does not provide enough flexibility and clarity. Other languages have many more ways of making decisions. (Such decision-making statements are called *control stuctures*. It would not be overstating the case to say that control structures are the very heart of programming, and that increasing their number and flexibility directly increases the power of a computer language.)

Finally, Standard BASIC and BASICA are confined to 64K of memory, which must serve both as the workspace and the storage space for the values of the variables. In 1981, that was a lot of room. Today, with VGA graphics and 10,000 cell spreadsheets, it ain't much. Oh, and one more thing, just to reiterate: that interpretation business we discussed earlier makes Standard BASIC and BASICA sloooooowwwww.

QBasic to the Rescue

As you have every right to expect, QBasic has gone a long way to address these shortcomings, without sacrificing the advantages of earlier BASIC versions.

Computer scientists are in unanimous agreement that a modern programming language should not require line numbers, but should have extensive control structures, *local variables* (that is, variables that apply only to a portion of the program), and the ability to pass and receive values from procedures. (A *procedure* is a portion of a program that performs a specific task; it's roughly equivalent to a subroutine.) All these features are available in QBasic. For most programs, QBasic can also access the computer's entire main memory, rather than just that 64K portion mentioned earlier. In addition, since QBasic is a compiled language, programs run faster.

What's more, getting at all of this power is not difficult, even for complete novices. In the next chapter, we show you how to do so, using the *QBasic Editor*.

Those of you who are familiar with previous versions of BASIC may wish to know more before we proceed to the editor. We cheerfully oblige you in the next section. (Novices may want to skim this material, or simply skip on to the beginning of Chapter 2.)

Experienced Users: Getting Started with QBasic

If you already know Standard BASIC, you can start programming almost immediately. About one hour is required to learn the essentials of entering, executing, and modifying programs. Then you can write short programs exactly as you would in Standard BASIC. After that you can read this book to explore the new possibilities that QBasic provides.

You may wonder about line numbers. In QBasic, line numbers are optional. As they aren't needed to keep track of the order statements come in, line numbers are used primarily in GOTO and GOSUB statements. Well, the availability of procedures and extensive control structures makes even these statements almost obsolete. (For years, instructors have been threatening to immediately fail any student who used a GOTO statement in a program turned in for credit.) Besides, another device, called a *label*, can be used as a substitute for a line number in a statement that is the target of a GOTO or GOSUB statement. You may have gotten used to line numbers, but trust us, you'll never miss them.

Yet even though QBasic does away with line numbers, and is compiled to boot, it's still mostly compatible with earlier BASIC versions. You can load and execute most programs written in BASICA, Microsoft BASIC, or GW-BASIC in QBasic. True, you must make slight modifications when using a few statements such as DRAW, PLAY, CLEAR, and CHAIN. (Note: Statements that apply to the program itself, such as LIST, EDIT, RENUM, and AUTO, cannot be used in QBasic. Sorry.)

Something you will have to get used to if you've already used other versions of BASIC is the differences between writing for an interpreted language and writing for a compiled one. For example, in an interpreted language, long variable names take up more space in memory than short names; however, for compiled languages, all variable names use the same amount of space. Thus, you're free to use descriptive names in QBasic. Not such a bad thing to have to get used to! (But don't go overboard; long variable names get tedious after the tenth time you have to type them out.)

For another thing, Standard BASIC uncovers errors only when the program is executed, and so certain errors will only be uncovered after several well-planned runs. (Under some conditions, you see, some types of errors won't reliably occur.) The QBasic editor and compiler, on the other hand, scan the entire program and uncover many types of errors prior to execution. This can save time and headaches down the road.

QBasic is a highly structured language, and as such makes an excellent introduction to *structured programming* if you aren't already used to programming that way. Structured programming is a strategy for creating programs that are easy to write, read, maintain, and debug. In this strategy, problems are broken down into smaller pieces, each of which is dealt with one at a time. This is sometimes called the *top-down* approach. Whatever you call it, it saves effort by giving you smaller problems to tackle and by allowing you to reuse these small solutions in other programs. Structured programming requires the modern control structures and procedures that QBasic provides.

Supposing we've sold you on using QBasic by now (which is a pretty safe assumption, since you bought this book), actually writing programs with QBasic is simplicity itself. In essence, you:

1. Invoke QBasic by typing QBASIC at the prompt and pressing <Enter>.
2. Press the <Esc> key to remove the startup window.
3. Type in the program as you would on a word processor.
4. After the program is written, press <Shift+F5> to run the program.

That's all there is to it. We'll go into more detail in the next chapter, to be sure.

But Wait, There's More

If you get seriously into QBasic, you may want to check out some of the advanced tools that are available for QBasic programmers. Microsoft has two: QuickBASIC and BASIC PDS.

QuickBASIC is an enhanced version of QBasic; BASIC PDS is an enhanced and expanded version of QuickBASIC. The main enhancement of QuickBASIC is the capability to compile programs into a form that can be executed directly from DOS, just like big-time applications such as 1-2-3, Microsoft Word, and dBASE. QuickBASIC has about 10 additional statements and further debugging capabilities. BASIC PDS adds extensive database management capabilities and features important to advanced programmers. Any program written in QBasic will run in QuickBASIC and BASIC PDS. You can develop applications in easy-to-use BASIC, and skip that previously necessary step of translating them into some other application.

Raring to go? Great. Let's take a closer look at what goes into QBasic. After that, we'll show you how to use the QBasic editor to write programs.

CHAPTER 2

A First Look at QBasic

Before your PC can step through a program that you create, performing in sequence each instruction you give it (in other words, before your computer can run your QBasic program) you have to get the program into the computer. Clearly, you're going to use your computer keyboard (and perhaps a mouse) to accomplish this task. But the text you type doesn't pour directly into QBasic; it needs a little massaging first. To help you with that task is the *QBasic Editor.*

The QBasic Editor is a kind of *word processing* program. Examples of this program genre include Microsoft Word, Wordstar, and WordPerfect. For those not familiar with these programs, or with the term word processor, such a program is a tool allowing you to type in, view, and arrange words — or text — on your PC.

A word processor makes your computer much more powerful than a typewriter; among other things, you can easily correct mistakes and insert new text in the middle of old without having to retype single lines or even whole pages. The editor in QBasic offers such capability for use in composing your QBasic programs.

By the way, we use the word *edit* to describe both the process of writing and the process of revising a program. This chapter presents the essential information that you need to know in order to edit and run a program using QBasic. Since the Editor is the place from which you perform these functions, the chapter serves as an introduction to the QBasic Editor. For those who need it, Chapter 3 presents further capabilities of the Editor. (Those who know Wordstar or other program-oriented editors can safely skip Chapter 3. By "program-oriented" editor, we mean a word processing program contained within another program. The most relevant examples would be the editors contained within most versions of other programming languages, such as Pascal and C. If you can use the editor from another programming language, the QBasic Editor should give you no trouble.)

Getting Started

Install DOS 5.0, or later version, on your computer as directed by the DOS manual. The two files needed for QBasic are QBASIC.EXE and QBASIC.HLP. (If you plan to do graphics and have a Hercules card, then MSHERC.COM is also essential.) With a hard disk, these files are most likely in the directory DOS. If you have these QBasic files on diskettes, you should first make a copy of the diskettes for day-to-day use and put the master copies away for safe keeping.

Invoke QBasic on your computer. (If you are unsure how to invoke QBasic, see Appendix H for the details.) After you invoke QBasic and remove the copyright notice by pressing the <Esc> key, the main screen appears as shown in Figure 2-1.

The Main Screen

Notice the menu bar at the top of the screen. There are eight menus of commands shown across this bar. (A menu, of course, is simply a list of available commands from which you may select.) The eight menu selections available from the Menu bar are:

File   Produces a pull-down menu of file-related tasks, such as loading or saving a program. By *file*, we mean a single, contiguous collection of data. Each file has a separate name. Each of your QBasic programs will be stored in a separate file.

Edit   Produces a pull-down menu of editing tasks, such as moving text from one place to another in your program.

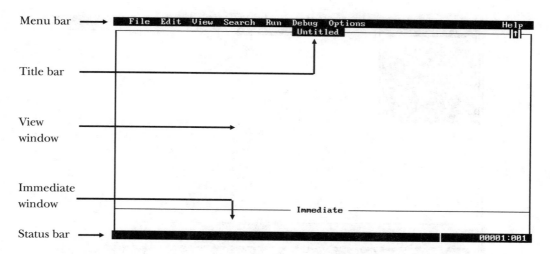

Menu bar ——→

Title bar ——→

View
window

Immediate
window

Status bar ——→

Figure 2-1. The main screen

View	Produces a pull-down menu of tasks allowing you to see specific program screens.
Search	Produces a pull-down menu of the standard word processing tasks "search" and "search and replace." With these, you may find where a particular word or phrase is located in your program, and you may replace that text with other text that you may specify.
Run	Produces a pull-down menu of tasks that affect program execution. This is the menu from which you put your programming work into action.
Debug	Produces a pull-down menu of assorted tasks for finding errors in a program.
Options	Produces a pull-down menu of commands you may use to customize QBasic. For example, there is a command to change the screen colors.
Help	Produces a pull-down menu of commands letting you get on-line help on selected topics.

When any one of these menu names is highlighted on the menu bar, as File is in Figure 2-2, QBasic is waiting for you to choose it or one of the other eight items from the Menu bar. To activate the menu bar, press the <Alt> key on your PC keyboard. Use the arrow keys (sometimes called cursor control keys) to move the highlight around. Press the <Enter> key to see the commands available within the highlighted menu.

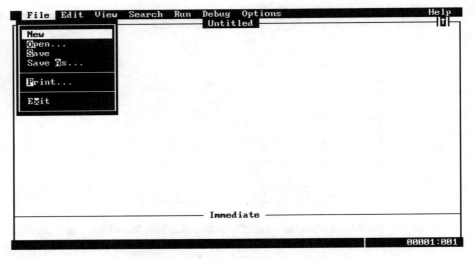

Figure 2-2.   The File menu

Now let's consider the remaining parts of the main screen.

Title bar   The title bar displays the word "Untitled" until you have
                       saved and named your work. Commands for saving your work
                       are contained in the File menu.

View window   All typing and editing of the program is done inside the View
                       window.

Immediate window   Press the <F6> key to active this window. A QBasic command
                       can then be typed into the Immediate window and executed
                       alone, immediately.

Status bar   The contents of the status bar include special key
                       combinations, the cursor position, and information on menu
                       options. The cursor, by the way, shows where text will go next
                       when you type at the keyboard. It appears as a small, blinking
                       underscore or square, depending on your system's setup.

Using QBasic's Menus

When you first enter (or *invoke*) QBasic, the View window is active. Pressing
the <Alt> key activates the menu bar, which means that one of the selections is

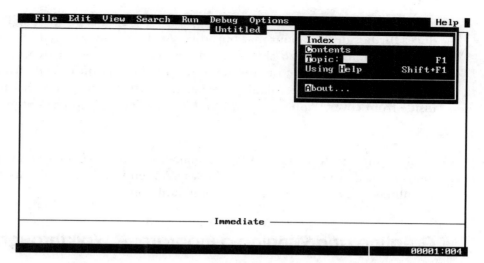

Figure 2-3. The Help menu

highlighted by a rectangular bar. QBasic now waits for you to make a selection. There are two methods for selecting an item from the menu bar:

Press the first letter of the item on your keyboard. (You can use either lowercase or uppercase.)

Use the direction keys to move the highlighted rectangle to the desired item, and then press the <Enter> key.

For example, with the menu bar active, pressing <F> selects File and pulls down a menu from under the word File. (See Figure 2-2.) This menu is called a pull-down menu. At this point, pressing <X> selects the Exit command and causes the computer to leave QBasic and return to DOS.

Here's another example of using the menus. Activate the menu bar by pressing the <Alt> key, and then press the <Right Arrow> key until the item Help is highlighted. Now, press the <Enter> key to produce the pull-down menu shown in Figure 2-3. At this point, pressing the <Down Arrow> key three times highlights the option "Using help"; selecting this option (press <Enter>) displays information about how to use on-line help.

For any option, the status bar explains its purpose, and pressing <F1> produces further details about that purpose. (As the pull-down menu indicates, pressing <Shift> and then <F1> without releasing <Shift> — we denote this as <Shift+F1> — selects the on-line help information option directly from the view window. There are many other such shortcuts shown on this book's inside front cover.) You can return to the view window by pressing the <Esc> key.

If this is your first time using QBasic, you may now wish to explore some other items from the menu bar. Take a look at Appendix E, which discusses the usefulness of most of the different menus and options.

Creating and Running a Program: A Walkthrough

Believe it or not, you are now ready to write your first QBasic program.

The text for your program must be typed into the View window. The View window is active — that is, anything you type will go there and not elsewhere — when the blinking cursor appears within the window. If necessary, press the <Esc> key (or possibly <F6>) until the cursor moves into the View window.

QBasic's editor has many convenient features to facilitate typing a program. However, for now the following elementary editing techniques will suffice:

- Type each line of the program as you would on a typewriter. After finishing a line, move to a new line by pressing the <Enter> key.

- You can use the direction keys (that is, the four keys marked with arrows) to move anywhere in the program.

- To erase a character, press either the <Backspace> key (located above Enter) to erase the character to the left of the cursor or the <Del> (Delete) key to erase the character at the cursor. Characters to the right of the deleted character will automatically move to the left to close up the space.

- To insert a character, position the cursor at the desired location (use the arrow keys) and type the character. Characters at and to the right of the cursor will automatically move to the right to accommodate the inserted character.

- To erase a line, make certain the cursor is anywhere on the line you wish erased. Now, hold down the <Ctrl> key (Ctrl stands for "Control") and press the <Y> key. We describe this combination as <Ctrl+Y>.

Now you know enough about controlling the QBasic Editor to enter your first program.

Entering a QBasic Program

The following walk-through is designed to introduce you to the mechanics of creating and running a program. Just follow the directions and observe the results. The QBasic statements used here will be explained later.

1. If necessary, use the direction keys and the combination <Ctrl+Y> (Erase Line) to clear the View window.

2. Type the "word"

   ```
   cls
   ```

   in lowercase letters and then press the Enter key. Notice that the word was automatically capitalized by QBasic.

   When the statement CLS is executed, the screen is cleared. CLS is an example of a *keyword* or *reserved* word. Keywords have special meanings to QBasic. (This also means you can't use them as, say, variable names.) There are about 200 keywords that QBasic understands.

   A *statement* (or instruction) consists of one of these keywords and possibly some parameters. Parameters are words or values that you supply to control exactly what a statement does. Each statement is written on a separate line and tells the computer to perform a specific task. A program consists of a collection of statements.

3. On the second line of the View window, type

   ```
   FOR i=1 TO
   ```

   and press the <Enter> key. (The number 1 in the line above is typed by pressing the "one" key, the key just above and left of the <Q> key, *not* the <L> key.)

   The box shown in Figure 2-4 appears on the screen to inform you that this is not a proper QBasic line. (Note: This box is called a *dialog* box. Dialog boxes come up at various times to point out errors or to offer assistance. The <Tab> key is used to move to different parts of a dialog box and the <Esc> key is used to remove a dialog box.)

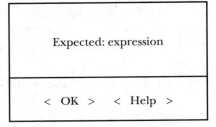

Figure 2-4. A dialog box

Press the <Esc> key to send away the dialog box and then continue typing on the same line to obtain

```
FOR i=1 TO 100
```

Now press the <Enter> key. Notice that spaces are added before and after the equal sign to make the line more legible.

4. Type a few more lines until the display in the View window is as shown below. This is our first example of a QBasic program. It consists of a sequence of lines that instruct the computer to perform certain tasks. This program causes the word "Hello" to be displayed 100 times. Like every program in this text, it finishes with an END statement. The computer is said to execute or *run* the program when it carries out the instructions one-by-one in sequence.

```
CLS
FOR i = 1 TO 100
PRINT "Hello",
NEXT i
END
```

5. To execute or "run" the program, hold down the <Shift> key and press the <F5> key. The display changes. The screen you are now viewing is called the Output screen. (Note: Throughout the rest of the book, when we want you to press the <Shift+F5> combination to run a program, we'll simply write [run]. Press <Shift+F5> whenever you see [run].)

6. Press any key to return to the View window, where you can continue editing the program.

7. Press <F4> to see the Output screen again. Press <F4> a second time to return to the View window. Pressing <F4> moves, or *toggles*, between the two windows.

8. You can run the program again if you wish by pressing <Shift+F5>.

9. Sometimes you are informed of errors after you press <Shift+F5>. To see an example of this, return to the View window and move the cursor to the fourth line of the program. Now delete the letter X from the word NEXT. [Run] the program. This time, a dialog box with the message "Syntax error" appears. The offending line of the program is highlighted.

   Press <H> to obtain some information about this type of error. Press <Esc> to return to editing. The cursor appears on the line to be corrected. After the correction is made, (put the "x" back into the word "next") the direction keys can be used to move the cursor off the corrected line.

10. Let's now modify the program by inserting the line

```
PRINT i;
```

    before the third line.

    To create space for the line, move the cursor to the end of the second line and press the <Enter> key. (Alternatively, move the cursor to the beginning of the third line, press the <Enter> key, and move the cursor up one line.) Now type the line. Moving the cursor off the line causes QBasic to check for certain types of errors, to capitalize keywords, and to adjust the spacing.

11. [Run] the new program. Now each of the "Hellos" will be numbered.

12. Press any key to return to the View window.

13. You can *store* the program on a formatted diskette or on your hard disk so you can run it later without having to retype it. To store, or *save* the program, press and release <Alt> to activate the menu bar, then press and release <F> to drop down the file menu, and then press <A> to access the command Save As. (This key combination is abbreviated <Alt/File/Save As> or <Alt/F/A>.)

    A dialog box appears, asking you to give a name to the program. Type a name of at most eight letters and/or numbers and then press the <Enter> key. For instance, you might type MYPROG1. The program will be stored on the diskette in the drive from which QBasic was started. It is stored in a file with the name MYPROG1.BAS. (The three letters after the name are called an extension. They identify this as a BASIC file.)

    This process is referred to as saving the program.

14. Now suppose you wish to write a new program. To clear MYPROG1.BAS from the View window, press and release <Alt>, (to activate the menu bar) then press and release <F> (to open the File menu), and then press

<N> (for "New"). (Note: If you press <Alt/F/N> before saving the previous program, a dialog box will appear to give you another chance to save it before it is removed. You can use the <Tab> key to highlight whether you care to save the file, and then press the <Enter> key to select the highlighted item.)

15. At any time, you can restore MYPROG1.BAS as the program in the View window by pressing <Alt/F/O> (Open), typing MYPROG1 at the cursor position, and then pressing the <Enter> key.

16. To exit from QBasic, simply press <Alt/F/X> (Exit). If changes have been made in the current program since the last time you Saved (if ever), QBasic gives you the option of saving the current form of the program before exiting.

So you can see, creating, modifying, running, and saving a program in the QBasic Editor is really quite easy. In the next chapter, we go into even more detail about the QBasic Editor, before introducing you to the language itself.

Before we go on to the next chapter, experienced BASIC users may wonder about some of the commands that they're accustomed to using from other versions of BASIC. We'll conclude this chapter by examining these commands and their QBasic equivalents. Commands are given under the names used in Standard BASIC. (Newcomers to BASIC should skip this section and proceed to Chapter 3.)

Experienced Users: How to Perform Standard BASIC Tasks

Here is a list of some common "direct" commands found in Standard BASIC. By "direct," we mean that BASIC executes them immediately as soon as you type them and press <Enter>. Following each command is a method to accomplish the same task when you use the QBasic Editor. (You may also perform some of these tasks outside of the Editor, as Appendix E describes.)

LIST In Standard BASIC, this command displays the entire contents of the current program. In QBasic, on the other hand, a portion of the current program is always visible in the View window. To see other parts of the program, make certain the cursor is in the View window and use <PgUp>, <PgDn>, <Ctrl+PgUp>, <Ctrl+PgDn>, or the direction keys.

Keep Pace with
Today's Micro-
computer
Technology with:

Brady
Publishing
and
Software

Brady Publishing books
and software are always up-
to-the-minute and geared
to meet your needs:

- Using major applications
- Beginning, intermediate,
  and advanced
  programming
- Covering MS-DOS and
  Macintosh systems
- Business applications
  software
- Star Trek™ games
- Typing Tutor

Available at your local book
or computer store or order
by telephone:
(800) 624-0023

///BradyLine

Insights into
tomorrow's technology
from the authors and
editors of Brady
Publishing

You rely on Brady Publishing's bestselling computer books
for up-to-date information about high technology. Now turn
to *BradyLine* for the details behind the titles.

Find out what new trends in technology spark Brady Publishing's authors
and editors. Read about what they're working on, and predicting, for the
future. Get to know the authors through interviews and profiles, and get to
know each other through your questions and comments.

BradyLine keeps you ahead of the trends with the stories behind the latest
computer developments. Informative previews of forthcoming books and
excerpts from new titles keep you apprised of what's going on in the fields
that interest you most.

- Peter Norton on operating systems
- Winn Rosch on hardware
- Jerry Daniels, Mary Jane Mara, Robert Eckhardt, and Cynthia Harriman
  on Macintosh development, productivity, and connectivity

Get the Spark. Get *BradyLine*.
Published quarterly. Free exclusively to our customers. Just fill out and mail this card
to begin your subscription.

Name _____

Address _____

City _____ State _____ Zip _____

Name of Book Purchased _____

Date of Purchase _____

Where was this book purchased? *(circle one)*

    Retail Store   Computer Store   Mail Order

F
R
E
E

*Mail this card for
your free subscrip-
tion to BradyLine*

70-66302

College Marketing Group
50 Cross Street
Winchester, MA 01890

ATT: **Cheryl Read**

SAVE   Press <Alt/F/S>. If you have not given a name to the program yet, QBasic will prompt you to type a name in a dialog box.

RUN   Press <Shift+F5>. QBasic will then compile and execute the program. After the program has finished running, you can return to the Editor by pressing any key.

LLIST   To print the entire current program on your current printing device, press <Alt/F/P/Enter>.

LOAD   Press <Alt/F/O> to execute the "Open a new program" command. Pressing this key sequence activates a dialog box entitled "Open" and displays "*.BAS" in the File Name rectangle. At this point there are two options. You can load a program into memory by typing the name of the program over "*.BAS" and pressing the <Enter> key. Alternatively, you can request a selected listing of file names on a disk, as you would in DOS, by typing the desired specification over "*.BAS" and pressing the <Enter> key. Use the DOS wildcard characters * and ? (Files matching the default specification "*.BAS" are initially listed.) You can then select the program that you want to load from the list by using the <Tab>, direction, and <Enter> keys. If QBasic queries you about saving the current program, respond as desired.

NEW   To erase the current program from memory and start work on a new program, press <Alt/F/N>. If QBasic asks you if you want to save the current program, respond as desired.

SYSTEM   To return to DOS, press <Alt/F/X>. If QBasic asks you if you want to save the current program, respond as desired.

Now you know what goes into creating and running a small QBasic program. All of this is done within the QBasic Editor. In the next chapter, we tell you more about the capabilities of this Editor. (If you know the word processing program WordStar, or are familiar with the editors used in languages such as QuickPascal, you can skip this chapter.) Chapter 4 introduces the language itself, and details the commands that QBasic offers you for manipulating numbers and characters.

The QBasic Editor

This chapter is for those who want additional experience with the QBasic Editor before learning more about the language itself. As we've said before, if you know Wordstar, or the editors included with QuickPascal, Turbo Basic, or Turbo Pascal, then you probably know enough to proceed with the next chapter. If you like, you can skim this chapter to refresh your memory, and to see what features are unique to the QBasic Editor.

New users, especially those of you who are new to computing in general, should definitely read this chapter. It offers a "hands-on" approach to learning the QBasic Editor. When you've finished, you'll be ready to tackle QBasic itself.

Take It from the Top

You create programs from the keyboard in much the same way you would write them with a typewriter. In computer lingo, we call this process of writing a program *editing* a program; so, as we've said, the part of QBasic used to create and alter programs is called the *Editor*.

Capabilities of the QBasic Editor

Before proceeding, let's talk about what the Editor can actually do. The main tasks that the Editor can perform are common to most word processors, as shown here. (A word processor, as we said in Chapter 2, is simply a program for entering and manipulating text.)

Cursor Movement   You can move the cursor to any location on the program screen. The direction keys on the numeric keypad move the cursor one position in the indicated direction. When used in conjunction with the <Ctrl key>, the <Left Arrow> and <Right Arrow> keys move the cursor to the beginning of the word to the left or right of the current cursor position. In addition, the Editor has commands that move the cursor to the beginning or the end of the current line, or to the top or bottom of the View window.

Scrolling   The process of moving all of the text up or down (or left or right) so that previously hidden text becomes visible is called scrolling. Think of the way a scroll (say, Isaiah from the Dead Sea Scrolls) works and you should get the picture. There are commands that scroll the program up or down one line, up or down an entire screen, and to the beginning or end of the program.

Search or Replace   The Editor can search the program for the first occurrence of any character or word that you specify. You can repeat this search to find subsequent occurrences. As an enhancement of this process, QBasic allows you to replace the found character or word (either automatically or with your consent) with specified text.

Block Manipulation   You can mark as a block all the material between two specified points in the program. (The text within the block will appear highlighted.) You can move a marked block to another place in the program or duplicate it elsewhere. You may also delete an entire block or print it.

Deletion   The <Backspace> and <Del> keys delete one character at a time. The Editor has commands to delete the line that contains the cursor, all the text from the cursor to the end of the line, or the word to the right of the cursor.

Restoration   When you delete something, it isn't quite gone forever. You can restore the text that has most recently been deleted. This protects you from, say, accidentally deleting a marked block of text that you really just wanted to move to another place in the program.

Save and Retrieve Programs   You can save on disk any program written with the Editor and retrieve it later.

At the Keyboard

We keep saying that programs are entered at the keyboard, but that's also something we oughtn't take for granted. So next, let's examine the workings of the keyboard itself.

There are several different styles of keyboards. Figure 3-1 shows a typical IBM PC-compatible keyboard. The keyboard is divided into three parts. The center portion functions like an ordinary typewriter keyboard.

The left-hand portion consists of ten keys labeled from <F1> through <F10>, called the *function keys*. (On some keyboards, the function keys are located across the top. Also, some keyboards have more than ten function keys.) Function keys are used to perform certain tasks with a single keystroke. For instance, pressing the function key <F1> causes a help screen to appear. (The commands associated with some of the keys will be discussed in this section.)

The right-hand portion of the keyboard, referred to as the *numeric keypad*, is used to move the cursor or to enter numbers. Press the <Num Lock> key a few times and notice the letter N appearing and disappearing in the right hand part of the Status bar. When the letter N is present, the numeric keypad produces numbers; otherwise, it moves the cursor. The <Num Lock> key is called a *toggle key* since it "toggles" between two states. When the numeric keypad is in the cursor-moving state, the four arrow keys each move the cursor one space.

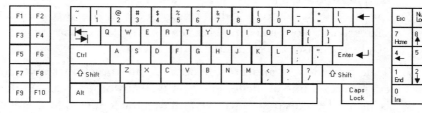

Figure 3-1.   IBM PC keyboard

Two very important keys may not have names printed on them. The <Enter> key is the key with the hooked arrow (or the word Enter). It is used to execute commands or to enter lines in a program. The <Backspace> key is the grey key with the left-pointing arrow, located above the <Enter> key. It moves the cursor one space to the left and erases any character in that location.

If you want more experience with the keyboard, start QBasic and work through the following routine:

1. Use the right and left direction keys on the numeric keypad to move the cursor. Notice that the cursor position number at the lower right corner of the screen changes each time one of these keys is pressed.

2. Press the <Home> key to move the cursor back to the beginning of the line. In general, the <Home> key moves the cursor to the leftmost position of the line on which it currently is located.

3. Type a few letters using the central "typewriter" portion of the keyboard. The <Shift> keys, marked with the symbol of an arrow pointing up, are used to obtain uppercase letters (or the uppermost character on keys showing two characters).

4. Press the <Caps Lock> key and then type some letters. The letters will appear in uppercase. We say the computer is in *uppercase mode.* To toggle back to lowercase mode, press the <Caps Lock> key again. Only alphabetic keys are affected by <Caps Lock>. (Note: When the Editor is in uppercase mode, the letter C appears in the rightmost part of the Status bar.)

5. Hold down the <Ctrl> key (Ctrl stands for "Control") and press the <Y> key. This combination erases the line containing the cursor. (Note: We designate this key combination <Ctrl+Y>.) The cursor itself returns to the leftmost column on the line.

6. Type some letters. Now press the <Backspace> key a few times. Pressing this key erases letters one at a time. Another method of deleting a letter is to move the cursor to that letter and press the <Del> key (Del stands for "Delete"). There's a difference between the two methods: The <Backspace> key erases the character to the left of the cursor, and the <Del> key erases the character at the cursor.

7. Type a few letters and use the appropriate direction key to move the cursor under one of the letters. Now type any other letter. Notice that it is inserted at the cursor position and that the letters following it move to the right. This is because *Insert* mode is active. The *Overwrite* mode, in

which a typed letter overwrites and thereby replaces the letter located at the cursor position, is invoked by pressing the <Ins> key (Ins stands for "Insert"). Pressing this toggle key a second time reinstates insert mode. You can tell from the size of the cursor which mode is active; a large cursor means overwrite mode.

8. Type a few more letters and move the cursor left a few spaces. Now press the <End> key (on the numeric keypad). The cursor moves to the end of the line.

9. The key to the left of the <Q> key is called the <Tab> key. It is marked with a pair of arrows, the top one pointing to the left and the lower one pointing to the right. In the View window, pressing the <Tab> key has the same effect as pressing the space bar several times.

10. Type more characters than can fit on one line of the screen. Notice that the leftmost characters scroll off the screen to make room for the new characters. Up to 255 characters can be typed on a line. Some of the programs in this text use long lines. When we cannot fit them on one line of a printed page, we break them up into two lines and use an underscore character "_" to indicate that they should be entered on one line of the screen.

11. The <Enter> key is used to begin a new line on the screen in much the same way that the carriage return lever is used on a manual typewriter. However, pressing the <Enter> key also "submits" the line to further processing. QBasic examines the line's contents. If the line is not a proper QBasic program line, a message appears pointing out the error. If the line is a proper QBasic program line, then certain spacings and capitalizations will be carried out to make the line conform to standards.

12. The <Alt> key activates the Menu bar. Then, pressing one of the highlighted letters, such as <F>, <E>, or <V>, selects a menu. (A menu can also be selected by pressing the <Right Arrow> key to highlight the name and then pressing the <Enter> key.) As shown in Figure 3-2, after opening a menu, each option has one letter highlighted. Pressing the highlighted letter selects the option. For instance, pressing <A> from the File menu selects the option "Save As." Here also, selections can be made with the direction keys and the <Enter> key.

13. The <Esc> key (Esc stands for "Escape") is used to return to the View window from the menu bar without selecting any menu options.

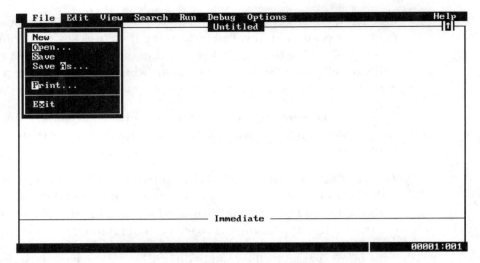

Figure 3-2.   A menu and its options

Editing Commands

There's a reason why we keep saying that those with WordStar experience will have little trouble with the QBasic editor. The QBasic command format was heavily influenced by WordStar, a widely popular word processing program.

Nearly every command can be issued by holding down the <Ctrl> key and then pressing one or two keys. For instance, holding down the <Ctrl> key and pressing <F> moves the cursor to the first character of the next word on the right. This command is written <Ctrl+F>. Holding down the <Ctrl> key and pressing <Q> and then pressing <D> moves the cursor to the end of the line containing the cursor. This combination is written <Ctrl+Q/D>. (The <Ctrl> key need only be held down while <Q> is pressed. Both keys can be released, if desired, before <D> is pressed.)

Table 3-1 contains some common key strokes and combinations recognized by the Editor.

Using the Clipboard

Ever wonder what happens to text once you delete it? In the case of QBasic, the text doesn't just disapperar. Rather, QBasic sets aside a part of memory, called the Clipboard, to accomodate deleted text, and this in turn assists in *moving* and *copying* selected portions of text.

Commands to Move Cursor	*Key strokes*
Left one character	Left Arrow
Right one character	Right Arrow
Left to start of word	Ctrl+[Left Arrow] or Ctrl+A
Right to start of word	Ctrl+[Right Arrow] or Ctrl+F
Left to start of line	Home or Ctrl+Q/S
Right to end of line	End or Ctrl+Q/D
Up one line	Up Arrow
Down one line	Down Arrow
Up to first line in program	Ctrl+Home
Down to last line in program	Ctrl+End

Commands to Scroll	
Up to a new page	PgUp
Down to a new page	PgDn
Scroll view up one line	Ctrl+[Up Arrow]
Scroll view down one line	Ctrl+[Down Arrow]

Commands to Delete Text	
Delete character left of cursor	Backspace
Delete character at cursor	Del
Delete from cursor to end of word	Ctrl+T
Delete from cursor to end of line	Ctrl+Q/Y
Delete entire line	Ctrl+Y

Table 3-1. The most common editing commands

Here's how it works: Whenever the current line is deleted (<Ctrl+Y>), the deleted text is placed in the Clipboard. At any subsequent time, pressing <Shift+Ins> *inserts* the contents of the Clipboard at the cursor position. Thus, you can delete text from one place (some folks call this operation a "cut") and insert it (i.e., "paste" it) some place else.

For example, use the following steps to move a line of code to a new location.

1. Place the cursor anywhere in the line of code to be moved.
2. Press <Ctrl+Y> to erase the line of code and place it into the Clipboard.
3. Move the cursor to the desired new location for the line of code.
4. Press <Shift+Ins> to insert the line of code at the cursor position.

NOTE   After the contents of the Clipboard are copied at the cursor position, the text *remains in the Clipboard* and therefore can be duplicated easily in several locations.

Larger portions of contiguous text, called *blocks*, also can be moved into the Clipboard. To select a segment of text as a block, move the cursor to the beginning of the segment you want to select, hold down the <Shift> key, move the cursor to the end of the segment of text, and then release the <Shift> key. The selected block is now highlighted. The following commands can be applied to the selected text block.

Shift+Del   Cuts the selected block from its current location and places it in the Clipboard.

Ctrl+Ins   Places a copy of the selected block in the Clipboard while leaving the block intact.

Del   Erases the selected block without placing it in the Clipboard.

(Taking any action other than the three actions above (for instance, moving the cursor) "deselects" the portion of text currently highlighted. That is, the highlighting disappears and the block is no longer marked for a subsequent operation.)

To move a block of text:

1. Select the block to be moved using the <Shift> key and the cursor keys.
2. Press <Shift+Del> to cut the block and place it into the Clipboard.
3. Move the cursor to the desired new location for the block.
4. Press <Shift+Ins> to insert the block at the cursor position.

The preceding should give you a reasonable idea of the commands available in the QBasic Editor, and how the Editor functions. Before you put that knowledge to the test, however, we've designed a brief tutorial to give you hands on experience with the commands and functions we've been talking about in this chapter.

An Editing Tutorial

This section presents a tutorial that introduces the most frequently used commands. To begin, start a new program (i.e., use <Ctrl+Y> or <Alt/F/N> to clear the View window) and carefully type the following line, including its obvious errors:

```
PRIMT "The ate is"; DATE$
```

The cursor should now be to the right of the dollar sign. Press either <Home> or <Ctrl+Q/S>. Note that the cursor has moved to the beginning of the line and is positioned under the P in PRIMT.

Let's change the M to an N so that the word is PRINT. To do this, press the <Right Arrow> key three times to move the cursor under M. Delete the M by pressing <Del> once. Now type N to make the correction.

Next, you should add a space immediately after the word "is." Press <Ctrl+Right Arrow> or <Ctrl+F> four times. Note that the cursor moves to the right to the beginning of a word each time you press one of these key combinations. The cursor should now be at the D in DATE$. Press the <Left Arrow> key three times to place the cursor under the quotation mark. Finally, press the space bar to insert a space after "is."

Now, you are ready to change "ate" to "date." Press <Ctrl+Left Arrow> or <Ctrl+A> twice. (Note that the cursor moves left to the beginning of a word each time that you press one of these key combinations.) The cursor should now be at the "a" in "ate." Type d to correct the word to "date."

Now press <End> or <Ctrl+Q/D> to move to the end of the line, and then press <Enter> to create a new line. (Note, pressing the <Enter> key with the cursor in the middle of the line can produce a mess.) Carefully type the following on the new line

```
PRINT "Time waits for no one."
```

Move the cursor back to the first line by pressing the <Up Arrow> key. Note that the cursor remains in the same column. Move the cursor back to the second line by pressing the Down Arrow key. Now press <Ctrl+Left Arrow> five times to move the cursor left to the beginning of the word "Time." Press <Ctrl+T>: Note that the Editor deletes the word Time. Press <Ctrl+T> again to delete the space that was present between "Time" and "waits." Press <Ctrl+T> a third time to delete the word waits. (<Ctrl+T> deletes from the cursor position to the right, to either the end of the current word or the end of the current group of spaces.)

Ooops! Suppose you reconsider and wish you had not deleted the words "Time waits." While you could retype it, use QBasic's unique restore-line command instead. Press <Ctrl+Q/L>. The line is restored to exactly the form it had when you moved the cursor back to the line with the <Down Arrow> key (second sentence of previous paragraph).

Now press <Ctrl+Right Arrow> or <Ctrl+F> twice to move the cursor to the beginning of the word "waits." Next, delete the remainder of the line by pressing <Ctrl+Q/Y>. Type in "is money," along with the second quotation mark, to complete the modifications to this line. The cursor should now be at the end of the line and the line should read

```
PRINT "Time is money"
```

Now let's combine QBasic's on-line help and text block manipulation capabilities. The help windows that provide information on a QBasic keyword often contain sample programs. These programs can be cut out of the help window, pasted into the View window, and used in your QBasic programs.

As an illustration, clear the View window, type the word FOR (without pressing the <Enter> key), and press <F1>. A help screen appears to explain FOR...NEXT loops. (Notice that the View window still remains on the screen, but is compressed to a single line.) The help screen includes an example program near the bottom of the screen. We will use part of this code as a program.

Press the <F6> key twice to active the help window. Now use the <Down Arrow> key to move to the line just under the word "Example." This line begins the text we want to copy. Now hold down the <Shift> key and move the cursor down until three lines of the program are highlighted. Release the

<Shift> key. Press <Alt/E/C>. This activates the Edit menu command "Copy," which places a copy of the highlighted text into the clipboard.

Press <Esc> to restore the View window. Press <Alt/F/N>, the "New" command from the File menu, to clear the View window. (Answer "no" when QBasic queries you about saving the program currently in the View window. That is, press <Tab> twice to select "No" and then press the <Enter> key.) In the new View window, first type CLS and press <Enter>. (When the program is executed, this statement will clear the output screen before any text is displayed.) Now press <Alt/E/P> (the Edit menu Paste command) to paste the contents of the Clipboard into the View window. Press <Alt/E/P> again to create a second copy. Finally, Press <Shift+F5> to run the program. The program counts from 1 to 15 two times.

Suppose you want the program to count to 15 just once. Press any key to return to the View window and move the cursor to the beginning of the second FOR statement. Now select the last three lines of the program as a block by holding down the <Shift> key, moving the cursor down three lines, and releasing the cursor. To clear the block, press <Alt/E/E> (Edit menu, Clear).

The one block option we did not try is "Cut," which is similar to Clear but retains the deleted text in the Clipboard. This option is used to move, instead of duplicate or delete, a block of text.

As a final editing command, let's apply QBasic's Change command. Press <Alt/S/C>. This activates the Change command in the search menu. Using this command, we can look for a specific word or words, and replace them.

As it turns out, a variable name used in the text we've copied ("i%") is not very descriptive. Let's change that. We presume you've activated the Change command with <Alt/S/C>. In response to the prompt for text to find, type "i%" and press <Tab>. In response to the prompt for text to change to, type "count%" and press <Enter>. The editor will highlight the first instance of "i%." Press the <Enter> key to make the change. Repeat two more times to change each occurrence of "i%." (Note: The three changes could have been made at once from the initial dialog box by using the <Tab> key to highlight "Change All" before pressing the <Enter> key.)

You will become very familiar with the QBasic Editor after writing a few programs. You'll probably find yourself memorizing many of the command shortcuts. The topics covered in this chapter are more than enough to get you up and running. But the Editor has other features to aid your creative programming. See the discussions of the Edit, View, and Search menu commands in Appendix E.

Now we are ready to see what QBasic can do. As we've said, all computer languages are intended to manipulate data; that's what a computer is for, after all. It stands to reason, however, that a computer must have places to store both data and results, just as the lines in the register of your checkbook record the facts about the checks you write (we hope!).

Before we get into specific commands, therefore, we have to examine the ways in which QBasic stores data. In so doing, we will introduce the concept of a computer *variable*, a concept that is central to programming. We'll examine the different types of variables available in QBasic, and discuss how each is used. After that, you'll be ready to begin tackling the real power of this language (or any other): the statements used to make decisions. First off, though, variables.

Manipulating Data

Introduction

We've seen how to use the QBasic Editor to create and modify programs. In so doing, however, we haven't done much more than take you inside the workshop and show you where the light switches and the power outlets are. As for the power tools themselves — and even more important, the kinds of things you can make with them — well, we haven't even *begun* to show you all of that yet.

Before we can proceed, though, we have to discuss the raw materials upon which a computer program operates. As a carpentry shop processes wood, a computer processes data. And like wood, data come in many forms. Even within the computer, data can be accomodated ("stored," if you will) in a variety of ways. All this is under your control. Matching the appropriate storage to your particular data is an important part of programming. In this chapter we explore the data storage options that are available to you in QBasic. We also show you some fundamental ways in which this data can be manipulated, including arithmetic operations and operations to manipulate text. Finally, we show you how to get data into a computer in the first place, and to get it back out when you're done. First, though, let's look more closely at how data is stored.

The In's and Out's of Computer Data

Think of all the things a computer can be programmed to do. It can process text, to yield precisely formatted documents. It can sort large lists of names or addresses in just about any way you choose. It can perform complex mathematical calculations.

Interestingly enough, all of these operations can be performed upon the same data; after all, the computer just sees the long sequences of 1's and 0's that we mentioned in the first chapter. Imagine "adding up" a list of names or "alphabetizing" a column of figures. Such things are possible although clearly undesirable. So how do we inform the computer of the differences between different types of data? How does the computer know that one series of bits represents a name, and another represents a number?

Within a computer's data storage area, or memory, data is kept in predefined locations. We say "predefined," but it is very important to note that it is you, the programmer, who defines these locations as they are needed. A good part of this chapter is taken up with showing you how to do so. For now, suffice it to say that there are two broad catagories of data storage locations: constants (sometimes called "literals") and variables.

Constants are easy. Such a location merely stores a value that does not change. An example would be the value of pi to five decimal places: 3.14159. When you enter a constant in a program, the computer sets aside a storage location and fills it with the appropriate value in "computer talk" i.e., that binary sequence of 1's and 0's we keep talking about. No matter. All you have to do is enter the number you want in the appropriate place. For example, if you wanted the computer to multiply pi times two, you would simply write:

   3.14159*2

As it turns out, the expression written above doesn't tell the computer anything. It also isn't very interesting. (Note: An *expression* is just a problem written out using mathematical symbols.) It would be of much more use to allow pi to be multiplied by any value we choose, without having to change the line each time. What's more, we need a place to store the result. This leads us to the concept of a computer *variable*.

A variable is a predefined storage location that can contain any value. Indeed, the value a variable holds can be changed at will. Each variable in a program has a name. This name is quite a bit like a label you might put on a box, to indicate its contents. Consider a more general form of the expression we wrote above: the formula for the circumference of a circle, given the circle's radius. This formula is usually written:

$C=2\pi r$

C stands for the circumference, which we don't know; 2, of course, is the constant 2; π is also a constant, which is approximately equal to 3.14159; and *r* is the radius of the circle, the distance from the circle's center to its edge. This value is known, although it is potentially different for each unique circle.

Now, if we wanted to write a simple program to find a circle's circumference, we could create two variables: one to hold the result (the circumference), and the other to hold the radius of the circle we're interested in. In this way, we could calculate the circumference of any circle.

In previous versions of BASIC, all we had to do to set up a variable was simply to use it in an expression. When the BASIC interpreter encountered the variable's name for the first time, it created it then and there. This can still be done in QBasic, but it isn't good programming practice. For one thing, there are actually several kinds of variables. These include variables that hold whole numbers (those without fractional parts that sometimes are called *integers* — examples include 2, 500, and -5), variables that hold fractions, as well as variables that hold text (a.k.a. *character strings*).

QBasic doesn't necessarily know which kind of variable you mean, so it makes an assumption. The assumption may be incorrect, leading to a kind of variable that can't store the data you want to put in it. (For example, you cannot store the number 3.14159 in an integer variable; the part to the right of the decimal simply disappears.) We discuss variable types at length later in the chapter.

Of course, a variable isn't much good if we can't get data into it or out of it. All programming languages have provisions for these operations, which fall under the general label *Input/Output*. (This is sometimes abbreviated I/O.)

The most common statements used to input a value into a variable are LET and INPUT. A statement of the form

```
LET variable = value
```

assigns the value to the variable. The word LET is usually omitted. Two examples are

```
wage = 4.25

total = 4 + 5
```

A statement in the form

```
INPUT "prompt", variable
```

displays the message *prompt,* waits until the user types in a response at the keyboard and presses the <Enter> key, and then assigns the response to the variable. An example is

```
INPUT "Enter your age: ", age
```

PRINT is the most used output statement. The statement

```
PRINT value
```

displays the value on the screen and the statement

```
PRINT "text"
```

displays the text on the screen. For instance, the output from the pair of statements

```
PRINT "The sum is"

PRINT 2+3
```

is

```
The sum is

 5
```

The PRINT statement displays positive numbers with a leading space and adds a trailing space to all numbers.

When a PRINT statement consists of the word PRINT followed by a sequence of items separated by semicolons, then the items are displayed one after the other. For instance, the statement

```
PRINT "The sum is"; 2+3
```

produces the output

```
The sum is 5
```

This gives us a broad outline of how computer data is input, stored, and output. Let's now turn our attention to the specifics. We'll start with numerical data, and the kinds of operations that can be done with them.

Numbers

When it comes to numbers, which is what a good deal of computing all boils down to, QBasic gives you quite a lot of flexibility. QBasic can perform calculations with numbers as small as about 10^{-324} and as large as about 10^{308}. The latter number, by the way, represents 10 followed by 307 zeroes. (To fully appreciate these magnitudes, consider that there are on the order of 10^{100} particles — photons, neutrinos, quarks, and electrons — in the known universe. If you lined all these particles up, and then constructed a cube with a side the same length as that line of particles, the cube could hold 10^{300} particles. 10^{308} is 100 million times more than that number.)

As we said earlier, a number can be used in QBasic either directly as a literal numeric value (e.g., 3.14159) or indirectly by storing the number in a named location within the computer's memory: a variable (e.g., PI). Once a variable storage location has been set up, we may use the name of the variable in statements.

We'll talk about the four types of number variables in the next section. For our present purposes, suffice it to say that all variable names must begin with a letter. They can consist of letters, digits and decimal points, up to 40 characters. The cases of the letters are irrelevant; for example, "pi" and "PI" refer to the same variable.

There are some words that you cannot use as variable names. You might recall that we have mentioned *reserved words* that QBasic has special meaning for;

Operator	Name	Example
+	Addition	2 + 3 is 5
-	Subtraction	3 - 2 is 1
*	Multiplication	2 * 3 is 6
/	Division	2 / 3 is .6666667
^	Exponentiation	3 ^ 2 is 9
-	Negation	-(1.5) is -1.5
\	Integer division	17 \ 5 is 3
MOD	Modulo	17 MOD 5 is 2

Table 4-1. Arithmetic operators

these cannot be used as variable names. Appendix F contains a list of words that QBasic reserves for its own use and that you cannot use as variable names.

A good variable name makes a program easy to understand by indicating how the variable is used and what kind of data it holds. Some suggestive names of variables are averagePrice, costOfMaterials, answer, and milesDriven. In this book we write variable names with lowercase letters. If a variable name is composed of more than one word, such as milesDriven, we indicate new words by capitalizing their first letter. This is just to make it easier for you to read and understand; QBasic doesn't care.

To manipulate number data, whether in the form of constants or variables, QBasic provides the eight arithmetic operations shown in Table 4-1. Since the *integer division* and *modulo* operators are not as well known as the others, some further explanation is in order.

Modulo Arithmetic

When two whole numbers are divided by long division, we obtain an integer quotient and a remainder. For instance, as shown here, 122 divided by 5 produces an integer quotient of 24 and a remainder of 2.

$$24$$
$$5 \overline{\smash{\big)}\, 122}$$
$$10$$
$$\overline{22}$$
$$20$$
$$\overline{2}$$

In general, if *M* and *N* are whole numbers and *M* is divided into *N* by long division, then

    N\M

denotes the integer quotient and

    N MOD M

denotes the remainder. For example, 122\5 is 24, and 122 MOD 5 is 2.

QBasic defines integer division and the operation MOD for any pair of numbers whose values are between -2,147,483,648 and +2,147,483,647. If *M* or *N* are not whole numbers, they are rounded to the nearest whole number. The value of $N \backslash M$ is the whole-number portion of the ordinary quotient, N/M. The value of N MOD M is $N - M \times (N \backslash M)$. The numbers *M* and *N* can be replaced by numeric variables of any type. However, unless the values assigned to the variables are in the proper range, the *error message* **Overflow** occurs. (An error message is something that appears on your screen whenever QBasic encounters a problem. It lets you know what the difficulty is, although fixing it is entirely up to you.)

Program 4-1 uses \ and MOD in an elementary change-making program that accepts an amount of money as input and calculates the number of nickels and pennies required to make that amount of change.

NOTE The error message, **Overflow**, will be displayed in a dialog box when the program is run with the last input value shown.

Remember, we say [run] when we want you to run a program by holding down the <Shift> key and pressing the <F5> key at the same time.

Program 4-1.   Integer division and MOD

```
REM Demonstrate integer division and MOD [4-1]
INPUT "Enter amount of money in cents: "; money
nickels = money \ 5
pennies = money MOD 5
PRINT nickels; "nickels and"; pennies; "pennies"
END

[run]
Enter amount of money in cents: 23
 4 nickels and 3 pennies

[run]
Enter amount of money in cents: 3000000000
{ Overflow }
```

(Program 4-1 starts with a REM statement and terminates with an END statement. REM stands for "remark." REM statements are not executed and serve to assist the person reading the program. END statements mark the end of a program. The user's response to the request for input is shown in italics.)

Variable Specifics

We've looked at some of the operations available in QBasic for working with numbers. Now let's take a closer look at the kind of numerical variables that QBasic offers.

To optimize execution time and make efficient use of memory, QBasic has four different types of numeric variables to which you can assign numbers. These types are known as *integer, long integer, single-precision floating-point,* and *double-precision floating-point.* The type of a numeric variable can be specified by appending one of the four type-declaration tags (%, &, !, #) to the end of the variable name. If no type-declaration tag is present, QBasic makes the variable single-precision. (This kind of decision-making is called "defaulting"; single-precision is the "default type" for variables. If you don't specify otherwise, that's what a variable ends up being.)

Integer and Long Integer Variables

Integer and long integer variables can only store whole numbers (both positive and negative) within restricted ranges. An integer variable can store whole

Program 4-2. Integer and long integer variables

```
REM Working with integers & long integers [4-2]
castOfBenHur% = 25452
wordsInBible& = 773692
US1990MedianAge% = 31.6
PRINT US1990MedianAge%
US1990NationalDebt& = 3000000000000
END

[run]
 32
{ Overflow }
```

numbers from -32,768 through 32,767, whereas long integer variables can store whole numbers from -2,147,483,648 through 2,147,483,647. The reason is simple. An integer variable occupies two bytes in the computer's memory; a long integer takes up four bytes.

Variables are designated as integer or long integer variables with the type declaration tags "%" or "&," respectively. Although long integers require more memory space and take longer to process than integers, long integers are often necessary. For instance, the exact populations of the states in the United States cannot be held by (short) integer variables. When a number outside of the allowable range is assigned to an integer or long integer, an overflow error message results, just like the one we saw above in Program 4-1.

When a number that is *not* whole (e.g., 2.5 or 3.14159) is assigned to an integer or long integer variable, the number is rounded to the nearest whole number. If the number has a decimal part equal to .5, then it is rounded to the nearest even whole number. For instance, 2.5 is rounded to 2, and 3.5 is rounded to 4. (This may not be what you're used to. In school, most of us are taught that a number with decimal part .5 is rounded up.)

Program 4-2 assigns values to numeric variables and displays the value of one of the variables. The last statement causes the error message "Overflow", because a number too big to be stored is assigned to a long integer variable.

Floating-point Variables

Integer variables are good for storing whole number amounts, presuming such values are below about 2.5 trillion. Still, that's less than the national debt.

To store larger amounts, and fractional values, you need additional variable types. QBasic has two kinds of floating-point variables to fill these needs. The two differ in the number of digits — or precision — and the magnitude of the values they can handle. Like long integers to regular integers, double precision variables occupy twice the storage space as single precision variables.

NOTE   Numbers expressed in scientific or engineering notation are examples of floating-point ("point" refers to the "decimal point") numbers. A floating-point number is a number written in the form $m{\times}10^e$. We refer to m as the *mantissa* and e as the *exponent*. The mantissa normally contains a decimal point at the far left or one digit from the left. The exponent is always a whole number, positive, negative, or zero. The number of *significant digits* in the floating-point number is the number of digits in the mantissa. For example, 186,000 can be expressed as the floating-point number $1.86{\times}10^5$, where the mantissa is 1.86, the exponent is 5, and there are three significant digits. As another example, the floating-point number $1.2{\times}10^{-15}$, is equivalent to 0.0000000000000012, but is much easier to write. The shorthand notation of floating-point numbers provides a way for writing, and storing, very large and very small numbers in a compact space. Imagine having to write out $3{\times}10^{26}$!

Single-precision numeric variables have names followed by the type-declaration tag "!" (or with no type-declaration tag — recall that single-precision is the default type if you don't specify otherwise with another tag). A single-precision numeric variable can store numbers — positive or negative — that have magnitude from 0 to $3.4{\times}10^{38}$. Values having magnitudes less than about 10^{-45} are treated as zero.

Double-precision numeric variables have names followed by the tag "#" and can store numbers — positive or negative — that have magnitude from 0 to $1.79{\times}10^{308}$. Values having magnitudes less than about 10^{-324} are treated as zero.

Although floating-point variables can hold very large and very small values, they are limited in accuracy. The values of single-precision variables are accurate to six (and sometimes seven) significant digits; whereas the values of double-precision variables are accurate to 16 significant digits.

Regardless of their precision, QBasic converts values of floating-point variables for storage to a special binary floating-point format. One bit is set aside for the sign of the mantissa, additional bits are set aside to hold the mantissa itself. Another bit holds the sign of the exponent, and the last bits hold the exponent's value.

QBasic converts floating point numbers back to base 10 format (i.e., in coventional form, where possible, or in the scientific notation format we discussed above for very large numbers) for display or printing. (The conversions to and from the base 2 format alter some numbers slightly. This is because the exact value of the mantissa can't always be precisely expressed in the number of bits assigned to it. The difference is very small.)

QBasic displays the values of floating-point variables either in scientific or standard notation. In scientific notation, as we explained, QBasic expresses each number as a number multiplied by 10 to a power, where 10 to a power is written as E followed by the power for single-precision variables, and D followed by the power for double-precision variables. For example, you can assign a value to a single-precision variable with a statement of the form

```
LET number = 1.36E-3
```

which in decimal form is 0.00136. Program 4-3 illustrates these ideas.

Note that we always begin a program with a descriptive REM statement. This is just to let us know something about the program; QBasic ignore remarks entirely. A remark can be added to the end of a line by preceding the remark with an apostrophe (').

Numeric Functions

Now you have places to store number. So what are you going to do with them? We've shown you the standard arithmetic operations that are available. QBasic also provides a wide variety of predefined numeric functions, which act upon numeric values to produce new values. Some of these functions are shown in Table 4-2. Appendix B contains a complete list of QBasic's built-in functions.

The function ABS can be used to obtain the magnitude of the difference between two numbers. Program 4-4 demonstrates a use of ABS in computing age differences.

Program 4-3. The use of numeric variables

```
REM Demonstrate the use of numeric variables [4-3]
num = .2
weightOfEarthInTons = 6588 * 10 ^ 21
balance = 1234567.89
balance# = 1234567.89
googol# = 1D+100
PRINT num
PRINT weightOfEarthInTons
PRINT balance
PRINT balance#
PRINT 1 / googol#
PRINT googol# ^ 5
END

[run]
 .2
 6.588E+24
 1234568
 1234567.89
 1D-100
 { Overflow }
```

The function INT can be used to round numbers. If *x* is any number, then

```
INT(x + .5)
```

is the value of *x* rounded to the nearest whole number. For any *x*,

```
INT(100 * x + .5) / 100
```

Function	Meaning	Example
ABS(x)	absolute value of x	|x|
FIX(x)	whole number part of x	FIX(3.2) is 3
INT(x)	nearest whole number < x	INT(3.2) is 3
SGN(x)	sign of x (-1, 0, or 1)	SGN(3.2) is 1

Table 4-2.   Some built-in numeric functions

Program 4-4.   Determining the difference between two ages

```
REM Determine age difference  [4-4]
INPUT "Enter age of first person: ", age1
INPUT "Enter age of second person: ", age2
difference = ABS(age1 - age2)
PRINT "The ages differ by"; difference; "years."
END


[run]
Enter age of first person: 7
Enter age of second person: 10
The ages differ by 3 years.
```

is the value of x rounded to two decimal places. To round x to n decimal places, replace 100 in the expression above by 1 followed by n zeroes. Thus, to round to 4 places, replace 100 with 10000, etc. Program 4-5 illustrates this technique.

Numeric Expressions

A *numeric expression* consists of numeric constants, variables, and/or functions combined by numeric operators. Parentheses are helpful in clarifying the order that QBasic uses to perform the operations. QBasic evaluates expressions within parentheses first. In the event that parentheses are nested one pair inside another pair, the innermost expression takes precedence. Unless

Program 4-5.   Rounding a number

```
REM Round a number [4-5]
INPUT "Enter number to be rounded:"; x#
INPUT "Enter number of decimal places"; n
roundedValue# = INT(10 ^ n * x# + .5) / 10 ^ n
PRINT "The rounded value is "; roundedValue#
END

[run]
Enter number to be rounded: -1.235
Enter number of decimal places: 2
The rounded value is -1.24
```

Expression	Interpretation	Value
2 + 3*4	2 + (3*4)	14
100 MOD 21/3	100 MOD (21/3)	2
-2^4	-(2^4)	-16
6*8/4+3	((6*8)/4)+3	15

Table 4-3.   Illustrations of operator hierarchy

altered by parentheses, the arithmetic operations are evaluated in the order following:

exponentiation
negation
multiplication and division
integer division
MOD
addition and subtraction

This so-called "sum of products" hierarchy is standard in mathematics.

First, QBasic evaluates all exponentiations from left to right, and then all negations from left to right. After that, QBasic evaluates the multiplications and divisions one after another from left to right. Then, after evaluating the integer divisions and MODs, QBasic carries out the additions and subtractions from left to right. Table 4-3 gives some expressions and their interpretations.

Character Data and Strings

Of course, you can work with more than numbers. Programs like the QBasic Editor are clearly set up to work with character data; you can too. But you need places to store such data. In QBasic (and elsewhere), character data such as words, sentences, etc., are stored in *character strings*.

A *string constant* is a sequence of characters. String constants in programs often appear surrounded by quotation marks. The string constant " ", which has length zero, is referred to as the *null string*. Variables holding string constants

Function	Meaning	Example
DATE$	Current date	DATE$ might be "08-26-1991"
INSTR(a$,b$)	First location of b$ in a$	INSTR("cat","a") is 2
LCASE$(a$)	a$ in lowercase letters	LCASE$("Cat") is "cat"
LEFT$(a$,n)	Leftmost n characters of a$	LEFT$("cat",2) is "ca"
LEN(a$)	Number of characters in a$	LEN("cat") is 3
MID$(a$,m,n)	n chars. of a$ beg. with mth	MID$("cat",2,1) is "a"
RIGHT$(a$,n)	Rightmost n characters of a$	RIGHT$("cat",2) is "at"
UCASE$(a$)	a$ in uppercase letters	UCASE$("Cat") is "CAT"
VAL(a$)	a$ as a number	VAL("1991") + 2 is 1993

Table 4-4. Some built-in string functions

follow the same naming rules as numeric variables, but use the type-declaration tag $. A string constant in QBasic can be as long as 32,767 characters.

The only operator available for strings is the concatenation operator, which is denoted by "+." If *a$* and *b$* are strings, then the string *a$* + *b$* is the string obtained by joining the two strings. For instance, "hand" + "book" is "handbook."

String Functions

QBasic provides numerous functions that take strings as arguments. Some of the string functions available in QBasic are shown in Table 4-4. See Appendix B for a complete description of these functions and other built-in string functions.

Program 4-6 uses string functions to extract a person's first name from his or her full name, while Program 4-7 determines a person's age.

NOTE The system clock in your computer must be set correctly for the function DATE$ to work.

Program 4-6. Extracting a first name

```
REM Extract first name [4-6]
INPUT "Enter your full name: ", fullName$
n = INSTR(fullName$, " ")  'Location of first space
firstName$ = LEFT$(fullName$, n - 1)
PRINT "Your first name is "; firstName$
END


[run]
Enter your full name: Scott H. Clark
Your first name is Scott
```

More about Variable Types

As we said earlier, placing a type declaration tag (%, &, !, # or $) at the end of a variable name explicitly specifies the type of the variable. It should also be noted that variables with the same name but different tags are distinct variables, as shown in Program 4-8.

Note that, as in Program 4-8, you can write several statements on the same line of a program as long as you separate them by using colons. Some claim this is not always a good programming habit to fall into, however. It makes the code harder to read.

Remember: QBasic specifies a variable whose name has no type declaration tag as a single-precision variable; that is, QBasic treats it as if the variable name

Program 4-7. Solving a person's age on this year's birthday

```
REM Solve person's age on this year's birthday [4-7]
INPUT "Enter your date of birth (mm/dd/yyyy): ", birthday$
age = VAL(RIGHT$(DATE$, 4)) - VAL(RIGHT$(birthday$, 4))
PRINT "Your age is"; age; "this year."
END

[run]  (Assume that this year is 1991.)
Enter your date of birth (mm/dd/yyyy): 04/06/1937
Your age is 54 this year.
```

Program 4-8. Different tags produce distinct variables

```
REM Different tags produce distinct variables [4-8]
a% = 5: a& = 987654321: a! = 2.5
a# = 3.14159265358979
a$ = "QBasic"
PRINT a%; a&
PRINT a!; a#
PRINT a$
END

[run]
 5   987654321
 2.5   3.14159265358979
QBasic
```

had the ! tag. Program 4-9 shows that QBasic considers a tagless variable to be the same as the single-precision tagged variable of the same name.

When You Tire of Playing Tag

If you find that using type-declaration tags is cumbersome, especially for numeric variables, you might be tempted to omit them, and thereby use only single-precision numeric variables. In some circumstances this is fine, but, in others, it can slow down a program or not provide adequate accuracy in calculations. QBasic provides a better solution through its *DEFtype* statements.

If x is any letter of the alphabet, then the statement

```
DEFINT x
```

Program 4-9. Tagged and untagged variables of the same name

```
REM Tagged and untagged variables of same name [4-9]
a = 2: b! = 3
PRINT a; a!; b; b!
END

[run]
 2   2   3   3
```

specifies that all variables with no declaration tags whose names begin with the letter *x* will be integer variables. If *x* and *z* are letters with *x* preceding *z* in the alphabet, then the statement

```
DEFINT x-z
```

specifies that all variables (without declaration tags) whose names begin with any letter from *x* through *z* will be integer variables. In general, DEFINT statements can contain several letters, ranges, or both, separated by commas.

For example,

```
DEFINT I
```

means the variable *income* will be an integer.

```
DEFINT I-K
```

means *income, jump,* and *kappa* will be integers. *kareem!,* however, would be a single-precision floating point variable, because it has an explicit type declaration tag.

Program 4-10 demonstrates the use of DEFINT. Notice that only uppercase letters appear in any DEFtype statement. (If lowercase letters are typed in, the Editor will convert them to uppercase.)

Program 4-10. The use of DEFINT

```
REM Populations of states in millions [4-10]
DEFINT C, I, M-R
california = 23.7
illinois = 11.4
maryland# = 4.2
newYork = 17.6
texas = 14.2
PRINT california; illinois; maryland#; newYork; texas
END

[run]
 24  11  4.199999809265137  18  14.2
```

Program 4-11. The peril of delaying type declaration

```
REM Demonstrate the peril of delaying type declaration [4-11]
cost1 = 123.45          'Processed as cost1!
DEFDBL C
cost2 = 67.89           'Processed as cost2#
PRINT cost1; cost2      'Processed as cost1# and cost2#
PRINT cost1!
END

[run]
 0   67.88999938964844
 123.45
```

Notice the third value printed in Program 4-10. 4.2 became 4.199999809265137 in the process of converting from standard notation to floating point format and back.

In an analogous manner, tagless variables can be designated as long integer, single-precision, double-precision, or string type with the statements DEFLNG, DEFSNG, DEFDBL, or DEFSTR, respectively.

Although DEFtype statements may appear anywhere in a program, good programming practice mandates that you place them near the top of the program. Doing so avoids mistakes such as the confusion with the variable *cost1* that occurs in Program 4-11.

In this case, what may look to you and me like one variable (COST1) can actually be two separate variables.

Arrays

The preceding variables are good for storing single values. Sometimes, though, you want someplace to store a large number of related values. QBasic can handle this, too, through arrays.

An array is a collection of variables of the same type. They share a common name. Each variable within the array is referred to by an *index*, which tells which place in the array that particular variable occupies. The individual variables are also called the *elements* of the array.

Program 4-12. Using a string array

```
REM Man of the Year award from Time magazine [4-12]
DIM manOfYear$(1979 TO 1982)
manOfYear$(1979) = "Ayatollah Khomeini"
manOfYear$(1980) = "Ronald Reagan"
manOfYear$(1981) = "Lech Walesa"
manOfYear$(1982) = "The Computer"
INPUT "Enter year from 1979 to 1982: ", year
PRINT manOfYear$(year); " was named Man of the Year."
END

[run]
Enter year from 1979 to 1982: 1982
The Computer was named Man of the Year.
```

One-Dimensional Arrays

One-dimensional arrays are used to hold a list of values. The elements in a one-dimensional array are indexed by a sequence of integers or integer expressions. If *arrayName* is the name of a one-dimensional array and the indices (or *subscripts*) range from M to N, then the elements of the array are written *arrayName*(M), *arrayName*($M+1$), an so on through *arrayName*(N). This array, and its range, is declared by the statement

```
DIM arrayName(M TO N)
```

If an array is used in a program without first being declared by a DIM statement, then a range of 0 through 10 is automatically assigned. Also, an array having a range of 0 through N can be declared with the statement

```
DIM arrayName(N)
```

Each element of an array must be of the same variable type. This type is usually specified by a type-declaration tag at the end of the array name. Program 4-12 uses a string array to record Time magazine's Man of the Year awards.

Two-Dimensional Arrays

If a one-dimensional array is thought of as holding the values from a list, then a two-dimensional array can be thought of as holding the values from a table.

	1981	*1982*	*1983*	*1984*
1. Percentage change in consumer price index	10.4	6.1	3.2	4.3
2. Unemployment rate	7.5	9.5	9.5	7.4
3. Median family income	25569	25216	25594	26433

Table 4-5.   United States economic statistics

Think of the rows of the table as labeled *M* through *N*, and the columns of the table labeled *S* through *T*. Then the value in the *r*th row and *c*th column of the table would be placed in *arrayName*(*r,c*). Such an array is declared by the statement

```
DIM(M TO N, S TO T)
```

Program 4-13 illustrates the use of a two-dimensional array that provides access to the information in Table 4-5.

Program 4-13. Using a two-dimensional array

```
REM United States economic statistics   [4-13]
DIM USstat#(1 TO 3, 1981 TO 1984)
USstat#(1, 1981) = 10.4
USstat#(1, 1982) = 6.1
USstat#(1, 1983) = 3.2
USstat#(1, 1984) = 4.3
USstat#(2, 1981) = 7.5
USstat#(2, 1982) = 9.5
USstat#(2, 1983) = 9.5
USstat#(2, 1984) = 7.4
USstat#(3, 1981) = 25569
USstat#(3, 1982) = 25216
USstat#(3, 1983) = 25594
USstat#(3, 1984) = 26433
INPUT "CPI, unemployment or income (1, 2, 3)"; category
INPUT "Year from 1981 through 1984"; year
PRINT USstat#(category,year)
END

[run]
CPI or unemployment or income (1 or 2 or 3)? 2
Year from 1981 through 1984? 1983
 9.5
```

Higher Dimensional Arrays

Arrays can be declared with up to 60 indices by a statement of the form

```
DIM arrayName(M TO N, S TO T, ..., U TO V)
```

(The three dots are a placeholder; there may or may not be additional indices as you desire.)

Such an array consists of $(N - M + 1) \times (T - S + 1) \times ... \times (V - U + 1)$ elements.

The name of each single element has the form

```
arrayName(a, b, ..., c)
```

where a is between M and N, b is between S and T, and c is between U and V. If a two- or higher-dimensional array is used in a program without first being declared by a DIM statement, then the range of 0 through 10 is automatically assigned to each index. Also, an array with the first index ranging from 0 to N, the second index ranging from 0 to T, and the last index ranging from 0 to V can be declared simply by the statement

```
DIM arrayName(N,T,...,V)
```

Arrays and Memory Considerations

When an array is declared by a DIM statement, a portion of memory is set aside for the elements of the array. The memory reserved for a numeric array has enough space to hold all of the values that can potentially be assigned to the array elements. On the other hand, the memory reserved for a string array has no room for the values of the elements. Instead, the memory locations allotted to each element are intended to store the length and location (in QBasic's 64K string storage space) of the string to be assigned. The maximum number of elements in each type of array per dimension is 32,768. QBasic imposes no restriction on the number of arrays that can be declared; the only limitation is caused by the amount of memory present in the computer.

Static Arrays versus Dynamic Arrays

DIM statements can specify the ranges of their variables' indices with numeric constants or expressions. For instance, the statements DIM *arrayName*(20) and DIM *arrayName*(3 TO 100, 2 TO 17) use only constants, whereas the statements DIM *arrayName*(*a* TO *b*, 15) and DIM *arrayName*(2 * *n*) use one or more expressions.

In QBasic there are two different ways that arrays are assigned portions of memory. *Static* arrays are allocated a portion of memory when the program is first processed by the compiler. Each time the program is run, this space will be the same size and cannot be used for any other purpose. *Dynamic* arrays are allocated a portion of memory each time the program is run. The size of this space might vary for each run of the program, and it can be liberated at any time. (In Standard BASIC you don't have the option: All arrays are dynamic.)

In QBasic, an array is static by default; however, it will be dynamic if one or more of the following is true:

1. The array is dimensioned using one or more variables to specify ranges of indices. E.g.,

    ```
    DIM arrayname (x)
    ```

2. The statement REM $DYNAMIC appears in the program prior to the dimensioning of the array.

NOTE Statements consisting of the remark keyword REM followed by one of the reserved words $DYNAMIC, $STATIC, or $INCLUDE are referred to as metacommands. They give instructions to the compiler. In this particular case, REM $DYNAMIC tells the compiler to make subsequent arrays dynamic.)

A dynamic array can be completely removed from memory with the ERASE statement. Specifically, the statement

```
ERASE arrayName
```

frees up the portion of memory that has been allocated to the named array. After a dynamic array is erased, it can be dimensioned a second time with different index ranges. However, the number of dimensions must be the same as before. That's because the original statement defining the dynamic array (e.g., DIM *arrayName*(x)) does not change.

When the ERASE statement is applied to a static array, the portion of memory is retained; however, all values that have been assigned to the elements are

Program 4-14. The creation of static and dynamic arrays

```
REM Demonstrate creation of static & dynamic arrays [4-14]
DIM a$(1 TO 25)                     'Static array
INPUT "Enter size of array:", n     'Input size
DIM c(n)                            'Dynamic array
REM $DYNAMIC
DIM d(17)                          'Dynamic array
REM $STATIC                        'Return to static as default
DIM b(50)                          'Static array
ERASE d
DIM d(20 TO 50)                    'Dynamic array
a$(22) = "ABC"
ERASE a$
PRINT a$(22) + "DEF"
END

[run]
Enter size of array: 5
DEF
```

reinitialized. (That is, these values become 0 for numeric arrays and " " — the null string — for string arrays.)

Dynamic arrays are more flexible than static arrays. A static array, after all, is always the same size; you have to change the program to change a static array. The size of a dynamic array can be determined when the program is run.

What's more, dynamic arrays are memory efficient since their memory space can be released for other purposes after the array is no longer needed by the program. However, static arrays have one important feature that justifies their inclusion in QBasic: they can be accessed faster. This quality produces a significant time saving when searching and sorting arrays.

Program 4-14 produces both static and dynamic arrays.

Inputting Data

Now we have data storage locations (variables and arrays) and we have operations to perform on them. But programs, to be meaningful, must have data to process. QBasic provides a wealth of statements for inputting data, including the LET, INPUT, READ/DATA, and INPUT$ statements, which are discussed below.

LET and INPUT

Data can be assigned to variables in many ways. The LET and INPUT statements, which have already been used in this book, are the best known. The statement

```
LET variable = expression
```

or its abbreviated form

```
variable = expression
```

assigns the value of the expression to the variable. E.g.,

```
LET pi = 3.14159
```

puts the value 3.14159 into the variable *pi*, and

```
LET name$ = "SCOTT"
```

puts the name "SCOTT" into the string variable *name$*.

The value and the variable must be either both string or both numeric. An error results if you try to assign a character string value to a numeric variable, or vice versa. If the two values are both numeric, but of different types, then the value is converted to the type of the variable. For example:

```
age% = 3.2
```

results in the value 3.2 being rounded down to 3 before it is stored in *age%*.

LET is used to assign values within a program. We also need a way to get values in from the outside world. The statement

```
INPUT variable
```

causes a question mark to be displayed on the computer screen, pauses until the user enters a response, and then assigns the response to the variable. The variation

```
INPUT "prompt"; variable
```

displays the message prompt prior to the question mark. If the semicolon in this variation is replaced by a comma, the message is displayed without the subsequent question mark. Variations of the form

```
INPUT "prompt"; variable1, variable2, ...
```

allow the user to assign values to several variables. The values are typed in, separated by commas, and then the <Enter> key is pressed. The statement

```
INPUT "Enter your age and weight: ", age%, weight%
```

when encountered, displays the prompt

```
Enter your age and weight:
```

without a question mark, and waits for the user to type in two numbers separated by commas and then to press <Enter>. The entered values are then placed into the integer variables *age*% and *weight*%.

READ and DATA

DATA statements list values that READ statements assign to variables. Specifically, a statement of the form

```
READ x
```

causes the computer to look for the first unassigned item of data in a DATA statement and assign it to the variable *X*. A sequence of statements such as

```
READ x
```

```
READ y
```

```
READ z
```

can be replaced by the single statement

```
READ x, y, z
```

Program 4-15. READ and DATA statements

```
REM Demonstration of READ & DATA statements [4-15]
READ person$, BirthYr
PRINT "When the U.S. constitution was signed,"
PRINT person$;" was"; 1776 - BirthYr; "years old."
READ person$
READ BirthYr
PRINT "When the Civil War began, "; person$;
PRINT " was"; 1861 - BirthYr; "years old."
REM -- Data: Person, Year of Birth
DATA Thomas Jefferson, 1743
DATA Abraham Lincoln, 1809
END

[run]
When the United States constitution was signed,
Thomas Jefferson was 33 years old.
When the Civil War began, Abraham Lincoln was 52 years old.
```

Each DATA statement holds one or more constants, with multiple constants separated by commas. Typically, each DATA statement holds several related items. It is good style to place DATA statements together at the end of the program and precede them with a REM statement that gives the categories of the information held in each DATA statement, as in Program 4-15.

INPUT$

If $a\$$ is a string variable and n is a whole number from 1 through 32,767, then the statement

```
a$ = INPUT$(n)
```

causes the program to pause until you type n characters on the keyboard. Then the string consisting of these n characters is assigned to the variable $a\$$ and the program continues with the next line.

The INPUT$($n$) function with $n = 1$ is often used to make a selection from a menu. Unlike making a selection with INPUT, the typed letter does not appear on the screen and you do not have to press the <Enter> key. Program 4-16 illustrates the technique.

Program 4-16. The INPUT$ function

```
REM Demonstrate the INPUT$ function [4-16]
PRINT "Type a letter."
letter$ = INPUT$(1)
PRINT "The letter you typed is "; letter$
END

[run]
Type a letter.                    {The user typed the letter T.}
The letter you typed is T
```

Input Type Mismatches

Each of the input statements above assigns a constant to a variable of a specified type. In the event that the constant is not of the same type as the variable, QBasic accommodates as best as possible.

If the variable has type integer and the constant has *single-* or *double-precision*, then QBasic rounds the constant, if possible, before assigning it to the variable. (An example of something that can't be rounded is $n\% = 41,234.56$. Such a statement causes the message "Overflow," because a short integer such as $n\%$ cannot hold a value greater than about 32,000.) Assigning a string constant to a numeric variable causes the message "Type mismatch" to be displayed. Character data and number data, are, after all, very different.

In a LET statement, the item on the right side of the equal sign can be either a constant or an expression. If this item is a numeric expression and the variable to the left of the equal sign is a string variable, then a "Type mismatch" error message results. Otherwise, assigning a numeric constant to a string variable with any input statement results in QBasic recognizing the number as a string.

Outputting Data to the Screen

We've talked about getting data into the computer, and manipulating it. Now let's talk about getting it back out again. The PRINT statement, with a little help from the functions TAB and LOCATE, can position data at specific places on the screen. A variation of the PRINT statement, PRINT USING, is custom-designed to display data in an orderly and familiar form.

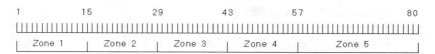

Figure 4-1. PRINT zones

PRINT Zones

The screen can hold 25 or more rows of text, with each row consisting of at most 80 characters. Each row can be thought of as being subdivided into five zones as shown in Figure 4-1.

When several items separated by semicolons follow the PRINT statement, QBasic displays the items one after the other. When commas are used instead of semicolons, QBasic displays the items in consecutive zones. Program 4-17 uses PRINT zones to produce a table that shows the various average annual expenditures for certain income groups. Note that the leading comma in the first PRINT statement below is used to skip the first print zone, so that the column headings line up over the numbers, and not over the row headings.

NOTE   Monitors attached to a graphics card, such as the Color/Graphics Adapter, Enhanced Graphics Adapter, or Video Graphics Array, can be put into a 40-column mode with the statement

```
WIDTH 40
```

The statement

```
WIDTH 80
```

reinstates 80-column mode. In 40-column mode, there are just two PRINT zones, one of length 14 and the other of length 26.

TAB Function

While the use of PRINT zones permits data to be organized into columns beginning at every 14th position of the line, the TAB function gives access to every position of the line. If an item in a PRINT statement is preceded by

```
TAB(n)
```

Program 4-17. Using PRINT zones

```
REM Annual expenditures of urban consumer units [4-17]
PRINT , "Food", "Housing", "Transportation"
PRINT "Highest 20%", 4838, 10188, 6949
PRINT "Middle 20%", 2877, 5032, 3451
PRINT "Lowest 20%", 1753, 1730, 1231
END

[run]
               Food              Housing           Transportation
Highest 20%    4838              10188             6949
Middle 20%     2877              5032              3451
Lowest 20%     1753              1730              1231
```

where *n* is a whole number from 1 to 80 (or 1 to 40 if the monitor is in 40 column mode), then QBasic will display that item, if possible, beginning in the *n*th position of the line. It won't be possible to print an item at the *n*th position in the line if the preceding item has already gone past this point, of course. Program 4-18 uses TAB to improve upon the output of Program 4-17.

Program 4-18. Using TAB to improve output

```
REM Annual expenditures of urban consumer units  [4-18]
PRINT TAB(17);"Food";TAB(26);"Housing";TAB(37);"Transportation"
PRINT "Highest 20%";TAB(16);4838;TAB(25);10188;TAB(36);6949
PRINT "Middle 20%";TAB(16);2877;TAB(25);5032;TAB(36);3451
PRINT "Lowest 20%";TAB(16);1753;TAB(25);1730;TAB(36);1231
END

[run]
               Food     Housing   Transportation
Highest 20%    4838     10188     6949
Middle 20%     2877     5032      3451
Lowest 20%     1753     1730      1231
```

Program 4-19. Displaying a message in the center of the screen

```
REM Display message in center of the screen [4-19]
a$ = "Happy Birthday"
CLS
LOCATE 12, (80 - LEN(a$)) \ 2
PRINT a$
END
```

LOCATE

For text purposes, the screen is subdivided into 25 or more horizontal rows (numbered 1, 2, 3, etc.) and 80 (or 40) vertical columns (numbered 1, 2, 3, etc.). The statement

```
LOCATE r, c
```

moves the cursor to the *r*th row, *c*th column of the screen. The next PRINT statement will display its data beginning at that location. Program 4-19 displays the string "Happy Birthday" in the center of an 80-column screen. (The CLS statement clears the screen. The LOCATE statement moves to the 12th row, and then determines what column to move to by determining the length of the message, subtracting the result from 80, which is the total width of the screen, and then dividing the resulting value by two. Its a technique typists use to center lines.)

PRINT USING

The PRINT USING statement is used to display numeric data in a familiar form (with commas, with an appropriate number of decimal places, and possibly preceded by a dollar sign) and to coordinate the combined display of string and numeric data. PRINT USING statements use a string, called a format string, to specify the form of the display.

A typical numeric format string is "##,###,###.##", a string of 13 characters. The statement

```
PRINT USING "##,###,###.##"; n
```

```
        n               Formatted Display

     1234                    1,234.00

     12.345                     12.35

     1234567.89          1,234,567.89
```

Figure 4-2.   Effect of PRINT USING "##,###,###.##"

reserves 13 positions, called a field, to display the number *n*. QBasic will display the number right-justified in that space, rounded to two decimal places, and containing appropriate commas preceding groups of three digits to the left of the decimal point. Figure 4-2 shows three possible values of *n* and their display with the statement just given.

If the first character in a numeric format string is a dollar sign, then QBasic will display the number with a dollar sign in the leftmost position of the field. If the first two characters are dollar signs, then QBasic will display the number with a dollar sign directly preceding the first digit. See Figure 4-3.

PRINT USING statements can combine text with numbers in several ways. One method is for the format string to contain the text with the special formatting characters. QBasic will display the text as it appears, and the numbers will conform to the rules of its formatting characters. Program 4-20 presents an example of this method.

The backslash character, \, can be used to format text with a format string. If *c$* is a string, then the statement

```
  PRINT USING "\          \"; c$
```

displays the first *n* characters of *c$*, where *n* is the length of the format string "\   \". That is, there are *n* - 2 blank spaces between the backslashes. The

```
     Statement                            Display

     PRINT USING "$####.##"; 45.78      $   45.78

     PRINT USING "$$###.##"; 45.78        $45.78
```

Figure 4-3.   Displaying dollar signs with PRINT USING

Program 4-20. Combining text and format in PRINT USING

```
REM  Growth of a bank deposit earning 6% interest [4-20]
INPUT "Enter amount of deposit: ", principal
a$ = "The balance after one year is $$###,###.##"
PRINT USING a$; 1.06 * principal
END

[run]
Enter amount of deposit: 1234.56
The balance after one year is     $1,308.63
```

exclamation mark, !, can be used to extract the first character from a string. Figure 4-4 shows examples that use the backslash character and the exclamation mark.

Program 4-21 shows that a format string can contain several groups of string formatting characters, numeric formatting characters, or both. In the program, the values to be formatted appear in a sequence in which the items are separated by commas.

The PRINT USING statement is often used to properly align numbers in columns. For instance, consider the Housing column in the output of Program 4-18. Ideally the numbers should be aligned so that their rightmost digits appear in the same column. Program 4-22 utilizes PRINT USING to achieve this goal and to improve readability by placing commas where appropriate.

Table 4-6, which shows the result of executing the statement PRINT USING *a$*; *n*, contains some additional symbols that can be used in formatting strings.

```
Statement                               Display

PRINT USING "\\smos"; "Computer"        Cosmos

PRINT USING "\   \"; "Computer"         Compu

PRINT USING "!"; "Computer"             C
```

Figure 4-4. Displaying leading characters with PRINT USING

Program 4-21. Several features of the PRINT USING statement

```
REM Demonstrate features of PRINT USING statement [4-21]
a$ = "!!! sold ###,### PC's in \ \ ####"
PRINT USING a$;"Int.","Bus.","Mach.",158000,"December",1984
END


[run]
IBM sold 158,000 PC's in Dec 1984
```

The ampersand character, &, can be used in a format string to display an entire string. If a single formatting character, such as # or \, appears in a format string preceded by an underline character, then the formatting character loses its special significance and is displayed literally. These two features are used to print the formatting characters. Program 4-23 illustrates the use of & and _.

Special Effects with a Monochrome Display — Using COLOR

Depending on the type of monitor used, text can be displayed on the screen with special effects (such as, underlining or blinking) or in color. A monochrome display is a special type of monitor that can be used with an IBM PC

Program 4-22.   Using PRINT USING to improve readability

```
REM Expenditures of urban consumer units [4-22]
PRINT "              Food      Housing     Transportation"
a$ =   "\          \   #,###     ##,###      #,###"
PRINT USING a$; "Highest 20%", 4838, 10188, 6949
PRINT USING a$; "Middle 20%", 2877, 5032, 3451
PRINT USING a$; "Lowest 20%", 1753, 1730, 1231
END


[run]
             Food      Housing     Transportation
Highest 20%  4,838     10,188      6,949
Middle 20%   2,877      5,032      3,451
Lowest 20%   1,753      1,730      1,231
```

Symbol(s)	Meaning	n	a$	Result
**	Inserts asterisks in place of leading blanks.	23	"**###"	***23
*	Displays an asterisk as the first character of the field.	23	"*####"	* 23
^^^^	Displays the number in exponential form.	23	"#.##^^^^"	2.30E+001
+	Reserves a space for the sign of the number.	-23	"###-"	23-

Table 4-6. Additional formatting strings for PRINT USING

or an IBM PC compatible. Monochrome displays produce sharper text than other monitors, but are restricted to two colors, referred to as white and black. (Most likely the actual colors will be green and black or amber and black.) For each character that is displayed on screen, the color of the character itself is called the foreground color and the color of the portion of the screen surrounding the character is called the background color.

The COLOR statement can be used to produce underlined, blinking, intense white, reverse video text, or certain combinations thereof on a monochrome display. Table 4-7 shows every possible combination and the QBasic COLOR statement that produces each one.

After one of these COLOR statements is executed, subsequent text will be displayed with the corresponding foreground and background until another COLOR statement is executed. Several different effects can appear on the

Program 4-23. Using & and _ with PRINT USING

```
REM Illustrate use of & and _ with PRINT USING [4-23]
b$ = "Forty-niners"
PRINT USING "The _#1 team in 1989 and 1990 was the &."; b$
END

[run]
The #1 team in 1989 and 1990 was the Forty-niners.
```

Foreground	Background	Statement
white	black	COLOR 7, 0
white, underlined	black	COLOR 1, 0
white, blinking	black	COLOR 23, 0
white, underlined, blinking	black	COLOR 17, 0
high intensity white	black	COLOR 15, 0
high intensity white, underlined	black	COLOR 9, 0
high intensity white, blinking	black	COLOR 31, 0
high int. wh., underlined, bkng.	black	COLOR 25, 0
black	white	COLOR 0, 7
black, blinking	black	COLOR 16, 0
black, blinking	white	COLOR 16, 7
black	black	COLOR 0, 0

Table 4-7. Special effects for displaying text on monochrome display

same screen. Program 4-24 demonstrates the different effects available with the monochrome display.

Displaying Color on a Color Monitor

Most color monitors are attached to either a Color/Graphics Adapter board (CGA), Enhanced Graphics Adapter board (EGA), or a Video Graphics Array adapter (VGA). With any of these boards, text can be displayed with foreground and background colors chosen from the sixteen colors in Figure 4-5.

Program 4-24. Some different effects on the monochrome display

```
REM Demonstrate effects on the monochrome display [4-24]
COLOR 17, 0
PRINT "The letters in this line are underlined & blinking."
COLOR 0, 7
PRINT "The letters in this line are in reverse video."
COLOR 0, 0
PRINT "This line will be unreadable."
COLOR 7, 0
PRINT "This is a standard line having white on black letters."
END
```

```
0  Black    4  Red       8  Gray         12  Light Red
1  Blue     5  Magenta   9  Light Blue   13  Light Magenta
2  Green    6  Brown    10  Light Green  14  Yellow
3  Cyan     7  White    11  Light Cyan   15  Intensity White
```

Figure 4-5. Available colors on a color monitor

Also, the foreground can be made to blink. With an EGA or VGA board, up to 48 additional colors are available.

If *f* is a number from 0 through 15 and *b* is a number from 0 through 7, then the statement

```
COLOR f, b
```

causes all further characters displayed on the screen to have a foreground of color *f* and a background of color *b* (i.e., the character itself will have color *f* and the small rectangle of screen space containing the character will have color *b*). Characters placed on the screen prior to this statement retain their original colors. Adding 16 to the number *f* causes the foreground to blink. Program 4-25 demonstrates the use of the COLOR statement.

Displaying Color on an Enhanced Graphics Display or VGA Monitor

The Enhanced Graphics Display and VGA monitors are special types of color monitors capable of displaying 64 colors in text mode. The colors are numbered 0 through 63. Each of the colors blue, green, cyan, red, magenta, and yellow are available in six shades. There are four shades of gray ranging from black to high intensity white. Table 4-8 gives the numbers of the colors in these groups. As a rule of thumb, in each group the higher numbers corre-

Program 4-25. The use of colors

```
REM Demonstrate the use of colors [4-25]
COLOR 14, 4
PRINT "The letters in this line are yellow on red."
COLOR 30, 4
PRINT "This is like the first, but has blinking letters."
COLOR 7, 0
PRINT "The is a standard line with white on black letters."
END
```

Color	Shades
Blues	1, 8, 9, 17, 25, 41, 57
Greens	2, 10, 16, 18, 24, 26, 34, 42, 48, 58
Cyans	3, 11, 27, 31, 35, 43, 59
Reds	4, 12, 32, 36, 44, 52, 53, 60
Magentas	5, 13, 21, 29, 45, 47, 61
Yellows	6, 14, 30, 54, 62
Grays	0 (black), 7, 15, 56, 63 (intensity white)

Table 4-8.   Shades of familiar colors

spond to lighter and/or brighter hues than the lower numbers. Brown has the number 20. The colors associated with the remaining 23 numbers are difficult to name. Program 4-26 displays all 64 colors. (This program uses statements that have not been discussed yet. You will understand it later. For now, just run it to behold the variety of colors at our disposal.)

QBasic uses two collections of numbers to control the choice of colors. The first collection is the set of numbers from 0 through 63 that identify the 64 different colors.

Figure 4-6 shows 16 paint jars labeled 0 through 15. For each jar, QBasic reserves a memory location that keeps track of the color in the jar. The list of jars and colors is referred to as a *palette*, by analogy with a painter's palette of

Program 4-26. The 64 colors available with an EGA or VGA

```
REM The 64 colors available on an EGA or VGA [4-26]
DEFINT i, j
FOR i = 0 TO 63 STEP 8
  CLS
  FOR j = 0 TO 7
    PALETTE j + 1, i + j
    COLOR j + 1, 0
    PRINT USING "Color ##"; i + j
    PRINT
  NEXT j
  SLEEP 4                   'Pause 4 seconds
NEXT i
END
```

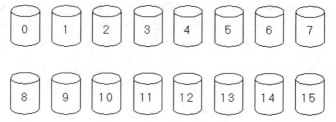

Figure 4-6. A palette

colors. The color in any jar can be changed at any time. If *m* is a number from 0 through 15 and *c* is a number from 0 to 63, then the statement

```
PALETTE m, c
```

replaces the color currently in jar *m* with the color *c*. The default colors (that is, the colors in the jars before any PALETTE statements are executed) are shown in Table 4-9. Note: The numbers 0 through 15 that label the jars are often called *attributes*.

If *f* and *b* are any numbers from 0 through 15 and 0 through 7, respectively, then the statement

```
COLOR f, b
```

causes all subsequent characters displayed on the screen to have the color in jar *f* of the palette as foreground and the color in jar *b* as background. Actually, the graphics board does not record two colors for each text position of the screen, but rather records the numbers of the two jars.

The monitor continually looks at the palette list to determine the colors to use. Characters placed on the screen prior to the execution of a COLOR statement retain their original colors. However, whenever a PALETTE statement is executed, QBasic will change every character whose foreground or background is specified by the jar whose color is changed.

Jar	0,	1,	2,	3,	4,	5,	6,	7,	8,	9,	10,	11,	12,	13,	14,	15
Color	0,	1,	2,	3,	4,	5,	20,	7,	56,	57,	58,	59,	60,	61,	62,	63

Table 4-9. The default palette

Program 4-27. The use of colors on an EGA or VGA monitor

```
REM Demonstrate colors on an EGA or VGA monitor [4-27]
COLOR 6, 7
PRINT "brown foreground, white background"
PALETTE 12, 1
COLOR 12, 7
PRINT "blue foreground, white background"
SLEEP 5                                  'Pause 5 seconds
PALETTE 7, 4
PRINT "All characters now have a red background."
END
```

At any time, at most 16 different colors can appear on screen. Program 4-27 shows the use of the COLOR and PALETTE statement with the EGA or VGA Monitor.

Outputting Data to a Printer

Clearly, you have a lot of options when it comes to outputting data on the screen. But the screen is not the only output device available to you. You can also LPRINT. The statement LPRINT sends data to the currently selected printer in much the same way that PRINT displays it on the screen.

Semicolons suppress the carriage-return/linefeed combination, commas format data into zones, the TAB function places data in specific positions on the line, and LPRINT USING formats the data with the same capabilities as PRINT USING. In addition, for appropriate printers, LPRINT can control character size, font, line spacing, and page length. Table 4-10 contains printer-controlling statements that hold for most dot-matrix printers. Table 4-11 lists some printer-controlling statements for most laser printers. (Be careful to distinguish between l (el) and 1 (one).)

The WIDTH statement specifies the maximum number of characters to be printed on each line before QBasic automatically performs a carriage return and line feed. If n is a positive integer, then the statement

```
WIDTH "LPT1:", n
```

specifies that each line contain at most n characters. The default value is 80 characters per line.

Statement	Effect
`LPRINT CHR$(7);`	Buzz the buzzer
`LPRINT CHR$(12);`	Form feed
`LPRINT CHR$(13);`	Carriage return and line feed
`LPRINT CHR$(14);`	Turn on double-width mode (5 chrs./inch) until line feed or LPRINT CHR$(20);
`LPRINT CHR$(15);`	Turn on compressed mode (16.5 chrs./inch) from Pica pitch
`LPRINT CHR$(18);`	Turn off compressed mode
`LPRINT CHR$(20);`	Turn off double-width mode
`LPRINT CHR$(27); "-"; CHR$(1);`	Turn on underline mode
`LPRINT CHR$(27); "-"; CHR$(0);`	Turn off underline mode
`LPRINT CHR$(27); "0";`	Set line spacing at 8 lines per inch
`LPRINT CHR$(27); "1";`	Set line spacing at about 10 lines per inch
`LPRINT CHR$(27); "2";`	Set line spacing at 6 lines per inch[*]
`LPRINT CHR$(27); "4";`	Turn on italics mode[*]
`LPRINT CHR$(27); "5";`	Turn off italics mode[*]
`LPRINT CHR$(27); "@";`	Reset printer to power-on condition[*]
`LPRINT CHR$(27); "E";`	Turn on emphasized mode
`LPRINT CHR$(27); "F";`	Turn off emphasized mode
`LPRINT CHR$(27); "G";`	Turn on double-strike mode
`LPRINT CHR$(27); "H";`	Turn off double-strike mode
`LPRINT CHR$(27); "S"; CHR$(1);`	Subscript on
`LPRINT CHR$(27); "S"; CHR$(0);`	Superscript on
`LPRINT CHR$(27); "T";`	Turn subscript/superscript off

[*]Epson printers and their compatibles only

Table 4-10. Printer-control statements for IBM and EPSON dot-matrix printers and their compatibles

In Conclusion

Now you know all of the fundamentals about variables: setting them up, getting data into them, manipulating them through various operations to get new results, and finally outputting these results to screen or printer. Now

Statement[*]	Effect
`LPRINT CHR$(27); "&13D";`	Select double spacing (3 lines per inch)
`LPRINT CHR$(27); "&14D";`	Select space and a half (4 lines per inch)
`LPRINT CHR$(27); "&16D";`	Select standard spacing (6 lines per inch)
`LPRINT CHR$(27); "&1nD";`	Set page length to *n* lines
`LPRINT CHR$(27); "&1nE";`	Set top margin to *n* lines
`LPRINT CHR$(27); "&1nL";`	Set left margin to column *n*
`LPRINT CHR$(27); "&1nR";`	Move cursor to line *n*
`LPRINT CHR$(27); "&1nC";`	Move cursor to column *n*
`LPRINT CHR$(27); "&1dD";`	Turn on text underlining
`LPRINT CHR$(27); "&1d@";`	Turn off text underlining
`LPRINT CHR$(27); "(s0P";`	Fixed spacing
`LPRINT CHR$(27); "(s1P";`	Proportional spacing
`LPRINT CHR$(27); "(snH";`	Select pitch of *n* characters/inch
`LPRINT CHR$(27); "(snV";`	Select characters of height *n* points
`LPRINT CHR$(27); "(s0S";`	Select upright characters
`LPRINT CHR$(27); "(s1S";`	Select italic characters
`LPRINT CHR$(27); "(snB";`	Select stroke weight *n* (-3 to 3)
`LPRINT CHR$(12);`	Form feed
`LPRINT CHR$(13);`	Carriage return and line feed
`LPRINT CHR$(27); "E"; CHR$(1);`	Reset printer to power-on condition
`LPRINT CHR$(27); "(snV";`	Set vertical height of scalable font to *n* points

[*] All l's (els) appear in boldface.

Table 4-11.   Printer-control statements for Hewlett-Packard LaserJet printers and their compatibles

we're ready to look at additional statements that control the way a QBasic program is executed, thereby giving a program the power to make decisions. Such power is at the very heart of computing.

Decisions and Repetition

—

It would not be exaggerating to say that almost all of the power of computer programming is found in the ability to evaluate conditions and to make decisions on processing based upon these evaluations. Even something as simple as the user making a choice from a menu involves such computer decision-making. What the computer does next in such a case depends entirely on the answer to the question "What choice did the user make?" and its corollary "What do I do next?"

The way such questions are phrased within a computer program is the subject of this chapter. For those not familiar with the subject, it may require an adjustment in your thinking. Consider: We know that everything within a computer's memory is stored in binary form, in strings of bits (*bi*nary digi*ts*, with eight of these in a byte). Up 'til now, we have called the two possible values that a bit can hold "1's and 0's." Yet the value of a bit could just as easily be interpreted in terms of any other pair of opposite concepts: "Yes" versus "No," "High" versus "Low," and, most importantly, "True" versus "False."

Decisions within a computer program are made based on the truth or falsity (the *truth value*) of a given *proposition*. A proposition is simply a declaration about reality that may or may not be true, but whose truth value can be determined. Consider an example:

The sky is blue.

Most people would say immediately that this proposition is true. (Except perhaps residents of the Pacific Northwest.) Of course, the sky isn't always blue, even in New Mexico. Clouds, which are white, sometimes obscure the blue of the sky. Since the blueness of the sky seems to depend on the presence of clouds, we could formulate a little test that would tell us whether the sky is blue on any particular day. We'd say:

If there are no clouds, then the sky is blue.

This is clearly a true statement. Mathematicians would say that it is *axiomatic*, which is as much as to say that it's not just a good idea, it's the law; you can depend on it. Now we ask the question:

Are there clouds?

Except that, in computer terms, we might want to phrase the question thusly:

Is it true that there are no clouds?

If it is true, then it follows that the sky is blue. If not, then the sky is not blue. We can sum the whole thing up thusly, in a form of argument called a syllogism:

If it is true that there are no clouds, then the sky is blue.
There are no clouds.
Therefore, the sky is blue.

What we've introduced you to here is called *elementary propositional logic*, a game that was being played before Aristotle's time and which came to full flower in late 19th and early 20th centuries. As with many things in math, it all started out as an exercise in pure thought, and ended up having real-world applications. To be specific, propositional logic is the very foundation of digital computing.

Let's consider a computer example, and go back to the menu we talked of earlier. How do we determine what to do next, based on a user's choice from a menu? We could phrase it like this:

> *If the user chose "A," then the program must stop.*
> *If the user chose "B," then the program must bake bread.*
> *If the user chose "C," then the program must cobble shoes.*
> <u>*The user chose A.*</u>
> *Therefore, the program must stop.*

All computer languages have provisions to phrase questions like these, and determine their answers, although of course the specifics regarding bread-baking and shoe-cobbling remain beyond the scope of our present technology. In this chapter, we're going to show you how to phrase questions in QBasic, and how to use their answers to accomplish specific tasks.

One more thing. We know that computers are particularly good at highly repetitive tasks; i.e., things that must be done over and over in order to get an answer. Human beings get bored really fast with such tasks, but computers eat them up. Adding up all the numbers in a checkbook register, for example. Based on the simple question "Have I reached the end of the list of numbers?" it's possible to design a simple program to add up a long list of numbers, based on repeating a single task (add the current number to the running total) without even knowing how many numbers there are.

It turns out, there are decision-making capabilities within most all computer languages, and certainly in QBasic, that make such repetition easy to program. A good part of this chapter will be devoted to examining the structures and statements used to accomplish repetitive tasks.

First things first, though. We start back with the fundamentals of computer logic with a set of symbols that you should remember from grade school.

Relational and Logical Operators

Computer programs are useful because of their ability to make decisions. In particular, a program can determine whether two numbers are the same and, if not, which number is the larger. Don't underestimate the power of this statement. Much of what we'll learn how to do in this chapter is tied up in this

Symbol	Meaning
<	less than
>	greater than
=	equal to
<= (or =<)	less than or equal to
>= (or =>)	greater than or equal to
<> or ><	not equal to

Table 5-1.   Relational operators

ability. You may remember exercises from grade school that made use of > as well, things like:

Is 2>6?

and

Is 2+1 > 2?

In a program, symbols such as <, =, and > are called *relational operators* and are used to construct conditions that are evaluated as either "true" or "false." (In the examples above, the first statement is false, the second, true.) Table 5-1 contains a complete list of the relational operators.

Remember the *number line* from grade school math? You can determine the order of two numbers by comparing their positions on the number line. The number a is said to be less than the number b if a appears to the left of b on the number line. Here are three examples:

2 < 7

-3 < 1.5

-5 < -2.

All of these statements, of course, are "true."

It's also possible to use the relational operators with character strings. The process of ordering strings is similar to alphabetizing words. A computer determines the order of two characters by their position in the *ASCII table* (see Appendix A). ASCII is a standard that relates 256 different characters and codes (these codes are used to control the computer) to the 256 different values a byte can hold, from 0 to 255. (00000000 to 11111111 in binary notation.) By convention, the character with the lower ASCII value precedes (or is less than) the other. (A *convention*, of course, just means that a bunch of folks got together and agreed on how something would be.) For instance, according to the ASCII table, these relations are true:

"a" < "g"

"9" < "A"

"Z" < "a"

Two strings are ordered by comparing their characters one at a time until two characters in the same position differ. For instance, "ball" < "bat", "Hard" < "disk", and "9W" < "nine". If the strings have different lengths, but agree for every position of the shorter string, then the shorter string is taken to be less than the longer string. For instance, "key" < "keyboard". If the strings have the same length and identical characters in each position, then the strings are said to be equal.

So, a relational expression or condition consists of two expressions (either both numeric or both string) separated by a relational operator. A condition is true if the values of the expressions satisfy the relationship. Some conditions and their truth values are shown in Table 5-2. (In the table, assume that the variables *a*, *b*, *a$*, and *b$* have been assigned the values 4, 6, "hello", and "Goodbye", respectively.)

Several of these examples show how such simple conditions are really powerful: through the use of variables. After all, anyone can tell the answer to

2>3

without thinking. Replace one of the numbers with a variable, however, as in

b >3

Condition	Truth Value
$2 < 3$	true
$INT(2.7) > 2$	false
$3 <= 3$	true
$a + 5 = b$	false
$-7 > a$	false
"bit" < "byte"	true
"two" = "TWO"	false
$b\$ > a\$$	false
$LEN(a\$) <> 5$	false

Table 5-2.   Truth values of relational expressions

and you get something that can be evaluated each time the program is run, based on the current value of *b*.

We can also formulate more complicated conditions, by building them up out of simple conditions such as those shown above. In this way, we can make a decision based on whether two or more things are true or not.

The computer uses *logical operators*, such as AND, OR, and NOT, to build complex conditions out of simple conditions. The truth value of a complex condition depends both on the truth values of the simple conditions and on the logical operators used to join the simple conditions. For example:

"The sky is blue" AND "There are no clouds."

This entire statement is only true if both simple conditions within it are true. If either is false (say, because there are clouds), then the entire statement is held to be false.

Table 5-3 gives the truth values of the simplest complex conditions using AND, OR, and NOT. The complex condition (*cond1* AND *cond2*) is true only when both of the simple conditions are true. NOT is called the negation operator and OR is called the inclusive OR operator. NOT *cond1* has the opposite truth value of *cond1*. The complex condition (*cond1* OR *cond2*) is true if either one or both of the two simple conditions are true.

cond1	cond2	cond1 AND cond2	cond1 OR cond2	NOT cond2
true	true	true	true	false
true	false	false	true	false
false	true	false	true	true
false	false	false	false	true

Table 5-3. Truth tables for AND, OR, and NOT

When evaluating complex conditions, it's useful to construct something called a truth table. Such a table, like the one given above, lists all the possibilities. For example, the first line in the table shows what happens to the other three possibilities when both *cond1* and *cond2* are true, etc.

To make certain we all understand, let's take another real-world example before we proceed. How about:

> *The sky is blue OR the grass is green*

The above statement is true if either of the simple statements are true. If the sky is blue, the entire statement is true, regardless of the color of the grass. If, on the other hand, the sky is cloudy and the grass is brown, then the entire statement is false.

Table 5-4 presents some conditions and their truth values. As before, assume that the variables *a*, *b*, *a$*, and *b$* have been assigned the values 4, 6, "hello", and "Goodbye".

(If you are unclear on the meaning of the string operators MID and LEN, then refer back to the section on character strings in the preceding chapter.) Let's consider the fifth line in detail. First, we'll substitute the actual values of the variables:

```
(LEN("Goodbye") = 7) AND ("hello" > "Goodbye")
```

The string operator LEN determines the length of a string; it produces an integer result. "Goodbye" has seven characters, so it's length is 7. Let's substitute that:

Condition	Truth Value
`(2 < 3) OR (0 > 1)`	true
`(2 < 3) AND (0 > 1)`	false
`NOT (0 > 1)`	true
`(MID$(a$, 2,1) < "Z") OR (a <> 4)`	false
`(LEN(b$) = 7) AND (a$ > b$)`	true
`NOT (a$ >= "hello")`	false

Table 5-4.   Truth values of complex conditions

```
(7 = 7) AND ("hello" > "Goodbye")
```

Clearly the first simple condition is true. That yields:

```
TRUE AND ("hello" > "Goodbye")
```

To evaluate the second condition, we recall that two strings are compare one character at a time, starting with the first. Since the ASCII table used to determine character orders is actually much like regular alphabetical order, it turns out that "h" is greater than "G". (That's because all small letters come together after all the capital letters.) Thus, the second simple condition is true also. We end up with:

```
TRUE AND TRUE
```

which itself, of course, is true.

But wait, there's more. Table 5-5 gives the truth values of the other logical operators available in QBasic. The operator XOR is known as *exclusive* OR. (The other OR operator is sometimes called *inclusive* OR.) The complex condition (*cond1* XOR *cond2*) is true if one or the other of the two simple conditions is true, *but not both*. That's what makes it exclusive; it excludes the possibility that both simple conditions are true. How about:

The sky is blue XOR the sky is cloudy.

cond1	cond2	cond1 XOR cond2	cond1 EQV cond2	cond1 IMP cond2
true	true	false	true	true
true	false	true	false	false
false	true	true	false	true
false	false	false	true	false

Table 5-5. Truth tables for XOR, EQV, AND IMP

That's an example of exclusive or. If both conditions are true, then the whole statement must be false, because the sky can't be both cloudy and blue at the same time.

The operators EQV and IMP are read "is equivalent to" and "implies," respectively. Two conditions are equivalent if they have the same truth values. For example:

The sky is blue EQV the sky is not cloudy

One condition is said to *imply* another provided that the second is true whenever the first is true. For example,

The grass is green IMP the grass is not brown

Expressions using operators appear in Table 5-6.

It's worth noting that QBasic itself has truth tables for these operators "built-in," as it were.

Condition	Truth Value
`(1 < 2) XOR (3 < 4)`	false
`(1 = 2) EQV ("A" > "B")`	true
`(1 < 2) IMP (1 = 2)`	false

Table 5-6. Expressions using XOR, EQV, and IMP

Let's consider some more examples:

Let's take each of these in turn, phrasing them in English. The first line says "One is less than two" or "three is less than four," exclusively. The claim is that one of the two statements is true, but not both. Clearly both are true, so the statement as a whole is false.

The second example says "The statement 'One equals two' is equivalent in truth value to the statement 'The letter A is greater than the letter B.'" One is not equal to two, and A is not greater than B. Therefore, the statement as a whole is true because the two simple statements have the same true value: They're both false.

The third one is trickier. In English, the statement reads: "The statement 'One is less than two' implies that 'One is equal to two.'" (Sometimes the reading takes the "If...then..." form, as in "If 1<2, then 1=2.") Clearly, 1<2 implies no such thing. Since the first statement is true, and the second false, the statement as a whole is false. It works like this: If the first statement is true, the second must actually be true for the whole thing to be true. If the first statement is false, then anything is possible, like:

If pigs can fly, then there'll be pork in the treetops by morning.

Complex conditions can involve a combination of several arithmetic, relational, and logical operators. In this book we make a generous use of parentheses in order to avoid any ambiguity and make the code easy to read. However, in the absence of parentheses, all versions of BASIC use the same *operator hierarchy*. Such a hierarchy determines which operations come first, and which come after, and in what order.

First, the arithmetic expressions are evaluated with the precedence discussed in Chapter 4. Then each relational operator is evaluated as either true or false. Finally, the logical operators are evaluated in the order NOT, AND, OR, XOR, EQV, and IMP. For instance,

```
NOT 2 + 3 < 6 AND "A" < "B" OR 4 * 5 + 2 < 23
```

is evaluated as

```
((NOT((2 + 3)<6))AND("A"<"B"))OR(((4 * 5)+2)<23).
```

In order, this complex condition is evaluated thusly: First, all arithematic is taken care of. This yields:

```
((NOT (5 < 6)) AND ("A" < "B")) OR (22 < 23)
```

Now the individual relational operations are evaluated, to yield:

```
((NOT (TRUE)) AND (TRUE)) OR (TRUE)
```

Next comes NOT, yielding:

```
((FALSE) AND (TRUE)) OR (TRUE)
```

Next comes AND, to give:

```
(FALSE) OR (TRUE)
```

And last comes OR, to give the final answer:

```
TRUE
```

Therefore, that entire thing written above is, as a whole, true. To take a stab at it, we might phrase the whole thing in English as:

> Either one, or both, of these two statements are true: That either the opposite of the truth value of the statement "two plus three is less than six" and the statement "capital 'A' is less than capital 'B'" are both true or four times five plus two is less than twenty-three.

Whew! Aren't you glad the computer gets to do that, and not you?

Summing Up

Again, the ability to make decisions that affect the flow of a program is important, indeed crucial, to problem solving. The 12 relational and logical operators presented in this section are sufficient to express any condition needed to make a decision.

Well, so we can test to see if some condition, or combination of conditions, is true or not? How do we put this knowledge to use? That's the subject of the next section.

Decision Structures

Do you remember our little menuing example from early in this chapter? If the user pressed "A," then stop the program...etc.? This simple construction is actually the most fundamental of computer decision-making structures. The general form is

```
IF condition THEN statement
```

The *condition* is evaluated. If it is true, then the *statement* (it can be any valid statement) is performed. If the condition is false, nothing happens and the program proceeds to the next statement. Using statements we already know, we could write:

```
IF 3>2 THEN PRINT "YES"
```

If this statement were encountered in a program, QBasic would display the string "YES" on the screen, because three is greater than two.

Suppose we want to take some other course of action if the condition is false? We can handle this as well, using the keyword ELSE. For example, consider this statement:

```
IF 3<2 THEN PRINT "YES" ELSE PRINT "NO"
```

If this statement were encountered in a program, QBasic would display the string "NO" on the screen, because the statement "3<2" is false. This type of decision making statement has the general form

```
IF condition THEN statement1 ELSE statement2
```

Most versions of BASIC, including QBasic, support this single-line IF...THEN...ELSE statement. Program 5-1 gives an example of a single line IF...THEN...ELSE statement.

IF Block

The actions in an IF *condition* THEN *statement1* ELSE *statement2* statement can consist of several QBasic statements. QBasic requires the separate statements to be separated by colons. For example:

```
IF 3>2 THEN PRINT "YES" : PRINT "CORRECT"    ELSE PRINT "NO"
```

Program 5-1. Single-line IF...THEN...ELSE

```
REM Determine eligibility to vote   [5-1]
a$ = "You are eligible to vote"
INPUT "Enter your age: ", age
IF age >= 18 THEN PRINT a$ ELSE PRINT a$+" in";18-age; "years"
END

[run]
Enter your age: 32
You are eligible to vote

[run]
Enter your age: 15
You are eligible to vote in 3 years
```

Now as you can see, the single line can be too long to fit into a single line of the View window or may be difficult to understand. A more readable way to handle this situation, rather than using colons, is to use the IF block supplied by QBasic. The format is

```
IF condition THEN
     statements
   ELSE
     statements
END IF
```

Each of the two "action" blocks can consist of as many statements as desired. They can even include other IF blocks. (We call this *nesting* IF blocks. It's a way of testing yet another condition once we know the result of the first. Nesting is an important part of programming.) Note that, in an IF block, no statement can follow THEN on the same line.

Program 5-2 accepts a year as input and decides if it is a leap year. Each year divisible by 4 is a leap year, with the exception of years that end in 00 and are not whole multiples of 400 — that is, those years that are divisible by 100 — and are not divisible by 400. (Recall that the MOD operator gives the remainder when a first number is divided by a second.)

Program 5-2. Using IF...THEN...ELSE blocks

```
REM Determine if a given year is a leap year   [5-2]
INPUT "Enter year (xxxx): ", year
IF year MOD 4 <> 0 THEN
    PRINT year; "is not a leap year."
  ELSE
    IF (year MOD 100 = 0) AND (year MOD 400 <> 0) THEN
        PRINT year; "is not a leap year."
      ELSE
        PRINT year; "is a leap year."
    END IF
END IF
END

[run]
Enter year (xxxx): 1800
 1800 is not a leap year.
```

ELSEIF statement

As Program 5-2 shows, the IF block can be used to select one of several possible options. This capability is made simpler with a further enhancement to the IF block, namely, the ELSEIF statement. A block of the general form

```
IF cond1 THEN
    statement(s)
  ELSEIF cond2 THEN
    statement(s)
  ELSEIF cond3 THEN
    statement(s)
  ELSE
    statement(s)
END IF
```

examines each condition in order, and executes the statement or statements that follow the *first* true condition. In the general example above, if *cond1* were false, but *cond2* and *cond3* were both true, only the statement(s) following *cond2* would be executed. Those following *cond3* and ELSE would be skipped.

If none of the conditions are true, the block executes the statement or statements following ELSE. The IF block can contain as many ELSEIF statements as desired. The ELSE statement at the end of the IF block is optional. If all of

Program 5-3. Using ELSEIF

```
REM Determine if a given year is a leap year   [5-3]
INPUT "Enter year (xxxx): ", year
IF year MOD 4 <> 0 THEN
    PRINT year; "is not a leap year."
  ELSEIF (year MOD 100 = 0) AND (year MOD 400 <> 0) THEN
    PRINT year; "is not a leap year."
  ELSE
    PRINT year; "is a leap year."
END IF
END

[run]
Enter year (xxxx): 1800
 1800 is not a leap year.

[run]
Enter year (xxxx): 1600
 1600 is a leap year.
```

the conditions are false and no ELSE statement is present, then the IF block takes no action.

Program 5-3 uses the ELSEIF statement to improve the readability of Program 5-2, which determines leap years. In the first run, the condition following IF was false, but the condition following ELSEIF was true. In the second run, the conditions following IF and ELSEIF were false and so the statement following ELSE was executed.

Program 5-4 uses ELSEIF in the computation of the FICA taxes that a company deducts from an employee's paycheck. FICA taxes have a social security and a medicare component. In 1991, social security taxes are paid at the rate of 6.2 percent on the first $53,400 of earnings in a year. Medicare taxes are paid at a rate of 1.45 percent on the first $125,000.

Avoiding Ambiguity

Now, in Standard BASIC, it can be really hard to understand statements that contain multiple IFs, THENs, and ELSEs. Consider

```
IF condition1 THEN IF condition2 THEN act1 ELSE act2
```

Program 5-4. Computing FICA taxes with ELSEIF

```
REM Calculate FICA taxes [5-4]
INPUT "Enter current earnings: ", pay
INPUT "Enter prior year-to-date earnings: ", prior
LET ficaTax = 0
IF prior + pay < 53400 THEN
     LET ficaTax = .062 * pay
   ELSEIF prior < 53400 THEN
     LET ficaTax = .062 * (53400 - prior)
END IF
IF prior + pay < 125000 THEN
     LET ficaTAX = ficaTax + .0145 * pay
   ELSEIF prior < 125000 THEN
     LET ficaTax = ficaTax + .0145 * (125000 - prior)
END IF
IF ficaTax = 0 THEN
     PRINT "No tax due."
   ELSE
     PRINT USING "Tax =$$#,###"; ficaTax
END IF

[run]
Enter current earnings: 2000
Enter prior year-to-date earnings: 60000
Tax =     $29.00
```

Does ELSE go with the first IF or the second IF? The general rule is that the first ELSE is associated with the closest preceding IF and each subsequent ELSE is associated with the closest unassigned preceding IF. Messy!

In QBasic, the IF block not only allows us to determine the correct associations without a possibly tedious application of this rule, but also allows us to associate an ELSE with whichever preceding IF we desire. Figure 5-1 gives two different interpretations to the statement just presented, using IF blocks. In the figure, the block on the left associates the ELSE with the first IF, whereas the block on the right associated the ELSE with the second IF.

SELECT CASE Structure

Often, the action to be taken depends solely on the numerical or character value of an expression. Hark back to the menu example we keep mentioning.

```
IF condition1 THEN                IF condition1 THEN
   IF condition2 THEN action1        IF condition2 THEN
ELSE                                    action1
   action2                          ELSE
END IF                                  action2
                                     END IF
                                  END IF
```

Figure 5-1. Nested IF...THEN blocks

We earlier phrased it in terms of a whole line of IF statements. While you *could* construct a logical statement to evaluate the value of the key the user pressed, and then use an IF block for each set of actions, the SELECT CASE structure is custom-made for this task.

Consider Program 5-5, which is written in Standard BASIC. (Note the line numbers.) When this program is rewritten with the SELECT CASE structure, as in Program 5-6, it is not only easier to write and read, but also has greater flexibility.

The general SELECT CASE block begins with a statement of the form

```
SELECT CASE expression
```

Program 5-5. A Standard BASIC program with many decisions

```
10 REM One, Two, Buckle My Shoe [5-5]
20 a = 7: b = 8
30 INPUT "Enter a number from 1 to 10: ", n
40 IF (n = 1) OR (n = 2) THEN PRINT "Buckle my shoe.": GOTO 90
50 IF (3<=n) AND (n<=4)  THEN PRINT "Shut the door.": GOTO 90
60 IF n <= 6 THEN PRINT "Pick up sticks.": GOTO 90
70 IF n = a OR n = b THEN PRINT "Lay them straight.": GOTO 90
80 PRINT "Start all over again."
90 END
RUN
Enter a number from 1 to 10: 5
Pick up sticks.
Ok
```

Program 5-6. Using SELECT CASE

```
REM One, Two, Buckle my shoe [5-6]
a = 7: b = 8
INPUT "Enter a number from 1 to 10: ", n
SELECT CASE n
 CASE 1, 2
    PRINT "Buckle my shoe."
  CASE 3 TO 4
    PRINT "Shut the door."
  CASE IS <= 6
    PRINT "Pick up sticks."
  CASE a, b
    PRINT "Lay them straight."
  CASE ELSE
    PRINT "Start all over again."
END SELECT
END
```

where the expression evaluates to either a numeric or a string value. The block ends with the statement

```
END SELECT
```

possibly preceded by the statement

```
CASE ELSE
```

The standard CASE statements inside the block consist of one or more possibilities for the value of the expression, with the different possibilities separated by commas. Each possibility is one of the following types:

A *constant*, such as 1 or "YES"

A *variable*, like $i\%$ or *result*

An *expression*, like *result* + 1

A *relational operator* preceded by IS and followed by a constant, variable, or expression (e.g., IS > 5)

A *range* expressed in the form "X TO Y," where X and Y are either constants, variables, or expressions (e.g., 1 TO 3)

Program 5-7. Using multi-statement actions and nested blocks

```
REM Determine the number of days in a given month  [5-7]
INPUT "Enter number of month (Jan = 1, Feb = 2, etc.): ", month
SELECT CASE month
  CASE 9, 4, 6, 11
    numberOfDays = 30
  CASE 2
    REM Determine if a given year is a leap year
    INPUT "Enter year (xxxx): ", year
    IF year MOD 4 <> 0 THEN
        numberOfDays = 28
      ELSEIF (year MOD 100 = 0) AND (year MOD 400 <> 0) THEN
        numberOfDays = 28
      ELSE
        numberOfDays = 29
    END IF
  CASE ELSE
    numberOfDays = 31
END SELECT
PRINT "The number of days in the month is"; numberOfDays
END

[run]
Enter number of month (Jan = 1, Feb = 2, etc.): 2
Enter year (xxxx): 2000
The number of days in the month is 29
```

When encountering a SELECT CASE block, QBasic evaluates the expression, and then looks for the first standard CASE statement that includes the value of the expression or otherwise for a CASE ELSE statement. If QBasic finds either one, it executes the statements associated with it. After that, or in the event neither is present, QBasic proceeds to the statement following the SELECT CASE block.

Program 5-7 contains multi-statement actions and nested blocks. After the month is entered as a number from 1 to 12, the number of days in the month is determined. To adjust for leap years, the year is also requested if the month is February. (By the way, we thought it would be good to remind you that using a comma, instead of a semicolon, between the prompt and the variable in an INPUT statement causes the prompt to be displayed without a question mark. When you use a semicolon, QBasic adds a question mark to the prompt, just as Standard BASIC does.)

Program 5-8. A SELECT CASE block with a string expression

```
REM Translate a given word into pig latin   [5-8]
INPUT "Enter a word: ", word$
SELECT CASE LEFT$(word$, 1)
  CASE "a", "e", "i", "o", "u", "A", "E", "I", "O", "U"
    pigword$ = word$ + "way"
  CASE "a" TO "z"
    pigword$ = MID$(word$,2,LEN(word$)) + LEFT$(word$,1) + "ay"
  CASE "A" TO "Z"
    pigword$ = UCASE$(MID$(word$,2,1))+MID$(word$,3,LEN(word$))
    pigword$ = pigword$ + LCASE$(LEFT$(word$,1)) + "ay"
END SELECT
PRINT "The pig latin translation is "; pigword$
END


[run]
Enter a word: Computer
The pig latin translation is Omputercay
```

Program 5-8, which translates words into "pig latin," uses a string expression in a SELECT CASE block. If the word to be translated into pig latin begins with an uppercase letter, the pig latin translation will also begin with an uppercase letter; the uppercase letter that is moved to the end of the word will now appear in lowercase.

Loops

The structures we have discussed up to now are good for tasks that can be completed in one pass. Sometimes, however, you want to repeat an action or a group of actions a specified number of times. You could type out the whole block of statements the number of times you want to perform it, but that's tedious. And what if you want to be able to repeat an action a varying number of times? All computer languages can handle this eventuality through the medium of a loop.

A loop repeats a sequence of statements either as long as or until a certain condition is true. The condition can be checked before or after the sequence of statements is executed. The standard loop in QBasic is the DO loop, which has several variations.

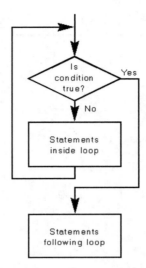

Figure 5-2. A flowchart (a diagram for indicating the flow of processing in a computer program) for a DO UNTIL loop with the condition checked at the top

When QBasic encounters the block

```
DO UNTIL condition
    statement(s)
LOOP
```

it first checks whether the condition is true or false. If the condition is true, then the statement(s) in the block will be skipped and the program will continue with the statement following the block. (The statement following LOOP, which marks the loop's end.) If the condition is false, the sequence of statements will be executed and then the entire process will be repeated. The flowchart in Figure 5-2 describes the process.

Program 5-9 computes the average of a list of numbers supplied by the user. The program uses a loop to continue asking for numbers until the user signals the end of the list by entering -1.

The Block

```
DO
    statements
LOOP UNTIL condition
```

Program 5-9. Using DO UNTIL

```
REM Find the average of a list of numbers  [5-9]
numItems = 0
sum = 0
PRINT "Enter -1 after the entire list has been entered."
INPUT "Enter a number: ", number
DO UNTIL number = -1
  numItems = numItems + 1
  sum = sum + number
  INPUT "Enter a number: ", number
LOOP
IF numItems > 0 THEN PRINT "The average is"; sum / numItems
END

[run]
Enter -1 after the entire list has been entered.
Enter a number: 89
Enter a number: 94
Enter a number: 87
Enter a number: -1
The average is 90
```

also executes the sequence of statements repeatedly until the specified condition is true. However, in this case, the condition is checked after the statements are executed. Therefore, the sequence of statements will always be executed at least once. The flowchart in Figure 5-3 describes the process.

Here is an example of the use of loops. Suppose that the 100 entries in the string array cities$( ) are in ascending alphabetical order. Also, suppose that the corresponding populations are contained in the array pop( ). Program segment 5-10 uses a *binary* search to find the population of a given city. Such a search is called *binary* because, at each pass, the program determines whether the thing being searched for is in the first half or the second half of the list. In this case, at each pass through the loop, the range of variables that could possibly contain the city is cut in half.

Instead of looping until a certain condition is true, DO loops can loop while (or as long as) a condition is true. The syntax is one of the following:

```
DO WHILE condition          DO
   statements                  statements
LOOP                        LOOP WHILE condition
```

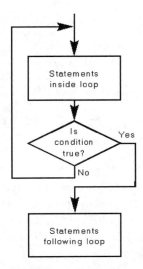

Figure 5-3. A flowchart for a DO UNTIL loop with the condition checked at the bottom

Any DO loop written with UNTIL can also be written with WHILE by replacing the condition with its negation. For instance, the DO loops in Program 5-9 and Program 5-10 can be rewritten as shown in Figure 5-4.

Program 5-10. A binary search

```
REM Binary Search  [5-10]
INPUT "Enter name of city: ", city
low = 1
high = 100
DO
  middle = INT((low + high)/2)
  SELECT CASE cities$(middle)
    CASE IS < city$
      low = middle + 1
    CASE IS > city$
      high = middle - 1
    CASE city$
      PRINT city$; " has population"; pop(middle)
  END SELECT
LOOP UNTIL (cities$(middle) = city$) OR (low > high)
IF cities$(middle) <> city$ THEN PRINT "City not found."
```

```
DO WHILE number <> -1
    .                    'Statements go here
LOOP
DO
    .                    'Statements go here
LOOP WHILE (cities$(middle) <> city$) AND (low <= high)
```

Figure 5-4.   DO WHILE loops

DO loops can also involve two conditions: one condition checked at the top (beginning) of the loop and the other checked at the bottom of the loop (end). However, such code can be difficult to understand and, if possible, should be rewritten. For instance, the code on the left in Figure 5-5 can be replaced by the code on the right.

```
DO UNTIL cond1            IF NOT cond1 THEN
    statements               DO
LOOP UNTIL cond2                 statements
                             LOOP UNTIL cond1 OR cond2
                         END IF
```

Figure 5-5.   Improving the readability of a DO Loop

Incidentally, the WHILE...WEND loop available in many enhanced versions of Standard BASIC performs the same as a DO loop that begins with the statement DO WHILE *condition*. For instance, the DO loop in Program 5-9 is equivalent to the WHILE...WEND loop shown in Figure 5-6.

```
WHILE number <> -1
  numberOfItems = numberOfItems + 1
  sum = sum + number
  INPUT "Enter a number: ", number
WEND
```

Figure 5-6.   A WHILE...WEND loop

Looping Based on Numbers

The loops considered so far are called *condition-controlled* loops. There are other ways to control loops. The FOR...NEXT loop, which some of you may be familiar with from earlier BASIC versions, is referred to as a *counter-controlled* loop. A counter (that is, a numeric variable) is given an initial value that is increased (or decreased) after each pass through the loop. Statements within the loop are executed repeatedly until the counter becomes greater than (or less than) a specified value. For example, the loop

```
FOR i = a TO b STEP s
   statement(s)
NEXT i
```

initially assigns the value *a* to the variable *i*. Next a test is done to see if *i* is less than or equal to *b*, when *s* is positive, or if *i* is greater than or equal to *b*, when *s* is negative. If so, the program executes the statements, replaces the value of *i* by *i* + *s*, and repeats the test. This process continues until the test fails, at which time the program exits the loop and executes the statement after the loop.

For example, the block

```
FOR i = 1 TO 10 STEP 1
   PRINT "BOO"
NEXT i
```

causes the word "BOO" to be displayed on the screen 10 times.

In a general FOR...NEXT loop, *a*, *b*, and *s* can be numeric expressions. However, the program executes faster if they are variables and fastest if they are constants. This is because numeric expressions must be evaluated, and the value of variables must be looked up, whereas constants are known. If STEP *s* is omitted from the FOR statement, the program increases the counter variable by 1 after each pass.

Program 5-11 uses a FOR...NEXT loop to add up the odd numbers from 1 to 99.

Program 5-11. A FOR...NEXT example

```
REM Sum the odd numbers from 1 TO 99   [5-11]
sum = 0
FOR number% = 1 TO 99 STEP 2
  sum = sum + number%
NEXT number%
PRINT sum
END
[run]
 2500
```

In many versions of Standard BASIC, the counter variable of a **FOR...NEXT** loop must be of either integer or single precision. QBasic permits the counter variable to be any numeric type. However, care must be taken to avoid rounding errors when using single- and double-precision counters. For instance, the statement

```
FOR n# = 1 TO 2 STEP .01
```

should be replaced by

```
FOR n# = 1 TO 2.005 STEP .01
```

since summing .01 one hundred times produces a number that is slightly larger than 1. This is another undesirable artifact of the way QBasic stores floating-point numbers internally. The internal binary representation of .01 is not precisely equal to .01.

The execution time of a FOR...NEXT loop depends on the numeric type of the counter variable. Execution is fastest with integer variables, and then decreases in speed with long integer variables, single-precision variables, and double-precision variables, in that order. The difference in speed between those loops that have integer counter variables and those that have double-precision counter variables is considerable. You should always use the fastest type possible.

Infinite Loops

The condition that causes a loop to stop executing is called the *terminal condition*. It usually involves a variable whose value can be altered by the statements in the body of the loop. However, if there is no terminal condition, or if the

```
DO
   PRINT "Hello";
LOOP

sum = 0
FOR i = 1 TO 5 STEP 0
   sum = sum + i
NEXT i

INPUT "Enter a number: ", n
DO UNTIL n * n < 0
```

Figure 5-7.   Infinite loops

truth value of the terminal condition cannot be changed by the body of the loop, then the loop *might* repeat indefinitely. Some examples of infinite loops are shown in Figure 5-7.

Any QBasic program, including those with infinite loops, can be terminated by pressing <Ctrl+Break>. QBasic returns to the View window and the line where the execution of the program was stopped is highlighted.

Many programs intentionally use infinite loops to keep repeating an operation until the user aborts the program with <Ctrl+Break>. This task is better handled by a control, or *decision structure* that repeats a loop until a special key is pressed.

For instance, Program 5-12 should be replaced with Program 5-13. (The sound statement **PLAY** *letter* produces the note corresponding to the letter.)

Program 5-12. A program requiring <Ctrl+Break> to terminate

```
REM Electronic keyboard [5-12]
CLS
PRINT "Press any keys from A through G"
DO
  a$ = INPUT$(1)
  IF UCASE$(a$)>="A" AND UCASE$(a$)<="G" THEN PLAY a$
LOOP
END
```

Program 5-13. An improvement over Program 5-12

```
REM Improved electronic keyboard [5-13]
CLS
PRINT "Press any keys from A through G"
PRINT "Press Q to terminate the program"
DO
  a$= INPUT$(1)
  IF UCASE$(a$) >= "A" AND UCASE$(a$) <="G" THEN PLAY a$
LOOP UNTIL UCASE$(a$) = "Q"
END
```

Exiting Loops and Decision Structures

Loops have a well-defined entry point and exit point. However, sometimes you might like to have the option of exiting a loop in the middle of a sequence of statements. This task can be accomplished in QBasic with the EXIT statement. The statements EXIT DO and EXIT FOR are used to exit DO...LOOP and FOR...NEXT loops, respectively, and jump to the statement after the loop.

```
DO
  statements1
  IF condition THEN EXIT DO
  statements2
LOOP
```

In the above syntax example, *statements1* are always executed. If *condition* is true, however, the loop is exited and the statement immediately following LOOP is executed. If *condition* is not true, then *statements2* are executed and the entire loop is executed again.

Program segment 5-14 does a sequential search of the 100 entries in the unordered string array cities$( ) to determine if a particular city is in the array. Note that when the program EXITs a FOR...NEXT loop prematurely, the value of the counter variable is not incremented.

Indentation and Nesting

When you use many IF and CASE blocks and loops in a program, and especially if you have some inside others (recall that we call this *nesting*), your code

Program 5-14.   Segment using an EXIT statement

```
REM Sequential search  [5-14]
INPUT "Enter name of city: ", city$
FOR i = 1 TO 100
  IF city$(i) = city$ THEN EXIT FOR
NEXT i
IF i = 101 THEN
    PRINT "City not found."
  ELSE
    PRINT "City is element"; i; "of the array."
END IF
```

gets difficult for other people — and even yourself later on — to read and understand. It helps to indent structures that appear inside other ones. You can do this using the TAB key, or simply by adding spaces, so that structures nested within others appear further to the right. You've indented things in this way before, we'll bet. Have you ever written an outline?

I.   Introduction
    A.   Why We're Writing This Book
    B.   Why You Should Read It
II.   Conclusion
    A.   Why We Wrote This Book
    B.   Why You Read It

QBasic will correctly compile a program even if it contains no indentation. However, indentation improves the readability of a program and, therefore, is good programming style. In this chapter, we have consistently indented the contents of each block and loop to clarify its structure.

Indentation is also used to show that one block or loop is contained, or nested, within another. Doing so allows the reader to pair up each DO statement with its associated LOOP statement and each FOR statement with its associated NEXT statement. Indentation also helps to prevent improper nesting, as shown in Figure 5-8. When loops are properly nested, the entire inner loop is contained within the outer loop.

Program segment 5-15 uses nested loops to rearrange the elements of an array into increasing order. The program uses a process called a *Shell sort*. It systematically compares distant elements and interchanges pairs that are out of

```
DO UNTIL condition          DO UNTIL condition
   FOR i = 1 TO 3              FOR i = 1 TO 3
LOOP                            NEXT i
   NEXT i                   LOOP

FOR i = 1 TO 5              FOR i = 1 TO 5
   FOR k = 3 TO 9              FOR k = 3 TO 9
NEXT i                         NEXT k
   NEXT k                   NEXT i
```

Improperly Nested Loops   **ProperlyNested Loops**

Figure 5-8. Nested loops

order. (The statement SWAP *array$*(*i*), *array$*(*i* + *gap*) exchanges the values of the two subscripted variables.) The distance over which pairs are compared, called the *gap*, is set to half the number of elements and successively halved until the entire array is ordered.

Now we've seen how to control the execution of a program's statements based on logical and numerical conditions, using IF and CASE blocks and DO loops. Sometimes, however, you will want to transfer to an entirely different location within a program if some condition is true. We'll show you how to do that, and why you'd want to, in the next chapter.

Program 5-15. Segment including a Shell sort

```
REM Shell sort of array$(), an array of n elements   [5-15]
gap = INT(n / 2)
DO WHILE gap > 0
  sorted$ = "no"
  DO WHILE sorted$ = "no"
    sorted$ = "yes"   'Innocent until proven guilty
    FOR i = 1 TO n - gap
      IF array$(i) > array$(i + gap) THEN
        SWAP array$(i), array$(i + gap)
        sorted$ = "no"
      END IF
    NEXT i
  LOOP
  gap = INT(gap / 2)
LOOP
```

Functions, Subroutines, and Subprograms

A programmer is a person who solves problems with the aid of a computer. The problem-solving process consists of the following four steps:

1. Define and understand the problem.

2. Devise a plan for solving the problem.

3. Code the solution as a program.

4. Test the program.

The first step requires that the programmer have a clear idea of what data (input) will be given to the computer, what results (output) are to be produced, and what relationships exist between them. The difficulty of the third step (coding a program) depends on the quality of the plan devised in the second step.

The original problem is broken down into a sequence of smaller sub-problems. If any of these subproblems are not manageable chunks, they are broken down into yet smaller subproblems. The programmer repeats the process until all subproblems are manageable. This process is sometimes known as "stepwise refinement." (Other jargony terms for this process include "top-down design," "iterative multilevel modeling," "hierarchical programming," and "divide and conquer programming.")

After breaking down the original problem, the programmer solves the manageable chunks one at a time and puts them together to produce a solution to the problem. Computer scientists agree that this is best method for solving complex problems.

Standard BASIC has two devices for coding subproblems and "manageable chunks" — subroutines and single-line user-defined functions. QBasic not only has these two devices, but has upgraded them into two of the most important structures of modern programming: subprograms and function procedures. In this chapter we'll briefly discuss the devices from Standard BASIC so that we can understand the enhancements to them found in QBasic.

Single-line Functions

QBasic has many predefined functions. Table 6-1 presents some of these functions that you have already encountered.

Although the input can involve several values, the output always consists of a single value. You can determine the type of output by looking at the name of the function. If a dollar sign follows the name, as in "CHR$", then the output is a string; if not, then the output is a number.

In addition to these predefined functions, you can define simple functions of your own, called FN functions. These new, user-defined functions must begin with the letters FN, and the names must conform to the rules of naming variables. Like variable names, they should be suggestive of the role per-

Function	Example	Input	Output
INT	`INT(2.6)` is 2	number	number
CHR$	`CHR$(65)` is "A"	number	string
LEN	`LEN("perhaps")` is 7	string	number
MID$	`MID$("perhaps", 4, 2)` is "ha"	string,number, number	string
INSTR	`INSTR("to be", " ")` is 3	string,string	number

Table 6-1. Some predefined functions

Program 6-1. A single-line FN function

```
REM Determine a person's first name  [6-1]
DEF FNFirstName$ (n$) = LEFT$(n$, INSTR(n$, " ") - 1)
INPUT "Person's name"; name$
PRINT "The person's first name is "; FNFirstName$(name$)
END


[run]
Person's name? Thomas Woodrow Wilson
The person's first name is Thomas
```

formed. You can define FN functions in programs by writing DEF followed by the function definition. Here are two examples.

```
DEF FNFirstName$ (n$) = LEFT$(n$, INSTR(n$, " ") - 1)

DEF FNDoublingTime (x) = 72 / x
```

The function FNFirstName$ takes the first name from a person's full name. The function FNDoublingTime estimates the number of years required for an investment to double in value when the investment earns interest at a rate of *x* percent. (The formula used is commonly known as the Rule of 72.) For instance, FNDoublingTime(8) is 9; that is, an investment that earns 8% interest will double in value in about nine years. Programs 6-1 and 6-2 illustrate the use of the two functions just discussed.

The variables *x* and *n$* that appear in the function definitions just given are called *parameters*. They have meaning only within the definition of the function. When you actually use, or invoke, an FN function in a program, con-

Program 6-2. Another example of an FN function

```
REM Calculate doubling time for an investment  [6-2]
DEF FNDoublingTime (x) = 72 / x
INPUT "Percent interest rate earned"; p
PRINT "Money will double in about"; FNDoublingTime(p); "years."
END

[run]
Percent interest rate earned? 8
Money will double in about 9 years.
```

stants, variables, or expressions appear in place of the parameters. These constants, variables or expressions are called *arguments*.

For example, in Program 6-2 the parameter is *x* and the argument is *p*. As with predefined functions, the only restrictions on the arguments used when you invoke a FN function are that there should be the proper number of them, and that each argument should be of the appropriate type: numeric or string.

For example, FNDoublingTime(5.5), FNDoublingTime(*rate*), and FNDoublingTime(*net*/7) are all proper invocations of FNDoublingTime since Program 6-2 defined FNDoublingTime with a single numeric parameter. However, FNDoublingTime(*rate, net*/7) and FNDoublingTime(*rate*$) are not proper invocations of FNDoublingTime.

Like predefined functions, user-defined FN functions have a single output that is either a number or a string. A dollar sign must follow the name of the function if the output is a string. In addition, you can use one of the numeric type declaration tags at the end of the name to specify a specific numeric type. (A DEFtype statement can also specify the type of the output.)

The input of an FN function can consist of one or more parameters. Two examples of FN functions with several parameters are as follows:

```
FNHypotenuse (a, b) = SQR(a ^ 2 + b ^ 2)

FNFutureValue (p, n, r) = p * (1 + r) ^ n
```

The function FNHypotenuse gives the length of the hypotenuse of a right triangle having sides of lengths *a* and *b*. The function FNFutureValue gives the balance in a savings account after *n* interest periods when *p* dollars is deposited at an interest rate of *r* per period. Program 6-3 uses the hypotenuse function.

Program 6-4 uses the future value function. With the responses shown below, the program computes the balance in a savings account when $100 is deposited for five years at 8% interest compounded quarterly. Interest is earned four times per year at the rate of 2% per interest period. There will be 4×5 or 20 interest periods.

Logical expressions can be used to define functions that perform some of the same tasks as IF...THEN statements. Logical expressions are either true or

Program 6-3. An example using the function FNHypotenuse

```
REM Find length of hypotenuse of a right triangle   [6-3]
DEF FNHypotenuse (a, b) = SQR(a ^ 2 + b ^ 2)
INPUT "Enter two legs of a right triangle: ", leg1, leg2
PRINT "Hypotenuse has length"; FNHypotenuse(leg1, leg2)
END

[run]
Enter two legs of a right triangle: 3,4
Hypotenuse has length 5
```

false. However, rather than use the values true and false, the computer evaluates false logical expressions to 0 and true logical expressions to -1. Program 6-5 illustrates the numeric evaluation of logical expressions. In the fourth line, the true expressions evaluate to the number -1 and are used as part of a numeric expression.

Program 6-6 uses logical expressions to define the function FNMax that determines the larger of two numbers. If x is greater than y, then $(x >= y)$ is true and so has the value -1, while $(y > x)$ is false and so has the value 0. Thus, in this case, the value of FNMax(x, y) will be

$$-(x >= y) * x - (y > x) * y$$
$$= -(\ -1\ ) * x - (\ 0\ ) * y$$
$$= x$$

Program 6-4. An example using the function FNFutureValue

```
REM Find the future value of a bank deposit   [6-4]
DEF FNFutureValue (p, n, r) = p * (1 + r) ^ n
INPUT "Amount of bank deposit"; p
INPUT "Number of interest periods"; n
INPUT "Interest rate per period"; r
PRINT USING "Balance is $####.##"; FNFutureValue(p, n, r)
END

[run]
Amount of bank deposit? 100
Number of interest periods? 20
Interest rate per period? .02
Balance is $ 148.59
```

Program 6-5. Numeric evaluation of logical expressions

```
REM Numeric evaluation of logical expressions   [6-5]
PRINT 2 = 1
PRINT 1 < 2
PRINT (1 < 2) * 3 + (4 < 5) * 6
END

[run]
 0
-1
-9
```

A similar analysis shows that the function evaluates to y when y is greater than x, and to x when x and y are equal.

Since QBasic treats *false* as 0 and *true* as -1, numeric functions can be defined whose possible values are thought of as "true" and "false", even though these values are really -1 and 0. As an example of how such a function might be useful, consider the problem of determining whether a character is an uppercase letter. If *a$* holds a single character, then the statement

```
IF (a$ >= "A") AND (a$ <= "Z") THEN action
```

causes the action to be performed when *a$* is an uppercase letter. To make the decision more obvious, we can define a function FNIsUppercase by the statement

```
DEF FNIsUppercase (c$) = (c$ >= "A") AND (c$ <= "Z")
```

Program 6-6. A function using logical expressions

```
REM Find the maximum of two numbers   [6-6]
DEF FNMAX (x, y) = -(x >= y) * x - (y > x) * y
INPUT "Enter two numbers separated by a comma: ", x, y
PRINT "The larger number is"; FNMax(x, y)
END

[run]
Enter two numbers separated by a comma: 3, 7
The larger number is 7
```

and then write the IF statement as

```
IF FNIsUppercase (a$) THEN action
```

It cannot be overemphasized that the parameters used to define a function are *just place holders* and have *no meaning* outside of the definition of the function. You can change the names of the parameters to any other name of the same type without affecting the definition.

Actually, the compiler creates special memory locations for the parameters that are only used when the function is invoked. The names that the compiler gives to these locations have nothing whatsoever to do with the variable names used in the program. Therefore, in the event that a FN function uses as a parameter a variable that appears in the program, the value of the variable *does not change* as the result of invoking the function. Program 6-7 demonstrates this feature. If you think that the second number in the output should have been 5, consider the fact that the definition of the function is, in effect, simply

```
DEF FNTriple (numericValue) = 3 * numericValue.
```

Some of QBasic's predefined functions, such as TIME$ and ERR, have no parameters. (TIME$ gives the current time and ERR gives the error code of the most recent error.) User-defined functions can also be parameterless. For instance, the function

```
DEF FNStateTime$ = "The time is now " + TIME$
```

gives the time preceded by a phrase. This function can be invoked by executing a statement such as PRINT FNStateTime$.

Program 6-7. Demonstrate the fact that parameters are dummy variables

```
REM Triple a number   [6-7]
x = 2
DEF FNTriple (x) = 3 * x
PRINT FNTriple(5)
PRINT x
END

[run]
 15
 2
```

Function Procedures

QBasic has a more powerful version of a function which is not found in Standard BASIC, the *function procedure.* Function procedures are defined in separate windows, consist of several lines of code, and are ideally suited to structured programming.

The block of statements that defines a function procedure begins with a statement of the form

```
FUNCTION FunctionName (list of parameters)
```

and ends with the statement END FUNCTION. Commas separate the parameters in the list. When a function is invoked, the computer assigns values of arguments to these parameters, and the statements within the block use the values to determine the function value. Normally, the statement immediately preceding the END FUNCTION statement has the form

```
FunctionName = value
```

and actually carries out the assignment of the function value. From now on, we use the word "function" to mean "function procedure."

Functions are not typed into the View window. Instead, a separate window is created to hold each function. The steps for creating a function are as follows.

1. Move the cursor to a new line.

2. If *FunctionName* is the name of the function, then type FUNCTION *FunctionName* and press <Enter>.

3. After the <Enter> key is pressed, a special window is set up for the function. The line FUNCTION *FunctionName* appears at the top of the screen, followed by a blank line, and the words END FUNCTION.

4. Type the function into this screen just as you would the main body.

5. To return to the main body of the program, press <Shift+F2> (that is, hold down <Shift> and press <F2>). Pressing <Shift+F2> a second time displays the function. (In general, successively pressing <Shift+F2> cycles through the main body and functions of the program.)

Program 6-8. A simple user-defined function

```
REM Triple a number   [6-8]
number = 5
PRINT Triple(number)
END

FUNCTION Triple (x)
   Triple = 3 * x
END FUNCTION
```

This book places all definitions of function procedures after the main program's END statement, and separates each definition from the others and the main body of the program by a blank line.

Program 6-8 contains an elementary function. Notice that when the statement Triple = 3 * x is used to assign a value to the function name, no parameters follow the function name.

Program 6-9 is the same as Program 6-6 except that a function procedure is used to define the function. The meaning is clearer in the function procedure definition.

Program 6-10 includes the definition of the true or false function IsALeapYear. To make the function definition clearer, the program assigns numeric variables named true and false appropriate values at the beginning of

Program 6-9. A function procedure version of the function from Program 6-6

```
REM Find the maximum of two numbers   [6-9]
INPUT "Enter two numbers separated by a comma:", x, y
PRINT "The larger number is"; Max(x, y)
END

FUNCTION Max (x, y)
   IF x >= y THEN
      Max = x
   ELSE
      Max = y
   END IF
END FUNCTION
```

Program 6-10. A user-defined function evaluating to true or false

```
REM Determine number of days in a given year  [6-10]
INPUT "What year are you interested in"; year
PRINT "The year"; year; "has ";
IF IsALeapYear(year) THEN
    PRINT "366 days."
  ELSE
    PRINT "365 days."
END IF
END

FUNCTION IsALeapYear (y)
  true = -1
  false = 0
  IF y MOD 4 <> 0 THEN
      IsALeapYear = false
    ELSEIF (y MOD 100 = 0) AND (y MOD 400 <> 0) THEN
      IsALeapYear = false
    ELSE
      IsALeapYear = true
  END IF
END FUNCTION

[run]
What year are you interested in? 1900
The year 1900 has 365 days.
```

the definition. Note also that you may assign a value to the function name in more than one statement within the function definition.

Program 6-11 uses a function that cannot be defined in a single line. The function determines the number of words in a sentence by counting the number of spaces and adding one.

Local, Static, and Shared Variables

When the same variable name appears in a function procedure and the main program, QBasic gives the variables separate identities and treats them as two different variables. The variables in a function procedure are said to be *local* to the block in which they reside. Each time that the function is invoked, QBasic sets aside new locations in memory to hold their values. When the program

Program 6-11. A user-defined function containing a loop

```
REM Count the number of words in a sentence   [6-11]
INPUT "Enter a sentence: ", sentence$
PRINT "The sentence contains";
PRINT NumberOfWords(sentence$); "words."
END

FUNCTION NumberOfWords (a$)
  FOR i = 1 TO LEN(a$)
    IF MID$(a$, i, 1) = " " THEN spaces = spaces + 1
  NEXT i
  NumberOfWords = spaces + 1
END FUNCTION

[run]
Enter a sentence: Inch by inch is a cinch; yard by yard is hard.
The sentence contains 11 words.
```

exits the block, QBasic forgets these memory locations. This process not only uses memory efficiently, but also sets local numeric variables to zero and local string variables to the null string whenever the function is invoked.

A variable that appears in the definition of a function procedure can also be declared as a *static* variable. Like local variables, static variables have no relationship to any variables outside of the block of statements defining the function. However, they retain their values from one evaluation of the function to the next. Therefore you can use or alter these values each time the function is invoked. The statement STATIC *list of variables* declares each variable in the list to be static.

Variables that appear in the definition of a function procedure and are recognized by the rest of the program are called *global*, or *shared*, variables. In the block of statements that defines a function, QBasic assumes that any variable that is not declared as static or shared and is not a parameter is actually a local variable. Thus, *true* and *false* in Program 6-10 are treated as local variables.

To make programs easier to decipher, QBasic allows variables to be declared as shared via a statement of the form SHARED *list of variables*. Like the STATIC declaration, SHARED declarations must follow the FUNCTION statement

```
REM n shared            REM n local             REM n static
n = 2                   n = 2                   n = 2
PRINT Triple(5);        PRINT Triple(5);        PRINT Triple(5);
PRINT n;                PRINT n;                PRINT n;
PRINT Triple(6);        PRINT Triple(6);        PRINT Triple(6);
PRINT a                 PRINT a                 PRINT a
END                     END                     END

FUNCTION Triple(x)      FUNCTION Triple(x)      FUNCTION Triple(x)
   SHARED a, n             SHARED a                SHARED a
   a = n                   a = n                   STATIC n
   n = 3 * x              n = 3 * x                a = n
   Triple = n             Triple = n               n = 3 * x
END FUNCTION            END FUNCTION               Triple = n
                                                END FUNCTION

[run]                   [run]                   [run]
 15  15  18  15          15  2  18  0             15  2  18  15
```

Figure 6-1. Programs distinguishing between SHARED, Local, and STATIC

and must precede every other executable statement in the definition block. Only REM and DEFtype statements can precede the declaration statements.

The outputs of the three programs in Figure 6-1 illustrate the effects of the two different declarations of the variable *n* in the definition of the function Triple.

Why Functions?

Seem like a lot of trouble to go to? Actually, there are many good reasons for employing functions. Each of the following objectives are easily achieved due to the capability of declaring variables as local, static, or shared.

1. The use of functions is consistent with the stepwise refinement approach to program design. Once you realize that you need a particular function, you can give it a name but save the task of figuring out the computational details until later.

2. Sometimes a single algorithm (a step-by-step plan that solves a particular problem) must be performed several times in a program. Specifying the algorithm as a function saves repeated typing of the same formula, improves readability, and simplifies debugging.

3. You can use functions that are derived for one program in other programs. As a programmer, you can maintain a collection, or *library*, of functions that might be needed. We are spared the concern of duplicating names by having local and static variables.

Subroutines

Sometimes, however, functions are not enough. Suppose you need more than one value back, for example. In that case, you could write a *subroutine*.

A subroutine is a portion of a program that lies outside of the main body of the program, ends with a RETURN statement, and is reached by a GOSUB statement. The first line of a subroutine must either have a line number or a label. A line number is a nonnegative whole number with at most 40 digits. A label is a name, similar to a variable name, but with a trailing colon. The line number or label can be placed either at the beginning of or preceding the identified line.

If, for example, a Standard BASIC program encounters the statement

```
GOSUB 1000
```

it immediately searches for, and then executes, the statement labeled 1000. The statements following line number 1000 are also executed, until the program encounters

```
RETURN
```

at which point, the statement following the original GOSUB 1000 statement is executed.

Whenever the statement GOSUB *labelName* (or GOSUB *lineNumber*) is executed, the program *branches* to the specified line. That is, the next statement executed by the program will be the specified line, not the one following the GOSUB statement. When QBasic reaches a RETURN statement, control branches back to the statement immediately following the GOSUB statement. You usually place subroutines at the end of the program and separated from the main body of the program by an END statement to prevent QBasic from executing the subroutines inadvertently.

Program 6-12.   Using GOSUB to make change

```
REM Make change  [6-12]
INPUT "Total cost of purchase"; cost
INPUT "Amount tendered by customer"; paid
ChangeDue% = 100 * (paid - cost)     'Change due in cents
PRINT " Change:"
unit% = 100                          '100 cents is 1 dollar
UnitName$ = "dollar"
GOSUB ReportNumberOfUnits
unit% = 25                           '25 cents is 1 quarter
UnitName$ = "quarter"
GOSUB ReportNumberOfUnits
unit% = 10                           '10 cents is 1 dime
UnitName$ = "dime"
GOSUB ReportNumberOfUnits
unit% = 5                            '5 cents is 1 nickel
UnitName$ = "nickel"
GOSUB ReportNumberOfUnits
unit% = 1
Name$ = "cent"
GOSUB ReportNumberOfUnits
END

ReportNumberOfUnits:
  number% = changeDue% \ unit%
  IF number% > 0 THEN
    IF number% > 1 THEN unitName$ = unitName$ + "s"
    PRINT number%; unitName$
  END IF
  changeDue% = changeDue% - (number% * unit%)
RETURN

[run]
Total cost of purchase? 1.65
Amount tendered by customer? 5.00
 Change:
 3 dollars
 1 quarter
 1 dime
```

Program 6-12 uses a subroutine to make change for a customer. The program first converts the amount of money due to cents, and then determines the number of bills and coins of each denomination. (To simplify matters, only dollar bills, quarters, dimes, nickels, and pennies are used.) The subroutine has the named label ReportNumberOfUnits.

The subroutine is Standard BASIC's principal device for dividing a program into small pieces that can be written one at a time. In addition to supporting subroutines, QBasic has a device, called a *subprogram,* that serves the same purpose as a subroutine, but is vastly improved. Subprograms are regarded as the single most important enhancement provided to Standard BASIC by QBasic.

Subprograms

A subprogram is a hybrid of a subroutine and a function. Like a subroutine, a subprogram is branched to from the main program and performs a specific task. Like a function, a subprogram has parameters and can pass values to these parameters when the subprogram is invoked. Also, you can declare variables that appear in a subprogram as STATIC or SHARED, as with function procedures. Each subprogram is defined by a block beginning with a statement of the form

```
SUB SubprogramName (list of parameters)
```

and ending with the statement END SUB. (Entering the line beginning with SUB invokes a window for the subprogram). A subprogram in invoked, or called, with the statement

```
CALL SubprogramName(list of arguments)
```

where the number and types of the entries in the argument list match those in the parameter list. As with functions, the argument list can contain constants, variables, and expressions. When a subprogram is called, the values of the arguments are passed to the parameters and used by the subprogram statements. After QBasic has executed all of the statements in the subprogram, or when QBasic encounters an EXIT SUB statement, program execution continues with the statement that follows the CALL statement.

Program 6-13 is similar to Program 6-12 but uses a subprogram instead of the subroutine. The new program passes values to the subprogram when the subprogram is called, whereas the original program had to assign these values to variables before GOSUBing to the subroutine.

On the surface, CALLing a subprogram and doing a GOSUB to a subroutine appear to be equivalent. Both statements cause a jump to a new section of the program, perform a task, and then jump back to the same location in the

Program 6-13. A rewrite of Program 6-12 using subprograms

```
REM Make change  [6-13]
INPUT "Total cost of purchase"; cost
INPUT "Amount tendered by customer"; paid
changeDue% = 100 * (paid - cost)
PRINT " Change:"
CALL ReportNumberOfUnits(100, "dollar")
CALL ReportNumberOfUnits(25, "quarter")
CALL ReportNumberOfUnits(10, "dime")
CALL ReportNumberOfUnits(5, "nickel")
CALL ReportNumberOfUnits(1, "cent")
END

SUB ReportNumberOfUnits (unit%, unitName$)
  SHARED changeDue%
  number% = changeDue% \ unit%
  IF number% > 0 THEN
    IF number% > 1 THEN unitName$ = unitName$ + "s"
    PRINT number%; unitName$
  END IF
  changeDue% = changeDue% - (number% * unit%)
END SUB
```

program. However, the similarity between the statements ends there. The following considerations reveal the important differences between them. (Throughout the remainder of this book we use subprograms exclusively.)

1. A GOSUB statement is essentially a jump to a new section of the main body of the program. QBasic can accidentally enter the statements that compose the subroutine without the use of a GOSUB. This can cause unpredictable results. CALL, however, invokes a protected section of statements that QBasic can never accidentally execute. (No harm would have been done if you omitted the END statement in Program 6-13. The same cannot be said for Program 6-12.)

2. Subroutines cannot have local variables. All variables are equivalent to the SHARED variables available in subprograms. Thus, when you are writing a subroutine, you have to be careful with temporary variables, especially loop counters and the like. It's possible the same variable or variables are being used elsewhere in your program. You could, for

example, destroy results from earlier in the program by accidentally assigning new values to such variables.

3. GOSUB does not allow your "manageable chunk" to be defined with generic variables (parameters). Before each use of a GOSUB statement, you must assign the values needed for this particular use of the subroutine to the appropriate variables hidden away in the subroutine. The programmer must answer the question "What names did I use for the variables when I wrote that subroutine?" However, subprograms allow you to define a task with generic variables, and execute it later by using the actual variables, values, or expressions that appear in the program at that time.

4. All variables in subroutines stay in memory throughout the program. Therefore valuable memory can be used up by temporary variables that have no use outside of the subroutine. However, subprograms use memory for local variables only when the subprogram is called.

5. Although QBasic allows the use of labels that are words and therefore have meaning, GOSUBing to one of these labels does not make it clear what variables will be affected by the subroutine. Thus you will find it harder to read through the main program at a later date and recall exactly what is happening each step of the way. Subprograms, with their parameter lists, do not suffer this shortcoming.

Pass by Reference versus Pass by Value

Programs 6-14 and 6-15 make assignments to the variables *state$* and *pop&*, and make no reassignments to these variables. Yet, when the values of the variables are displayed at the end of Program 6-14, the values have changed.

As in Program 6-14, when the CALL of a subprogram uses a variable as an argument, QBasic performs a "pass by reference." QBasic uses (or references) the variables in the CALL statement in place of the parameters that appear in the subprogram definition. In Program 6-14 for example, the statement CALL DisplayInfo(*state$, pop&*) effectively executes the following statements:

```
state$ = LEFT$(state$, 2)
pop& = pop& / 1000000
PRINT pop&; "million people live in "; state$
```

Only one memory location is involved for each argument. You can see the use of memory for the variable *pop&* in Figure 6-2. Initially, the main program

Program 6-14.   Demonstration of pass by reference

```
REM Display population of the golden state   [6-14]
state$ = "CALIFORNIA"
pop& = 24000000
CALL DisplayInfo(state$, pop&)
PRINT state$; pop&
END

SUB DisplayInfo (a$, b&)
  a$ = LEFT$(a$, 2)
  b& = b& / 1000000
  PRINT b&; "million people live in "; a$
END SUB

[run]
 24 million people live in CA
CA 24
```

allocates a memory location to store the value of *pop&* (Figure 6-2a). When QBasic calls the subprogram, the parameter b& becomes the subprogram's name for this memory location (Figure 6-2b). When the value b& is divided by 1,000,000, the value in this memory location becomes 24 (Figure 6-2c). After

Program 6-15.   Demonstration of pass by value

```
REM Display population of the golden state   [6-15]
state$ = "CALIFORNIA"
pop& = 24000000
CALL DisplayInfo(state$ + "", pop& + 0)
PRINT state$; pop&
END

SUB DisplayInfo (a$, b&)
  a$ = LEFT$(a$, 2)
  b& = b& / 1000000
  PRINT b&; "million people live in "; a$
END SUB

[run]
 24 million people live in CA
CALIFORNIA 24000000
```

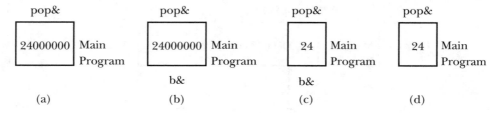

Figure 6-2. Passing a variable by reference to a subprogram

the completion of the subprogram, the parameter b& is forgotten; however, its value lives on in *pop&* (Figure 6-2d). The variable *pop&* is said to be "passed by reference."

One immediate consequence of pass by reference is that, within the subprogram, you can give new values to the arguments used in the CALL of the subprogram, thus explaining the output of Program 6-14.

When you use a constant or expression in the CALL of a subprogram, as in Program 6-15, QBasic makes a "pass by value:" QBasic places the constant or the value of the expression in a new memory location created for the associated parameter. The effect is the same as if the parameter is assigned the value of the constant or expression at the beginning of the subprogram. For example, in Program 6-15, the statement CALL DisplayInfo(*state\$* + " ", *pop&* + 0) effectively executes the following statements:

```
a$ = state$ + ""
b& = pop& + 0
a$ = LEFT$(a$, 2)
b& = b& / 1000000
PRINT b&; "million people live in "; a$
```

Two memory locations are involved for each argument. You can see the use of memory for the variable *pop&* when it is "passed by value" in Figure 6-3. Initially, the main program allocates a memory location to store the value of *pop&* (Figure 6-3a). When QBasic calls the subprogram, a temporary second memory location for the parameter b& is set aside for the subprogram's use and the value of *pop&* is copied into this location (Figure 6-3b). When the value b& is divided by 1,000,000, the value of b& becomes 24 (see Figure 6-3c). After the completion of the subprogram, b&'s memory location disappears

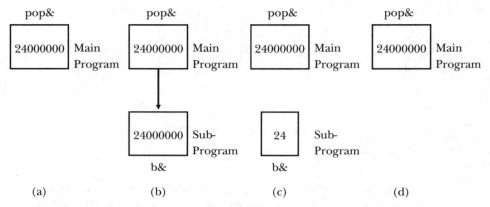

Figure 6-3. Passing a variable by value to a subprogram

(Figure 6-3d). The value of the variable *pop&* in the main program remains the same.

From these explanations, you can see why Program 6-15 did not change the values of *state$* and *pop&*. In a pass by value situation, since only the values of the arguments are made available to replace the parameters, QBasic does not give to the subprogram the actual variables to use and change.

As a further example, consider Program 6-16, which CALLs the subprogram Insert with a constant as the first argument. The subprogram displays the string Jonathan Livingston Sea Gull, but the string is not available for use in the main body of the program. However, if the CALL statement in Program 6-16 is replaced by the two statements

```
item$ = "Jonathan Sea Gull"
CALL Insert(item$, "Livingston ", 10)
```

so that the program uses a variable as the first argument, then the subprogram Insert not only displays the string Jonathan Livingston Sea Gull, but also passes this string back as the new value of the variable *item$*. Subsequent statements in the main program can then use the string in *item$*.

Occasionally, you may have data stored in a variable that you wish to pass to a subprogram, and yet you do not want the subprogram to change the value of the variable. Program 6-15 achieves this result for the variable *state$* and *pop&*

Program 6-16. Pass by value versus pass by reference

```
REM Add in Jonathan's middle name  [6-16]
CALL Insert("Jonathan Sea Gull", "Livingston ", 10)
END

SUB Insert (first$, second$, spot)
  REM Insert second$ into first$, starting at spot
  first$ = LEFT$(first$,spot-1) + second$ + MID$(first$,spot)
  PRINT first$
END SUB

[run]
Jonathan Livingston Sea Gull
```

by using the expressions *state$*+" " and *pop&*+0 as arguments, thus causing a pass by value. QBasic provides a cleaner solution: If a variable argument is enclosed in an extra pair of parentheses when a subprogram is called, then the value of the variable will be passed by value to the subprogram. After executing the subprogram, QBasic guarantees the variable to have its original value. For example, if you replace the CALL statement in Program 6-16 by three statements

```
item$ = "Jonathan Sea Gull"
CALL Insert((item$), "Livingston ", 10)
PRINT item$
```

then the program will display

```
Jonathan Livingston Sea Gull
Jonathan Sea Gull
```

As we have seen, functions and subprograms have many similarities. Because they are similar, we will henceforth use the word *procedure* to identify these two building blocks of structured programs.

Symbolic Constants

QBasic has two kinds of constants, literal constants and symbolic constants. Literal constants appear throughout this book as the concrete values assigned to variables. Examples of literal constants are 5, 7.2E+23, 678&, and "hello".

Symbolic constants also are known as *named constants*, since they are constants that are given a name. If *lit* is a numeric or string literal constant, then the statement

```
CONST ConstantName = lit
```

assigns the value *lit* to the name *ConstantName*. The CONST statement is said to declare the symbolic constant *ConstantName*.

A symbolic constant declared in the main body of a program is recognized by every procedure in the program. Within procedures, the constant is treated as if it was passed by value. In fact, attempting to reassign a value to a symbolic constant, either with an assignment statement or with another CONST statement, produces the error message "Duplicate definition." Also, a symbolic constant declared inside a procedure is local to that procedure. That is, it is not recognized by the main body of the program or any other procedure.

Passing Arrays to Procedures

We have seen many examples of simple numeric and string variables being used as procedure parameters. QBasic also supports the passing of an entire array. To define a function or subprogram so that you can pass an array, the parameter used in the FUNCTION or SUB statement must contain the name of the array followed by an empty pair of parentheses. The calling statement must contain the actual name of the array to be passed followed by an empty pair of parentheses. Arrays are always passed by reference.

In Program 6-17, the subprogram MergeLists merges two sorted lists of words into one sorted list. The parameters *listA$( )*, *listB$( )*, and *newList$( )* in the subprogram definition tell QBasic that these string arrays will be used whenever MergeLists is called. In the CALL statement, a set of empty parentheses follows each array name. The empty parentheses allow QBasic to distinguish between arguments like *oldNames$* and *oldNames$( )* which QBasic interprets as a regular string variable and an entire string array, respectively.

Program 6-17. Passing arrays to a procedure

```
REM Merge two sorted lists [6-17]
DIM oldNames$(1 TO 5), newNames$(1 TO 7), combinedList$(1 TO 12)
FOR index = 1 TO 5
  READ oldNames$(index)
NEXT index
FOR index = 1 TO 7
  READ newNames$(index)
NEXT index
CALL MergeLists(oldNames$(), newNames$(), combinedList$())
CLS
FOR index = 1 TO 12
  PRINT combinedList$(index); " ";
NEXT index
PRINT
DATA Alan, Bill, Jim, Sue, Tina
DATA Adam, Bob, Chris, Gail, Kim, Mike, Steve
END

SUB MergeLists (listA$(), listB$(), newList$())
  REM Each array must have been dimensioned by a
  REM statement of the form DIM arrayName(1 TO m),
  REM where m is a positive whole number
  sizeA = UBOUND(listA$)
  sizeB = UBOUND(listB$)
  sizeNew = UBOUND(newList$)
  REM If array newList$() is not large enough
  REM for combined lists, do not try to merge.
  IF sizeNew < sizeA + sizeB THEN
    PRINT "Result array not large enough for merge"
    EXIT SUB
  END IF
  aNow = 1
  bNow = 1
  newNow = 1
  DO WHILE (aNow <= sizeA) AND (bNow <= sizeB)
    IF listA$(aNow) < listB$(bNow) THEN
        newList$(newNow) = listA$(aNow)
        aNow = aNow + 1
      ELSE
        newList$(newNow) = listB$(bNow)
        bNow = bNow + 1
```

(continued)

Program 6-17. *(continued)*

```
      END IF
      newNow = newNow + 1
   LOOP
   REM Logically, one array, listA$() or listB$(),
   REM has been exhausted, and so, of the following two
   REM loops, only one will actually have work to do.
   FOR index = aNow TO sizeA
      newList$(newNow) = listA$(index)
      newNow = newNow + 1
   NEXT index
   FOR index = bNow TO sizeB
      newList$(newNow) = listB$(index)
      newNow = newNow + 1
   NEXT index
END SUB

[run]
Adam Alan Bill Bob Chris Gail Jim Kim Mike Steve Sue Tina
```

Declaring Arrays

Like other variables, an array declared inside a procedure is local by default and can be made static or shared. This is best accomplished by including the words STATIC or SHARED in the DIM statement. Figure 6-4 shows the beginning of a subprogram that declares and dimensions several arrays.

Local arrays are always dynamic. A local array, like any other local variable, is initialized to zero or the null string each time the subprogram or function is invoked, and is removed from memory when execution of the subprogram or function is complete.

If a FUNCTION or SUB statement is followed by the word STATIC, then a static array dimensioned inside the function or subprogram will retain its values between calls. Note however, that even though such a static array continues to occupy memory after execution of the subprogram or function is complete, the program cannot access the array from outside the declaring subprogram or function. Also recall that a static array must be dimensioned

```
SUB UseManyArrays
  REM count() is a local array
  DIM count(1 TO 20)
  DIM STATIC totals(1 TO 10)
  DIM SHARED lastCounts(1 TO 20)
  .
  .
  .
END SUB
```

Figure 6-4. Declaring arrays in a procedure

using constants to specify the lower and upper bounds; variables are not allowed. The DIM statements for local arrays and static arrays in STATIC procedures can be executed repeatedly without causing an error message.

Arrays dimensioned in the main body of the program can be shared with a particular procedure by including the statement SHARED *arrayName*( ) in the procedure before using the array.

In the subprogram of Program 6-18, the array *count*( ) is dimensioned as a local array.

Program 6-19 shows a simple mechanism, know as a last-in-first-out, or LIFO, stack. This stack permits the program to store values in the order received and then to bring them back for processing in reverse order. In the subprogram LifoStackControl, the array *stack*( ) and the variable *top*% must be allocated permanent memory, and not be created and initialized each time LifoStackControl is called. The word STATIC at the end of the SUB statement mandates that all variables used in the subprogram retain their values between calls. These variables are only initialized once. This initialization of numeric variables to zero and string variables to null can be thought of as occurring when the subprogram is first called.

The Differences between Functions and Subprograms

All tasks that are performed by functions can also be performed by subprograms. However, when the objective is solely to calculate a single value, func-

Program 6-18.   A procedure using a local array

```
REM Count occurrences of various letters in a string   [6-18]
INPUT "Enter string to analyze: ", a$
CALL LetterCount(a$)
END

SUB LetterCount (info$)
  'a       holds the ASCII value of "A"
  'z       holds the ASCII value of "Z"
  'place   keeps track of our current position in info$
  'char    stores the ASCII value of the character found at
  '        place in info$, and serves as the index into the
  '        count array
  'count() is an array to hold the count of the number of times
  '        a letter occurs in info$ (case of letters is ignored)
  a = ASC("A")
  z = ASC("Z")
  DIM count(a TO z)
  REM The array count should initially be filled with zeros.
  REM QBasic does this automatically
  REM Scan across info$, count occurrences of each letter
  FOR place = 1 TO LEN(info$)
    char = ASC(UCASE$(MID$(info$, place, 1)))
    'If the character is a letter, count it, otherwise ignore it.
    IF char >= a AND char <= z THEN count(char) = count(char) + 1
  NEXT place
  REM Print results, put letter on first line and count on second
  FOR char = a TO z
    PRINT USING " !"; CHR$(char);
  NEXT char
  PRINT
  FOR char = a TO z
    PRINT USING " #"; count(char);
  NEXT char
  PRINT
END SUB

[run]
Enter string to analyze: Don't count time; make time count.
 A B C D E F G H I J K L M N O P Q R S T U V W X Y Z
 1 0 2 1 3 0 0 0 2 0 1 0 3 3 3 0 0 0 0 5 2 0 0 0 0 0
```

Program 6-19. A subprogram with a static array

```
REM Demonstrate a Last-In-First-Out stack   [6-19]
CALL LifoStackControl("push", 5, status$)
PRINT status$
CALL LifoStackControl("push", 8, status$)
PRINT status$
CALL LifoStackControl("pop", num, status$)
PRINT status$; num
CALL LifoStackControl("pop", x, status$)
PRINT status$; x
'All pushed values have been popped, so status$
'will report an error for calling pop again.
CALL LifoStackControl("pop", wrong, status$)
PRINT status$; wrong
END

SUB LifoStackControl (operation$, value, status$) STATIC
  REM Implementation of a Last In First Out (LIFO) stack
  DIM stack(1 TO 256)
  'operation$ is the action to be taken, PUSH or POP
  'value      is the data to be PUSHed onto the stack or
  '           the data that  POPped off the stack
  'status$    "OK" if operation$ is successful
  '           or an error message if not
  'top%       records the last location into which data
  '           has been placed
  'stack      is a STATIC array to hold the values being
  '           PUSHed & POPped
  SELECT CASE UCASE$(operation$)
    CASE "PUSH"
      IF top% < 256 THEN
          top% = top% + 1
          stack(top%) = value
          status$ = "OK"
        ELSE
          status$ = "Stack is Full"
      END IF

    CASE "POP"
      IF top% > 0 THEN
          value = stack(top%)
          top% = top% - 1
          status$ = "OK"
        ELSE
          status$ = "Stack is Empty"
```

(continued)

Program 6-19. *(continued)*

```
      END IF
    CASE ELSE
      status$ = "Stack Operation Error"
  END SELECT
END SUB

[run]
OK
OK
OK 8
OK 5
Stack is Empty 0
```

tions are more natural to work with. The main differences between subprograms and functions are:

1. While subprograms are invoked by a CALL statement, functions are invoked by using the function in a place where QBasic would otherwise expect to find a constant or expression.

2. While a subprogram name serves only to identify the subprogram, and ideally describes its task, a function name identifies the function, describes the task, and is assigned a value by the statements within its definition. We say that when a function is invoked, it returns a value. That value can be a string or any of the four numeric types, in accordance with the type indicated by the name of the function.

3. Functions primarily are used to calculate a single value.

The first two differences are illustrated by Program 6-20, which uses both a string function and a subprogram to reverse the order of the characters in a sentence input by the user.

Subprograms and Functions That Invoke Each Other: Stepwise Refinement

As discussed at the beginning of this chapter, a programmer's key problem-solving strategy is stepwise refinement. As a programmer, you break down a large problem into a sequence of smaller problems. You then deal with each

Program 6-20. A program showing some differences between functions and subprograms

```
REM Show difference in using a function and a subprogram   [6-20]
REM to reverse the order of the characters in a string.
INPUT "Enter a phrase: ", phrase$
PRINT "  "; RevLine$(phrase$)
CALL ReverseLine(phrase$, answer$)
PRINT "  "; answer$
END

FUNCTION RevLine$ (info$)
  FOR index = LEN(info$) TO 1 STEP -1
    temp$ = temp$ + MID$(info$, index, 1)
  NEXT index
  RevLine$ = temp$
END FUNCTION

SUB ReverseLine (info$, result$)
  FOR index = LEN(info$) TO 1 STEP -1
    result$ = result$ + MID$(info$, index, 1)
  NEXT index
END SUB

[run]
Enter a phrase: LEVEL is a palindrome
  emordnilap a si LEVEL
  emordnilap a si LEVEL
```

subproblem in a subprogram or function. Whenever the task assigned to a subproblem is still complicated, you should break the subproblem into a sequence of still-smaller subproblems. Since QBasic allows subprograms and functions to call other subprograms and functions, it is easy to code this type of solution. Let's illustrate this process by using stepwise refinement to solve a specific problem.

The current calendar, known as the Gregorian calendar, was introduced in 1582. Imagine that you want to convert any numeric date after the year 1582 into an improved form that gives the day of week and spells out the month. Figure 6-5 gives a breakdown of the problem into subproblems. Each rectangle, except the top one, corresponds to a subprogram or a function. This diagram is called a stepwise refinement chart.

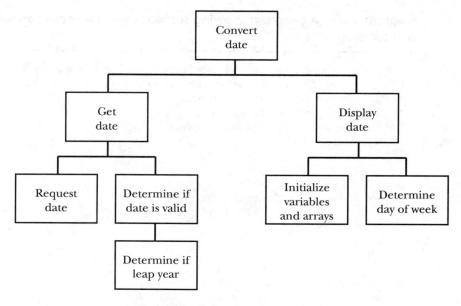

Figure 6-5. A stepwise refinement chart

By solving the problem in pieces rather than in its entirety, the main body of Program 6-21 is short and easily understood. The subprogram GetDate not only requests the month, day, and year, but also checks that the given input is valid. The names for the subprograms and functions invoked in GetDate readily reflect these tasks.

Note that DateIsValid is assigned the result of a logical expression that is true or false. The value of the function DateIsValid is best thought of as true or false, even though QBasic actually considers the value as either -1 or 0.

The function DateIsValid also invokes the true or false valued function IsALeapYear that was introduced in Program 6-10. Further, DateIsValid demonstrates that a function can do more that just compute a value. Part of DateIsValid's job is to print an error message to the user when the given date is not valid.

The subprogram PrintFancyDate first dimensions two local arrays, one for holding the names of the days of the week, the other the names of the months, and then calls the subprogram Initialize to assign values to the arrays. By

Program 6-21. A program written with stepwise refinement

```
REM Convert numeric date to day-of-week, month, day, year   [6-21]
CALL GetDate(month, day, year)
CALL PrintFancyDate(month, day, year)
END

FUNCTION DateIsValid (month, day, year)
  yearOk = (year >= 1582)
  monthOk = (month >= 1) AND (month <= 12)
  SELECT CASE month
    CASE 2
      IF ThisIsALeapYear(year) THEN
          dayOk = (day >= 1) AND (day <= 29)
        ELSE
          dayOk = (day >= 1) AND (day <= 28)
      END IF
    CASE 4, 6, 9, 11
      dayOk = (day >= 1) AND (day <= 30)
    CASE ELSE
      dayOk = (day >= 1) AND (day <= 31)
  END SELECT
  DateIsValid = yearOk AND monthOk AND dayOk
  IF NOT (yearOk AND monthOk AND dayOk) THEN
    PRINT "Date is not valid. Press any key to continue."
    temp$ = INPUT$(1)
  END IF
END FUNCTION

FUNCTION DayOfWeek (m, d, y)
  REM m is month, d is day, y is year
  IF m <= 2 THEN
    m = m + 12
    year = year - 1
  END IF
  DayOfWeek=(d+2*m+3*(m+1)\5+y+y\4-y\100+y\400+2) MOD 7
END FUNCTION

SUB GetDate (month, day, year)
  DO
    CALL RequestDate(month, day, year)
  LOOP UNTIL DateIsValid(month, day, year)
END SUB
```

(continued)

Program 6-21. *(continued)*

```
SUB Initialize (d$(),    m$())
  d$(0) = "Saturday":    d$(1) = "Sunday"
  d$(2) = "Monday":      d$(3) = "Tuesday"
  d$(4) = "Wednesday":   d$(5) = "Thursday"
  d$(6) = "Friday"
  m$(1) = "January":     m$(2) = "February"
  m$(3) = "March":       m$(4) = "April"
  m$(5) = "May":         m$(6) = "June"
  m$(7) = "July":        m$(8) = "August"
  m$(9) = "September":   m$(10) = "October"
  m$(11) = "November":   m$(12) = "December"
END SUB

SUB PrintFancyDate (m, d, y)
  DIM day$(0 TO 6), month$(1 TO 12)
  CALL Initialize(day$(), month$())
  IF d < 10 THEN
      f$ = "&_, & #_, ####"
    ELSE
      f$ = "&_, & ##_, ####"
  END IF
  PRINT USING f$; day$(DayOfWeek(m, d, y)); month$(m); d; y
END SUB

SUB RequestDate (month, day, year)
  CLS
  INPUT "Month (1-12)"; month
  INPUT "Day (1-31)"; day
  INPUT "Year (1582-->)"; year
END SUB

FUNCTION ThisIsALeapYear (year)
  true = -1:
  false = 0
  IF year MOD 4 <> 0 THEN
      ThisIsALeapYear = false
    ELSEIF (year MOD 100 = 0) AND (year MOD 400 <> 0) THEN
      ThisIsALeapYear = false
    ELSE
      ThisIsALeapYear = true
  END IF
END FUNCTION
```

(continued)

Program 6-21. *(continued)*

```
[run]
Month (1-12)? 7
Day (1-31)? 4
Year (1582-->)? 1776
Thursday, July 4, 1776
```

putting these assignments in a subprogram by themselves, the program avoids cluttering up the subprogram PrintFancyDate. Note also the compact and readable way in which PrintFancyDate calls upon the function DayOfWeek. Since QBasic allows you to use a function in any place where you can use a constant value, it is perfectly legitimate to obtain the subscript for the array day$ by invoking the function DayOfWeek.

The function DayOfWeek itself makes use of a rather strange looking but effective formula for determining the day of the week corresponding to a given month, day, and year. Note that, in order for the formula to work, the program considers January and February as months 13 and 14 of the previous year.

If you have written programs in languages that allow you to nest subprogram and function definitions, note that QBasic does not allow this style of program construction; you must define each subprogram and function separately.

Recursion

A procedure can not only invoke other procedures, but it can also invoke itself. This process is called *recursion*. There are some problems that have a recursive flavor and therefore are most naturally defined recursively. As an example, suppose that a country of 6 million people is experiencing an annual population growth rate of 2% and a steady immigration of 20,000 people each year. You can use this simple formula that gives the population at the beginning of any year in terms of the population at the beginning of the previous year:

```
(pop_at_beg_of_year)=1.02*(pop_at_beg_of_previous_year) +20000.
```

(Since 2% is 0.02, you can think of the number 1.02 as 1 + 0.02, or 1 plus 2%. Therefore, multiplying the population by 1.02 is the same as adding 2% to the current population.) Next, you can define a function, Population(n), that will give the population at the beginning of any year. The parameter n will assume values such as 0, 1, 2, and so on, that correspond to the present year, 1 year hence, 2 years hence, and so on, respectively. Population(0) has the value 6,000,000. You can use the formula just given to compute population sizes for successive years, as follows:

```
Population(1) = 1.02*Population(0) + 20000
Population(2) = 1.02*Population(1) + 20000
  :
  :
Population(n) = 1.02*Population(n-1) + 20000
```

Suppose that you wanted to know the value of Population(3). You could use the following calculations:

```
Population(3) = 1.02*Population(2) + 20000
```

Now,

```
Population(2) = 1.02*Population(1) + 20000
```

and

```
Population(1) = 1.02*Population(0) + 20000
```

But Population(0) is known to be 6,000,000. You can now trace through the equations one at a time until you obtain the value of Population(3):

```
Population(1) = 1.02*6000000 + 20000 = 6140000

Population(2) = 1.02*6140000 + 20000 = 6282800

Population(3) = 1.02*6282800 + 20000 = 6428456
```

Program 6-22 follows this process. Each time that the function is invoked, the program decreases the value of $n\%$ by 1, and therefore the value of $n\%$ will eventually reach 0. At this point the recursion will terminate. Whenever recursion is used in a procedure, you *must* provide a way to stop the recursion. If you do not, QBasic will display an "Out of stack space" error message, because eventually you're going to run out of room: QBasic must store all values for each iteration through the recursive procedure.

Program 6-22. A recursively defined function

```
REM Compute future populations [6-22]
INPUT "Number of years in future"; numberOfYears%
PRINT "The population will be"; Population&(numberOfYears%)
END

FUNCTION Population& (n%)
  IF n% = 0 THEN
      Population& = 6000000
    ELSE
      Population& = 1.02 * Population&(n% - 1) + 20000
  END IF
END FUNCTION

[run]
Number of years in future? 3
The population will be 6428456
```

Program 6-23 uses a recursively defined subprogram to guess the number that a person is thinking of. The main body of the program gives directions to the user and then calls the subprogram Guess to begin making guesses. The main program also provides for repeated play.

The subprogram Guess makes and displays a guess halfway between the lowest value and the highest value that the player could possibly be thinking of. Initially this value is between 1 and 1,000. The subprogram Guess then asks the player to indicate whether the displayed guess is high, low, or correct. If the current guess is high, then a value that is one less than the current guess becomes the new value for the highest number the player can be thinking of. The subprogram Guess is called again with this new highest possible value. Similarly, if the current guess is low, the subprogram Guess is called again with a value that is one more than the current guess used as the new lowest possible value. The program maintains a count of the number of guesses made, which allows the program to report the number of guesses made before a correct answer is given.

With these kinds of tools — and the patience to use them in a methodical, stepwise process — you can solve very complex problems. Complex problems call for more complex data. The structures to deal with such data are outlined in the next chapter.

Program 6-23.   A recursively defined procedure

```
REM Guess my number [6-23]
REM User thinks of number, computer does guessing
DO
  PRINT "Think of a number between 1 and 1000, "
  PRINT "but don't tell me what it is."
  PRINT "I will guess your number in 10 tries or less."
  PRINT "Press any key when you've decided on your number."
  response$ = INPUT$(1)
  tries = 1
  CALL Guess(1, 1000, tries)
  PRINT "Want to play again (Y,N)?"
  response$ = UCASE$(INPUT$(1))
  CLS
LOOP UNTIL response$ = "N"
END

SUB Guess (low, high, tries)
  currentGuess = INT((low + high) / 2)
  PRINT
  PRINT USING "My guess is ####!"; currentGuess; ".";
  PRINT "Is my guess High, Low, or Correct (H,L,C)?"
  DO
    response$ = UCASE$(INPUT$(1))
  LOOP UNTIL (response$="H") OR (response$="L") OR (response$="C")
  SELECT CASE response$
    CASE "H"
      high = currentGuess - 1
      CALL Guess(low, high, tries + 1)
    CASE "L"
      low = currentGuess + 1
      CALL Guess(low, high, tries + 1)
    CASE "C"
      PRINT
      PRINT "I guessed your number in"; tries; "tries."
  END SELECT
END SUB

[run]
Think of a number between 1 and 1000,
but don't tell me what it is.
I will guess your number in 10 tries or less.
Press any key when you've decided on your number.
```

(continued)

Program 6-23. *(continued)*

```
My guess is  500.
Is my guess High, Low, or Correct (H,L,C)? H
My guess is  250.
Is my guess High, Low, or Correct (H,L,C)? L

My guess is  375.
Is my guess High, Low, or Correct (H,L,C)? C

I guessed your number in 3 tries.
Want to play again (Y,N)? N
```

Data Files

In previous chapters, data processed by a program was either assigned by LET statements, stored in DATA statements, or supplied by the user in response to INPUT statements. These methods are sufficient for small quantities of data to be used in only one program. However, large amounts of data, data that many programs will access, or data that users will update (such as stock prices and employee payroll information) must be kept on a disk.

QBasic offers three different ways to organize disk-based data files. The resulting three types of files are called sequential, random-access, and binary. Each type of file has advantages and disadvantages. Sequential files use space efficiently, but are not easily updated and are difficult to search for a single piece of information. Random-access files provide rapid access to individual pieces of information, but require considerable effort to program and maintain. Binary files offer the greatest flexibility, but have no structure and, therefore, place considerable responsibility on the programmer to make sure the data are interpreted correctly.

This chapter discusses the creation and use of all three types of data files. The creation process physically records data onto a disk. The computer can then read this data from the disk and assign it to variables in much the same way that the computer can read from DATA statements.

143

Sequential Files

The ASCII table in Appendix A contains 256 characters. While not all of these characters can be displayed on the screen or printed on the printer, they can all be used in files. The characters with ASCII values ranging from 0 through 31 are referred to as control characters.

Of special importance for sequential files are the control characters numbered 10 and 13, which are the line feed and carriage-return characters. The pair of characters that consists of a carriage-return character followed by a line feed character is called a carriage-return/line feed pair, and is written <CR/LF>.

The carriage-return/line feed is a standard way of denoting the end of a line. For example, you indicate the end of a line of a QBasic program by pressing the <Enter> key. Doing this sends a carriage-return/line feed instruction to the screen, which causes the cursor to move to the beginning of the next row on screen.

A sequential file can be thought of as a long sequence of characters. Sequential files normally contain a number of carriage-return/line feed pairs that subdivide the file into blocks called *records*. In most of the sequential files discussed in this section, each record consists of several pieces of related data, called *fields*, that are separated from each other by commas.

The sequential file in Figure 7-1 holds employee payroll data for a company. The record for each employee contains four fields: a name field, a social security number field, an hourly wage field, and an earnings-to-date for the current year field. Each string appears in quotation marks and each amount of money is given in cents as an integer or long integer. If this file were displayed on the screen from DOS with the TYPE command, the screen would appear as in Figure 7-2.

Creating a Sequential File

There are many ways to organize and place data into a sequential file. The technique presented here is easy to visualize and apply. Other techniques are discussed later.

1. Choose a file name. Recall that a file name is a string that consists of two parts: (a) a name of at most eight characters followed by (b) an optional

```
"Smith,John","123-45-6789",17000,19091000<CR/LF>"Johnson,Robert",
"456-98-7654",1350,1537650<CR/LF>"Williams,David","238-91-2355",8
25,934725<CR/LF>
```

Figure 7-1. An employee payroll file

extension that consists of a period and at most three characters. You can use letters, digits, and a few other characters - & ! _ @ ' ' ~ ( ) { } - # % $ - in either the name or the extension. Some examples of file names are "INC&EXP.87", "CUSTOMER.DAT", and "FORT_500".

2. Choose a number from 1 through 255 to be the *reference number* of the file. While in use by QBasic, the file will be identified by this number.

3. Execute the statement

    ```
    OPEN filename FOR OUTPUT AS #n
    ```

    where *n* is the reference number. This is referred to as *opening* a *file* for *output.* The procedure opens a communications line between the computer and the disk drive for storing data onto the disk. The statement allows the computer to output data and record it in the specified file.

WARNING You should execute this statement only once and that is when you first create a file. If you open an already existing sequential file for output, the computer will erase the existing data. We'll discuss how to modify an existing file later in this chapter.

4. Record data into the file with the WRITE# statement. If *a$* is a string, then the statement

    ```
    WRITE #n, a$
    ```

    writes the string *a$* in quotation marks into the file. (Remember that *n* is the reference number of the file.) If *c* is a number, then

    ```
    WRITE #n, c
    ```

    ```
    "Smith,John","123-45-6789",17000,19091000
    "Johnson,Robert","456-98-7654",1350,1537650
    "Williams,David","238-91-2355",825,934725
    ```

Figure 7-2. The employee payroll file as displayed by the DOS command TYPE.

writes the number *c*, without any leading or trailing spaces, into file number *n*. The statement

```
WRITE #n, a$, c
```

enters *a$* and *c* as before, and uses a comma to separate them. Similarly, if several strings, or numbers, or a combination of these, which are separated by commas, follow the statement WRITE #*n*, all of the strings and numbers appear as before, with commas separating them. After executing each WRITE# statement, QBasic places the pair <CR/LF> into the file.

5. After you have recorded all of the data into the file, execute

```
CLOSE #n
```

where *n* is the reference number of the file. This disassociates the number *n* from the file and tells DOS where the file ends. This procedure is referred to as closing the file. (Omitting the file number after the CLOSE statement closes all open files.)

Program 7-1 creates the file that was given in Figure 7-1. The values in the last DATA statement are known as *sentinel values*. They signal that the computer has read all of the data.

Adding Items to a Sequential File

Data can be added to the end of an existing sequential file with the following steps.

1. Choose a number from 1 through 255 to be the reference number for the file. This number need not be the same number that was used when creating the file.

2. Execute the statement

```
OPEN filename FOR APPEND AS #n
```

where *n* is the reference number. This procedure is referred to as opening a file for append. The statement allows the computer to output data and record it at the end of the specified file. (If the specified file does not exist, a new file will be created.)

3. Record data into the file by using the WRITE# statement.

4. After you have recorded all of the data into the file, close the file with the statement CLOSE #*n*.

Program 7-1. Create the sequential file PAYROLL.91

```
REM Create the file PAYROLL.91 and record some data into it.[7-1]
OPEN "PAYROLL.91" FOR OUTPUT AS #1    'Name file & assign a number
READ nom$, ssn$, hourlyWage%, yearToDate&
DO UNTIL nom$ = "EOD"                 'Loop until End of Data
   WRITE #1, nom$, ssn$, hourlyWage%, yearToDate&
   READ nom$,ssn$,hourlyWage%,yearToDate& 'Read next set of data
LOOP
CLOSE #1
REM -- Data:name, soc. sec. num., hourly wage, yr-to-date earnings
DATA "Smith,John", 123-45-6789, 17000, 19091000
DATA "Johnson,Robert", 456-98-7654, 1350, 1537650
DATA "Williams,David", 238-91-2355, 825, 934725
DATA "EOD", "", 0, 0
END
```

Program 7-2 adds new records to the end of the PAYROLL.91 file. Figure 7-3 shows the contents of PAYROLL.91 after the computer has executed the program and been given the italicized input.

Program 7-2. Add a new record to the end of PAYROLL.91

```
REM Place an additional record into the file PAYROLL.91    [7-2]
OPEN "PAYROLL.91" FOR APPEND AS #1
CLS
INPUT "First name"; firstName$
INPUT "Last name"; lastName$
INPUT "Social security number"; ssn$
INPUT "Hourly wage (in cents)"; hourlyWage%
INPUT "Year to date earnings (in cents)"; yearToDate&
nom$ = lastName$ + "," + firstName$
WRITE #1, nom$, ssn$, hourlyWage%, yearToDate&
CLOSE #1
END

[run]
First name? Al
Last name? Jones
Social security number? 450-21-3678
Hourly wage (in cents)? 1325
Year to date earnings (in cents)? 1275975
```

```
"Smith,John","123-45-6789",17000,19091000<CR/LF>"Johnson,Robert",
"456-98-7654",1350,1537650<CR/LF>"Williams,David","238-91-2355",8
25,934725<CR/LF>"Jones,Al",450-21-3678,1325,1275975<CR/LF>
```

Figure 7-3.   The contents of the appended file PAYROLL.91.

Reading Information from a Sequential File

Data stored in a sequential file can be read in order (that is, sequentially) and assigned to variables with the following steps.

1.   Choose a number from 1 through 255 to be the reference number for the file. This number need not be the same number that was used when recording the file.

2.   Execute the statement

```
OPEN filename FOR INPUT AS #n
```

where n is the reference number. This procedure is referred to as opening a file for input. The statement opens a communications line between the computer and the disk drive for copying data from the diskette. Data can then be input from the specified file to the computer.

3.   Read data from the file by using the INPUT# statement. The INPUT# statement assigns data from a file to variables in much the same way that INPUT assigns data from the keyboard. Correct use of the INPUT# statement requires a knowledge of the WRITE# statement that recorded the data on the disk. That is, you must know what order the values were written in, so you can be sure the correct values are placed into your variables. The statement

```
INPUT #n, var1, var2, ...
```

assigns to each of the variables (*var1*, *var2*, and so on) one of the items of the file. (Commas or the pair of characters carriage-return/line feed separate the items in the file.) The number and type of the variables in the INPUT# statement should be the same as those of the variables in the WRITE# statement that created each record.

4.   After the computer has found the items that it was searching for or after it has read all of the data from the file, close the file with the statement CLOSE #n.

Program 7-3. Calculate hours worked by each employee

```
REM Process  PAYROLL.91 to find hours worked in 1990   [7-3]
OPEN "PAYROLL.91" FOR INPUT AS #1
CLS
PRINT "Name"; TAB(20); "Hours Worked"
PRINT "--------------"; TAB(20); "------------"
DO UNTIL EOF(1)            'Process the entire file
  INPUT #1, nom$, ssn$, hourlyWage%, yearToDate&
  PRINT nom$; TAB(20);
  PRINT USING "   #####"; yearToDate& / hourlyWage%
LOOP
CLOSE #1
END

[run]
Name                 Hours Worked
--------------       ------------
Smith,John               1123
Johnson,Robert           1139
Williams,David           1133
Jones,Al                  963
```

QBasic has a useful function, EOF, that tells you if you have reached the end of a file. At any time, the condition

```
EOF(n)
```

will be true if you have reached the end of open file referenced by the number *n*, and false if you have not.

Program 7-3 gives the number of hours worked by each employee in the file PAYROLL.91. By using the DO UNTIL EOF(1) statement, the programmer does not have to know the number of records in the file. The PRINT USING format prevents the computer from displaying fractional parts of hours.

The EOF function serves the same role for a file that a sentinel value (such as EOD or -1) does for a set of DATA statements. However, there are some important differences. A typical program segment for READing DATA statements must read a record before entering a loop and then again at the bottom of the loop, as in Figure 7-4a. This construction is necessary because QBasic

```
READ info$, etc.
DO UNTIL info$ = "EOD"              DO UNTIL EOF(1)
  'process info$, etc.               INPUT #1,info$, etc.
          :                          'process info$, etc.
          :                                    :
  READ info$, etc.                             :
LOOP                               LOOP
    (a)                                (b)
```

Figure 7-4. Typical READ/DATA and file INPUT# loops

detects the End-Of-Data condition by reading an extraneous sentinel value
that is not to be processed.

In contrast, a typical program segment for INPUTting from a file must check
for the End-Of-File condition *first*, and *then* input a record as the first action
inside the loop, as in Figure 7-4b. This construction is necessary because the
End-Of-File condition is true *as soon as* QBasic sees that no more data exists in
the file. Executing INPUT# when no more records are available results in an
error.

Program 7-4 illustrates an error common when reading a sequential file. The
program will not process the last item in the file. In addition, if the file
contains no data, then the third line will produce the error message "Input
past end of file."

Sequential files can be quite large. Rather than list the entire contents, we
often search the file for a specific piece of information. Program 7-5 allows a
user to input a Social Security number, and finds the corresponding person in

Program 7-4. A flawed file-reading program

```
REM Display names/employees earning more than $10 per hour   [7-4]
OPEN "PAYROLL.91" FOR INPUT AS #1
CLS
INPUT #1, nom$, ssn$, hourlyWage%, yearToDate&
DO UNTIL EOF(1)
  IF hourlyWage% > 1000 THEN PRINT nom$
  INPUT #1, nom$, ssn$, hourlyWage%, yearToDate&
LOOP
CLOSE #1
END
```

Program 7-5. A sequential search of a sequential file

```
REM Find individual PAYROLL.91 using soc. sec. #.  [7-5]
OPEN "PAYROLL.91" FOR INPUT AS #1
CLS
INPUT "Social Security Number"; a$
ssn$ = ""
DO UNTIL (ssn$ = a$) OR EOF(1)    'Examine until person found
   INPUT #1, nom$, ssn$, hourlyWage%, yearToDate&
LOOP
IF ssn$ = a$ THEN
    PRINT nom$; " has the number "; a$
  ELSE
    PRINT a$; " is not in the file PAYROLL.91"
END IF
CLOSE #1
END

[run]
Social Security Number? 238-91-2355
Williams,David has the number 238-91-2355

[run]
Social Security Number? 222-33-4444
222-33-4444 is not in the file PAYROLL.91
```

the file PAYROLL.91 by examining each record until it finds the desired one. Since a particular Social Security number may not be in the file, the DO UNTIL statement must check the function EOF(1) to determine if QBasic reached the End-Of-File without finding a match.

Other Methods of Outputting and Inputting Data to Sequential Files

There are statements other than WRITE# and INPUT# that can be used to place data into and retrieve data from sequential files.

The statements PRINT# and PRINT# USING place data into files in much the same way that their counterparts, PRINT and PRINT USING, display information on the screen. With PRINT#, QBasic records numbers with trailing and possibly leading spaces; semicolons cause subsequent data to be displayed in the next position, and commas cause subsequent data to be recorded in the next 14-character zone. Unless you terminate PRINT# and PRINT# USING statements with a comma or semicolon, QBasic automatically records a carriage-return and a line feed.

The statements LINE INPUT# and INPUT$ can be used to read data from a sequential file. The statement

```
LINE INPUT #n, a$
```

reads all characters to the next carriage-return/line feed in the file referenced by the number *n* and assigns this string of characters to the variable *a$*. The statement

```
a$ = INPUT$(m, n)
```

reads the next *m* characters from the file referenced by the number *n*, and assigns them to the string variable *a$*. (The statement reads all characters, including commas and carriage-returns.) LINE INPUT# is usually used to retrieve data that has been recorded with PRINT#.

Sorting a Sequential File

In addition to accessing sequential files for information, you regularly update them by modifying certain pieces of data, removing some records, and adding new records. You can perform these tasks most efficiently if you first sort the files. By sort, we mean arrange the file's records in some logical order. You must choose a field to order the file by, we call this sorting on a particular field.

You can sort the records of a sequential file on any field, by first reading the data into several arrays (one array per field) and then sorting on one array while carrying out each SWAP statement on every array. Program 7-6 uses this technique to sort the sequential file PAYROLL.91 by employee name.

By the way, harking back to Chapter 6, Program 7-6 provides a good example of top-down design. The main body of the program is short and consists primarily of calls to subprograms whose names describe the different tasks to be performed. The subprogram CountRecords determines the number of records in the payroll file so that it can dimension sufficiently large parallel arrays. (There will be an array for each field, and arrays with the same subscript will hold fields from the same record.) The program gives the user the opportunity to save processing time by entering the number of records in the payroll file, if known.

If the user does not know the number, the program uses the LINE INPUT# statement to read everything up to the next <CR/LF> pair, thus, the program can read an entire record without regard for fields. Counting the number of LINE INPUT# statements executed before the End-Of-File is reached gives the number of records in the payroll file.

The subprogram LoadArrays uses the INPUT# statement to read the four fields of each record of the payroll file directly into the appropriate array elements. The program uses the loop FOR i = 1 TO count ... NEXT i rather than the loop DO UNTIL EOF(1) ... LOOP since the program already knows the number of records to be processed. In addition, if the user gave an incorrect count and the program used a DO UNTIL loop, there would be the danger of trying to read more data than the arrays were dimensioned to hold.

The subprogram SortByName uses a *modified bubble sort* to put the *nom$* array in order. In such a sort, "higher" values are allowed to "bubble" to the top of the file. The sort procedure compares values in the array. When it finds two that are out of order, it swaps them. Whenever the program interchanges the values of two elements of the *nom$* array, it must also interchange the values in the corresponding elements of the other three arrays. Doing so assures that array elements with the same subscript continue to hold information from the same record.

The subprogram WriteArrays does the opposite of LoadArrays. WriteArrays uses the WRITE# statement to put the sorted data from the arrays back into a new version of the payroll file. Like each of the other subprograms, WriteArrays prints a message before starting to process. This message reassures the user that the sort is proceeding properly.

There is another method of sorting a file by the first field. DOS has a command called SORT that orders the records of a sequential file. The command

```
SORT <filename1 >filename2
```

sorts the records of *filename1* in ascending order by the first field, and places them into a new file called *filename2*. The DOS command

```
SORT <filename1 >filename2  /R
```

produces a descending-order sort.

Program 7-6. Sort the file PAYROLL.91

```
REM Sort records in PAYROLL.91 file by employee names   [7-6]
DEFINT a-z   'cause all tagless variables to be of type integer
CLS
CALL CountRecords(total)
DIM nom$(total),ssn$(total),hourlyWage%(total),yrToDate&(total)
CALL LoadArrays(total,nom$(),ssn$(),hourlyWage%(),yrToDate&())
CALL SortByName(total,nom$(),ssn$(),hourlyWage%(),yrToDate&())
CALL WriteArrays(total,nom$(),ssn$(),hourlyWage%(),yrToDate&())
PRINT "Sort complete"
END

SUB CountRecords (number)
  PRINT "How many records are in PAYROLL.91?"
  INPUT "(Enter 0 to have me count them.) ", number
  IF number = 0 THEN
    PRINT "Counting records"
    OPEN "PAYROLL.91" FOR INPUT AS #1
    number = 0
    DO UNTIL EOF(1)
      LINE INPUT #1, temp$
      number = number + 1
    LOOP
    CLOSE #1
  END IF
END SUB

SUB LoadArrays(count, n$(), s$(), hw%(), ytd&())
  OPEN "PAYROLL.91" FOR INPUT AS #1
  PRINT "Reading from file"
  FOR i = 1 to count
    INPUT #1, n$(i), s$(i), hw%(i), ytd&(i)
  NEXT i
  CLOSE #1
END SUB

SUB SortByName (count, n$(), s$(), hw%(), ytd&())
  PRINT "Sorting"
  FOR i = 1 TO count        'At most count loops needed for sort
    swapped = 0             'Set flag indicating no swaps yet
    FOR k = 1 TO count - i
      IF n$(k) > n$(k + 1) THEN   'Swap successive elements
        SWAP n$(k), n$(k + 1)     'in all arrays whenever
```

Program 7-6. *(continued)*

```
           SWAP s$(k), s$(k + 1)        'successive elements in the
           SWAP hw%(k), hw%(k + 1)      'nom$ array are out of order
           SWAP ytd&(k), ytd&(k + 1)
           swapped = 1            'Set flag indicating a swap occurred
        END IF
      NEXT k
      IF swapped = 0 then EXIT FOR 'If no swaps in the FOR k loop
   NEXT i                              'then arrays are sorted, so EXIT
END SUB

SUB WriteArrays (count, n$(), s$(), hw%(), ytd&())
   PRINT "Writing sorted file"
   OPEN "PAYROLL.91" FOR OUTPUT AS #1
   FOR i = 1 TO count
     WRITE #1, n$(i), s$(i), hw%(i), ytd&(i)
   NEXT i
   CLOSE #1
END SUB
```

Program 7-7 produces the same result as did Program 7-6. The second line changes the name of the file PAYROLL.91. The SHELL statement invokes DOS and carries out the indicated SORT command.

NOTE On systems without hard disk drives, the computer will ask you to insert the DOS diskettes containing COMMAND.COM and SORT.EXE.

Suppose that the sorted file PAYROLL.91 is quite large and that the company has hired new employees. Also, suppose that the payroll data for the new people is contained in the sorted sequential file NEWEMP. Program 7-8 merges these two files into one sorted file. The merge is accomplished by copying the records of the file PAYROLL.91 into another file while inserting each record from NEWEMP in the proper place. This program can be modified to perform similar tasks, such as deleting the records of employees who leave the company and changing the hourly wages of some of the employees.

Program 7-7.   Sort PAYROLL.91 with DOS's SORT command

```
REM Sort records in PAYROLL.91 file by employee names   [7-7]
NAME "PAYROLL.91" AS "TEMPFILE"
SHELL "SORT <TEMPFILE >PAYROLL.91"
KILL "TEMPFILE"           'Delete Tempfile from Disk
END
```

Program 7-8.   Merge two files

```
REM Update the file PAYROLL.91 by inserting new employees   [7-8]
REM Merge NEWEMP into PAYROLL.91 (both files sorted by name)
CALL OpenFiles
CLS
PRINT "Merging NEWEMP into PAYROLL.91"
nom1$ = ""    'Null value indicates next record needs to be read
nom2$ = ""
DO UNTIL (EOF(1) AND nom1$ = "") OR (EOF(2) AND nom2$ = "")
   'Read next record if required
   IF nom1$ = "" THEN
       INPUT #1, nom1$, ssn1$, hourlyWage1%, yearToDate1&
   END IF
   IF nom2$ = "" THEN
       INPUT #2, nom2$, ssn2$, hourlyWage2%, yearToDate2&
   END IF
   'Write out the record having the "lesser" name
   'and indicate that the next record needs to be read
   IF nom1$ < nom2$ THEN
       WRITE #3, nom1$, ssn1$, hourlyWage1%, yearToDate1&
       nom1$ = ""
    ELSE   'nom2$ <= nom1$
       WRITE #3, nom2$, ssn2$, hourlyWage2%, yearToDate2&
       nom2$ = ""
   END IF
LOOP
'Either tempfile or newemp has now been completely processed.
'Any additional data from the other file must now be written out.
IF nom1$ <> "" THEN
    WRITE #3, nom1$, ssn1$, hourlyWage1%, yearToDate1&
END IF
DO UNTIL EOF(1)
  INPUT #1, nom1$, ssn1$, hourlyWage1%, yearToDate1&
  WRITE #3, nom1$, ssn1$, hourlyWage1%, yearToDate1&
LOOP
```

Program 7-8. *(continued)*

```
IF nom2$ <> "" THEN
    WRITE #3, nom2$, ssn2$, hourlyWage2%, yearToDate2&
END IF
DO UNTIL EOF(2)
  INPUT #2, nom2$, ssn2$, hourlyWage2%, yearToDate2&
  WRITE #3, nom2$, ssn2$, hourlyWage2%, yearToDate2&
LOOP
CLOSE
KILL "TEMPFILE"
PRINT "Merge complete"
END

SUB OpenFiles
  'Tempfile must not exist in order for renaming to succeed,
  'but tempfile must exist in order that KILL not cause an error.
  'Create tempfile in case it doesn't exist, then KILL it for
  'sure.
  OPEN "TEMPFILE" FOR OUTPUT AS #1
  CLOSE #1
  KILL "TEMPFILE"
  NAME "PAYROLL.91" AS "TEMPFILE"
  OPEN "TEMPFILE" FOR INPUT AS #1
  OPEN "NEWEMP" FOR INPUT AS #2
  OPEN "PAYROLL.91" FOR OUTPUT AS #3
END SUB
```

Comments about Sequential Files

You can use a string variable for the file name in an OPEN statement. Doing this is advantageous for programs that process data from several different data files. In response to an INPUT statement, the user can identify the data file to be processed.

So far, this chapter has assumed that you will be sorting files on the disk in the default drive, the current drive at the time that you invoked QBasic. To work with a file from another disk drive, place the letter of the drive and a colon before the name of the file. For instance, if the file PAYROLL.91 is on a diskette in drive B, then the statement

```
OPEN "B:PAYROLL.91" FOR INPUT AS #1
```

gives us access to the file. A file name or a file name preceded by a drive letter and a colon is referred to as a *filespec*. If you are using subdirectories, the filespec should also contain the path to the subdirectory.

The maximum number of files that can be open at any time varies from about four to fifteen. The number of files DOS can handle simultaneously is determined by a command of the form "FILES = *n*" in the CONFIG.SYS file. (In the absence of a FILES command, the value is 8.) However, three file slots are used by DOS; other file slots might be for certain devices. In order for QBasic to be able to have 15 files open at the same time, the value of *n* in CONFIG.SYS should be set to at least 20.

Sequential files make efficient use of disk space and are easy to create and use. Their disadvantages are as follows:

- Often a large portion of the file must be read in order to find one specific item.

- An individual item of the file cannot be changed or deleted easily. A new file must be created by reading each item from the original file and recording it, with the single item changed or deleted, into the new file.

Another type of file, known as a random-access file, has neither of the above listed disadvantages of sequential files. However, random-access files tend to use more disk space and require greater effort to program. Before introducing random-access files, we must introduce two new types of variables, fixed-length strings and records.

Fixed-length String and Record Variables

Normally, the data type of a string variable is declared by adding a dollar sign to the variable name. The absence of a dollar sign or the use of one of the suffixes %, &, !, or #, declares the variable as numeric. The DIM statement provides an alternate way of declaring these data types. The appropriate statements are

```
DIM var AS STRING
DIM var AS INTEGER
DIM var AS LONG
DIM var AS SINGLE
DIM var AS DOUBLE
```

where the name of the variable is written without any type-declaration suffix.

Program 7-9. DIM statement used to declare variable types

```
REM Demonstrate the declaration of variable types with DIM   [7-9]
CLS
DIM city AS STRING
city = "New York"
DIM pop AS SINGLE
pop = 7000000
PRINT city; pop
END


[run]
New York 7000000
```

Program 7-9 uses the DIM statement to declare and assign values to variables. Although the program still would be correct without the statement DIM pop AS SINGLE, we will soon see a situation where an analogous kind of declaration is necessary.

Fixed-length string variables do not have a trailing dollar sign. They are specified by statements of the form

```
DIM var AS STRING * n
```

where n is a positive integer. After such a declaration, the value of *var* will always be a string of length n. (The initial value is a string of n CHR\$(0) characters.) Suppose that *a\$* is an ordinary string and that a statement of the form

```
var = a$
```

is executed. If *a\$* has more than n characters, then only the first n characters will be assigned to *var*. If *a\$* has less than n characters, then spaces will be added to the end of the string to guarantee that *var* has length n.

Program 7-10 uses fixed-length strings. In the output, San Francisco is truncated to a string of length 9, and Detroit is padded on the right with two blank spaces.

Care must be taken when comparing an ordinary (variable length) string with a fixed-length string or comparing two fixed-length strings of different

Program 7-10. DIM statement used to declare a fixed-length string

```
REM Illustrate fixed-length strings   [7-10]
CLS
PRINT "123456789"
DIM city AS STRING * 9
city = "San Francisco"
PRINT city
city = "Detroit"
PRINT city; "MI"
PRINT LEN(city)
END

[run]
123456789
San Franc
Detroit  MI
  9
```

lengths. In Program 7-11, the strings assigned to *city, town$,* and *municipality* have lengths 9, 7, and 12, respectively, and therefore are all different.

There are times when we want to consider the values assigned to variables as being the same, such as *city* and *town$* in Program 7-11. In this situation, the function RTRIM$ comes to the rescue. If *a$* is an ordinary string or a fixed-length string, then the value of

```
RTRIM$(a$)
```

is the (variable-length) string consisting of *a$* with all right-hand spaces removed. For instance, the value of RTRIM$("hello   ") is the string "hello". In Program 7-11, if the IF block is changed to

```
IF (RTRIM$(city)=town$) AND (RTRIM$(city)=RTRIM$(municipality)) THEN
    PRINT "same"
  ELSE
    PRINT "different"
END IF
```

then the first line of the output will be "same."

An array of fixed-length strings is declared by a statement of the form

```
DIM arrayname(a TO b) AS STRING * n
```

Program 7-11. The difference between ordinary and fixed-length strings

```
REM Illustrate fixed-length strings  [7-11]
CLS
DIM city AS STRING * 9
DIM municipality AS STRING * 12
town$ = "Chicago"
city = "Chicago"
municipality = "Chicago"
IF (city = town$) OR (city = municipality) THEN
    PRINT "same"
  ELSE
    PRINT "different"
END IF
PRINT "123456789012345"
PRINT city + "***"
PRINT town$ + "***"
PRINT municipality + "***"
END

[run]
different
123456789012345
Chicago   ***
Chicago***
Chicago      ***
```

When fixed-length strings are passed to and from procedures, the parameter in the SUB or FUNCTION statement must be a variable-length string.

Record Variables

We have worked with four different data types in this text: numbers, strings, arrays, and fixed-length strings. Strings and numbers are built-in data types that can be used without being declared. On the other hand, arrays and fixed-length strings are user-defined data types that must be declared with a DIM statement before being used.

NOTE The only exceptions are arrays with range 0 to 10 that can be dimensioned implicitly.

Now, a record is a user-defined data type that is a grouping of related variables of these different types.

```
  Name: _ _ _ _ _ _ _ _ _ _ _ _ _ _ _ _ _ _ _ _ _ _ _ _ _ _ _ _ _ _
  State: _ _
  Year Founded: _ _ _ _
```

Figure 7-5. An index card having three fields

Figure 7-5 shows an index card that can be used to hold data about colleges.
The three pieces of data, name, state, and year founded, are called fields. The
length of a field is the number of spaces that have been allocated to it. We see
that the three fields of the index card have lengths 30, 2, and 4, respectively.
Each field is actually a variable in which information can be stored. The layout
of the index card can be identified by a name such as CollegeData, which is
referred to as a *record type*.

For programming purposes, the layout of the record is declared by the block
of statements

```
TYPE CollegeData
  nom AS STRING * 30
  state AS STRING * 2
  yearFounded AS SINGLE
END TYPE
```

A record variable capable of holding the data for a specific college is declared
by a statement such as

```
DIM college AS CollegeData
```

which creates the three variables *college.nom*, *college.state*, and *college.yearFounded*
to hold the information.

In general, a record type is created by a TYPE block of the form

```
TYPE RecordType
  fieldName AS fieldType
  fieldName AS fieldType
    :
END TYPE
```

and a record variable is declared to be of that type by a statement of the form

```
DIM recordName AS RecordType
```

Program 7-12. Using records

```
REM Demonstrate use of records   [7-12]
CLS
TYPE CollegeData
  nom AS STRING * 30
  state AS STRING * 2
  yearFounded AS SINGLE
END TYPE
DIM college AS CollegeDATA
INPUT "Name"; college.nom
INPUT "State"; college.state
INPUT "Year Founded"; college.yearFounded
century = 1 + INT(college.yearFounded / 100)
PRINT RTRIM$(college.nom); " was founded in the"; century;
PRINT "th century in "; college.state
END

[run]
Name? Boston University
State? MA
Year Founded? 1839
Boston University was founded in the 19 th century in MA
```

where *RecordType* is the name of the user-defined data type, *fieldName* is the name of one of the fields of the record variable, *fieldType* is either STRING * *n*, for some *n*, or one of the numeric types: INTEGER, SINGLE, LONG, or DOUBLE.

Program 7-12 shows the use of records.

TYPE statements can only appear in the main body of a program, never in functions or subprograms. However, DIM statements can be used in functions and subprograms to declare a variable to be a record variable. When records are passed to and from functions and subprograms, the parameter in the FUNCTION or SUB statement must have the form

```
parameter AS recordtype
```

Program 7-13 uses subprograms to perform the same tasks as Program 7-12.

Record variables are similar to arrays in that they both store and access data items using a common name. However, the elements in an array must be of

Program 7-13. Passing records to subprograms

```
REM Demonstrate use of records with procedures   [7-13]
CLS
TYPE CollegeData
  nom AS STRING * 30
  state AS STRING * 2
  yearFounded AS SINGLE
END TYPE
DIM college AS CollegeData
CALL GetData(college)
CALL DisplayStatement(college)
END

SUB GetData (school AS CollegeData)
  REM Request the name, state, and year founded
  INPUT "Name"; school.nom
  INPUT "State"; school.state
  INPUT "Year Founded"; school.yearFounded
END SUB

SUB DisplayStatement (school AS CollegeData)
  REM Display the name, century founded, and state of a school
  century = 1 + INT(school.yearFounded/100)
  PRINT RTRIM$(school.nom); " was founded in the"; century;
  PRINT "th century in "; school.state
END SUB
```

the same data types, whereas the fields in a record variable can be a mixture of different data types. Also, the different elements of an array are identified by their indices, whereas the fields of a record are identified by a name following a period.

Each character of a string is stored in a piece of memory known as a byte. Therefore, a field of type STRING * n requires n bytes of memory. Integers, long integers, single-precision numbers, and double-precision numbers are stored in 2, 4, 4, and 8 bytes of memory, respectively. If *recVar* is a user-defined record variable, then the value of LEN(*recVar*) is the sum of the number of bytes required for the fields of *recVar*.

In addition to being declared as numeric or fixed-length string data types, the elements of a user-defined record variable can also be declared as other types of records. Program 7-14 uses this feature.

Program 7-14. A user-defined record variable with a record as an element

```
REM Demonstrate use of records with records as elements   [7-14]
TYPE NameType
  first AS STRING * 15
  last AS STRING * 15
END TYPE
TYPE AddressType
  street AS STRING * 30
  city AS STRING * 15
  state AS STRING * 2
  zipCode AS STRING * 5
END TYPE
TYPE PersonData
  nom AS NameType
  address AS AddressType
END TYPE
DIM president AS PersonData
CLS
CALL GetData(president)
CALL DisplayData(president)
END

SUB DisplayData (person AS PersonData)
  PRINT
  PRINT RTRIM$(person.nom.first); " ";
  PRINT RTRIM$(person.nom.last)
  PRINT RTRIM$(person.address.street)
  PRINT RTRIM$(person.address.city); ", ";
  PRINT person.address.state; " "; person.address.zipCode
END SUB

SUB GetData (person AS PersonData)
  REM Request the name, address, and phone number
  INPUT "Enter First Name: ", person.nom.first
  INPUT "Enter Last Name: ", person.nom.last
  INPUT "Enter Street: ", person.address.street
  INPUT "Enter City: ", person.address.city
  INPUT "Enter State: ", person.address.state
  INPUT "Enter Zip Code: ", person.address.zipCode
END SUB

[run]
Enter First Name: George
Enter Last Name: Bush
Enter Street: 1600 Pennsylvania Avenue NW
```

(continued)

Program 7-14. *(continued)*

```
Enter City: Washington
Enter State: DC
Enter Zip Code: 20500

George Bush
1600 Pennsylvania Avenue NW
Washington, DC 20500
```

Random-Access Files

Information that resides in a random-access file is comparable to data that is organized on an accountant's pad with rows numbered 1, 2, 3, and so on. Any row can be read or written on without first looking through every other row of the pad. In Figure 7-6, each row is partitioned into four regions. Each row is called a record and each region is called a field. Of the four fields in the Figure 7-6, two contain string data and two contain numeric data. (The numeric data have been encoded into two-character and four-character strings.) By adding up the spaces allocated to the fields, the total number of characters that can be placed in each record is 44 (27 + 11 + 2 + 4 = 44). We say that each record has length 44.

A user-defined record variable is used to read and write the records of a random-access file. The fields of the record variable are the same as the fields of the random-access file. For instance, for the file in Figure 7-6, an appropriate TYPE statement is

```
TYPE EmployeeType
  nom AS STRING * 27
  ssn AS STRING * 11
  hourlyWage AS INTEGER    'hourly wage in cents
  yearToDate AS LONG       'year to date earnings in cents
END TYPE
```

and the appropriate DIM statement is

```
DIM employee AS EmployeeType
```

where *employee* is a record variable of type EmployeeType.

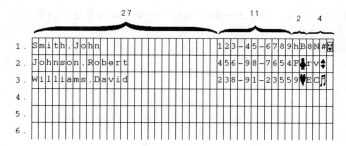

Figure 7-6. An accountant's pad

For a random-access file, one statement suffices to open the file for any purpose: creating, writing, appending, or reading. Suppose the reference number chosen for the file is *n*. Then executing the statement

```
OPEN filename FOR RANDOM AS #n LEN = LEN(recVar)
```

permits records to be written, read, added, or changed in the specified file. The function LEN(*recVar*) gives the length of the record.

Suppose a random-access file has been opened and a TYPE statement has been executed. The two-step procedure for entering data into a record is as follows:

1. Assign a value to each of the fields of the record variable.
2. Place the data into record *r* of the file whose reference number is *n* with the statement

    ```
    PUT #n, r, recVar
    ```

Program 7-15 produces the random-access file in Figure 7-6. Note that the processing loop within the program is controlled by a sentinel value even though the number of data records is easily determined. This design technique has the advantage that no changes need be made to the body of the program if new data statements are added to the end of the program.

Suppose the record variable *recVar* has been declared and a random-access file has been opened with reference number *n*. The statement

```
GET #n, r, recVar
```

assigns record *r* of the file referenced by the number *n* to *recVar*.

Program 7-15.   Create the random-access file PAYROLL.91R

```
REM Create the random-access file PAYROLL.91R   [7-15]
TYPE EmployeeType
  nom AS STRING * 27
  ssn AS STRING * 11
  hourlyWage AS INTEGER   'hourly wage in cents
  yearToDate AS LONG      'year to date earnings in cents
END TYPE
DIM employee AS EmployeeType
OPEN "PAYROLL.91R" FOR RANDOM AS #1 LEN = LEN(employee)
recordNumber = 1
READ employee.nom, employee.ssn
READ employee.hourlyWage, employee.yearToDate
DO UNTIL RTRIM$(employee.nom) = "EOD"
  PUT #1, recordNumber, employee
  recordNumber = recordNumber + 1
  READ employee.nom, employee.ssn
  READ employee.hourlyWage, employee.yearToDate
LOOP
CLOSE #1
REM--Data:name,soc. sec. number,hourly wage,year-to-date earnings
DATA "Smith,John",123-45-6789,17000,19091000
DATA "Johnson,Robert",456-98-7654,1350,1537650
DATA "Williams,David",238-91-2355,825,934725
DATA EOD,"",0,0
END
```

The total number of characters in the file of reference number n is given by the value of the function

```
LOF(n)
```

Dividing the value of the LOF function by the record length, LEN(*recVar*), gives the number of records in a random-access file. Program 7-16 uses this technique in order to display the complete contents of the random-access file PAYROLL.91R.

Comments about Random-Access Files

1. Random-access files also are know as *direct access* or *relative* files. Since each record has the same number of characters, the computer can

Program 7-16. Exhibit the contents of PAYROLL.91R

```
REM Getting records from a random-access file PAYROLL.91R    [7-16]
DEFINT I
TYPE EmployeeType
   nom AS STRING * 27
   ssn AS STRING * 11
   hourlyWage AS INTEGER    'hourly wage in cents
   yearToDate AS LONG       'year to date earnings in cents
END TYPE
DIM employee AS EmployeeType
OPEN "PAYROLL.91R" FOR RANDOM AS #1 LEN = LEN(employee)
CLS
PRINT "                           Social                    Year to"
PRINT "                           Security      Hourly      Date"
PRINT "Name                       Number        Wage        Wages"
PRINT "------------------- ----------- ------ ---------"
fm$ = "\                   \ \          \       ###.##      ######.##"
FOR i = 1 TO LOF(1) / LEN(employee)
   GET #1, i, employee                          'Bring forward record i
   PRINT USING fm$; employee.nom; employee.ssn; _
        employee.hourlyWage / 100; employee.yearToDate / 100
NEXT i
CLOSE #1
END


[run]
                    Social                    Year to
                    Security      Hourly      Date
Name                Number        Wage        Wages
------------------- -----------   ------      ---------
Smith,John          123-45-6789   170.00      190910.00
Johnson,Robert      456-98-7654    13.50       15376.50
Williams,David      238-91-2355     8.25        9347.25
```

calculate where to find a specified record and therefore does not have to search for it.

2. Unlike sequential files, random-access files needn't be closed between placing information into them and reading from them.

3. Records do not have to be filled in order. For instance, a file can be opened and the first PUT statement can be PUT #*n*, 9, *recVar*.

4. A field variable retains its current value unless the value is altered by a GET or LET statement.

5. If the record number *r* is omitted from a PUT or GET statement, then the record number used will be the one following the number most recently used in a PUT or GET statement (or the first record if no PUT or GET statements have been used.) For instance, if the statement PUT #1, *recVar* is added to Program 7-15 just before the file is closed, then the information on David Williams will be duplicated in record 4 of the file PAYROLL.91R.

6. Users often enter records into a random-access file without keeping track of the record numbers. If file *#n* is open, then the value of the function

   ```
   LOC(n)
   ```

   is the number of the record that has most recently been copied into or out of file *n* with a PUT or GET statement.

7. An alternate method of reading and writing data to a random-access file is provided by the buffer method. (The buffer method is the only method available in Standard BASIC and versions of QuickBASIC prior to 4.0.) Although the buffer method requires more programming effort, it is the only way a database program can be written when the file layout varies at run-time. With the buffer method, a FIELD statement is used to give each field a name and specify its width. Information is entered into the file via a two-step process. A portion of memory, referred to as a buffer, is automatically set aside for the file. The information for a single record is placed into the buffer one field at a time. This is accomplished with the statements LSET and RSET. Then the total record is copied into the file as record number *r* by the statement

   ```
   PUT #n, r
   ```

   Records also are read from random-access files with a two-step process. The statement

   ```
   GET #n, r
   ```

   places a copy of record number *r* into the buffer. Individual fields are then accessed by referring to them by their names. Numeric data must be converted to string data before being placed in the file. The functions MKI$, MKL$, MKS$, and MKD$ are used to convert numbers to strings, and the functions CVI, CVL, CVS, and CVD are used to convert these strings back to numbers. Program 7-17 is a version of Program 7-16 that uses the buffer method.

Program 7-17.   Using the buffer method with a random-access file

```
REM Getting data from PAYROLL.91R   [7-17]
OPEN "PAYROLL.91R" AS #1 LEN = 44
FIELD #1, 27 AS nom$, 11 AS ssn$, 2 AS hrWg$, 4 AS yrToDt$
CLS
PRINT "                         Social                    Year to"
PRINT "                         Security        Hourly    Date"
PRINT "Name                     Number          Wage      Wages"
PRINT "------------------       ----------      ------    ---------
f$ = "\                  \ \            \     ###.##      ######.##"
FOR i = 1 TO LOF(1) \ 44
  GET #1, i                                'Bring forward record i
  PRINT USING f$; nom$, ssn$, CVI(hrWg$)/100, CVL(yrToDt$)/100
NEXT i
CLOSE #1
END
```

Binary Files

A binary file is the most rudimentary type of file. It offers the greatest flexibility of any type of file, but makes the greatest demands upon the programmer. A binary file can be thought of as a sequence of characters that has *no structure* imposed by delimiters or records. The characters are said to occupy positions 1, 2, 3, and so on. We can jump to any position and read or write any number of characters. QBasic overwrites characters that previously occupied positions currently being written to.

Like random-access files, binary files have just one, all-purpose OPEN statement. The statement

```
OPEN filename FOR BINARY AS #n
```

assigns reference number *n* to the specified binary file, which then may be both written to and read. At any time, there is a location in the file called the *current file position*. Initially the current file position is 1. The primary tasks of accessing a binary file are accomplished by the three statements SEEK, PUT, and GET, with a little help from the functions SEEK and LOF.

For a file with reference number *n*, the statement

```
SEEK #n, r
```

changes the current file position to *r*. The statement

```
PUT #n, r, var
```

places the value of *var* in the file beginning at position *r* and moves the current file position a distance equal to the length of *var*. The statement

```
GET #n, r, var
```

begins at the file position *r*, reads a number of bytes equal to the length of *var*, assigns them to *var*, and moves the current file position a distance equal to the length of *var*.

At any time, the value of the function

```
SEEK(n)
```

is the current file position in the binary file with reference number *n*, while the value of

```
LOF(n)
```

is the length of the file. Program 7-18 shows several examples of the use of these functions. Each comment after a PUT statement shows the contents of the file at that point.

Any file can be OPENed as a binary file and accessed with SEEK, GET, and PUT. For instance, a sequential file can be opened as a binary file and have certain pieces of data changed without the entire file being recopied. As an example, Program 7-19 alters the sequential file PAYROLL.91 appearing in Figure 7-1. Note that in Figure 7-1, the pay rate for John Smith, $170.00, is given beginning with the 28th character in the file.

Files created outside of QBasic will have their own special formats. This will be the case, for instance, with the files created by popular spreadsheet and database programs. Such files can be opened as binary files and examined or changed. Program 7-20 uses the binary file mode to permit the contents of an

Program 7-18. Working with a binary file

```
REM Demonstrate the use of a binary file  [7-18]
OPEN "DEMOFILE" FOR BINARY AS #1
abcde$ = "abcde"
fgh$ = "fgh"
FGHIJ$ = "FGHIJ"
b$ = "  "                  'LEN(b$) = 2
a$ = "A"
PUT #1, 1, abcde$          'abcde
PUT #1, 6, fgh$            'abcdefgh
SEEK #1, 3                 'Move to position 3
GET #1, , b$              'Read 2 characters; the value of b$ is "cd"
PRINT SEEK(1)             'Display the current file position, 5
PUT #1, , FGHIJ$          'abcdFGHIJ
SEEK #1, 1                'Move to beginning of file
PUT #1, , a$             'AbcdFGHIJ
SEEK #1, LOF(1)          'Move to last byte in of file
b$ = "kl"
done$ = "done"
PUT #1, , b$             'AbcdFGHIkl
SEEK #1, SEEK(1) - 5    'Move current file position 5 positions left
PUT #1, , done$         'AbcdFdonel
CLOSE #1                 'Close the file
END

[run]
 5
```

arbitrary (i.e., any old) file to be displayed. Each line of this display consists of two parts. The left side displays the ASCII values of 15 characters from the file. The right shows the 15 characters themselves, with a period in place of each character that is not one of the 96 standard keyboard characters.

Program 7-19. Use the binary file mode to cheat

```
REM Give John Smith a $15.00 pay raise  [7-19]
OPEN "PAYROLL.91" FOR BINARY AS #1
SEEK #1, 28               'move file pointer to 28th character
pay$ = "18500"
PUT #1, , pay$     'change 28th through 32nd character
CLOSE #1
END
```

Program 7-20. Use the binary file mode to snoop

```
REM Decode any file into ASCII code & standard characters   [7-20]
DIM byte AS STRING * 1
CLS
INPUT "Source File: ", filename$
OPEN filename$ FOR BINARY AS #1
text$ = ""
FOR index = 1 TO LOF(1)       'process entire file
  'Read a single character from the file
  GET #1, index, byte
  'Print the ASCII value of the character
  PRINT USING "\  \"; STR$(ASC(byte));
  'If character is not a regular character, change it to a
  'period
  IF (ASC(byte) < 32) OR (ASC(byte) > 127) THEN byte = "."
  'Add the character in byte$ onto the string in text$
  text$ = text$ + byte
  'After printing 15 ASCII values, print corresponding text
  IF index MOD 15 = 0 THEN
    PRINT "  "; text$
    text$ = ""
  END IF
NEXT index
PRINT TAB(63); text$    'Print out text for last (partial) line
CLOSE #1
END
```

Program 7-21 not only allows the contents of an arbitrary file to be viewed, but also allows characters to be changed. Characters are displayed vertically one per line along with their positions in the file. A maximum of 19 characters from the file can be viewed at one time. The most recently displayed character can be altered.

The subprogram DisplayCommands lists the five commands understood by this file-editing program in the lower portion of the screen. To prevent this command menu from being erased, any other items displayed by the program are restricted to the first 19 lines of the screen.

The subprogram AdvanceToNextByte uses the GET function to read the character at the current file position after first checking that the current file position is not past the last character of the file. This character is then

Program 7-21. A file editor

```
REM Examine and change a file byte by byte  [7-21]
DIM SHARED byte AS STRING * 1
DEFINT A-Z
bottomLine = 19
CLS
INPUT "Source File: ", filename$
OPEN filename$ FOR BINARY AS #1
CALL DisplayCommands
currentLine = 1
GET #1, 1, byte
CALL Display(byte)
CALL ReadIn(action$)
DO UNTIL action$ = "Q"
  SELECT CASE action$
    CASE "N", CHR$(13)
       CALL AdvanceToNextByte
    CASE "R"
       CALL ReplaceCurrentByte
    CASE "G"
       CALL GoToByteRelativeToStart
    CASE "J"
       CALL JumpToByteFromHere
  END SELECT
  CALL ReadIn(action$)
LOOP
CLOSE #1
END

SUB AdvanceToNextByte
  SHARED currentLine
  IF NOT EOF(1) THEN               'if not at the end of the file
    GET #1, , byte                 'advance to next byte
    CALL Display(byte)
  END IF
END SUB

SUB Display (byte AS STRING)
  SHARED currentLine, bottomLine
  LOCATE currentLine, 1
  'Display position of byte in file and its ASCII value
  PRINT USING "##########  \   \";SEEK(1)-1; STR$(ASC(byte));
  'Display a 1 to 3 character description of byte
  SELECT CASE byte
```

(continued)

Program 7-21. *(continued)*

```
      CASE CHR$(0) TO CHR$(31)
        PRINT "^"; CHR$(ASC(byte) + 64);
      CASE CHR$(32) TO CHR$(127)
        PRINT byte;
      CASE CHR$(128) TO CHR$(159)
        PRINT "@^"; CHR$(ASC(byte) - 64);
      CASE CHR$(160) TO CHR$(255)
        PRINT "@"; CHR$(ASC(byte) - 128);
    END SELECT
    PRINT "          ";
    'Advance to a new line and clear line below it
    currentLine = (currentLine MOD bottomLine) + 1
    LOCATE currentLine, 1: PRINT SPACE$(30);    ' Print 30 spaces
    LOCATE currentLine, 1
  END SUB

  SUB DisplayCommands
    SHARED bottomLine
    CLS
    LOCATE bottomLine + 2, 1
    PRINT "N or [ENTER] =move to next byte"
    PRINT "J            =jump forwards or backwards from here"
    PRINT "G            =go to specific byte (1 to";STR$(LOF(1));")"
    PRINT "R            =replace this byte"
    PRINT "Q            =save file and quit";
  END SUB

  SUB GoToByteRelativeToStart
    SHARED currentLine
    INPUT "go to offset --> ", size
    IF (size >= 1) AND (size <= LOF(1)) THEN
        SEEK #1, size                'change current file position
        GET #1, , byte               'to position given by user and
        CALL Display(byte)           'display the byte read
      ELSE
        CALL ReportError
    END IF
  END SUB

  SUB JumpToByteFromHere
    SHARED currentLine
    INPUT "size of jump --> ", size
```

Program 7-21. *(continued)*

```
    IF (size + SEEK(1) >= 1) AND (size + SEEK(1) <= LOF(1)) THEN
        SEEK #1, size + SEEK(1)      'change current file position
        GET #1, , byte               'relative to LOC(1) which is
        CALL Display(byte)           'position of last byte read
      ELSE
        CALL ReportError
    END IF
END SUB


SUB ReadIn (action$)
  SHARED currentLine
  PRINT "action?";                   'display prompt then read
  action$ = UCASE$(INPUT$(1))        'one key and capitalize it
  LOCATE currentLine, 1: PRINT "      "; 'erase prompt
  LOCATE currentLine, 1
END SUB


SUB ReplaceCurrentByte
  SHARED currentLine, bottomLine
  currentLine = currentLine - 1     'back cursor up one line
  IF currentLine = 0 THEN
      currentLine = bottomLine       'then loop to bottom of screen
  END IF
  LOCATE currentLine, 1              'place cursor and
  PRINT "replace with -->";          'print prompt
  text$ = INPUT$(1)                  'read in replacement character
  SEEK #1, SEEK(1) - 1               'Undo auto advance of current
                                     'file position due to last GET
  PUT #1, , text$                    'replace last byte displayed
  CALL Display(text$)
END SUB


SUB ReportError
  SHARED currentLine
  'Display error message on next line then erase it
  '& current line
  LOCATE currentLine + 1, 1: PRINT "Not in file";
  SLEEP 1
  LOCATE currentLine + 1, 1: PRINT SPACE$(30);
  LOCATE currentLine, 1: PRINT SPACE$(30);
  LOCATE currentLine, 1
END SUB
```

displayed on the screen. Since the GET function automatically moves the current file position ahead one position, any action that is to affect the character just displayed must begin by using the SEEK statement to move the current file position back one position.

The subprogram ReplaceCurrentBtye repositions the cursor on the line containing the last character that was displayed and prompts for a replacement character. Once a new character is given, the SEEK statement is used to move the current file position back one position to the point from which the GET function read the old character. The PUT statement then replaces the old character with the new one.

The subprogram GoToByteRelativeToStart prompts the user to enter a new value for the current file position. This position is to be given relative to the beginning of the file. The command menu shows the allowed range of values, from 1 for the beginning of the file to LOF(1) for the end of the file. If the user supplies a valid position, the SEEK statement is used to move the current file position and the character at the new position is then displayed.

The subprogram JumpToByteFromHere prompts the user to a enter a value that is used to move the current file position relative to its current location. Negative values move the current file position towards the beginning of the file, and positive values move it towards the end of the file. The user is told if the newly specified position is not in the file. Otherwise, the SEEK statement is used to move the current file position, and the character at the new position is displayed.

The subprogram ReadIn prompts the user to give one of the five commands listed in the lower portion of the screen. Once a key is pressed, the prompt is erased.

The subprogram DisplayByte displays the current file position, the ASCII value of the character passed to it, and a description of the character, and then erases the "next line" on screen. (If *currentLine* is 19, the "next line" is 1; if *currentLine* is any other number, the "next line" is one more than *currentLine*.) The description displayed for a character depends upon its ASCII value. The 96 standard keyboard characters (ASCII values 32 through 127) are displayed as themselves. Each control character (ASCII values 0 through 31) is displayed as a caret (^) followed by the character whose ASCII value is 64 more than the ASCII value of the control character. For example, the character with ASCII value 7 displays as ^G (character G has ASCII value 71). DisplayByte displays each high ASCII character (ASCII values 128 through 255) as an "at symbol" (@) followed by the description of the character whose ASCII value is 128 less than the ASCII value of the high ASCII character. For example, the character with ASCII value 135 displays as @^G, while the character with ASCII value 193 displays as @A (character A has ASCII value 65).

The program uses the subprogram ReportError to tell the user that the given G (Go) or J (Jump) command resulted in a position not in the file. ReportError displays an error message, waits one second, and then clears the message and the user input that caused the error.

We've seen how to create and modify files, and even how to peek into and change files created by programs other than QBasic. Granted, the concepts introduced are a bit difficult. Let's now turn to topics in the next chapter that are a little less rigorous and more fun, Graphics and Sound.

Graphics and Sound

QBasic has the capacity to produce dazzling graphics displays and a wide range of musical notes and sound effects. This chapter explains the way to create still and animated images on the screen in both color and black-and-white. Later Chapter 9 shows the way to obtain mathematical graphs, and Chapter 10 explains how to display business data with bar and pie charts.

Graphics

Graphics can be produced on a graphics monitor or a monochrome display attached to a Hercules adapter. When a Hercules adapter is used, the program MSHERC.COM must be executed from DOS before QBasic is invoked. All discussions of graphics in this text assume that a graphics adapter and compatible monitor are being used.

Monitors that can be used with an IBM PC, or an IBM PC compatible, are primarily of four types: IRGB monitors, enhanced graphics monitors, monochrome monitors, and composite monitors. (Standard TV sets are composite monitors.) Such a monitor is plugged into either a CGA (Color/Graphics Adapter) board, an EGA (Enhanced Graphics Adapter) board, or a VGA (Video Graphics Array) board.

The most powerful of these configurations is an enhanced graphics monitor with a VGA board. This chapter initially discusses graphics techniques that work for every configuration, and then addresses the additional capabilities of the EGA and VGA.

Graphics Modes

The two graphics modes available on all graphics monitors are referred to as medium-resolution and high-resolution graphics modes. Medium-resolution graphics mode allows the use of up to four colors at any time, whereas high-resolution graphics mode permits only black and white. On the other hand, high-resolution graphics mode permits finer detail.

Specifying Points on the Screen

The graphics screen is divided into an array of small rectangles, called points or pixels. (Pixel stands for "**pic**ture **el**ement.") In both medium- and high-resolution modes there are 200 pixels vertically. Horizontally, there are 320 pixels in medium-resolution graphics mode and 640 pixels in high-resolution graphics mode. (See Figure 8-1.)

> **NOTE**   With a monochrome monitor attached to a Hercules adapter, there are 348 pixels vertically and 720 pixels horizontally.

A pair of numbers called coordinates identify each pixel. The upper left-hand point has coordinates (0, 0). You reach the point with coordinates (x, y) by starting at the upper-left point, and then by moving x points to the right and y points down, as shown in Figure 8-2. For instance, the center of the screen has the coordinates (160, 100) in medium-resolution graphics mode and (320, 100) in high-resolution graphics mode.

> **NOTE**   With a monchrome monitor attached to Hercules card, the center of the screen has coordinates (360, 174).)

The primary graphics statements available in QBasic are SCREEN, PSET, PRESET, LINE, CIRCLE, DRAW, PAINT, COLOR, GET, PUT, POINT, VIEW, WINDOW, and PMAP. The SCREEN statement is used to specify one of the graphics modes. Points, lines, and circles are displayed with the statements PSET, LINE, and CIRCLE. The DRAW statement produces figures on the

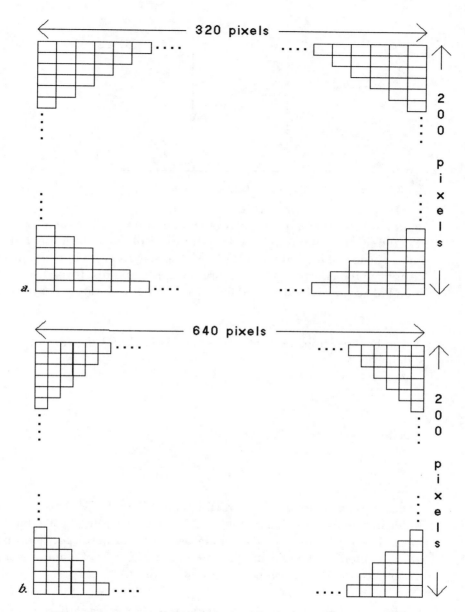

Figure 8-1. Graphics modes: (a) medium-resolution and (b) high-resolution

screen in much the same way that we draw them on paper with a pencil. In medium-resolution graphics mode, the COLOR statement can be used to select colors for the displayed objects and for the background. Animation is

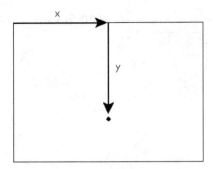

Figure 8-2.   The coordinates of a point

achieved by storing a rectangular portion of the screen with GET and placing
it in different locations with PUT. Graphics displays can be limited to a rectangular portion of the screen with VIEW. The WINDOW statement allows you to
customize the coordinate system used to specify points. If you use WINDOW,
then PMAP translates back and forth from one coordinate system to the other.

A number identifies each SCREEN mode. Table 8-1 lists the numbers. The
statement

```
SCREEN 0, 1
```

specifies text mode and the statement

```
SCREEN n, 0
```

where $n > 0$ specifies graphics SCREEN mode number n. Text characters are
wider in mode 1 (40 characters per line) than in mode 2 (80 characters per
line). The remainder of this chapter assumes you have specified one of the
graphics modes. (The second parameter in the SCREEN statement enables or
disables color when a composite monitor is used.)

When a monochrome display is attached to a Hercules card, the statement

```
SCREEN 3
```

must be used to invoke graphics. This SCREEN mode is similar to SCREEN
mode 2.

Number	Screen mode	Capabilities
0	text mode	text only
1	medium-resolution graphics mode	text and graphics
2	high-resolution graphics mode	text and graphics
3	Hercules graphics mode	text and graphics

Table 8-1. Screen modes

Points, Lines, Rectangles, and Circles

The statement

```
PSET (x, y)
```

turns on the point with coordinates (*x, y*) and the statement

```
PRESET (x, y)
```

turns the point off. The statement

```
LINE (x1, y1)-(x2, y2)
```

draws a line from the point (*x1, y1*) to the point (*x2, y2*). The statement

```
LINE (x1, y1)-(x2, y2), , B
```

draws a rectangle having the points (*x1, y1*) and (*x2, y2*) as opposite corners. The statement

```
LINE (x1, y1)-(x2, y2), , BF
```

draws the same rectangle, but solid. The statement

```
CIRCLE (x, y), r
```

draws the circle with center (*x, y*) and radius *r*. (The radius is measured in terms of the number of pixels from the center of the circle horizontally to its boundary.) Figures 8-3 through 8-7 show the effects produced by these statements in medium-resolution graphics mode. Variations of the **CIRCLE** state-

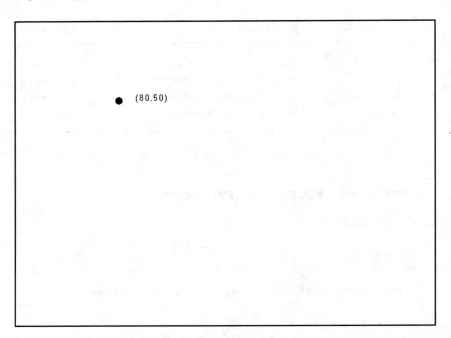

Figure 8-3.   The result of PSET (80, 50)

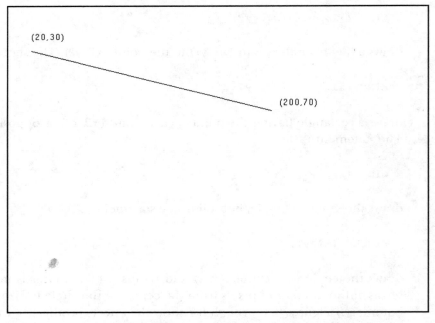

Figure 8-4.   The result of LINE (20, 30)-(200, 70)

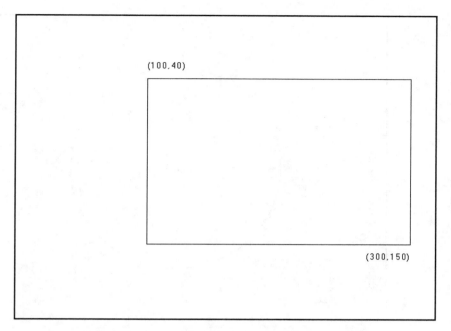

Figure 8-5. The result of LINE (300, 150)-(100, 40), , B

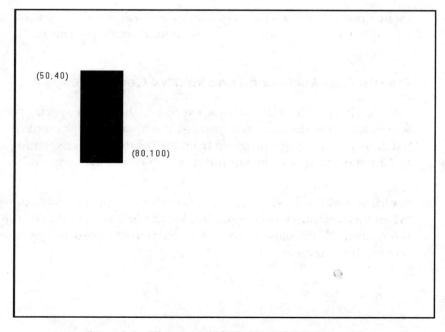

Figure 8-6. The result of LINE (50, 40)-(80, 100), , BF

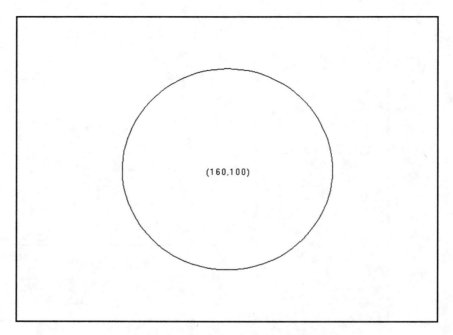

Figure 8-7.   The result of CIRCLE (160, 100), 80

ment draw ellipses and arcs of circles and ellipses. These features are discussed in Chapter 10, where they are used to create pie charts.

The Last Point Referenced and Relative Coordinates

After each graphics statement is executed, there is a special point on the screen known as the *last point referenced*. It is always the last point referred to in a statement. Running a program from the beginning, or executing a SCREEN or CLS statement, sets the last point referenced to the center of the screen.

A variation of the LINE statement allows for one of the points to be omitted. When this variation is used, QBasic takes the omitted point to be the last point referenced. For instance, if the last point referenced is the center of the screen, the statement

```
LINE -(100, 50)
```

draws a line from the center of the screen to the point (100, 50).

Statement	Last Point Referenced
`CIRCLE (80, 70), 30`	$(80, 70)$
`LINE (0, 0)-(40, 50)`	$(40, 50)$
`LINE (50, 80)-STEP (20, 10)`	$(70, 90)$
`PSET (20, 30)`	$(20, 30)$
`PSET(10, 20): CIRCLE STEP (30, 40), 10`	$(40, 60)$

Table 8-2. Examples of the last point referenced and relative coordinates

The coordinates used to identify points in the examples above are called absolute coordinates. Points can also be identified by using *relative* coordinates. These coordinates are given relative to the last point referenced and are preceded by the word STEP. QBasic evaluates

```
STEP (r, s)
```

by starting at the last point referenced, moving r units horizontally (to the right if r is positive or to the left if r is negative), and then moving s units vertically (down if s is positive or up if s is negative). Therefore, if the last point referenced has absolute coordinates (a, b), then STEP (r, s) designates the point with coordinates $(a + r, b + s)$. Table 8-2 gives some statements and the last point referenced after the statement is executed.

The DRAW Statement

The DRAW statement provides a small graphics language that sketches figures by drawing a sequence of lines, each one emanating from the last point referenced to a specified point or in a specified direction. These figures can be rotated, colored, duplicated, and enlarged or reduced.

The M Subcommand of the DRAW Statement

The statement

```
DRAW "M x, y"
```

draws a straight line from the last point referenced to the point with coordinates (x, y). After the statement has been executed, the point (x, y) becomes the new last point referenced. For instance, the statements

```
CLS: DRAW "M 200,50": DRAW "M 300,150"
```

produce a line from the center of the screen to the point (200, 50) and a line from (200, 50) to (300, 150). The last two statements can be condensed into the single statement

```
DRAW "M 200,50 M 300,150"
```

If the letter N precedes the letter M in a DRAW statement, the last point referenced will be the same as it was before the line was drawn. For example,

```
CLS: DRAW "NM 200,50  M 300,150"
```

draws a line from the center of the screen to the point (200, 50) and then from the center of the screen to (300, 150). (The point (300, 150) will be the last point referenced for future DRAW statements.) We often think of the lines as being drawn by a moving point, and say that the point drew the first line and then returned to the original position before drawing the second line.

If the letter B precedes the letter M in a DRAW statement, the point moves without drawing the line. That is, the statement DRAW "BM x,y" merely makes (x, y) the new last point referenced. For example,

```
DRAW "BM 200, 50  M 300, 150"
```

draws a single line from the point (200, 50) to the point (300, 150). The statement DRAW "BM x,y" is used extensively to set the starting point before tracing a figure with a DRAW statement.

The coordinates of the specified point also can be given in relative form. If r and s are nonnegative numbers, then the statement

```
DRAW "M +r, s"
```

draws a line from the last point referenced to the point that is r units to the right and s units down. For instance, in medium-resolution graphics mode,

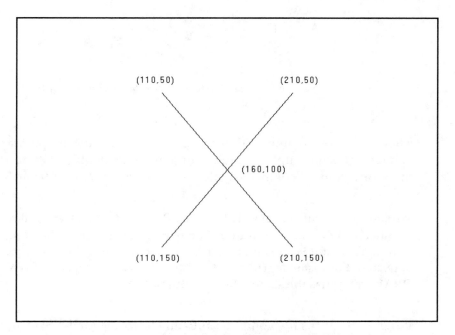

Figure 8-8. The letter X as produced with the DRAW statement

```
CLS: DRAW "M +40,50"
```

draws a line from the point (160, 100) to the point (200, 150). The statements DRAW "M -*r,s*", DRAW "M +*r,-s*", and DRAW "M -*r,-s*" have analogous interpretations. The presence of the + or - sign in front of the first coordinate provides the tip-off that relative coordinates are being used.

The following statements (in medium-resolution graphics) all draw the large letter X shown in Figure 8-8.

```
CLS: DRAW "NM 210, 50   NM 210,150   NM 110,150   M 110, 50"
CLS: DRAW "BM 110, 50   M 210, 150   BM 210,50   M 110, 150"
CLS: DRAW "BM 110, 50   M +100, 100   BM +0, -100   M -100, 100"
```

The DRAW Direction Subcommands U, D, L, R, E, F, G, and H

A statement of the form

```
DRAW "U n"
```

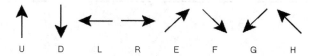

Figure 8-9.   Eight directions used by the DRAW statement

where *n* is a positive integer draws a line by starting at the last point referenced and moving *n* units up. It is equivalent to the statement DRAW "M +0,-*n*". The other direction subcommands operate as shown in Figure 8-9 and Table 8-3.

Whenever the subcommands U, D, L, R, E, F, G, or H are followed by the number 1, the 1 can be omitted. The parameter *n* in the subcommands U, D, L, R, E, F, G, and H can also assume negative integer values. The results are as expected. For instance, DRAW "U -9" has the same effect as DRAW "D 9" and DRAW "E -9" has the same effect as DRAW "G 9".

Program 8-1 turns the computer into an electronic Etch-A-Sketch. While the program is running, you can control a moving dot by pressing the eight keys U, D, L, R, E, F, G, or H and holding them down for as long as you like. To terminate the program press Q. Pressing a key other than one of those mentioned produces a beep. Program 8-2 produces the cube shown in Figure 8-10.

Using the prefixes N and B with the direction subcommands produces the same results as before. For instance, the statement DRAW "BU20" moves the

Subcommand	Moves	Equivalent to
U *n*	*n* units up	M +0,-*n*
D *n*	*n* units down	M +0,*n*
L *n*	*n* units left	M -*n*,0
R *n*	*n* units right	M +*n*,0
E *n*	*n* units NE	M +*n*,-*n*
F *n*	*n* units SE	M +*n*,*n*
G *n*	*n* units SW	M -*n*,*n*
H *n*	*n* units NW	M -*n*,-*n*

Table 8-3.   The DRAW Direction Subcommands

Program 8-1. An electronic Etch-A-Sketch

```
REM Convert the screen into a drawing pad   [8-1]
SCREEN 1, 0     ' Use SCREEN 3 with Hercules adapter
PRINT "Draw using U D L R E F G H."
PRINT "To quit press Q."
a$ = ""
DO WHILE a$ <> "Q"
  SELECT CASE a$
    CASE "U", "D", "L", "R", "E", "F", "G", "H", ""
      DRAW a$
    CASE ELSE
      PRINT CHR$(7);        'Beep!
  END SELECT
  a$ = UCASE$(INPUT$(1))
LOOP
END
```

last point referenced up 20 units without drawing a line. The letter X shown
in Figure 8-8 also can be drawn by each of the following statements.

```
CLS: DRAW "E50   G100   E50   H50   F100"
CLS: DRAW "NE50   NF50   NG50   H50"
CLS: DRAW "BE50   G100   BU100   F100"
```

The DRAW statements given so far have consistently used uppercase and have
included spaces to improve readability. Neither of these conventions is necessary. For instance, the statement that draws the cube in the Program 8-2 can
be written

```
DRAW "160u60r60d60e20u60g20e20160g20"
```

Program 8-2. DRAW a cube

```
REM Draw a cube   [8-2]
SCREEN 1, 0
DRAW "L60 U60 R60 D60 E20 U60 G20 E20 L60 G20"
END
```

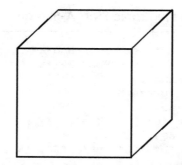

Figure 8-10. The cube drawn by Program 8-2

The Angle Subcommands

The statement

```
DRAW "A n"
```

tells QBasic to draw all subsequent figures rotated counterclockwise through $n \times 90$ degrees, where n is 0, 1, 2, or 3. The statement

```
DRAW "TA n"
```

tells QBasic to draw all subsequent figures rotated through n degrees, where n is between -360 and 360.

Program 8-3 draws the cube given earlier in Figure 8-10. The cube has been rotated through a counterclockwise angle of 45 degrees.

The Scale Subcommand

Figures created with DRAW statements can be enlarged using the scale subcommand. The statement

```
DRAW "S n"
```

Program 8-3. Illustrate the Angle Subcommand of DRAW

```
REM Draw a cube on an angle  [8-3]
SCREEN 1, 0
DRAW "TA45 L60 U60 R60 D60 E20 U60 G20 E20 L60 G20"
END
```

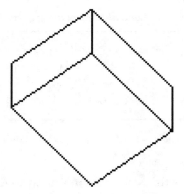

Figure 8-11.   The cube produced by Program 8-3

specifies that QBasic should draw all subsequent segments at $n/4$ times their stated size until you specify another scale. The number n can range from 1 to 255. For instance, the statement DRAW "S8 U10 L15 D10 R15" is equivalent to the statement DRAW "U20 L30 D20 R30". They both draw a rectangle of height 20 and width 30.

Using Variables and Substrings in DRAW

The string in a DRAW statement can be assigned to a string variable, and then the string variable can be used to represent the string. For instance, the statement DRAW "U20 L30 D20 R30" is equivalent to

```
a$ = "U20 L30 D20 R30": DRAW a$
```

The + operator for strings can also be used to combine strings for the DRAW statement. For example, the DRAW statement in Program 8-3 can be replaced by

```
cube$ = "L60 U60 R60 D60 E20 U60 G20 E20 L60 G20": DRAW "TA45 " + cube$
```

Until now, the numbers appearing in DRAW strings were all numeric constants. You can place a numeric variable into a DRAW statement by converting the value to a string with STR$ and then using + to place the string into the DRAW command string. Table 8-4 shows several DRAW statements and their equivalent forms using a variable.

Statement	Equivalent form using variables
DRAW "U 20"	a=20: DRAW "U" + STR$(a)
DRAW "TA 45"	angle = 45: DRAW "TA" + STR$(angle)
DRAW "NL5 D2"	a=5: b=2: DRAW "NL" + STR$(a) + "D" + STR$(b)
DRAW "M +40,50"	a=40: b=50: DRAW "M +" + STR$(a) + "," + STR$(b)

Table 8-4. Examples of DRAW statements with variables

Program 8-4 uses the Scale subcommand to draw cubes of various sizes. (The cube will not completely fit in the screen if the scale is greater than about 180.)

Color

Table 8-5 shows the 16 principal colors that are available on a color monitor. A number from 0 to 15 identifies each color. This section considers the use of color in medium-resolution graphics mode. Later, this chapter presents the enhancements that are possible if you use the monitor with an EGA or VGA adapter.

A palette can be thought of as a collection of four paint jars numbered 0, 1, 2, and 3 with each jar containing a color of paint. Medium-resolution graphics mode offers two palettes, palette 0 and palette 1, that you can use at any time. Table 8-6 gives the colors contained in the jars. Only four colors can appear on the screen at one time, and all of these colors must be from the same palette.

Program 8-4. Illustration of the use of variables in a DRAW string

```
REM Draw various size cubes   [8-4]
SCREEN 1, 0
INPUT "SCALE (1-255) "; scale
DRAW "S" + STR$(scale)
DRAW "BM +0,2 L3 U3 R3 D3 E1 U3 G1 E1 L3 G1"
END
```

0 Black	4 Red	8 Gray	12 Light Red
1 Blue	5 Magenta	9 Light Blue	13 Light Magenta
2 Green	6 Brown	10 Light Green	14 Yellow
3 Cyan	7 White	11 Light Cyan	15 High-Intensity White

Table 8-5. The 16 Principal Colors

The COLOR statement is used to select either palette 0 or palette 1 as the current palette, and to assign a background color to the jars numbered 0. The statement

```
COLOR b, p
```

where *b* is a number from 0 to 15 and *p* is either 0 or 1 makes *b* the new background color (the color in the 0 jars) and specifies that QBasic should take the color of each point on the screen from palette *p*. Text always appears in the color from jar 3 of the current palette. Any figure produced by one of the following statements will appear in the color from jar *m* of the current palette.

```
PSET (x, y), m
LINE (x1, y1)-(x2, y2), m
CIRCLE (x, y), r, m
DRAW "C m" + draw string
```

If you omit the parameter *m* in any of these statements, then QBasic will draw the figure in the third color of the current palette.

	Palette 0		Palette 1
Jar#	Assigned Color	Jar#	Assigned Color
0	b (background color)	0	b (background color)
1	2 (green)	1	3 (cyan)
2	4 (red)	2	5 (magenta)
3	6 (brown)	3	7 (white)

Table 8-6. The Two Standard Palettes

| NOTE | We often refer to the color assigned to jar *m* of the current palette as the *m*th color. Some books use the word attribute to refer to the number *m*. |

Program 8-5 produces figures and text in several different colors. Program 8-6 draws the cube given earlier in Figure 8-10 in magenta with cyan front edges and a white background.

Not only can QBasic draw colored lines and curves, but it can also fill in, or paint, enclosed regions with a color selected from the current palette. A region to be painted is identified by giving the coordinates of a point inside the region and the color of the boundary. If the point (*x*, *y*) is inside an enclosed region whose boundary has the *b*th color of the current palette, then the statement

```
PAINT (x, y), m, b
```

fills in the region with the *m*th color of the current palette. For example, Program 8-7 creates a dart board. The inner circle is black and the three rings are cyan, magenta, and white.

The DRAW statement has a paint command that can be incorporated into its command string. The statement

```
DRAW "P m, b"
```

Program 8-5. Display text and figures in color

```
REM Demonstrate the use of colors  [8-5]
SCREEN 1, 0
COLOR 8, 0                      'Gray background, palette 0
PRINT "Hello"                   'Brown greeting
PSET (50, 50)                   'Brown point
PSET (100, 100), 1              'Green point
LINE (10, 20)-(30, 40), 2       'Red line
CIRCLE (100, 100), 50, 3        'Brown circle
PSET (150, 150)
DRAW "C1 R6 U5 L6 D5"           'Green square
END
```

Program 8-6. Drawing in color

```
REM Draw the cube of Figure 8-10 with different colors   [8-6]
SCREEN 1, 0
COLOR 7, 1
CLS
DRAW "C1 L60 U60 R60 D60 C2 E20 U60 G20 E20 L60 G20"
END
```

has the same effect as the statement PAINT (x, y), m, b where the point (x, y) is the last point referenced.

Program 8-8 creates a cube with a red front face, a brown top and a green right face against a white background. Each of the last three lines of the program uses B and a move command to place the last point referenced inside one of the cube faces before painting it.

Styling and Tiling

QBasic has two graphics enhancements that substitute for and complement colors. A styled line is a line made up of a repeating pattern of dots and dashes. A tiled region is an enclosed region of the screen that is filled in with a repeating rectangular pattern, which resembles a tiled floor.

Line styling requires the ability to convert a binary number (a sequence of 0's and 1's) to hexadecimal form (beginning with &H and using the digits 0

Program 8-7. Illustration of the PAINT statement

```
REM Create a dart board   [8-7]
SCREEN 1, 0
COLOR 0, 1
FOR n = 1 TO 4
  CIRCLE (160, 100), 20 * n, 3
NEXT n
FOR n = 1 TO 3
  PAINT (170 + 20 * n, 100), n, 3
NEXT n
END
```

Program 8-8. Illustrate painting with the DRAW statement

```
REM Paint a cube   [8-8]
SCREEN 1, 0
COLOR 7, 0
a$ = "L60 U60 R60 D60 E20 U60 G20 E20 L60 G20"
DRAW a$
DRAW "BF5 P 2,3"
DRAW "BR60 P 1,3"
DRAW "BH10 P 3,3"
END
```

through 9 and the letters A through F). In every situation arising in line styling, the binary number is given as a 16 place string (a "sixteen-tuple") of zeros and ones. The following process will determine the hexadecimal form:

1. Partition the 16-tuple into four 4-tuples.

2. Replace each 4-tuple with the digit or letter shown in Table 8-7.

3. Place &H onto the front of the derived string of four characters.

For example, the 16-tuple 0101111110100010 is partitioned as 0101 1111 1010 0010, and then written &H5FA2.

Figure 8-12 shows four styled lines. The style of each line is a 16-point pattern that is repeated as many times as necessary. To draw a styled line from (a, b) to (c, d), we consider the pixels lying on the straight line between the two specified points and turn on some of these pixels. Suppose that we begin with the point (a, b) and, of the first 16 pixels, turn on the 1st, 5th, 10th, and 14th pixels. We can represent this pattern by the 16-tuple

```
1000100001000100
```

0000	0	0100	4	1000	8	1100	C
0001	1	0101	5	1001	9	1101	D
0010	2	0110	6	1010	A	1110	E
0011	3	0111	7	1011	B	1111	F

Table 8-7. Binary numbers and their hexadecimal equivalents

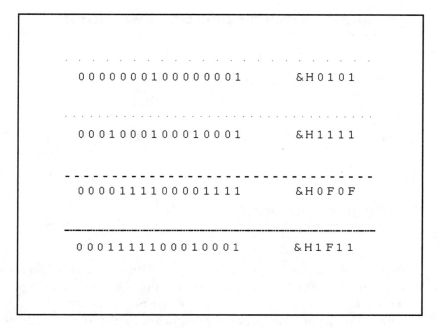

Figure 8-12. Styled lines

Counting from left to right, this 16-tuple has ones in its 1st, 5th, 10th, and 14th positions, and zeroes in all other positions. The 16-tuple is the binary representation of the hexadecimal number &H8844. The statement

```
LINE (a, b)-(c, d), , , &H8844
```

draws the line from (a, b) to (c, d) by beginning at (a, b) with the first 16 pixels as just described, and then repeating the same pattern in each successive 16-tuple until reaching the point (c, d). In general, if s is the hexadecimal representation of a 16-tuple of zeros and ones, then the statement

```
LINE (a, b)-(c, d), , , s
```

draws the line from (a, b) to (c, d) with the pattern determined by the 16-tuple. The number s is referred to as the style of the line. Figure 8-12 shows a few patterns with their associated 16-tuples and styles. The parameters m, B, or both may be inserted between the appropriate commas to obtain color, a styled rectangle, or both.

Program 8-9. Illustrate the effect of the style parameter

```
REM Determine the pattern of a styled line   [8-9]
SCREEN 1, 0
LINE (20, 170)-(300, 170), , , &H1F11
FOR n = 0 TO 15
  PRINT POINT(20 + n, 170);
NEXT n
END

[run]
  0  0  0  3  3  3  3  3  0  0  0  3  0  0  0  3

{ Styled line not shown }
```

Program 8-9 draws the last styled line in Figure 8-12 and displays descriptive numbers. The POINT function has the value 3 if the indicated pixel is on and the value 0 if it is off. The pattern of zeroes and threes is the same as the pattern of zeroes and ones that appears in the binary representation of &H1F11.

Figure 8-13 shows two examples of enclosed regions PAINTed with tile patterns. The method for designing patterns is different for high-resolution graphics than for medium-resolution graphics. This section will discuss each case separately.

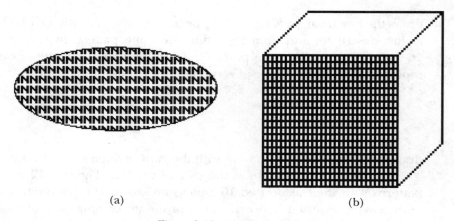

(a)   (b)

Figure 8-13. Examples of tiling

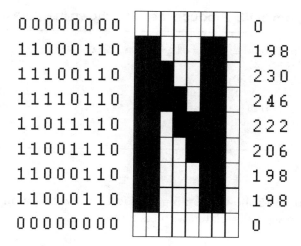

Figure 8-14. The tile used in Figure 8-13a

In high-resolution graphics, each tile is 8 pixels horizontally and from 1 to 64 pixels vertically. You specify a tile by identifying each pixel as on or off. You can associate each row of the tile with an 8-tuple of zeroes and ones, where the ones correspond to the pixels to be turned on and the zeroes correspond to the pixels to be turned off. Each 8-tuple corresponds to an integer from 0 through 255.

Figure 8-14 shows the tiling used in Figure 8-13a, along with the binary 8-tuples and integers associated with each row. The tile in Figure 8-14 is specified by the string

```
t$=CHR$(0)+CHR$(198)+CHR$(230)+CHR$(246)+CHR$(222)+_
    CHR$(206)+CHR$(198)+CHR$(198)+CHR$(0)
```

where $t\$$ is the tile specifier. Program 8-10 uses the tile in Figure 8-14 to tile a circle with the same tiling as the ellipse in Figure 8-13a.

In medium-resolution graphics, each tile is 4 pixels horizontally, and from 1 to 64 pixels vertically. You specify a tile by giving the number of the jar (0, 1, 2, or 3) to be used to color each pixel. Then, you translate each of the four numbers into binary notation: 0 is 00, 1 is 01, 2 is 10, and 3 is 11. You can then associate each row of the tile with an 8-tuple of zeroes and ones, by stringing together the four binary numbers in the row. Each of the 8-tuples is the binary representation of a decimal integer from 0 to 255.

Program 8-10.   Produce the tiling shown in Figure 8-13a

```
REM Produce a circle filled with N's   [8-10]
SCREEN 2, 0
CIRCLE (100, 75), 90
t$ = CHR$(0) + CHR$(198) + CHR$(230) + CHR$(246) + CHR$(222) + _
     CHR$(206) + CHR$(198) + CHR$(198) + CHR$(0)
PAINT (100, 75), t$
END
```

Figure 8-15 shows the tiling used in Figure 8-13b, along with the binary 8-tuple and integer associated with each row.

The tile in Figure 8-15 is specified by the string

```
t$ = CHR$(70) + CHR$(85) + CHR$(78)
```

In either high- or medium-resolution graphics, suppose that a tile has r rows with associated integers $n1$, $n2$, ..., nr. Then the string

```
t$ = CHR$(n1) + CHR$(n2) + ... + CHR$(nr)
```

specifies the tile. If an enclosed region contains the point (x, y) in its interior and has a boundary drawn in the bth color of the current palette, then the statement

```
PAINT (x, y), t$, b
```

fills in the region by tiling it with the tile *t$*.

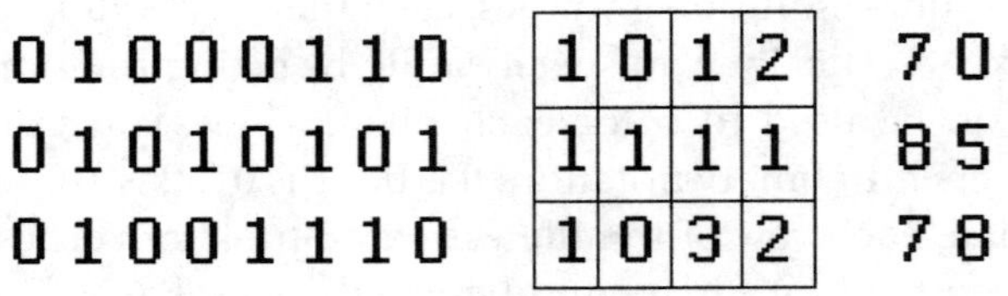

```
0 1 0 0 0 1 1 0    1 0 1 2    7 0
0 1 0 1 0 1 0 1    1 1 1 1    8 5
0 1 0 0 1 1 1 0    1 0 3 2    7 8
```

Figure 8-15.   The tile used in Figure 8-13b

Program 8-11. Produce the tiling shown in Figure 8-13b

```
REM Cube with tiled face   [8-11]
SCREEN 1, 0
COLOR 0, 0
DRAW "L60 U60 R60 D60 E20 U60 G20 E20 L60 G20"
t$ = CHR$(70) + CHR$(85) + CHR$(78)
PAINT (150, 90), t$
END
```

Program 8-11 uses the tile in Figure 8-15 to obtain the tiling shown in Figure 8-13b.

In medium-resolution graphics, the statement PAINT (*x, y*), *t$, b* is not always able to tile over a region that has already been PAINTed with a tile pattern or color. A general solution to this problem is possible as long as the border of the region in question does not have the background color (that is, *b* is not 0). In this case, the statement PAINT (*x, y*), 0, *b* should precede the PAINT statement given earlier. The first PAINT statement clears the region to the background color, thereby allowing the next PAINT statement to execute its tiling properly.

Program 8-12 presents an example of the retiling problem. To solve the problem, you should place the statement PAINT (30, 50), 0, 3 before PAINT (30, 50), *t$*, 3.

The tile specifier, *t$*, is just a string. Hence, any string of length at most 64 can be used for *t$*. Program 8-13 tiles the entire screen in a pattern that the user-supplied string determines.

Animation

Animation is accomplished by using the GET statement to take a snapshot of a rectangular portion of the screen and then repeatedly using the PUT statement to place the snapshot at nearby locations.

The graphics GET statement stores a copy of a rectangular portion of the screen in memory. The rectangular portion of the screen is designated by giving the coordinates of its upper-left corner (*x1, y1*) and its lower-right corner (*x2, y2*), as shown in Figure 8-16. The information saved consists of the

Program 8-12.   A tiling problem

```
REM Draw a red rectangle and then paint it with stripes   [8-12]
SCREEN 1, 0
COLOR 0, 0
LINE (10, 10)-(50, 90), , B
PAINT (30, 50), 2, 3
t$ = CHR$(255) + CHR$(255) + CHR$(0) + CHR$(0) + _
     CHR$(170) + CHR$(170) + CHR$(0) + CHR$(0)
PAINT (30, 50), t$, 3
END
```

jar number associated with each point of the region. (Remember that your palette choice and the jar number determine the point color.) The statement

```
GET (x1, y1)-(x2, y2), arrayName
```

stores a description of the specified rectangle in the named array. You may use any numeric array type. For simplicity, the rest of this section discusses only integer arrays.

You must first dimension the array with a statement of the form

```
DIM arrayName(n)
```

Program 8-13.   The patterns generated by strings

```
REM Experiment with different tile patterns   [8-13]
SCREEN 1, 0
COLOR 0, 0
INPUT "Type in any string of characters: ",t$
PAINT (5, 5), t$
END

[run]
Type in any string of characters: FUN
```

{ The pattern produced is the same one that appears in the cube in Figure 8-13b. }

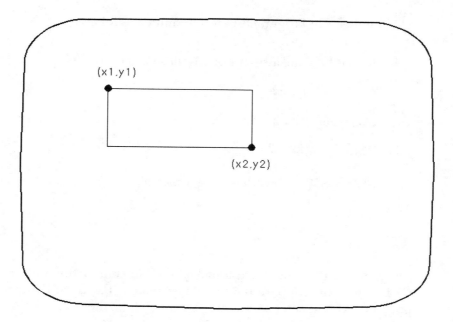

Figure 8-16. A rectangular region captured by a GET statement

(Normally, arrays with a size *n* less than 11 do not have to be specifically dimensioned. However, this is not the case if you will first use the array with a GET statement.) In medium-resolution graphics mode, the size, *n*, of the integer array is determined in the following manner:

1. Let *h* be the number of pixels in a horizontal side of the rectangle, and *v* be the number of pixels in a vertical side. Thus,

    $h = x2 - x1 + 1$

    and

    $v = y2 - y1 + 1$

2. Calculate the number $(2 \times h+7)/8$, multiply its integer part by *v*, and then add 4. Call the result *b*.

3. The value of *n* must be at least $(b/2) - 1$.

In high-resolution graphics mode, the procedure for determining the value of *n* is the same, except that you replace the number 2 in step 2 by the number 1.

The number n in Program 8-14 is determined as follows:

1. Using the same assumptions as those in step 1,

   $h = 25 - 4 + 1 = 22$

   $v = 60 - 20 + 1 = 41$

2. $2*h + 7 = 2*22 + 7 = 51$

   $51/8 = 6.375$, which has integer part 6

   $b = 6*v + 4 = 6*41 = 250$

3. $n = (250/2) - 1 = 124$

The graphics PUT statement usually is used in conjunction with the graphics GET statement. Suppose that a GET statement has recorded a rectangular portion of the screen into an integer array. Then, the statement

```
PUT (x, y), arrayName, PSET
```

will place an exact image of the rectangular region on the screen, positioned with its upper left-hand corner at the point (x, y). In Program 8-15, H_2O is displayed on the screen. The number 2 will appear as a subscript of the H.

Program 8-16 draws a truck, as shown in Figure 8-17, and then moves it across the screen. The rectangular region chosen is a little larger than is necessary to include the truck. On the left, the region has a small blank border, which erases the overhanging part of the previous truck drawing each time that the program places a new picture of the truck on the screen.

Program 8-14. Illustrate the dimensioning of an array to be used with GET

```
REM Capture a rectangular region of the screen   [8-14]
SCREEN 1, 0
n = 124
DIM a%(n)
GET (4, 20)-(25, 60), a%
END
```

Program 8-15. Use PUT to display a subscript

```
REM Display the formula for water   [8-15]
SCREEN 1, 0
LOCATE 1, 1
PRINT "2"
DIM two%(9)
GET (0, 0)-(7, 7), two%
CLS
LOCATE 1, 1
PRINT "H O"
PUT (8, 4), two%, PSET
END
```

The word PSET, which appears at the end of the PUT statements just given, is referred to as the action of the statement. There are four other possible actions: PRESET, AND, OR, and XOR. We first consider the effects of these actions for high-resolution graphics mode.

In high-resolution graphics mode, each point is colored either black or white. Suppose that a GET statement has recorded a rectangular portion of the

Program 8-16. A demonstration of animation

```
REM Move a truck across the screen   [8-16]
SCREEN 1, 0
CALL DrawTruck
DIM truck%(629)
GET (20, 21)-(119, 70), truck%
CLS
FOR n = 1 TO 200
  PUT (n, 100), truck%, PSET
NEXT n
END

SUB DrawTruck
  CIRCLE (105, 60), 10              'Draw front tire
  PAINT (105, 60), 3               'Paint front tire
  CIRCLE (35, 60), 10              'Draw rear tire
  PAINT (35, 60), 3                'Paint rear tire
  LINE (21, 21)-(101, 40), , BF    'Draw back of truck
  LINE (21, 40)-(119, 60), , BF    'Draw hood
END SUB
```

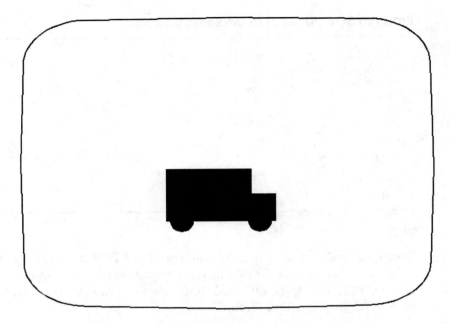

Figure 8-17. The truck created by Program 8-16

screen into an array. Then each of the actions effect the rectangular region having the point (*x*, *y*) as its upper left-hand corner and having the same size as the original rectangle.

The statement

```
PUT (x, y), arrayName, PRESET
```

displays a reversed image of the original rectangular region. Every point that was originally white will be black, and vice versa.

The remaining three actions interact with whatever images are already in the rectangular part of the screen that will be PUT upon. The action AND results in a point being white only if it is already white and is also white in the image being transferred. The action OR results in a point being white if it is already white or if it is white in the image being transferred. The action XOR results in a point being white if it is either already white or if it is white in the image

Program 8-17. Illustrate the use of XOR

```
REM Move a ball around the screen   [8-17]
DIM ball%(10)
t0 = TIMER
FOR i = 1 TO 500: NEXT i
loopsPerSec = 500 / (TIMER - t0)
'loopsPerSec = # of passes through the loop to delay about 1 sec.
SCREEN 2, 0
'Get an image of the ball
CIRCLE (20, 20), 4
PAINT (20, 20), 3
GET (16, 16)-(24, 24), ball%
'Specify initial position of ball
'and increments for finding new position
horizontal = 16
vertical = 16
hIncrement = 1
vIncrement = 1
PRINT " Press any key to quit."
DO WHILE INKEY$ = ""
  'If ball is at edge of screen, reverse the value of increment
  IF vertical>190 OR vertical<1 THEN vIncrement=-vIncrement
  IF horizontal>630 OR horizontal<1 THEN hIncrement=-hIncrement
  'Save old position for later PUT that erases ball
  oldHorizontal = horizontal
  oldVertical = vertical
  'Compute new position
  horizontal = horizontal + hIncrement
  vertical = vertical + vIncrement
  'Erase ball from old position
  PUT (oldHorizontal, oldVertical), ball%, XOR
  'Place ball at new position
  PUT (horizontal, vertical), ball%, XOR
  'Control speed of ball
  FOR i = 1 TO loopsPerSec * .004: NEXT i   'Delay .004 seconds
LOOP
END
```

being transferred, but not both. If no action is specified in a PUT statement, then XOR is automatically invoked.

XOR is commonly used in animation. PUTting an image on top of itself with XOR has the effect of erasing the image and restoring the original background. Program 8-17 results in a ball moving around the screen and bouncing off the sides. Press any key to terminate the program.

To create a variation of Program 8-17, add the following line before the DO WHILE loop:

```
LINE (320, 0)-(410, 199), , BF
```

The program will then draw a solid vertical rectangle in the middle of the screen. After the ball passes through the rectangle, the rectangle will still be intact.

In medium-resolution graphics mode, the action PSET causes an exact copy of the original rectangle to be displayed (unless you have changed the current palette, in which case, points colored from jar *m* of the old palette will now be colored from jar *m* of the new palette). The action PRESET displays a reverse image: points that were colored from jar 3 are now colored from jar 0 of the current palette, and vice versa. Similarly, points colored from jar 1 are now colored from jar 2, and vice versa.

Every point of the screen has an associated jar number. This number is 0 until the point is affected by a graphics or PRINT statement. The remaining three PUT actions interact with the colors that are already in the rectangular part of the screen that will be PUT upon. The new jar number of each point is determined by its old jar number, the jar number of the corresponding point in the stored rectangle, and the action. The resulting jar numbers (which determine the colors) are given in Table 8-8.

You can also obtain the resulting jar numbers if you understand logical operators and the binary representation of numbers. For example, to determine the result of combining jars 2 and 3 with respect to the action XOR, write the two jar numbers in binary notation and apply the logical operator XOR to the components. The numbers 2 and 3 are 10 and 11 in binary notation, respectively. Since 10 XOR 11 is 01 or 1, the action XOR combines jars 2 and 3 to produce jar 1.

You can use the POINT function in animation to determine if two objects are about to collide. The value of

```
POINT (x, y)
```

Old Jar Number		Stored Jar Number		
		0 1 2 3	0 1 2 3	0 1 2 3
	0	0 0 0 0	0 1 2 3	0 1 2 3
	1	0 1 0 1	1 1 3 3	1 0 3 2
	2	0 0 2 2	2 3 2 3	2 3 0 1
	3	0 1 2 3	3 3 3 3	3 2 1 0
		AND	**OR**	**XOR**

Table 8-8. Jar numbers that result from the actions AND, OR, and XOR

is the jar number of the point with coordinates (x, y). (In high-resolution graphics mode, points that are black (off) have a jar number of 0, while points that are white (on) have a jar number of 1.)

In Program 8-18 a barrier of user-specified position and length appears, and a ball moves from left to right across the screen. Figure 8-18 shows the barrier and the ball. If the ball hits the barrier, the ball's direction will be reversed. The program repeats the DO loop until the ball either reaches the right side of the screen, or reaches the left side of the screen while moving to the left. The POINT function detects objects in the path of the ball and tells the program whether it should reverse the direction of the ball. The upper left-hand corner of the rectangle that contains the ball is 3 pixels to the left and 3 pixels above the center of the ball. If the length of the barrier is less than 100, then the ball will cross the entire screen. Otherwise, the ball will appear to bounce off the barrier.

The Use of an EGA Board

You can attach any of three types of monitors to an EGA (Enhanced Graphics Adapter) board: an EGM (Enhanced Graphics Monitor), an IRGB monitor (an ordinary color monitor whose letters stand for Intensity Red Green Blue), or a monochrome display.

You can realize the full power of the EGA if you use an EGM. 64 colors and three additional SCREEN modes are available. (Chapter 4 presents a discussion of the 64 colors available on an EGM.) With an IRGB monitor, you can change the colors assigned to the jars in the two medium-resolution graphics mode palettes to any four of the 16 standard colors; in high-resolution graphics mode, you can specify the foreground and background colors. With a

Program 8-18. Illustrate the use of POINT to detect a collision

```
REM Move a ball across a screen with a barrier  [8-18]
DEFINT D, X
SCREEN 1, 0
t0 = TIMER
FOR i = 1 TO 500: NEXT i
loopsPerSec = 500 / (TIMER - t0)
'Get the image of a ball
DIM ball%(9)
CIRCLE (3, 100), 2
PAINT (3, 100), 3
GET (0, 97)-(6, 103), ball%
'Get size and location of barrier then draw it
INPUT "Enter a position from 10 to 300: ", position
INPUT "Enter a length from 1 to 199: ", length
CLS
LINE (position, 0)-(position + 20, length), , BF
'Move ball across screen. If ball hits, reverse its direction
d = 1           '1=right, -1=left
x = 3           'x-coordinate of center of ball
DO
  IF POINT(x + 4, 99) <> 0 THEN d = -1
  x = x + d
  PUT (x - 3, 97), ball%, PSET
  FOR i = 1 TO loopsPerSec * .004: NEXT i
LOOP UNTIL x > 315 OR (x < 4 AND d = -1)
END
```

monochrome display, you can display graphics in a special SCREEN mode. Each SCREEN mode supported by QBasic is described below:

- SCREEN mode 1 (320×200 graphics resolution, 40 characters per line)

  IRGB monitor: The situation is the same as with a CGA board, except that you may now use the PALETTE statement to change the colors assigned to the palettes. If m is a number from 0 to 3 and c is a number from 0 to 15, then the statement PALETTE m, c changes the color in jar m of the current palette to color c as shown in Table 8-5. Note that selecting a palette with a COLOR statement restores the default color assignments of that palette. Program 8-19 prepares to work in SCREEN mode 1 with a light blue background and the colors yellow, magenta, and light green for the foreground.

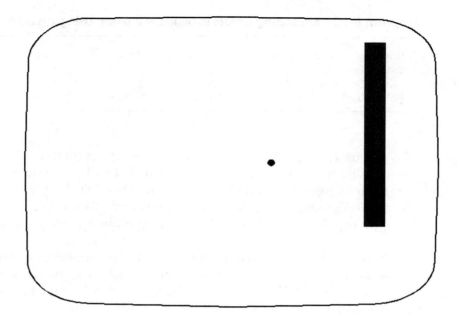

Figure 8-18. The ball and the barrier

EGM monitor: The situation is the same as with an IRGB monitor, except that there are 64 colors available to the COLOR statement for the background color *b* and to the PALETTE statement for the assigned color *c*.

• SCREEN mode 2 (640 × 200 graphics resolution, 80 characters per line)

IRGB monitor: The situation is the same as with a CGA board, except that the PALETTE statement can be used to change both the foreground

Program 8-19. Setting up a new palette in SCREEN mode 1

```
REM New colors for palette 0 on IRGB Monitor with an EGA
[8-19]
SCREEN 1, 0
COLOR , 0       'Select palette 0
PALETTE 0, 9    'Put light blue in jar 0 (as background color)
PALETTE 1, 14   'Put yellow in jar 1
PALETTE 2, 5    'Put magenta in jar 2
PALETTE 3, 10   'Put light green in jar 3
```

Program 8-20. Changing colors in SCREEN 2 when using an EGA

```
REM New colors in SCREEN 2 on an IRGB Monitor with an EGA    [8-20]
SCREEN 2, 0
PALETTE 0, 9    'Make the background light blue
PALETTE 1, 0    'Make the foreground black
```

and background colors to any one of the 16 standard colors. If c is a number from 0 to 15, then the statement PALETTE 0, c selects color c as the background color and the statement PALETTE 1, c selects color c as the foreground color. Program 8-20 sets up SCREEN mode 2 to have a light blue background with all text and graphics appearing in black.

EGM monitor: Any two of the 64 EGA colors are available as foreground or background. If c is a number from 0 to 63, then the statement PALETTE 0, c selects color c as the background color and the statement PALETTE 1, c selects color c as the foreground color.

- SCREEN mode 3 (720×348 graphics resolution, 80 characters per line)

Monochrome monitor: This mode can be used only with the Hercules monochrome graphics adapter. It is similar to SCREEN mode 2, with the exception that the PALETTE statement is not supported.

- SCREEN mode 7 (320×200 graphics resolution, 40 characters per line)

EGM or IRGB monitors: A single palette with 16 jars, numbered 0 through 15, is available. Initially jar m is assigned color m from Table 8-5. However, the PALETTE statement can be used to assign any of the 16 principle colors to any of the 16 jars. The statement COLOR f, b specifies that the color in jar f of the palette be used for foreground (that is, the color used for text and the default color for graphics) and that the color in jar b of the palette be used for background. The parameter m in the graphics statements PSET, LINE, CIRCLE, DRAW, and PAINT can range from 0 through 15. When a GET statement is used to capture a rectangular region of the screen in an integer array, step b of the procedure for determining the size of the array must be changed as follows: the number 2 should be changed to 1, and v should be replaced by 4*v.

- SCREEN mode 8 (640 × 200 graphics resolution, 80 characters per line)

  EGM or IRGB monitor: This mode performs the same as SCREEN mode 7.

- SCREEN mode 9 (640 × 350 resolution, 80 characters per line)

  EGM monitor: A single palette with 16 jars, numbered 0 through 15, is available. Initially, jar m is assigned a color number that closely matches the colors of Table 8-5. The COLOR, PALETTE, and GET statements perform the same as in SCREEN modes 7 and 8, except that 64 colors are available to assign to the 16 jars. However, if there is only 64K of memory on the EGA board, the palette will consist of just the four jars numbered 0 to 3. The parameter m in the graphics statements PSET, LINE, CIRCLE, DRAW, and PAINT can range from 0 to 3 or 0 to 15, depending on the amount of memory.

- SCREEN mode 10 (640 × 350 graphics resolution, 80 characters per line)

  Monochrome monitor: A single palette with four jars is available. Nine pseudo-colors (see Table 8-9) can be assigned to these jars with the PALETTE statement. If m is a number from 0 to 3 and c is a number from 0 to 8, then the statement PALETTE m, c assigns pseudo-color c to jar m of the palette. The statement COLOR f, b specifies that the pseudo-color in jar f of the palette be used for foreground (that is, the pseudo-color used for text foreground and the default pseudo-color for graphics), and

0	black
1	blinking (black to white)
3	blinking (black to high intensity white)
4	white
5	blinking (white to high intensity white)
6	blinking (high intensity white to black)
7	blinking (high intensity white to white)
8	high intensity white

Table 8-9. Pseudo-colors available on the monochrome display

that the pseudo-color in jar *b* of the palette be used for background. This mode performs the same as SCREEN modes 7 and 8 with respect to the GET statement. The parameter m in the graphics statements PSET, LINE, CIRCLE, DRAW, and PAINT can range from 0 through 3.

The Use of a VGA Board

With a VGA board and monitor, SCREEN modes 1 through 10 emulate the performance of an EGA board. VGA boards support three additional graphics SCREEN modes — 11, 12, and 13. Since the COLOR statement is not available in these modes, colors are altered with PALETTE statements. Each of the 256K colors available to fill jars has the form $c = (65536 * b) + (256 * g) + r$, where *b*, *g*, and *r* range from 0 to 63, and represent varying intensities of blue, green, and red.

- SCREEN mode 11 (640×480 resolution, 80 characters per line): Screen mode 11 is an enhancement of SCREEN mode 2. Any two of 256K colors can be assigned to the foreground and background. If *c* is a valid color number, then the statement PALETTE 0, *c* sets the background color to *c* and the statement PALETTE 1, *c* sets the foreground color to *c*. The parameter *m* in the graphics statements PSET, LINE, CIRCLE, DRAW, and PAINT can be either 0 or 1. When a GET statement is used to capture a rectangular region of the screen in an integer array, the number 2 in step 2 of the procedure for determining the size of the array should be changed to 1.

- SCREEN mode 12 (640×480 resolution, 80 characters per line): A single palette with 16 jars, numbered 0 through 15, is available. Initially, jar *m* is assigned a color number that closely matches the colors of Table 8-5. Any 16 of 256 colors can be assigned to the jars. If *c* is a valid color number, then the statement PALETTE *j*, *c* fills jar *j* with color *c*. (Jars 0 and 15 hold the default background and foreground colors.) The parameter *m* in the graphics statements PSET, LINE, CIRCLE, DRAW, and PAINT can range from 0 through 15. When a GET statement is used to capture a rectangular region of the screen in an integer array, step 2 of the procedure for determining the size of the array must be changed as follows: the number 2 should be changed to 1, and *v* should be replaced by 4*v*.

- SCREEN mode 13 (320×200 resolution, 40 characters per line): A single palette with 256 jars, numbered 0 through 255 is available. Any 256 of 256K colors can be assigned to the jars. If *c* is a valid color number, then the statement PALETTE *j*, *c* fills jar *j* with color *c*. The parameter *m* in the graphics statements PSET, LINE, CIRCLE, DRAW, and PAINT can range from 0 through 255. When a GET statement is used to capture a rectangular region of the screen in an integer array, the number 2 in step 2 of the procedure for determining the size of the array should be changed to 8.

User-defined Coordinate Systems

The coordinates discussed in the beginning of this chapter are known as physical coordinates. The use of physical coordinates has two disadvantages. First, the coordinates of an actual point on the physical screen depends on the SCREEN mode. For example, the center of the screen has coordinates (160,100) in SCREEN mode 1, (320,100) in SCREEN mode 2, and (320,175) in SCREEN mode 9. Second, the coordinate systems are difficult to use in many applications, such as displaying data in bar graphs or graphing mathematical functions. You can eliminate these limitations by using the WINDOW statement, which allows you to design your own coordinate system. The statement

```
WINDOW (x1, y1)-(x2, y2)
```

sets up a standard x-y coordinate system for the screen. The points of the plane have x coordinates ranging from *x1* rightward to *x2*, and y coordinates ranging from *y1* up to *y2*, as shown in Figure 8-19a. The statement

```
WINDOW SCREEN (x1, y1)-(x2, y2)
```

embeds the screen in a nonstandard x-y coordinate system. The points of the plane have x coordinates ranging from *x1* rightward to *x2*, and y coordinates ranging from *y1* down to *y2*, as shown in Figure 8-19b. These user-defined coordinate systems are referred to as *natural coordinate systems*. After either of these statements has been executed, the graphics statements PSET, PRESET, LINE, CIRCLE, GET, and PUT will use the new natural coordinates. After having specified natural coordinates with a WINDOW statement, you can return to physical coordinates by executing a WINDOW statement without the word SCREEN and without specifying coordinates. You will also return to physical coordinates if you change the SCREEN mode.

The WINDOW statement does not affect the size and location of text characters, the DRAW statement, or the scale of a LINE style or a PAINT tile. Also, the WINDOW statement sets the last point referenced to the center of the

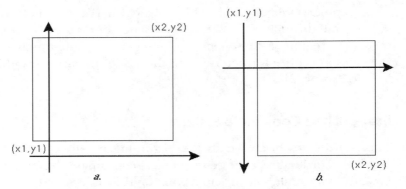

Figure 8-19.   The coordinate systems specified by the WINDOW statement

screen. The PMAP function (described in Appendix G) can be used to convert from physical coordinates to natural coordinates, and vice versa.

Program 8-21 specifies a standard x-y coordinate system in which the x coordinates range from -5 to 5, and the y coordinates range from -5 to 100. The outcome of this program appears in Figure 8-20.

Program 8-22 specifies a nonstandard x-y coordinate system in which the x coordinates range from -200 to 2,000 and the y coordinates range from -500 to 500. The outcome of this program appears in Figure 8-21.

Program 8-21. Illustrate the use of the WINDOW statement

```
REM Using the WINDOW Statement  [8-21]
SCREEN 2, 0
WINDOW (-5, -5)-(5, 100)
'Draw y axis and arrow
LINE (0, -5)-(0, 100)
LINE (0, 100)-(.3, 95)
LINE (0, 100)-(-.3, 95)
'Draw x axis and arrow
LINE (-5, 0)-(5, 0)
LINE (5, 0)-(4.7, 5)
LINE (5, 0)-(4.7, -5)
'Draw an example circle and rectangle
CIRCLE (1, 60), 2
LINE (-4, 8)-(1, 20), , B
END
```

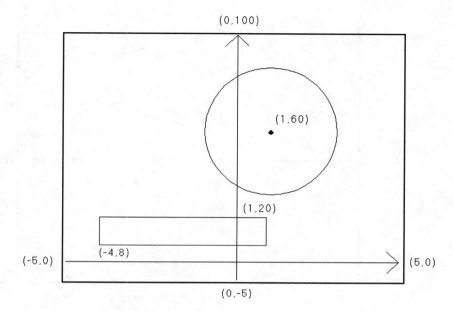

Figure 8-20. The result of Program 8-21

Each time you specify a natural coordinate system in a program, the coordinate system determines how points will be placed until another WINDOW statement is executed. By varying the coordinate system, you can enlarge,

Program 8-22. Illustrate the Use of WINDOW SCREEN

```
REM Using the WINDOW SCREEN statement   [8-22]
SCREEN 2, 0
WINDOW SCREEN (-200, -500)-(2000, 500)
'Draw y axis and arrow
LINE (0, -500)-(0, 450) 'Leave room for message at the bottom
LINE (0, 450)-(70, 400)
LINE (0, 450)-(-70, 400)
'Draw x axis and arrow
LINE (-200, 0)-(2000, 0)
LINE (2000, 0)-(1930, 50)
LINE (2000, 0)-(1930, -50)
'Draw an example circle and line
CIRCLE (1100, 100), 400
LINE (100, -100)-(900, -400)
END
```

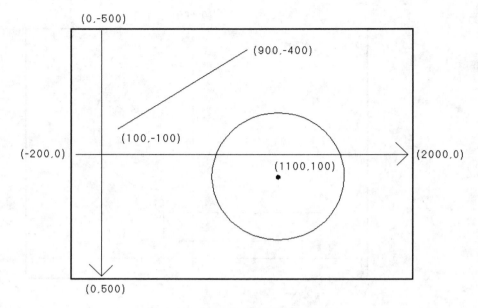

Figure 8-21.   The result of Program 8-22

shrink, and move figures to different parts of the screen. Program 8-23 produces Figure 8-22.

Viewports

QBasic provides the capability of setting aside a rectangular portion of the screen and specifying that all subsequent graphics appear only in this region. Such a rectangular region is called a viewport. Viewports make it easy to enlarge or contract rectangular portions of the screen and to place a scaled picture wherever we choose.

Consider the rectangular portion of the medium-resolution graphics screen having $(x1,y1)$ as its upper-left corner and $(x2,y2)$ as its lower-right corner. The statement

```
VIEW (x1, y1)-(x2, y2)
```

will cause all graphics drawn by PSET, PRESET, LINE, and CIRCLE to be displayed inside the specified rectangular region. That is, the rectangular region becomes a viewport and works like a second screen enclosed within the

Program 8-23. Illustrate the use of WINDOW to enlarge, shrink, and move figures

```
REM Draw a stick figure in different sizes and locations  [8-23]
SCREEN 1, 0
CALL DrawFigure
WINDOW SCREEN (0, 0)-(900, 600)
CALL DrawFigure
WINDOW SCREEN (-50, 50)-(190, 190)
CALL DrawFigure
END

SUB DrawFigure
   CIRCLE (160, 80), 20
   PAINT (160, 80), 2, 3
   LINE (160, 97)-(160, 150)
   LINE (160, 120)-(190, 110)
   LINE (160, 120)-(130, 110)
   LINE (160, 150)-(190, 180)
   LINE (160, 150)-(130, 180)
END SUB
```

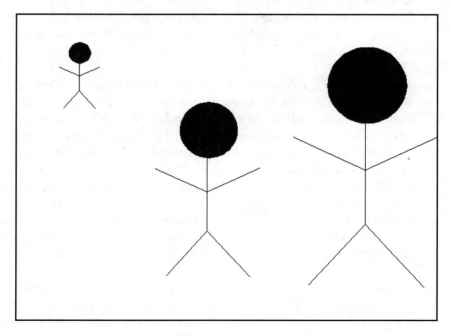

Figure 8-22. Output of Program 8-23

physical screen. Color can be added to the viewport and its boundary with the statement

```
VIEW (x1, y1)-(x2, y2), v, b
```

which causes the interior of the viewport to have the color in jar *v*, and the boundary to have the color in jar *b*. If either *v* or *b* is omitted, the viewport assumes the background color.

Program 8-24 shows the effects of several different VIEW statements. You should not be surprised to find that when the program pauses the first time, it appears as in Figure 8-23a. After pressing <Enter>, the first VIEW statement is executed. It defines a viewport with upper-left corner at (100, 75) and lower-right corner at (639, 199) of the physical screen. Since 1 was specified as the border parameter, the border is visible as shown in Figure 8-23b. After pressing <Enter> a second time, the second pair of LINE and CIRCLE statements is executed. Notice that they are identical to the first two LINE and CIRCLE statements but that their output appears as in Figure 8-23c. This occurs because the VIEW statement causes the point (100, 75) on the physical screen to be regarded as (0, 0) of the viewport. It's as if the monitor slid down 75 pixels and across 100 pixels. We say the bottom-right corner of the second image is "clipped" since it does not fit into the viewport. Notice that the VIEW statement and subsequent graphics statements did not affect images already on the screen.

A viewport, once defined, "respects" the natural coordinate system defined by WINDOW statements. Program 8-25 draws a line graph two times: once after setting suitable natural coordinates with a WINDOW statement, and then again in a small viewport (see Figure 8-24). Notice that the viewport boundaries were given in absolute pixel coordinates, but the graph was drawn as if the viewport was an entire screen. This occurs because the effects of the WINDOW statement remain active and are transferred to the new viewport. The graph appears "stretched" because the viewport coordinates set by VIEW do not have the same aspect ratio as the screen. If this graph had been drawn without a WINDOW statement, the viewport would have simply clipped out any portions of the line graph that did not fit within its boundaries.

When a VIEW statement is followed by another VIEW statement, only the second viewport will be active. That is, subsequent graphics statements address themselves to the second viewport. Program 8-26 uses the VIEW statement

Program 8-24. Illustrate the effects of the VIEW statement

```
REM Draw a circle and diagonal line in different viewports [8-24]
SCREEN 2
LINE (0, 0)-(639, 199)
CIRCLE (320, 100), 175
LOCATE 2, 40
INPUT "Press Enter to set viewport...", dummy$
VIEW (100, 75)-(639, 199), , 1
LOCATE 2, 40
INPUT "Press Enter to draw identical image...", dummy$
LOCATE 2, 40: PRINT SPACE$(39)    ' Print 39 spaces
LINE (0, 0)-(639, 199)
CIRCLE (320, 100), 175
END
```

with the WINDOW statement to vary the size of a star. The output is shown in Figure 8-25.

If the statement VIEW $(x1, y1)$-$(x2, y2)$, v, b is replaced by the statement

```
VIEW SCREEN (x1, y1)-(x2, y2), v, b
```

then no scaling or relocation occurs. Instead, when a figure is drawn, only the portion of the figure inside the viewport will be visible. Consider the cube drawn in Program 8-2. Program 8-27 draws a portion of the cube by executing a VIEW SCREEN statement before drawing. The output of the program is shown in Figure 8-26.

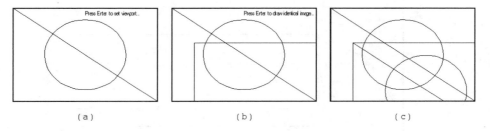

Figure 8-23. Output of Program 8-24

Program 8-25.   Illustrate the scaling effect of using WINDOW with VIEW

```
REM Draw a line chart and then the same line chart scaled by
VIEW [8-25]
SCREEN 2
WINDOW (-.5, -4)-(7.5, 16)
CALL LineChart          'Line graph drawn first time
VIEW (130, 117)-(550, 180), , 1
CALL LineChart          'Line graph drawn again in new viewport
DATA 0, 14, 7, 9, 6, 12
END

SUB LineChart
  CLS
  RESTORE
  LINE (0, 0)-(7, 0)     'x-axis
  LINE (0, 14)-(0, 0)    'y-axis
  READ a
  PSET (1, a)
  FOR m = 2 TO 6
    READ a
    LINE -(m, a)
  NEXT m
END SUB
```

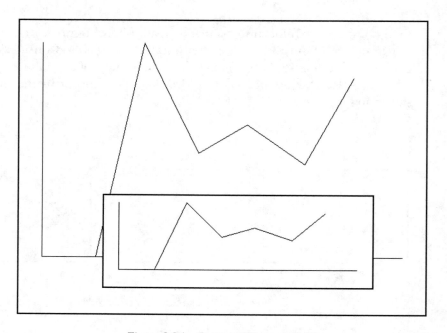

Figure 8-24.   Output of Program 8-25

Program 8-26. Illustrate the use of the VIEW statement

```
REM Draw four graphs of a star   [8-26]
SCREEN 1, 0
COLOR , 1
WINDOW (-8, -8)-(8, 8)
VIEW (1, 1)-(159, 99), , 3
CALL DrawStar(1)
VIEW (161, 101)-(240, 149), , 1
CALL DrawStar(2)
VIEW (242, 151)-(282, 176), , 2
CALL DrawStar(3)
VIEW (284, 178)-(304, 190), , 3
CALL DrawStar(1)
END

SUB DrawStar (starColor)
  PSET (0, 8)
  LINE -(5, -8), starColor
  LINE -(-7, 2), starColor
  LINE -(7, 2), starColor
  LINE -(-5, -8), starColor
  LINE -(0, 8), starColor
END SUB
```

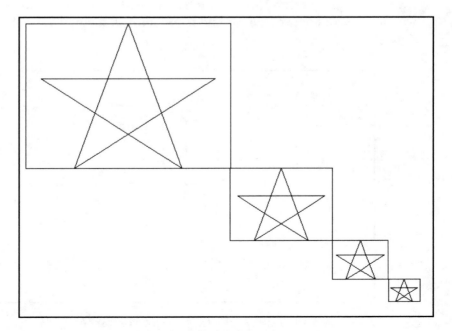

Figure 8-25. The result of Program 8-26

Program 8-27.   Illustrate the use of VIEW SCREEN

```
REM Clip a picture of a cube   [8-27]
SCREEN 1, 0
VIEW SCREEN (135, 35)-(195, 105), , 3
DRAW "L60 U60 R60 D60 E20 U60 G20 E20 L60 G20"
END
```

The VIEW statement does not affect the size and location of text characters, the DRAW statement, or the scale of a LINE style or a PAINT tile. If a CLS statement is executed while a VIEW statement is active, only the contents of the viewport will be cleared. This applies to text as well as to graphics. To clear the entire screen without altering active WINDOW and VIEW statements, execute PRINT CHR$(12). To clear the entire screen and also deactivate the viewport, use the statements VIEW: CLS.

Sound

QBasic can play musical compositions on your PC via the PLAY statement. You designate the notes and their lengths, the tempo of the composition, and whether or not the program should pause until all the notes are played.

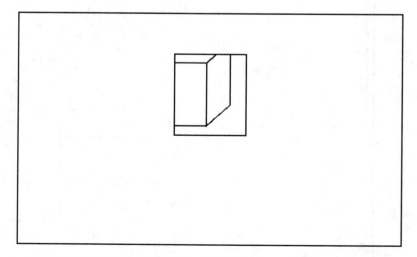

Figure 8-26.   The result of Program 8-27

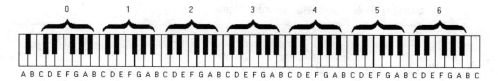

Figure 8-27. Piano keyboard

A piano keyboard consists of 88 keys. 84 of these keys can be played on the computer. In Figure 8-27, these 84 keys are grouped into seven octaves labeled 0 to 6.

Each note is identified by its octave (0 to 6) and letter (A to G). Sharps and flats are denoted by trailing the letter with "#" or "+" for a sharp and "-" for a flat. PLAY statements contain the word PLAY followed by a string containing information about the notes to be played. A typical statement is

```
PLAY "O3 C"
```

which results in middle C being played. The statement

```
PLAY "O2 DE O4 E+B-"
```

results in four notes being played in succession, the first two being from octave 2 and the second two from octave 4. In general, the letter O followed by one of the numbers 0 to 6 mandates that all subsequent notes will be from the designated octave, until another octave is specified. Even subsequent PLAY statements will be affected by the designated octave. If no octave is specified before the first note is PLAYed, the note will be taken from octave 4. The octave can be increased or decreased at any time by inserting the character ">" or "<," respectively, into the PLAY string.

Program 8-28 turns the computer into an electronic piano. While the program is running, you can play notes by pressing any of the keys <A> through <G> and holding them down for as long as you like. The octave can be changed by pressing ">" or "<" an appropriate number of times. To terminate the program press <Q>.

Program 8-29 plays a few notes. Since no octave is specified before the first PLAY statement, the first two notes (E and F sharp) will be from octave 4, the default octave. The remaining five notes (C, D flat, E, E, and F sharp) are all

Program 8-28.   An electronic piano

```
REM Convert the screen into an electronic piano   [8-28]
CLS
PRINT "I can play A B C D E F and G. Use < or > to ";
PRINT "change octaves. Press Q to quit."
a$ = ""
DO UNTIL a$ = "Q"
  SELECT CASE a$
    CASE "A", "B", "C", "D", "E", "F", "G", ">", "<", ""
        PLAY a$
    CASE ELSE
        LOCATE 3, 1: PRINT "I Can't play that!";
  END SELECT
  a$ = UCASE$(INPUT$(1))
  LOCATE 3, 1: PRINT SPACE$(18);        ' Print 18 spaces
LOOP
END
```

from octave 1. The octave designation O1 continues to affect future PLAY statements until another octave designation is made. The three PLAY statements could have been condensed into the single statement PLAY "EF+ O1 CD-EEF#". Program 8-30 plays the D minor scale.

The PLAY statement can choose one of two execution modes. In the Music Foreground (MF) mode, whenever a PLAY statement is encountered, the designated notes are played before the next statement of the program is executed. In the Music Background (MB) mode, the computer stores up to 32 notes (and pauses) in a buffer and plays them while continuing to execute the program. (The pauses between successive notes are counted as notes.) These modes are invoked with the statements PLAY "MF" and PLAY "MB". The default mode is Music Foreground.

Program 8-29.   Specifying pitch

```
REM Play 7 notes   [8-29]
PLAY "EF+"
PLAY "O1 CD-E"
PLAY "EF#"
END
```

Program 8-30. PLAY the scale of D minor

```
REM Scale of D Minor  [8-30]
PLAY "D E F G A B- O5 C D"
END
```

When Program 8-31 is run, the words appear as soon as the tune begins playing. If the MB in the third line is replaced by MF, the words will not appear until the tune finishes playing.

The standard musical notes are whole notes (1/1), half notes (1/2), quarter notes (1/4), eighth notes (1/8), 16th notes (1/16), 32nd notes (1/32), and 64th notes (1/64). The computer not only can produce all of these lengths but can produce $1/n$th notes for any n from 1 to 64.

When one of the letters A to G in a PLAY statement is trailed by the number n, that note will have the length of a $1/n$th note. For instance, the statement

```
PLAY "C2 C1 C25"
```

results in the note of C (above middle C) being played three times, first as a half note, then as a whole note, and finally as a 25th note.

Lengths of notes also can be specified by the letter L followed by a number from 1 to 64, which mandates that (until another length is specified) all subsequent notes that don't carry their own trailing length designation will have that length. Even subsequent PLAY statements will be affected by the specified length. If no length is specified before the first note is PLAYed, notes

Program 8-31. Demonstration of Music Background mode

```
REM Play beginning of Happy Birthday  [8-31]
CLS
PLAY "MB"
PLAY "CCDCFE"
PRINT "Happy Birthday to You"
END
```

Statement	Equivalent form Using a Variable
PLAY "C4"	a = 4: PLAY "C" + STR$(a)
PLAY "L2 D"	length = 2: PLAY "L" + STR$(length) + "D"

Table 8-10. Using variables to specify lengths

will be played as quarter notes until otherwise specified. For instance, the statement

```
PLAY "CC8 L16 CCC L1 CCC2"
```

results in the note of C being played eight times, first as a quarter note, then as an eighth note, three times as a sixteenth note, twice as a whole note, and finally as a half note.

To insert the value of a numeric variable into a PLAY statement, you need to convert the variable's value to a string with STR$ and put the resulting string in the proper position using +. Table 8-10 shows several PLAY statements and equivalent forms that use variables. You can use variables with other PLAY command parameters in an analogous way. Program 8-32 uses the variable from a FOR/NEXT loop to play middle C in 64 different lengths.

Following the letter P with a number n from 1 to 64 produces a pause (or rest) of duration $1/n$. For instance, the statement

```
PLAY "C P2 C P16 C"
```

plays the note C three times, separated by half and 16th note pauses.

In standard musical notation, a small dot after a note or rest means it should last one and a half times its normal length. Following a note or pause in a PLAY statement with a period produces the same effect. For instance, the statement

```
PLAY "C C. C8. C.. L15 P4. C2. C."
```

plays C six times with lengths 1/4, 3/8, 3/16, 9/16, 3/4, and 1/10. There is a pause of length 3/8 between the fourth and fifth notes.

Program 8-32. Demonstrate the different lengths of notes

```
REM Vary the lengths of notes [8-32]
CLS
LOCATE 12, 1
PRINT "This is a whole note."
PLAY "MF O3 C1"
FOR n = 2 TO 64
  LOCATE 12, 10
  PRINT " 1 /"; n; "note."
  PLAY "L" + STR$(n) + "C"
NEXT n
END
```

In standard musical notation, a small dot over or under a note means that the note should be short and sharp, with a pause between each note and the next one. This is called *staccato*. A curved line over or under several notes means that they should be played smoothly with no pause between each note and the next. This is called *legato*. You can induce staccato and legato within PLAY statements by using the pairs of letters MS and ML, respectively. The pair MN refers to normal music. The pair of letters MS within a PLAY statement ensures that the computer plays all subsequent notes staccato until QBasic encounters one of the pair of letters MN or ML. Similar considerations apply to ML.

Program 8-33 plays the first part of "Happy Birthday" in staccato mode, then in normal mode, and finally in legato mode. Notice that, in the legato mode, the first two C notes blend into a single long note. Program 8-34 plays the beginning of the song "Frère Jacques" by using the length of notes that the user designates.

The speed or tempo of a composition is usually given in Italian words. Some common tempos are shown in Table 8-11. In the PLAY statement, you can specify the tempo of a composition by following the letter T with a number n from 32 to 255, which ensures that QBasic will play all subsequent notes at the speed of n quarter notes per minute until you specify another tempo. If you do not specify a tempo before the computer PLAYs the first note, the tempo will be 120 quarter notes per minute until you specify otherwise. For instance, the statement

```
PLAY "C T60 C"
```

Program 8-33. Staccato, normal, and legato modes

```
REM Happy Birthday in three styles   [8-33]
b$ = "CCDCFE"
PLAY "MS" + b$
PLAY "MN" + b$
PLAY "ML" + b$
END
```

plays C twice — first for 1/2 second and then for 1 second. Program 8-35 plays the scale of C major at each of the tempos in Table 8-11.

In this discussion, each of the 84 notes available to the PLAY statement has been identified by a combination of octave (0 to 6) and letter (A to G with possible + or -). These notes can also be identified by the letter N followed by one of the numbers from 1 to 84, as shown in Table 8-12.

You use the combination N0 to identify a pause (this combination is useful because, unlike the combination Pn, N0 uses the default note length). For example, the statement

```
PLAY "N37 N0 N38"
```

plays middle C, a pause, and then C sharp. Program 8-36 uses numbers to identify notes.

QBasic has another statement for producing tones. The statement

```
SOUND f, d
```

Program 8-34. Demonstrate the use of STR$ in PLAY statements

```
REM Play the beginning of Fre're Jacques   [8-34]
CLS
INPUT "Length of notes (1-64)"; n
f$ = "CDEC"
PLAY "L" + STR$(n) + f$ + f$ + "EFG P" + STR$(n) + "EFG"
END
```

Tempo	Translation	Approximate number of quarter notes per minute
Largo	Very slow	50
Adagio	Slow	70
Andante	Slow and flowing	90
Moderato	Medium	110
Allegro	Fast	130
Vivace	Lively	150
Presto	Very fast	170

Table 8-11. Music tempos

produces a sound of pitch *f* hertz with a duration of *d* ×.055 seconds. Although the frequency can range from 37 to 32767 hertz, the human ear can only hear up to about 20,000 hertz. Program 8-37 uses the SOUND statement to create special effects, such as falling bombs, sirens, and clock ticks.

In this chapter, we've looked at the wealth of graphics-drawing and sound-generating capabilities that QBasic has to offer. In the last two chapters of this book, we'll examine the scientific and financial calculation tools available, and consider examples of their use.

Program 8-35. Demonstrate different tempos

```
REM Scale of C   [8-35]
CLS
PLAY "MF"
FOR n = 50 TO 170 STEP 20
  PRINT n; "quarter notes per minute"
  PLAY "T" + STR$(n) + "O3 CDEFGAB O4 C"
NEXT n
END
```

Octave 0		Octave 1		Octave 2		Octave 3		Octave 4		Octave 5		Octave 6	
Note	Number	Note	Number	Note	Number	Note	Number	Note	Number	Note	Number	Note	Number
C	1	C	13	C	25	C	37	C	49	C	61	C	73
C+	2	C+	14	C+	26	C+	38	C+	50	C+	62	C+	74
D	3	D	15	D	27	D	39	D	51	D	63	D	75
D+	4	D+	16	D+	28	D+	40	D+	52	D+	64	D+	76
E	5	E	17	E	29	E	41	E	53	E	65	E	77
F	6	F	18	F	30	F	42	F	54	F	66	F	78
F+	7	F+	19	F+	31	F+	43	F+	55	F+	67	F+	79
G	8	G	20	G	32	G	44	G	56	G	68	G	80
G+	9	G+	21	G+	33	G+	45	G+	57	G+	69	G+	81
A	10	A	22	A	34	A	46	A	58	A	70	A	82
A+	11	A+	23	A+	35	A+	47	A+	59	A+	71	A+	83
B	12	B	24	B	36	B	48	B	60	B	72	B	84

Table 8-12.   The number associated with each note

Program 8-36.   PLAY a tune by numbers

```
REM Jingle Bells  [8-36]
CLS
PRINT "Jingle bells, Jingle bells"
PLAY "MF L8 N41 N41 L4 N41 L8 N41 N41 L4 N41"
PRINT "Jingle all the way"
PLAY "L8 N41 N44 N37. L16 N39 L4 N41 N0"
PRINT "Oh what fun it is to ride in a"
PLAY "L8 N42 N42 N42. L16 N42 L8 N42 N41 N41 L16 N41 N41"
PRINT "One horse open"
PLAY "L4 N44 N44 N42 N39"
PRINT "Sleigh"
PLAY "L1 N37"
END
```

Program 8-37. Special effects using the SOUND statement

```
REM Falling bomb, clock, and siren  [8-37]
t0 = TIMER
FOR i = 1 TO 500: NEXT i
loopsPerSec = 500 / (TIMER - t0)
'loopsPerSec = # of passes through loop to delay about 1 second
CLS
'Bomb
PRINT "Falling Bomb"
FOR n = 1000 TO 700 STEP -5
  SOUND n, 1
NEXT n
SOUND 37, 3
SLEEP 1
'Clock
PRINT "Clock"
FOR n = 1 TO 5
  SOUND 500, .1
  FOR i = 1 TO loopsPerSec * .4: NEXT i
  SOUND 2000, .1
  FOR i = 1 TO loopsPerSec * .4: NEXT i
NEXT n
SLEEP 1
'Siren
PRINT "Siren"
FOR n = 1 TO 5
  SOUND 1700, 5
  SOUND 1000, 5
NEXT n
END
```

Mathematical and Scientific Programming

We now move from the lighter subjects of graphics and sound into the realm of computing might. You might not expect it, but QBasic has some powerful tools for scientists and engineers. Used singly or in combination, these tools can be harnessed to solve sophisticated problems.

Because scientific computing is limited almost exclusively to numerical calculations (although graphics is gaining considerable prominence, as a subscription to *Scientific American* will quickly reveal), the functions we introduce in this chapter are designed to work with and upon numerical data, although not without graphical applications, as you'll see. We'll show you functions beyond those revealed earlier in the book, and discuss their applications.

Built-in Mathematical Functions

Chapter 4 discussed the built-in arithmetic functions ABS, FIX, INT, and SGN. This chapter explores the predefined square-root function (SQR), trigonometric functions (ATN, COS, SIN, and TAN), the exponential function (EXP), and the logarithmic function (LOG). This chapter gives the definition of each of these new functions.

The Square Root Function

For any nonnegative number x, the value of

```
SQR(x)
```

is the nonnegative number whose square is x. For example, SQR(25) is 5 and SQR(1) is 1. The SQR of most numbers are not integers, so you must be careful about the type of variable you store such a result in.

Quadratic Formula   The roots (i.e., answers) of the quadratic equation

$$ax^2 + bx + c = 0$$

are

```
(-b + SQR(b^2 - 4*a*c)) / 2*a
```

and

```
(-b - SQR(b^2 - 4*a*c)) / 2*a
```

provided that $b^2 - 4ac >= 0$.

Hypotenuse of a Right Triangle   The length of the hypotenuse (longest side) of a right triangle (one angle = 90, hypotenuse is opposite this angle) that has sides of lengths a and b is

```
SQR(a^2 + b^2)
```

Trigonometric Functions

A circle of radius 1 is called a unit circle. The circumference of a unit circle is 2*pi, (usually written 2π) where pi (to a pretty darned good approximation) is 3.141592653589793. Figure 9-1 shows a unit circle with an angle having one leg along the positive part of the x-axis.

You can measure angles either in degrees or in radians. When you measure in radians, the size of the angle is the length of the arc of the unit circle that the angle subtends (or sweeps out). For example, since a right angle subtends one-quarter of the unit circle, a right angle consists of $(2*\pi)/4$ or $\pi/2$ radians. Another way to obtain the radian measure of an angle is to multiply the

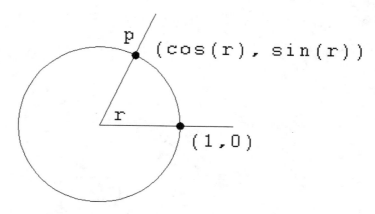

Figure 9-1. An angle drawn in a unit circle

number of degrees of the angle by $\pi/180$. For example, since a right angle has 90 degrees, its radian measure is $90*(\pi/180)$ or $\pi/2$.

Each of the trigonometric functions assigns a number to an angle. Consider an angle of r radians that is placed in the unit circle as in Figure 9-1 and that intersects the circle at the point P. The value of COS(r) is the first coordinate of the point P and the value of SIN(r) is the second coordinate of P. The value of TAN(r) is SIN(r)/COS(r). These three functions are called the sine, cosine, and tangent functions. If x is any number, then the value of ATN(x) is an angle (in radians) whose tangent is x. (If you need to, you can make a good approximation of the number π by using $4*$ATN(1).)

Surveying   The height of the tree shown in Figure 9-2 is $d*$TAN(r).

Periodic Phenomena   The trigonometric functions can help to model certain cyclical natural occurrences. For example, the temperature of the tap water in Dallas, Texas on the nth day of the year is approximately 59 + $14*$COS((n-208)$*\pi/183$). Program 9-1 uses this formula.

Projectile Motion   If a golf ball is hit at an angle of r radians with the ground at a speed of s feet per second, then the distance traveled by the ball is s^2*COS(r)$*$SIN(r)/16. (Note that this formula assumes minimum wind resistance.) Program 9-2 employs a respectable speed of 170 feet per second in this formula to give the driving range for a pro golfer.

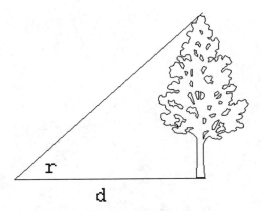

Figure 9-2. Finding the height of a tree

Exponential Functions

Any function of the form

$$b^x$$

is called an exponential function. The number *b* is called the base and the number *x* is called the exponent. If the base has value e, where e is approximately 2.718281828459045 (the same number of significant digits that double-precision variables can handle), then you can use the QBasic function EXP(*x*) instead of explicitly computing 2.718281828459045# ^ *x*. (The num-

Program 9-1. An example using the cosine and arctangent functions

```
REM Predict tap water temperature in Dallas  [9-1]
CLS
INPUT "Day of the year (1-365)"; day%
pi = 4 * ATN(1)
t = 59 + 14 * COS((day% - 208) * pi / 183)
PRINT USING "The tap water temperature will be ## degrees"; t
END

[run]
Day of the year (1-365)? 180
The tap water temperature will be 71 degrees
```

Program 9-2. Using trigonometric functions with angles given in degrees

```
REM Give horizontal distance traveled by a golf ball   [9-2]
REM starting off with a speed of 170 feet per second
CLS
PRINT "At what angle (in degrees) with respect to the ground"
INPUT "was the golf ball hit (0-90)"; degrees
pi = 4 * ATN(1)
radians = degrees * pi / 180
PRINT "A ball starting off at a speed of 170 feet per second"
PRINT "at an angle of";degrees;"degrees will travel a distance"
PRINT USING "of ### feet";170^2*COS(radians)*SIN(radians)/16
END


[run]
At what angle (in degrees) with respect to the ground
was the golf ball hit (0-90)? 45
A ball starting off at a speed of 170 feet per second
at an angle of 45 degrees will travel a distance
of 903 feet
```

ber e is similar to the number pi. You cannot write its exact value, but you can approximate it to any degree of accuracy.) For example, the statement

```
PRINT EXP(3)
```

calculates e^3 and produces the output 20.08554.

Normal Curve   The so-called *normal curve* of statistics is used to estimate the likelihood of a measurement appearing in a certain range. For a population with mean m (sometimes called "average") and standard deviation s (a measure of how far away from average the different values tend to get), the normal curve is the graph of the function (1/(s*SQR(2*pi)))*EXP(-.5*((x-m)/s)^2).

For normally distributed measurements, the percentage of the measurements that lie between the values a and b is the area under the normal curve from $x=a$ to $x=b$. Given the mean and standard deviation of a population, Program 9-3 does a numeric integration (area-finding) of the area under the normal curve to estimate the probability of an event occurring within a given range of values.

Program 9-3.   Application of EXP to probability

```
REM Find the area of a region under a normal curve   [9-3]
CLS
INPUT "Mean and standard deviation of data"; mean, sd
INPUT "Range of data over which to compute probability"; xLow, xHigh
pi = 4 * ATN(1)
sum = 0
FOR i = xLow TO xHigh STEP sd / 100
  sum = sum + NormalCurve(i)
NEXT i
PRINT "Probability of an event occurring in the given range is"
PRINT USING "approximately ###.## percent"; sum * sd;
PRINT USING " or 1 in #####"; 100 / (sum * sd)
END

FUNCTION NormalCurve (x)
  SHARED mean, sd, pi
  NormalCurve = (1 / (sd*SQR(2*pi))) * EXP(-.5*((x-mean)/sd)^2)
END FUNCTION

[run]
Mean and standard deviation of data? 80, 10
Range of data over which to compute probability? 95, 100
Probability of an event occurring in the given range is
approximately   4.50 percent or 1 in    22
```

(We can give a real-world interpretation to the above result. Let's say the numbers represent a test given to a programming class. The average, or mean test score was 80 out of 100. About two-thirds of the students who took the test had scores within 10 points of the mean (average). (Roughly speaking, that describes a standard deviation: how far out from the mean you have to go to get about 2/3 of the population.) How many students made A+'s — that is, scored 95 or above? The answer is, one out of 22 students. This was a tough test!)

Continuous Interest   Most banks pay interest that is compounded either quarterly, monthly, or daily. However, many banks compound their interest continuously. If you deposit P dollars in a bank that pays interest rate r compounded continuously, then the balance in the account after t years is $P*EXP(r*t)$. For example, if you deposit 1,000 dollars at 5% interest compounded continuously, then the balance after t years is $1000*EXP(.05*t)$.

Program 9-4. Application of EXP to continuous interest

```
REM Calculate the balance in a savings account   [9-4]
CLS
INPUT "Amount originally deposited"; amount
INPUT "Annual rate of continuously compounded interest"; intr
INPUT "Number of years that have elapsed"; years
'Compensate for interest that was given as a percent
IF intr > 1 THEN intr = intr / 100
balance = amount * EXP(intr * years)
PRINT USING "The current balance is $$##,###.##"; balance
END

[run]
Amount originally deposited? 2000
Annual rate of continuously compounded interest? 8
Number of years that have elapsed? 20
The current balance is    $9,906.06
```

Program 9-4 further illustrates the use of EXP in continuous interest problems.

Quality Control Suppose that you have a large quantity of light bulbs and that the average lifetime of a light bulb is a hours. Then the percentage of light bulbs still remaining after t hours is approximately $EXP(-t/a)$. Program 9-5 shows how many light bulbs out of 100 you can expect to shine after various multiples of the average lifetime.

The result is surprising, isn't it? After the average lifetime, you might expect half the light bulbs to be still shining, not just 37% of them. This confirms the observation that nothing lasts as long as it's supposed to.

Logarithmic Functions

There is a logarithmic function corresponding to each exponential function. For any base b,

$$\log_b (x)$$

Program 9-5. Application of EXP to quality control

```
REM How many bulbs will remain?  [9-5]
DEF FNLeft (t, avgL) = 100 * EXP(-t / avgL)
CLS
INPUT "Average lifetime (in hours) of a light bulb"; avgLife
PRINT "Starting with 100 light bulbs, you can expect to have"
FOR i = avgLife / 2 TO 3 * avgLife STEP avgLife / 2
   PRINT USING "## left after ##### hours"; FNLeft(i, avgLife), i
NEXT i
END

[run]
Average lifetime (in hours) of a light bulb? 5000
Starting with 100 light bulbs, you can expect to have
61 left after  2500 hours
37 left after  5000 hours
22 left after  7500 hours
14 left after 10000 hours
 8 left after 12500 hours
 5 left after 15000 hours
```

is the power to which *b* must be raised to get *x*. QBasic has defined the logarithmic function LOG for the base e, also called the *natural logarithm*. For example, LOG(2) is .69314718, LOG(e) is 1, and LOG(1) is 0.

The logarithm to the base *b* can be obtained from LOG by using the formula

$$\mathrm{Log}_b(x) = \mathrm{LOG}(x) \ / \ \mathrm{LOG}(b)$$

In particular,

$$\begin{aligned}
\mathrm{Log}_{10}(x) &= \mathrm{LOG}(x) \ / \ \mathrm{LOG}(10) \\
&= \mathrm{LOG}(x) \ / \ 2.302585 \\
&= .4342945 * \mathrm{LOG}(x)
\end{aligned}$$

In double-precision, $\mathrm{Log}_{10}(x) = .4342944819032518*\mathrm{LOG}(x)$

Continuous Interest   An investment at the interest rate *r* compounded continuously will increase *n*-fold in LOG(*n*)/*r* years. For instance, an investment that earns 8 percent interest compounded continuously will triple in LOG(3)/.08, or 13.7326536084, years.

Techniques for Graphing Functions

No program is guaranteed to produce a good graph for every conceivable function. No matter how carefully a program is written, a clever mathematician can devise a function that the program cannot do justice to. The main program presented in this section incorporates safeguards against several of the idiosyncrasies that you commonly encounter when graphing functions, and will produce an adequate graph for many types of functions.

Program 9-6 is a no-frills function graphing program. You specify the *domain* (the interval on the x-axis over which the program will graph the function) and the *range* (the smallest and largest y coordinates of points that will appear on the screen). The program gives the appropriate WINDOW statement, draws the coordinate axes, and then draws 640 points on the graph.

Program 9-6 has the following shortcomings:

1. The program must be changed each time a new function is considered. Ideally, you would like the user to specify the function interactively during the execution of the program.

2. The x-axis, y-axis, or both may not appear on screen. For example, this will occur if either *xLow* or *yLow* is a positive number.

3. You might not be able to provide good values for *yLow* and *yHigh*. In the most extreme case, making a poor choice can result in a completely blank screen.

4. There might be certain points in the domain at which the function is undefined (such as $x=0$ for the function $1/x$) or has a value that is too large and causes an overflow (such as $x=2,000$ for the function $EXP(x)$). Either of these situations will terminate the program and may lock up the system.

5. If the graph increases rapidly, two successive points might be far apart on the screen with a substantial gap between them.

Program 9-7 is a sophisticated function graphing program that corrects the five shortcomings of Program 9-6 in the following ways.

1. Program 9-7, which must be named GRAPH.BAS on disk, actually writes another program, called EVALUATE.BAS, which is used to calculate all the values of the function. After the user enters the function, GRAPH writes the second program EVALUATE that will evaluate the function at

Program 9-6. A rudimentary graphing program

```
REM Sketch the graph of a function  [9-6]
DEF FNF (x) = 1 / x
'Request the domain of the function
CLS
INPUT "Graphing should begin with x = ", startGraph
INPUT "Graphing should  end  with x = ", endGraph
'Request the range of function values to appear on the screen
INPUT "What is the lower bound"; yMin
INPUT "What is the upper bound"; yMax
'Initialize the screen
SCREEN 2
VIEW (0, 0)-(639, 180) 'Leave room for 'Press any key' at bottom
WINDOW (startGraph, yMin)-(endGraph, yMax)
LINE (startGraph, 0)-(endGraph, 0)    'Draw x-axis
LINE (0, yMin)-(0, yMax)              'Draw y-axis
'Draw the graph
increment = (endGraph - startGraph) / 639
FOR x = startGraph TO endGraph STEP increment
  y = FNF (x)
  PSET (x, y)
NEXT x
END
```

the range of values input by the user. The first program, GRAPH, fills an array with the values at which the function is to be evaluated, and then executes EVALUATE, passing the array of x values. EVALUATE in turn fills a second array with all the function values. The last statement executed by EVALUATE is to reexecute GRAPH.BAS and to pass the filled array of function values. Notice in GRAPH how *flag%* is used to execute the statements associated with the IF condition only once. When EVALUATE executes GRAPH, *flag%* tells GRAPH that it is being called by EVALUATE, that is, the arrays are filled and ready to be plotted. The CHAIN statement allows one program to invoke another, and the two program's matching COMMON statements allows them to share the arrays and the flag variable.

2. To guarantee that the y-axis appears on screen, the WINDOW statement in Program 9-7 uses the x values entered by the user to set the horizontal limits only when they are negative and positive, respectively. In any other case, one of the limits is replaced by a number that guaran-

Program 9-7. A generic curve sketching program

```
REM Draw the graph of a function input by the user [9-7]
REM Be sure to name this program GRAPH.BAS
COMMON flag%, x(), y()          'Variables shared between programs
CONST Mode = 2                  'Screen mode
CONST MaxX = 639                'Right-most pixel for screen mode
CONST MaxY = 199                'Bottom-most pixel for screen mode
CONST Overflow = 3.402822E+38   'Overflow flag
CONST True = -1
CONST False = 0
IF flag% = 0 THEN
    CLS
    DIM x(0 TO MaxX)
    DIM y(0 TO MaxX)
    INPUT "Input function: y = ", function$
    INPUT "Graphing should begin with x = ", x(0)
    INPUT "Graphing should end with   x = ", x(MaxX)
    increment = (x(MaxX) - x(0)) / (MaxX + 1)
    FOR i% = 1 TO MaxX - 1          'Fill the array of x values
       x(i%) = x(i% - 1) + increment
    NEXT i%
    OPEN "EVALUATE.BAS" FOR OUTPUT AS #1  'Write a program to
    PRINT #1, "COMMON flag%, x(), y()"    '  fill the array of
    PRINT #1, "ON ERROR GOTO Errhandler"  '  y values
    PRINT #1, "FOR i% = 0 TO " + STR$(MaxX)
    PRINT #1, "   x = x(i%)"
    PRINT #1, "   y(i%) = " + function$
    PRINT #1, "NEXT i%"
    PRINT #1, "Errhandler:"
    PRINT #1, "IF ERR THEN"
    PRINT #1, "     y(i%) = " + STR$(Overflow)
    PRINT #1, "     RESUME NEXT"
    PRINT #1, "END IF"
    PRINT #1, "CHAIN " + CHR$(34) + "GRAPH" + CHR$(34)
    CLOSE #1
    flag% = -1
    PRINT : PRINT "Evaluating function. Please wait..."
    CHAIN "EVALUATE"             'CHAIN to the new program
  ELSE
    ON ERROR GOTO SkipPoint 'If LINE or PSET can't plot a point
    CALL SetAxes(x(), y(), yLow, yHigh)
    i% = 0
    pointOk% = False
    DO WHILE i% <= MaxX
      DO WHILE NOT pointOk% AND i% <= MaxX
```

(continued)

Program 9-7. *(continued)*

```
               IF y(i%) <> Overflow AND y(i%) >= yLow AND y(i%) <= yHigh THEN
                  PSET (x(i%), y(i%))
                  pointOk% = True
               END IF
               i% = i% + 1
           LOOP
           DO WHILE pointOk% AND i% <= MaxX
             IF y(i%) <> Overflow AND y(i%) >= yLow AND y(i%) <= yHigh THEN
                  LINE -(x(i%), y(i%))
               ELSE
                  pointOk% = False
             END IF
             i% = i% + 1
         LOOP
       LOOP
END IF
END
SkipPoint:
pointOk% = False
RESUME NEXT

SUB ScaleExtrema (lo, hi)
  REM Forces low and high values to positive and negative
  IF lo >= 0 THEN lo = -hi / 20
  IF hi <= 0 THEN hi = -lo / 20
END SUB

SUB SetAxes (x(), y(), yLow, yHigh)
  REM Sets window scale and draws axes
  xLow = x(0)
  xHigh = x(MaxX)
  CALL ScaleExtrema(xLow, xHigh)
  PRINT : PRINT "Do you wish to give lower and upper bounds ";
  PRINT "for the graph (Y/N)"
  PRINT "  (If not, the minimum and maximum value of the function"
  PRINT "   on the given interval will be computed and used.)"
  answer$ = UCASE$(INPUT$(1))
  IF answer$ = "Y" THEN
      INPUT "What is the lower bound"; yLow
      INPUT "What is the upper bound"; yHigh
    ELSE
      yLow = y(0)
      yHigh = y(0)
      FOR i% = 1 TO MaxX
```

Program 9-7. *(continued)*

```
          SELECT CASE y(i%)
            CASE Overflow
            CASE IS < yLow: yLow = y(i%)
            CASE IS > yHigh: yHigh = y(i%)
            CASE ELSE
          END SELECT
        NEXT i%
        CALL ScaleExtrema(yLow, yHigh)
      END IF
      SCREEN Mode
      VIEW (0, 0)-(MaxX, MaxY * .9)
      WINDOW (xLow, yLow)-(xHigh, yHigh)
      LINE (xLow, 0)-(xHigh, 0)       'Draw x-axis
      LINE (0, yLow)-(0, yHigh)       'Draw y-axis
    END SUB

    [run]
    Input function: y = (x/300)*(x^2-45)*(x^2-10)
    Graphing should begin with x = -7
    Graphing should end with   x = 7

    Evaluating function. Please wait...

    Do you wish to give lower and upper bounds for the graph (Y/N)?
      (If not, the minimum and maximum value of the function
    on the given interval will be computed and used.)

    [User pressed N]
    (graph is shown in Figure 9-3)
```

tees the horizontal limits will have different signs. For instance, if the lower bound on the x values is positive, then the lower bound is replaced with a number that allows at least 5% of the visible x-axis to have negative values (thus ensuring the y-axis will appear on the screen). A similar calculation and replacement is done for the y values if they are not directly entered by the user.

3. The program gives the user the option of either supplying values for the lower and upper bounds of the function or letting the program do it automatically. The program sets the bounds by examining all the function values, taking the lowest and highest values, and then using them to set the natural coordinates for the graph.

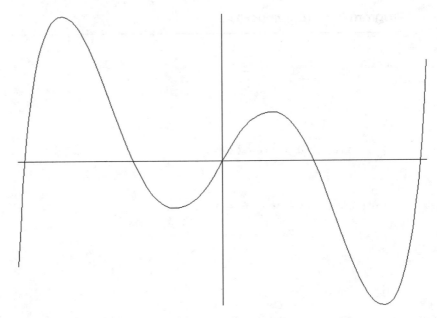

Figure 9-3. A graph of f(x) = (x/300)(x^2-45)(x^2-10) as produced by Program 9-7

4. **EVALUATE** and **GRAPH** both use an error-trapping routine to handle undefined values. The statement **ON ERROR GOTO ErrHandler** causes any error to transfer control to the error-handling routine that follows the label ErrHandler. When the function cannot be computed for a certain value of *x*, or when **LINE** and **PSET** are passed a very large number, an error occurs. If the function cannot be computed, the constant value Overflow is assigned to the offending array element. Then the FOR loop continues computing the function at the remaining x values. Later, when GRAPH is plotting the function, it skips any array values marked by the Overflow constant.

5. To avoid gaps, Program 9-7 does not simply plot points; it draws lines between successive points on the graphs with the statement **LINE -(x,y)**. This statement draws a line from the last point referenced to the point (*x, y*). However, there are certain exceptions to this action. The first point plotted must be displayed with PSET since the last point referenced is not a function value. Thereafter, LINE is used to connect valid points. If the program finds that the y coordinate of a point cannot be plotted in the current window, then the program skips this point and uses PSET on the next displayable point. Then LINE is used again until another invalid point is discovered.

Random Numbers

Consider a specific collection of numbers. We say that a process selects a number at random from this collection if any number in the collection is just as likely to be selected as any other and if the number cannot be predicted in advance. Some examples are shown in Table 9-1.

The function RND, which acts like the spinner in Figure 9-4, gives QBasic the capability of selecting a number at random from any collection of numbers. The value of the function is a number from 0 up to, but not including, 1. Each time that RND appears in the program, it will be assigned a different number, and any number greater than or equal to 0 and less than 1 is just as likely to be generated as any other.

At this time, there is "good news" and "bad news." The good news is that thinking of the value produced by RND as resulting from the flip of a spinner is exactly what is needed to design applications of RND. The bad news is that successive repetitions of RND always generate the same sequence of numbers. (This feature of RND is intentional and is important in debugging programs that do simulations.) However, QBasic has another function, RANDOMIZE TIMER, that uses the computer's built-in clock to change the sequence of numbers that RND generates. The sequence of numbers generated by RND is not truly random since, in practice, each number actually determines the next number. However, the sequence has the appearance of a randomly generated sequence.

Okay, stay with us now. For any subinterval of the interval [0,1], (e.g., 1/4 to 1/2) the likelihood of generating a number in that subinterval is the same as for any other subinterval of the same length (e.g., 1/2 to 3/4). The sequence of numbers that RND generates is said to be pseudo-random.

Collection	*Process*
1, 2, 3, 4, 5, 6	Toss a balanced die
0 or 1	Toss a coin: 0 = tails, 1= heads
-1, 0, 1, ..., 36	Spin a roulette wheel (interpret 00 as -1)
1, 2, ..., N	Write numbers on slips of paper, and pull one from hat
Numbers from 0 to 1	Flip the spinner in Figure 9-4

Table 9-1. Methods of selecting numbers at random from various collections of numbers

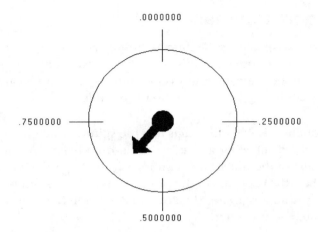

.0000000

.7500000

.2500000

.5000000

Figure 9-4.   A spinner to select a number between 0 and 1 randomly

Program 9-8 uses the RND function to select a number at random from each of the collections of numbers in Table 9-1. Since the value of RND lies between 0 and 1 (exclusive of 1), 6*RND lies between 0 and 6 (exclusive of 6). Therefore, INT(6*RND) is 0, 1, 2, 3, 4, or 5, while INT(6*RND) + 1 is 1, 2, 3, 4, 5, or 6. The program simulates a coin toss by finding an event that is likely to occur half of the time. Half of the time, the value of RND will lie in the left half of the interval from 0 to 1. The spin of the roulette wheel was handled analogously to the toss of the die. In general, the value of INT(n*RND) will be one of the numbers 0, 1, 2, and so on to n-1, and the value of INT(n*RND) + m will be one of the numbers m, m+1, and so on to m+n-1. Therefore, you can use this technique to select an integer from any consecutive set of integers.

Program 9-9 uses the RND function to shuffle a deck of cards and deal five cards from the top of the deck. The program places the 52 cards initially into a "fresh deck" array with all of the hearts first, followed by the diamonds, clubs, and spades. Therefore, cards 1 to 13 will be hearts, cards 14 to 26 will be diamonds, cards 27 to 39 will be clubs, and cards 40 to 52 will be spades. Each suit is in the order of ace, 2, 3, and so on to king. The program identifies each card by using a string that consists of the denomination and the suit. The symbols for heart, diamond, club, and spade have ASCII values 3, 4, 5, and 6, respectively, and can be generated as CHR$(3), CHR$(4), CHR$(5), and CHR$(6). The program shuffles the cards by successively interchanging the card at each position in the deck with a randomly selected card.

Program 9-8. Illustration of RND

```
REM Select a number at random   [9-8]
RANDOMIZE TIMER
d% = INT(6 * RND) + 1
PRINT "The number showing on the die is"; d%
IF RND < .5 THEN result$ = "heads" ELSE result$ = "tails"
PRINT "The coin landed "; result$
r% = INT(38 * RND) - 1
PRINT "The roulette wheel shows the number";
IF r% = -1 THEN PRINT " 00" ELSE PRINT r%
PRINT "The spinner landed on the number";
PRINT USING " .###"; RND
END


[run] (results will vary)
The number showing on the die is 4
The coin landed heads
The roulette wheel shows the number 32
The spinner landed on the number .072
```

Program 9-9 presents a method for selecting a set of five cards from a deck of 52 cards. This is a special case of the problem of selecting *m* objects from a set of *n* objects or, equivalently, of selecting *m* integers from the integers 1 to *n*. A brilliant algorithm for accomplishing this task is shown in Program 9-10. (For details, see D. E. Knuth, *The Art of Computer Programming* Volume 2, p. 121, Addison-Wesley, 1969.) This algorithm has the additional feature of ordering the set of *m* numbers. Do a few pencil-and-paper walk-throughs that use small values of *m* and *n* to convince yourself that the algorithm does indeed produce the appropriate quantity of numbers.

You have seen the uses of the RND function in sampling (when you selected five cards from a deck) and simulation (when you created a model of the outcome of spinning a roulette wheel). Some other uses are as follows.

Testing Programs for Correctness and Efficiency Selecting randomly chosen items of data avoids any bias of the tester.

Numerical Analysis The areas under certain curves, such as the normal curves of statistics, have important interpretations. One method for determin-

Program 9-9. Using RND to randomly permute the elements of a set

```
REM Shuffle a deck of cards   [9-9]
DIM card$(1 TO 52)              'Array to hold deck of cards
CLS
CALL SetUpDeck(card$())         'Set up fresh deck
CALL Shuffle(card$())           'Shuffle deck of cards
CALL DisplayFive(card$())       'Display first five cards
REM ---------- Data for fresh deck: denomination
DATA A, 2, 3, 4, 5, 6, 7, 8, 9, 10, J, Q, K
END

SUB DisplayFive (card$())
  FOR i = 1 TO 5
    PRINT card$(i) + "   ";
  NEXT i
  PRINT
END SUB

SUB SetUpDeck (card$())
  hearts = 3: spades = 6
  ace = 1: king = 13
  FOR suit% = hearts TO spades
    RESTORE
    FOR denomination% = ace TO king
      READ denom$
      cardNumber = 13 * (suit% - hearts) + denomination%
      card$(cardNumber) = denom$ + CHR$(suit%)
    NEXT denomination%
  NEXT suit%
END SUB

SUB Shuffle (card$())
  RANDOMIZE TIMER
  FOR i = 1 TO 52
    SWAP card$(i), card$(INT(52 * RND) + 1)
  NEXT i
END SUB

[run] (results will vary)
8♥   9♠   6♦   K♠   4♣
```

ing the area under a curve consists of enclosing the area with a rectangle, selecting points at random from the rectangle, and counting the percentage that falls under the curve. You can then estimate the area to be this percentage of the area of the rectangle.

Program 9-10. Using RND to randomly select a subset of a set

```
REM Select m numbers between 1 and n   [9-10]
CLS
INPUT "Numbers are to lie between 1 and "; n
INPUT "Number of numbers to be selected"; m
RANDOMIZE TIMER
needed = m
remaining = n
FOR i% = 1 TO n
  IF RND < needed / remaining THEN
      PRINT i%;
      needed = needed - 1
  END IF
  remaining = remaining - 1
NEXT i%
PRINT
END

[run] (results will vary)
Numbers are to lie between 1 and ? 10
Number of numbers to be selected? 3
 1  7  8
```

Recreation   You can write programs that play games such as blackjack. In addition, you can use programs to simulate games of chance and analyze various strategies.

Decision Making   In Game Theory, a branch of mathematics sometimes applied to economics, some strategies use RND to simulate decisions.

Creating Custom-designed Mathematical Characters

In graphics mode, you can create a custom-designed character set to replace the characters in the upper half of the ASCII table — CHR\$(128) through CHR\$(255). Since the character set will be stored in memory, we must first discuss the way that memory locations are specified.

Specifying Memory Locations

In computerese, the letter K stands for 1,024. Therefore, 64K is 65,536 and K^2 is 1,048,576. Main memory locations are numbered from 0 to K^2-1; that is, from 0 to 1,048,575. Certain 64K blocks of memory are called segments as shown below:

Segment 0 consists of memory locations 0, 1, 2, ..., 65,535
Segment 1 consists of memory locations 16, 17, 18, ..., 65,551
Segment 2 consists of memory locations 32, 33, 34, ..., 65,567
  :
  :
Segment m consists of memory locations $16*m$, $16*m+1$, ..., $16*m+65535$

Within each segment, the locations are said to have offsets 0, 1, 2, ..., 65,535. Any memory location can be specified by giving a segment number and an offset within that segment. These two numbers are usually written in the form *segment:offset*. A specific memory location has several *segment:offset* representations. For example, memory location 35 can be specified as 0:35, 1:19, or 2:3.

At any time, a certain segment of memory is declared as the current segment. Statements and functions that read data from and write data to memory locations identify a location by its offset in the current segment. The statement

```
DEF SEG = m
```

declares the *m*th segment to be the current segment.

Each memory location contains an 8-tuple (string of eight) of zeroes and ones, called a *byte*. This 8-tuple is the binary representation of a number from 0 to 255. Therefore, we say that each memory location holds a number from 0 to 255. The value of the function

```
PEEK(n)
```

is the number in the memory location of offset *n* in the current segment. The statement

```
POKE n, r
```

places the number *r* into the memory location with offset *n* in the current segment. The number *r* can be given in decimal or hexadecimal notation. Numbers written in hexadecimal notation are preceded by &H. The use of hexadecimal notation simplifies the task of placing a specific 8-tuple of zeroes and ones into a memory location.

The memory locations in segment 0 give useful information about the hardware components of the computer, the status of the keyboard and screen, and the whereabouts of special portions of memory. In particular, memory locations of offset 124, 125, 126, and 127 point to the offset and segment of the beginning of the portion of memory that generates the characters associated with the upper ASCII values. This portion of memory is called a *character table.* The offset and segment used for the beginning of the character table are PEEK(124)+256*PEEK(125) and PEEK(126)+256*PEEK(127), respectively.

Specifying Characters in Graphics Mode

In the graphics screen modes 1 and 2, each character is displayed in an eight by eight rectangular array of pixels. Figure 9-5 shows the user-defined character 1/3. To the right of each row of the array is the 8-tuple of zeros and ones that describes the row. Ones denote pixels that are on, and zeroes denote pixels that are off. The sequence of eight binary numbers describes the character 1/3.

The steps for specifying characters for the upper ASCII values are as follows:

1. Create a fixed-length string variable to hold the character table. (A fixed-length string variable is convenient since once its memory location is assigned, the location is not moved by QBasic. Also, the functions VARSEG and VARPTR are available to give the segment and offset of the value of the variable.)

2. Set the numbers in memory locations 124, 125, 126, and 127 of segment 0 to point to the fixed-length string variable. If the variable begins at location $s{:}f$, in *segment:offset* form, then the values POKEd into memory locations 124, 125, 126, and 127 should be $f \bmod 256$, $f \setminus 256$, $s \bmod 256$, and $s \setminus 256$, respectively.

3. POKE the eight binary numbers that describe character 128 into the first eight locations of the fixed-length string. POKE the eight binary numbers that describe character 129 into the next eight locations of the character table. Continue in this manner to put the descriptors for up to 128 characters into the table.

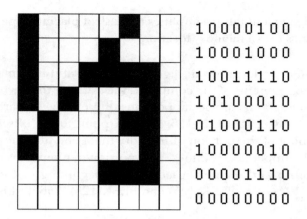

Figure 9-5. How the character 1/3 will appear on the screen

Program 9-11 defines character 128 to be the fraction 1/3, and character 129 to be a solid right triangle. Although only 16 bytes of memory are needed to describe these two characters, the program sets aside a character table of 1,024 bytes that can potentially hold the descriptions of 128 characters. The descriptors for the two characters are stored in DATA statements and are POKEd into the character table. The program can easily be extended to define additional characters.

The data for each character consists of a sequence of eight numbers selected in exactly the same way that an eight-by-eight tile is specified in screen 2 graphics mode. See the discussion of PAINT for details. (Figure 9-5 shows the binary representations of the numbers used in the above program to define the character "1/3.")

Mathematical Characters

The upper 128 ASCII characters in Appendix A contain a number of mathematical characters. Some of these characters are described in Table 9-2.

Program 9-11. Demonstration of user-defined characters

```
REM Save four bytes from low memory [9-11]
SCREEN 1
DEF SEG = 0
DIM store(0 TO 3) AS INTEGER
FOR i = 0 TO 3
   store(i) = PEEK(124 + i)
NEXT i
REM Fill those four bytes with new values
CONST numChars = 128
CONST length = 8 * numChars
DIM chars AS STRING * length
offset = VARPTR(chars)
POKE 124, offset MOD 256
POKE 125, offset \ 256
segment = VARSEG(chars)
POKE 126, segment MOD 256
POKE 127, segment \ 256
REM Place data for characters in memory
DEF SEG = segment
FOR i = 0 TO 15
   READ a%
   POKE offset + i, a%
NEXT i
REM Each DATA statement describes one character
DATA 132,136,158,162,70,130,14,0: 'one-third
DATA 2,6,14,30,62,126,254,0: 'solid rt triangle
REM Display newly defined characters
PRINT CHR$(128) + "   ";
PRINT CHR$(129)
REM Restore status of four bytes in low memory
DEF SEG = 0
FOR i = 0 TO 3
   POKE 124 + i, store(i)
NEXT i
END

[run]
 ⅓  ◢
```

ASCII Value	Description	ASCII Value	Description
171	1/2	239	Intersection
172	1/4	241	Plus or minus sign
224–235	Greek letters	244–245	Integral sign
236	Infinity	251	Square root symbol
238	Is an element of	253	2 as a small exponent

Table 9-2.   Some mathematical characters in the ASCII table

Saving Graphs

The Color/Graphics Adapter reserves 4,000 locations in memory to hold the contents of the screen. After you draw a graph, you can save the contents of these memory locations in a disk file and then reload them to reproduce the graph. The statements

```
DEF SEG = &HB800

BSAVE filename, 0, 4000
```

save the bytes in these memory locations into the specified file; whenever you are in the same SCREEN mode that you saved the file from, you can use the statements

```
DEF SEG = &HB800

BLOAD filename
```

to restore the original screen.

Matrices

An $m \times n$ matrix is a two-dimensional array declared by a statement of the form

```
DIM arrayName(1 TO m, 1 TO n)
```

The matrix will have m rows and n columns. Some versions of BASIC have built-in functions that add, multiply and invert matrices. Although QBasic does not have these functions, they can easily be defined as subprograms.

Matrix Addition

You must dimension all three of the matrices passed to the subprogram in Program Segment 9-12 — even the one that will eventually hold the sum — prior to calling the subprogram. Inside the subprogram, the two matrices to be added are named *first* and *second*, and their sum is named *sum*.

The subprogram begins by verifying that the three matrices passed to the subprogram have the same number of rows and columns. After the verification, the subprogram adds the matrices with a pair of nested FOR...NEXT loops.

Program Segment 9-12. A subprogram that forms the sum of two matrices

```
SUB MatrixAddition (first(), second(), sum())      '[9-12]
   'the assumption is made that each matrix has been
   'dimensioned in the form arrayName(1 TO m, 1 TO n)
   rowsFirst = UBOUND(first, 1)
   colsFirst = UBOUND(first, 2)
   rowsSecond = UBOUND(second, 1)
   colsSecond = UBOUND(second, 2)
   rowsSum = UBOUND(sum, 1)
   colsSum = UBOUND(sum, 2)
   'Verify that first two matrices have the same size
   IF (rowsFirst<>rowsSecond) OR (colsFirst<>colsSecond) THEN
      PRINT "sizes not appropriate for addition"
      EXIT SUB
   END IF
   'Verify that the sum array has the correct size
   IF (rowsFirst <> rowsSum) OR (colsFirst <> colsSum) THEN
      PRINT "Sum matrix not correct size."
      EXIT SUB
   END IF
   'Carry out the addition
   FOR i1% = 1 TO rowsSum
     FOR i2% = 1 TO colsSum
       sum(i1%, i2%) = first(i1%, i2%) + second(i1%, i2%)
     NEXT i2%
   NEXT i1%
END SUB
```

Matrix Multiplication

You must dimension all three of the matrices passed to the subprogram in Program Segment 9-13, even the one that will eventually hold the product, prior to calling the subprogram. Inside the subprogram, the two matrices to be multiplied are named *first* and *second*, and their product is named *product*.

The subprogram begins by verifying that the three matrices passed to the subprogram have suitable sizes; that is, the number of columns of the first matrix must be the same as the number of rows of the second matrix, the number of rows of the product matrix must be the same as the number of rows of the first matrix, and the number of columns of the product matrix must be the same as the number of columns of the second matrix. After the verifications, the entries in the product matrix are obtained one at a time. Each entry is a sum, accumulated in the variable total, of products of numbers taken from the appropriate row of the first matrix and the appropriate column of the second matrix.

Matrix Inversion

The two matrices passed to the subprogram in Program Segment 9-14, even the one that will eventually hold the inverse of the other, must be dimensioned prior to calling the subprogram. Inside the subprogram, the matrix to be inverted is named *original#* and the matrix that will eventually hold its inverse is named *inverse#*. The computation used to obtain the inverse of a matrix is very sensitive to roundoff errors. Therefore, double-precision is used throughout the subprogram.

The subprogram begins by verifying that the two matrices passed to the subprogram have proper sizes. Both matrices must be square matrices of the same size. The subprogram carries out the inversion with a variation of the Gauss-Jordan elimination algorithm. The subprogram places the matrix to be inverted in the left half of a large matrix named *b#*, whose right half contains an identity matrix. The subprogram then carries out elementary row operations on *b#* to transform the left half of *b#* into a diagonal matrix. In an attempt to minimize round-off errors, the algorithm postpones performing any divisions until the end. After appropriate divisions, the right half of *b#* will contain the inverse of the original matrix.

Program Segment 9-13. A subprogram that forms the product of two matrices

```
SUB MatrixMultiply (first(), second(), product())     '[9-13]
   'The assumption is made that each matrix has been
   'dimensioned in the form arrayName(1 TO m, 1 TO n)
   rowsFirst = UBOUND(first, 1)
   colsFirst = UBOUND(first, 2)
   rowsSecond = UBOUND(second, 1)
   colsSecond = UBOUND(second, 2)
   rowsProduct = UBOUND(product, 1)
   colsProduct = UBOUND(product, 2)
   'Verify that first and second matrices can be multiplied
   IF colsFirst <> rowsSecond THEN
       PRINT "Sizes not appropriate to multiply matrices"
       EXIT SUB
   END IF
   'Verify that product array is proper size
   IF (rowsFirst<>rowsProduct) OR (colsSecond<>colsProduct) THEN
       PRINT "Product matrix not correct size"
       EXIT SUB
   END IF
   'Carry out the multiplication
   FOR i1% = 1 TO rowsProduct
     FOR i2% = 1 TO colsProduct
        total = 0
        FOR i3% = 1 TO colsFirst
           total = total + first(i1%, i3%) * second(i3%, i2%)
        NEXT i3%
        product(i1%, i2%) = total
     NEXT i2%
   NEXT i1%
END SUB
```

We've now looked at a number of operations that may interest the scientifically and engineering inclined. In the last chapter of this book, we look at the QBasic capabilities that are of interest to business.

Program Segment 9-14.   A subprogram that obtains the inverse of a matrix

```
SUB MatrixInversion (original#(), inverse#())    '[9-14]
  'Arrays are assumed to be square with subscripts
  'that range from 1 to UBOUND(original#())
  'Verify that both matrices are square and of same size
  IF UBOUND(original#, 1) <> UBOUND(original#, 2) THEN
      PRINT "Matrix to be inverted is not square."
      EXIT SUB
  END IF
  IF UBOUND(inverse#, 1) <> UBOUND(inverse#, 2) THEN
      PRINT "Matrix to hold inverse is not square."
      EXIT SUB
  END IF
  IF UBOUND(original#, 1) <> UBOUND(inverse#, 1) THEN
      PRINT "The matrix to hold the inverse has the wrong size."
      EXIT SUB
  END IF
  'Dimension an array that is twice as wide as the given array,
  'copy the given array into the left half of this new array,
  'and make the right half an identity matrix
  size% = UBOUND(original#, 1)
  DIM b#(size%, 2 * size%)
  FOR row% = 1 TO size%
    FOR col% = 1 TO size%                 'col is column
      b#(row%, col%) = original#(row%, col%)
    NEXT col%
    b#(row%, size% + row%) = 1
  NEXT row%
  'Use a modified Gauss-Jordan elimination to invert the matrix
  FOR i% = 1 TO size%
    'If diagonal element is zero, swap row with a later row
    'to obtain a non-zero diagonal element.
    IF b#(i%, i%) = 0 THEN
      switched% = 0
      FOR testRow% = i% + 1 TO size%
        IF b#(testRow%, i%) <> 0 THEN
          FOR col% = 1 TO 2 * size%
            temp# = b#(i%, col%)
            b#(i%, col%) = b#(testRow%, col%)
            b#(testRow%, col%) = temp#
          NEXT col%
          switched% = -1
        END IF
      NEXT testRow%
```

(continued)

Program Segment 9-14. *(continued)*

```
      IF NOT switched% THEN
         PRINT "Matrix has no inverse."
         EXIT SUB
      END IF
   END IF
   'Reduce all non-diagonal elements in the index column to zero
   FOR row% = 1 TO size%
     IF row% <> i% THEN
         hold# = b#(row%, i%)
         FOR col% = 1 TO 2 * size%
            b#(row%, col%) = b#(i%, i%) * b#(row%, col%)
            b#(row%, col%) = b#(row%, col%) - hold# * b#(i%, col%)
         NEXT col%
     END IF
   NEXT row%
 NEXT i%
 'Divide each row by value on diagonal and
 'assign values to inverse array
 FOR row% = 1 TO size%
   FOR col% = 1 TO size%
     inverse#(row%, col%) = b#(row%, col% + size%) / b#(row%, row%)
   NEXT col%
 NEXT row%
END SUB
```

Business Programming

The previous chapter was devoted to scientific calculations. QBasic also has power for the business user to harness. In fact, we're going to bring together just about everything we've learned so far right here in this chapter, and design a full-blown database management program. Take that, Lotus!

First though, we need to cover some subtleties that are needful to know, if we're going to keep our calculations accurate and in balance.

Financial Calculations

After justifying the value of long integers in financial calculations, this section gives a detailed analysis of the amortization of a loan.

The Importance of Long Integers

Many financial calculations are best performed by converting all amounts to cents and using long integer variables. Not only does this result in faster calculations, it actually ensures accuracy. Don't believe us? We'll give you an example. Below, Program 10-1 uses long integer variables to calculate interest earned, and then automatically rounds the interest to the nearest cent.

Program 10-1. Using long integers in financial computations

```
REM Calculate interest with long integers   [10-1]
CLS
p& = 123456
interestRate = .05
interestEarned& = interestRate * p&
PRINT "The interest earned is"; interestEarned& / 100
END


[run]
The interest earned is 61.73
```

Program 10-2, on the other hand, uses double-precision variables to perform the same calculation as Program 10-1. The function FNRound is used to round numbers to two decimal places. While FNRound does its best, its effort is partly undone by the peculiarities of the way QBasic stores and displays double-precision numbers.

In Program 10-2 you can display the amount of interest correctly with a PRINT USING statement. However, this is only a cosmetic cure since the value of the variable is not exactly what you might want if you continued the program and performed further calculations with the earned interest.

Noninteger variables, therefore, give you problems with fractions of a cent. In some cases, especially when working with large numbers, the errors can continue to compound until we're talking about significant numbers of dollars.

Program 10-2. Rounding difficulties with double-precision numbers

```
REM Calculate interest with double-precision numbers   [10-2]
DEF FNRound (x#) = INT(100 * x# + .5) / 100
p# = 1234.56
interestRate = .05
interestEarned# = FNRound(interestRate * p#)
PRINT "The interest earned is"; interestEarned#
END

[run]
The interest earned is 61.72999954223633
```

Amortization of a Loan

The standard method of amortizing a loan is to make equal payments for a specified number of months, at which time the loan is paid off. The following terms describe a specific amortization.

Amount	The amount of the loan, or the quantity of money borrowed
Rate	The annual rate of interest (given as a percentage); such as 12 or 10.5.
Duration	The number of months over which the loan is to be paid off
Payment	The monthly payment

Given the values of any three of these variables, you can determine the value of the fourth variable by using a mathematical formula. The most common situation is for you to know the amount, rate, and duration, and for you to determine the payment.

At any time, the *balance* of the loan is the amount outstanding on the loan — that is, the amount you must pay to retire the debt at that time. The initial balance is the amount of the loan, and the balance decreases to 0 after you make all the monthly payments. Part of each monthly payment consists of interest on the balance, and the remainder of the payment goes toward reducing the balance.

interest paid for month	=	monthly rate of interest * balance at beginning of month
reduction of debt for month	=	payment - interest paid for month
balance at end of month	=	balance at beginning of month - reduction of debt for month

Program 10-3 requests that the user input the terms of a loan — the amount, annual interest rate, duration, and monthly payment. If the user omits the amount, duration, or monthly payment, the program will automatically calculate it. (The calculation of the interest rate from the other terms is rather complex and has been omitted.) After all of the terms are known, the user can request an amortization schedule that shows a year's transactions at a time.

Program 10-3. Amortization of a loan (output shown in Figures 10-1 and 10-2)

```
REM Calculate terms and display an amortization schedule  [10-3]
CLS
DEFDBL A-Z
PRINT "Give a zero value for amount, duration, or payment"
PRINT "in order to have that value computed."
INPUT "Amount of loan"; amount
INPUT "Annual interest rate (percent)"; rate
PRINT "Number of months over which loan will be paid off";
INPUT duration%
INPUT "Amount of each payment"; payment
i = rate / 1200    'Interest rate per month
IF amount = 0 THEN
    CALL FindAmount
  ELSEIF duration% = 0 THEN
    CALL FindDuration
    CALL FindPayment   'adjust payment for whole number duration
  ELSEIF payment = 0 THEN
    CALL FindPayment
END IF
PRINT "Display loan amortization schedule (Y/N)?"
answer$ = UCASE$(INPUT$(1))
IF answer$ = "Y" THEN CALL Amortize
END

SUB Amortize
  SHARED amount, i, duration%, payment
  CLS
  PRINT "PAY#   PAYMENT   INTEREST   RED. OF DEBT    BALANCE"
  balance& = 100 * amount
  payment& = 100 * payment
  FOR payNum% = 1 TO duration%
    interest& = i * balance&
    'If this is the last payment on loan, recompute payment
    IF payNum% = duration% THEN payment& = interest& + balance&
    reductionOfLoan& = payment& - interest&
    balance& = balance& - reductionOfLoan&
    PRINT USING "####  #####.##    "; payNum%, payment& / 100;
    PRINT USING "#####.##    "; interest& / 100;
    PRINT USING "#####.##    "; reductionOfLoan& / 100;
    PRINT USING "#####,###.##"; balance& / 100
    IF (payNum% MOD 12 = 0) AND (payNum% <> duration%) THEN
        PRINT
```

Program 10-3. *(continued)*

```
    PRINT "Press any key to continue."
    a$ = INPUT$(1)
    CLS
    PRINT "PAY#    PAYMENT    INTEREST    RED. OF DEBT      BALANCE"
    END IF
 NEXT payNum%
END SUB

FUNCTION Ceil (x)
  REM The smallest whole number greater than or equal to x
  Ceil = -INT(-x)
END FUNCTION

SUB FindAmount
  SHARED amount, i, duration%, payment
  amount = (payment / i) * (1 - (1 + i) ^ -duration%)
  PRINT USING "The amount of the loan is $$####,###.##"; amount
END SUB

SUB FindDuration
  SHARED amount, i, duration%, payment
  duration% = Ceil(LOG(payment/(payment - i * amount))/LOG(1 + i))
  PRINT USING "Loan is paid off after ### months"; duration%
END SUB

SUB FindPayment
  SHARED amount, i, duration%, payment
  payment = (i * amount) / (1 - (1 + i) ^ -duration%)
  PRINT USING "Each payment will be $$,###.##"; payment
END SUB

[run]
Give a zero value for amount, duration, or payment
in order to have that value computed.
Amount of loan? 100000
Annual interest rate (percent)? 9.5
Number of months over which loan will be paid off? 360
Amount of each payment?  0
Each payment will be  $840.85
Display loan amortization schedule (Y/N)? Y
```

PAY#	PAYMENT	INTEREST	RED. OF DEBT	BALANCE
1	840.85	791.67	49.18	99,950.82
2	840.85	791.28	49.57	99,901.25
3	840.85	790.88	49.97	99,851.28
4	840.85	790.49	50.36	99,800.92
5	840.85	790.09	50.76	99,750.16
6	840.85	789.69	51.16	99,699.00
7	840.85	789.28	51.57	99,647.43
8	840.85	788.88	51.97	99,595.46
9	840.85	788.46	52.39	99,543.07
10	840.85	788.05	52.80	99,490.27
11	840.85	787.63	53.22	99,437.05
12	840.85	787.21	53.64	99,383.41

Press any key to continue.

Figure 10-1.   Amortization of year 1 from Program 10-3

Note that the formula used in the program to determine the monthly payment is accurate. However, since the smallest unit of currency is one cent, our currency system itself introduces inaccuracy. You can't pay fractions of a cent, and rounding the monthly payment to the nearest cent throws off the amortization schedule slightly. This inaccuracy is compensated for by adjusting the last payment so that it completely pays off the balance. Normally, the adjustment will be a small amount.

PAY#	PAYMENT	INTEREST	RED. OF DEBT	BALANCE
349	840.85	75.99	764.86	8,833.35
350	840.85	69.93	770.92	8,062.43
351	840.85	63.83	777.02	7,285.41
352	840.85	57.68	783.17	6,502.24
353	840.85	51.48	789.37	5,712.87
354	840.85	45.23	795.62	4,917.25
355	840.85	38.93	801.92	4,115.33
356	840.85	32.58	808.27	3,307.06
357	840.85	26.18	814.67	2,492.39
358	840.85	19.73	821.12	1,671.27
359	840.85	13.23	827.62	843.65
360	850.33	6.68	843.65	0.00

Figure 10-2.   Amortization of year 30 from Program 10-3

Pie Charts

Data achieves its greatest impact when you present it graphically. This section presents a generic program that creates a pie chart. This program has been designed both to present the essential programming techniques and to be flexible.

Pie charts are appropriate for showing the relative sizes of from 3 to 10 quantities. (Displays that involve more than 10 categories are usually more readable in the form of a bar chart. Bar charts are discussed in the next section.) Program 10-4 is a special case of a general program that draws pie charts for up to 10 categories. The only necessary modification to change the chart is the replacement of the numbers and their categories in the DATA statements at the top of the program. In the event that the names of the individual categories are long, you can reduce the size of the pie chart by decreasing the value assigned to the variable scale.

Figure 10-3 contains the output from Program 10-4. The figure presents the percentages of the people in the world who speak each of the major languages. The sectors of the circle appear on screen in three different colors,

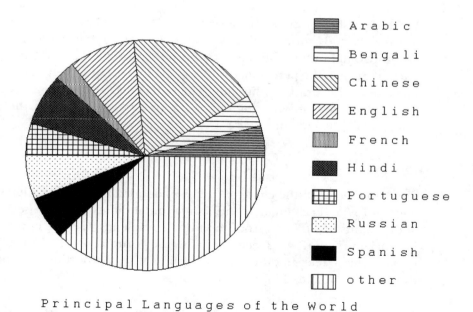

Principal Languages of the World

Figure 10-3. A pie chart displayed by Program 10-4

and each sector has a different pattern. To change the patterns that appear in Figure 10-3, use the information presented in the discussion of tile patterns in Chapter 8, and change the characters to the right of the equal signs in the subprogram AssignTilingPatterns in Program 10-4.

In a pie chart, each sector of the pie represents a percentage of the entire pie. Therefore, the program must convert the numeric data into percentages. In Program 10-4, the subprogram CountAndTotalData counts the number of different entries in the first DATA statement and totals these numbers.

NOTE   The last entry in this DATA statement, -1, serves as a sentinel to signal the end of the items.

The variable *count* gives the number of sectors that will appear in the pie chart, and the variable *total* will be used to convert each number from the first DATA statement into percentages.

The subprogram DrawChart draws and fills the sectors of the pie chart. An understanding of this subprogram requires a further discussion of the CIRCLE statement.

Figure 10-4 shows a circle that is segmented by several radius lines. The radius line that extends horizontally from the center of the circle to the right is called the horizontal radius line. Each radius line is assigned a number between 0 and 1 that gives the percentage of the circle that is found between the chosen line and the horizontal radius line. The radian measure of the angle from the horizontal radius line to any radius line is $2*\pi$ multiplied by the assigned number. The statement

```
CIRCLE (x, y), r, , -r1, -r2
```

draws the sector of the circle of radius *r* bounded by the radius lines making angles of *r1* and *r2* radians with the horizontal radius line. The sector begins at the radius line that is associated with *r1*, and ends with the radius line that is associated with *r2*. This sector contains the portion $(r2\text{-}r1)/(2*\pi)$ of the area of the entire circle. In other words, starting at *r1*, the portion *p* of the area of the circle is contained in the sector from *r1* to *r2*, where *r2* is $r1 + 2*\pi*p$.

Now, back to our program. Program 10-4 creates a pie chart one sector at a time, beginning with the sector just above the horizontal radius line. For this

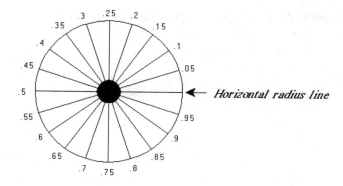

Figure 10-4. The portions of a circle

sector, *r1* is 0 and the CIRCLE statement involves -0. The computer cannot distinguish between -0 and 0 and therefore will not produce the intended result. This situation is remedied by using a very small number, such as -.00001, instead of -0. The program will then draw the sectors of the pie chart one after the other. The program uses the ending radius line for each sector as the beginning radius line for the next.

In Program 10-4, the PAINT statement, which is used to fill a sector with a pattern, requires the coordinates of a point inside the sector. One way to find such a point is to select the midpoint of the radius line that bisects the sector. If the sector is bounded by the radius lines having radian measures *r1* and *r2*, then the radian measure associated with the bisecting radius line is $t = (r1 + r2)/2$. You can then use the trigonometric functions to find the midpoint of this radius line. The coordinates of the point are $x + (r/2)*COS(t)$ and $y + (r/2)*SIN(t)$, where (x, y) is the center of the circle and *r* is the radius.

There is one more fine point to attend to. A WINDOW statement must be used to specify a coordinate system. After that, the circle drawn by the statement CIRCLE $(x,y),r$ will have a horizontal radius line of length *r*. The vertical radius line will appear on the screen with the same length. However, the length in terms of the y scale that the WINDOW statement sets will most likely be different than *r*. In order for the trigonometric formulas just given to hold, these two lengths must agree. They will agree if the WINDOW statement specifies the lengths of the x-axis and the y-axis in a 4-to-3 ratio. (This is due to the fact that the lengths of the two sides of the screen are in a 4-to-3 ratio.) A suitable WINDOW statement is WINDOW (0,0)-(4,3).

Program 10-4.   A generic pie chart program

```
REM Illustrate the relative usages of the major languages   [10-4]
scale = 1
'The size of the pie chart may be adjusted by varying the value
'of scale. The smaller the value of scale, the more room for
'the item descriptions. A scale of 1 gives the pie chart a
'diameter equal to half the width of the screen.
DIM tile$(1 TO 10)
CALL AssignTilingPatterns(tile$())
CALL CountAndTotalData(itemCount, sumOfData)
CALL DrawChart(itemCount, sumOfData, tile$(), scale)
CALL DisplayLegend(itemCount, tile$(), scale)
REM -- Data: number of people (in millions) that speak language
DATA 177, 171, 974, 420, 114, 300, 164, 285, 296, 2000, -1
REM -- Data: the major languages
DATA Arabic, Bengali, Chinese, English, French
DATA Hindi, Portuguese, Russian, Spanish, other
REM -- Data: title for pie chart
DATA Principal Languages of the World
END

SUB AssignTilingPatterns (tile$())
  'the following tiling patterns may be changed as desired
  tile$(1) = CHR$(136) + CHR$(136) + CHR$(170)
  tile$(2) = CHR$(85) + CHR$(0)
  tile$(3) = CHR$(128) + CHR$(32) + CHR$(8) + CHR$(2)
  tile$(4) = CHR$(3) + CHR$(12) + CHR$(48) + CHR$(192)
  tile$(5) = CHR$(170) + CHR$(170) + CHR$(0) + CHR$(0)
  tile$(6) = CHR$(17)
  tile$(7) = CHR$(168) + CHR$(168) + CHR$(0)
  tile$(8) = CHR$(1) + CHR$(16)
  tile$(9) = CHR$(255)
  tile$(10) = CHR$(5)
END SUB

SUB CountAndTotalData (count, total)
  count = 0
  total = 0
  READ itemValue
  DO UNTIL itemValue < 0
    total = total + itemValue
    count = count + 1
    READ itemValue
  LOOP
END SUB
```

Program 10-4. *(continued)*

```
SUB DisplayLegend (count, tile$(), scale)
  heightInRows = 25
  widthInColumns = 40
  WINDOW SCREEN (0, 0)-(widthInColumns, heightInRows)
  boxWidth = 2
  boxHt = 1
  legendTop = (heightInRows - (boxHt + 1) * count) \ 2
  leftEdge = widthInColumns * (scale / 2) + 2
  FOR i = 1 TO count
    READ itemName$
    boxBottom = legendTop + (boxHt + 1) * i
    boxTop = boxBottom - boxHt
    rtEdge = leftEdge + boxWidth
    LINE (leftEdge, boxTop)-(rtEdge, boxBottom), , B
    PAINT (leftEdge + boxWidth / 2, boxBottom-boxHt / 2), tile$(i)
    LOCATE boxBottom, leftEdge + boxWidth + 2: PRINT itemName$
  NEXT i
  'display title
  READ title$
  LOCATE heightInRows - 1, (widthInColumns - LEN(title$)) / 2
  PRINT title$;
END SUB

SUB DrawChart (count, total, tile$(), scale)
  'Display results are independent of the values of
  'windowWidth and windowHeight. All that is important
  'is that these values be in the ratio of 4 to 3.
  windowWidth = 4
  windowHeight = 3
  SCREEN 1, 0
  COLOR , 0
  WINDOW (0, 0)-(windowWidth, windowHeight)
  twoPi = 8 * ATN(1)                    '2*pi
  radius = scale * windowWidth / 4
  xcenter = radius
  ycenter = windowHeight / 2
  startSector = .00001
  RESTORE    'use first data statement again
  FOR index% = 1 TO count
    READ itemValue
    endSector = startSector + twoPi * (itemValue / total)
    IF endSector > 6.283 THEN endSector = 6.283
    CIRCLE (xcenter, ycenter), radius, , -startSector, -endSector
    theta = (startSector + endSector) / 2
```

(continued)

Program 10-4. *(continued)*

```
    x = xcenter + radius * COS(theta) / 2
    y = ycenter + radius * SIN(theta) / 2
    PAINT (x, y), tile$(index%)
    startSector = endSector
  NEXT index%
  READ itemValue   'read the sentinel value
END SUB
```

After Program 10-4 draws the pie chart, the subprogram DisplayLegend draws legend boxes giving the identifying pattern to the left of each category name. The subprogram draws each rectangular box by using the LINE statement, and the PAINT statement uses the center of the rectangle to fill the rectangle. The program centers the rectangles vertically on the right side of the screen. After displaying all of the legends, Program 10-4 displays the title of the pie chart centered at the bottom of the screen.

Bar Charts

The other primary graphical device for displaying data is the bar chart. This section develops a generic bar chart program that both displays a bar chart on screen and produces a high-quality printed version.

Figure 10-5 shows a printout obtained by using the bar chart program.

Some of the features of this chart are as follows:

- The text looks like text produced by a printer in text mode, rather than text produced by a graphics screen dump (i.e., by a utility program included with DOS that simply copies the contents of the screen to the current printer).

- The tick marks on the y-axis are evenly spaced and aligned with their labels. (Each of these labels can contain up to four digits.)

- The labels under the bars are vertical and centered. (On the screen display, each label is limited to a maximum of three characters. However, there is no limit to the number of characters for each label on the printed version.)

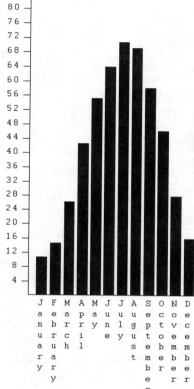

Figure 10-5. A bar chart created with Program 10-8

We first analyze each of the tasks that go into creating a bar chart and then put them together in a complete program.

Setting Up a Coordinate System, Axes, and Tick Marks

The first step in designing any graphics program is to select a convenient screen mode and coordinate system. The high-resolution graphics mode is most appropriate for bar charts since it uses smaller text characters than medium-resolution graphics mode. This minimizes the amount of space that labels require, which is one of the most important considerations in formatting bar charts. The statement

```
WINDOW (-40, -27)-(599, 172)
```

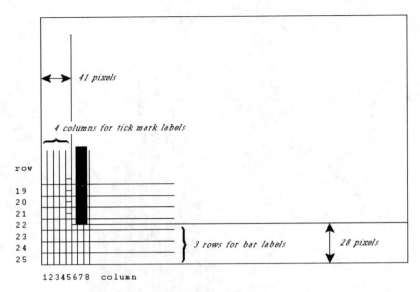

Figure 10-6.   Choosing coordinates for a bar chart

establishes a well-suited coordinate system. Since the screen is divided into 640 × 200 pixels in high-resolution screen mode, each pixel corresponds to a point with integer coordinates; that is, a unit in this coordinate system is exactly one pixel wide or high.

Figure 10-6 shows the rationale for the choices of the numbers -40 and -27 in the WINDOW statement. Since each character is 8 pixels high and 8 pixels wide, space exists for four digits and a tick mark to the left of the y-axis, and space exists for three characters below the x-axis. By placing the x-axis at the 28th pixel from the bottom of the screen, the x-axis will be vertically centered in the 22nd text line. If you start from the x-axis, moving up 8 pixels for each successive tick mark guarantees that each tick mark will be centered vertically in a text line. Therefore, even though QBasic draws the tick marks with graphics statements and displays the labels as text, the tick marks and labels will be perfectly aligned.

The statements

```
LINE (0, 0)-(599, 0)
LINE (0, 0)-(0, 164)
```

draw the axes. The y-axis extends up only 164 pixels so that the program can use the top 8 pixels, which form the top row, to display a title. Finally, the statements

```
FOR verticalPosition% = 8 TO 160 STEP 8
  LINE (0, verticalPosition%)-(-8, verticalPosition%)
NEXT verticalPosition%
```

place 20 tick marks — each pair of tick marks separated by 8 pixels — directly to the left of the y-axis.

Determining a Scale for the Y-Axis

The numbers used as labels for the tick marks on the y-axis depend on the value that the highest bar represents. Let's refer to this value as maximumDataValue. One way to determine the scale is to label the top tick mark with this value, label the lowest tick mark with 1/20 of this value, and so on. Another way is to label the lowest tick mark with a rounded up value of maximumDataValue/20 and label the others accordingly. The first way can result in some strange labels. Although the second way is reasonable, graph makers prefer to have successive labels that differ by numbers such as 5, 10, or 100. Program Segment 10-5 selects reasonable values for the tick labels by choosing a reasonable value for the interval between tick marks. The program segment also specifies a PRINT USING format string that will display the labels appropriately.

Displaying Vertical Bar Labels

The labels that are placed under the bars could be placed horizontally if the bars are sufficiently wide and the labels short. However, you gain more flexibility if you display the labels vertically under each bar. This format permits bars to be centered over every other character position and, in the printer version of the chart, allows labels of any length to be printed. As mentioned earlier, the program will display only the first three letters of each bar label on screen.

If the labels for each bar are held in the array *names$*( ) and you place successive bars so that they are centered over character columns 7, 9, 11, and so on, then the bar labels can be displayed with the statements in Program Segment 10-6. The code uses the MID$ function to select the *letter%*th letter from each label. If there is no *letter%*th letter in a given label, MID$ will give the null

Program Segment 10-5.   A segment that chooses a reasonable tick mark interval

```
s = maximumDataValue / 20
SELECT CASE s
  CASE IS >= 100
    interval = Ceil(s / 100) * 100
    format$ = "####"
  CASE IS >= 10
    interval = Ceil(s / 10) * 10
    format$ = "####"
  CASE IS >= 1
    interval = Ceil(s / 1) * 1
    format$ = "####"
  CASE IS >= .1
    interval = Ceil(s * 10) / 10
    format$ = "##.#"
  CASE IS >= .01
    interval = Ceil(s * 100) / 100
    format$ = "#.##"
  CASE ELSE
    interval = Ceil(s * 1000) / 1000
    format$ = ".###"
END SELECT
FOR tick% = 1 TO 20
  LOCATE 22 - tick%, 1
  PRINT USING format$; interval * tick%;
NEXT tick%

FUNCTION Ceil (x)
  REM The smallest whole number greater than or equal to x
  Ceil = -INT(-x)
END FUNCTION
```

string. To preserve the spacing of the other labels, the segment converts this null value to a space.

Positioning and Displaying the Bars

The height of each bar reflects the value that the bar represents. Since the height of a single pixel is *interval*/8, the height of a bar (in pixels) should be

```
value represented by the bar / (interval / 8)
```

Program Segment 10-6. A segment that displays vertical labels

```
FOR bar% = 1 TO barCount%
  FOR letter% = 1 TO 3
    LOCATE 22 + letter%, 7 + 2 * (bar% - 1)
    letter$ = MID$(names$(bar%), letter%, 1)
    IF letter$ = "" THEN letter$ = " "
    PRINT letter$;
  NEXT letter%
NEXT bar%
```

Since only one space separates the labels under the bars, the maximum width that each bar could have is 16 pixels. For the moment, suppose that each bar is 16 pixels wide. Then the first bar would begin at the fourth pixel of the x-axis and extend to the 19th pixel. The second bar would extend from the 20th pixel to the 35th, and so on. The bars could then be drawn by the statements in Program Segment 10-7, which assumes that the labels and values of the bars are stored in the arrays *name$*( ) and *values*( ), respectively. The BF parameter in the LINE statement draws a solid rectangle that has the two given points as opposite corners.

The bars drawn by Program Segment 10-7 are correct, but they run together. The chart would be easier to read if space existed between successive bars. Therefore, the LINE statement should be replaced by

```
LINE (leftEdge% + 1, 0)-(leftEdge% + barWidth% - 1, height%), , BF
```

Program Segment 10-7. A segment that draws the bars

```
leftEdge% = 4
barWidth% = 16
FOR bar% = 1 TO barCount%
  height% = values(bar%) / (interval / 8)
  LINE (leftEdge%, 0)-(leftEdge%+barWidth%-1, height%), , BF
  leftEdge% = leftEdge% + barWidth%
NEXT bar%
```

Printing the Bar Chart on a Dot-Matrix Printer

The standard method to print the contents of the screen is to use a screen-dumping utility. DOS contains a program of this type called GRAPH-ICS.COM. You normally load the program from DOS before you run any programs; at any time thereafter, pressing <Shift-PrtSc> produces a screen dump. However, this method has some shortcomings. First, it is rather slow, particularly when a bar chart contains only a few bars and most of the screen is empty. Second, the printed image is distorted in comparison to the image on the screen.

There is another method to print a bar chart which not only corrects the shortcomings of a screen dump but also allows you to print all of the letters in the bar labels. This method involves writing a set of custom routines that use the original data to graph the bar chart directly on the printer, as opposed to using a screen dump to copy the image from the screen to the printer. The printing subprograms presented in Program 10-8 form one example of such a set of routines. The main print subprogram, PrintChart, first invokes Pre-pareToPrint to set up the printer for graphics printing and then prints the bar chart title and uses the subprogram PrintLine to produce the body of the chart. The program then calls the subprogram PrintLastLine to print the horizontal axis and the pieces of bars just above this axis. Finally, the program calls the subprogram PrintBarLabels to print, in a vertical column, the full label for each bar.

The printing subprograms of Program 10-8 use a scale of *interval*/16 to help the printed bar chart have the same shaped as the displayed chart. As a result, each displayed row becomes two print lines. The subprograms print the tick mark labels, the tick marks, a portion of the vertical axis, and an appropriate portion of each bar as the first of the two lines. The second line prints just a portion of the vertical axis and an appropriate piece from each bar.

In standard printing, no more than 80 characters are printed on a line, and successive lines have a gap between them. For graphics printing, you may use nearly 1,000 characters on a single line to form an 8-inch-wide image. Also, you must eliminate the gap between lines. In Program 10-8, the subprogram PrepareToPrint sets the printing width to 255, the maximum QBasic allows, so that QBasic will not insert a carriage return and line feed before all the graphics characters for a given line have been sent to the printer.

PrepareToPrint also sets line spacing to 8/72 inch to cause successive lines to print without a gap between them. PrepareToPrint also gives the strings that define the three graphics characters used in printing the vertical axis.

The subprogram PrintLine handles the printing of a given line. PrintLine prints either a four-digit tick label or four spaces, followed by a string of graphics data. The graphics data for a given line begins with either a tick mark and a portion of the vertical axis or only a portion of the vertical axis. This data is followed by appropriate sets of 24 patterns of dots, one set for each bar in the chart. (A standard printed character is 12 dots wide, so a 2-character-wide bar is 24 printed dots wide.)

The function Pattern% determines the patterns to be printed for each bar, as well as how much of a given bar the current line of print contains. If a particular bar extends above the current line being printed, then the value of the function is 255, which results in a solid rectangle being printed as the print head moves over that bar's position. If a particular bar does not reach as high as the current line being printed, then the value of the function is 0, which results in nothing being printed as the print head moves over the bar's position. When a particular bar extends partially into the line being printed, the function returns a value between 1 and 127, which results in the appropriate portion of a rectangle being printed as the print head moves over the bar's position.

A Generic Bar Chart Program

Program 10-8 incorporates the various features discussed earlier in this section. The program allows the graphing of a maximum of 37 bars from values supplied interactively by the user during run-time. The program has been designed with four characters allocated for tick mark labels. This design does not actually limit the magnitude of the quantities that you can represent. For example, if the quantities are in the hundreds of thousands, then you can drop the last three digits from each quantity (in order to produce data between 1 and 999) and you can add "in thousands" to the title of the graph.

Program 10-8. A generic bar chart program

```
REM Display and print a barchart with up to 37 bars  [10-8]
CONST maxBars = 37  'Center over columns 7, 9, 11, ..., 79
DIM values(1 TO maxBars), names$(1 TO maxBars)
'These subprograms share the variables values(),
'names$(), title$, interval, maxLength%, and barCount%
CALL GetInfo
CALL PrepareScreenAxisAndTickMarks
CALL DrawBars
CALL LabelBars
LOCATE 1, 1: PRINT title$;
LOCATE 1, 50: PRINT "Print chart on printer (Y/N)?"
IF UCASE$(INPUT$(1)) = "Y" THEN CALL PrintChart
END

FUNCTION Ceil (x)
  Ceil = -INT(-x)
END FUNCTION

SUB DrawBars
  SHARED values(), interval, barCount%
  leftEdge% = 4
  barWidth% = 16
  FOR bar% = 1 TO barCount%
    height% = values(bar%) / (interval / 8)
    LINE (leftEdge%+1, 0)-(leftEdge%+barWidth%-1,height%), ,BF
    leftEdge% = leftEdge% + barWidth%
  NEXT bar%
END SUB

SUB FindNiceInterval (s)
  SHARED interval, format$
  SELECT CASE s
    CASE IS >= 100
      interval = Ceil(s / 100) * 100
      format$ = "####"
    CASE IS >= 10
      interval = Ceil(s / 10) * 10
      format$ = "####"
    CASE IS >= 1
      interval = Ceil(s / 1) * 1
      format$ = "####"
    CASE IS >= .1
      interval = Ceil(s * 10) / 10
      format$ = "##.#"
```

Program 10-8. *(continued)*

```
      CASE IS >= .01
        interval = Ceil(s * 100) / 100
        format$ = "#.##"
      CASE ELSE
        interval = Ceil(s * 1000) / 1000
        format$ = ".###"
  END SELECT
END SUB

SUB GetInfo
  SHARED values(),names$(),title$,interval,maxLength%,barCount%
  maxValue = 0
  maxLength% = 0
  barCount% = 0
  CLS
  CALL GiveInstructions
  INPUT "Name"; newName$
  DO WHILE newName$ <> ""
    IF LEN(newName$)>maxLength% THEN maxLength%=LEN(newName$)
    INPUT "Value"; newValue
    IF newValue > maxValue THEN maxValue = newValue
    barCount% = barCount% + 1
    values(barCount%) = newValue
    names$(barCount%) = newName$
    IF barCount% = maxBars THEN EXIT DO
    'Redisplay instructions at bottom of screen
    'when they scroll off the top.
    IF barCount% MOD 10 = 0 THEN CALL GiveInstructions
    INPUT "Name"; newName$
  LOOP
  LINE INPUT "Title? "; title$
  'Compute a nice value for the vertical interval between tick
  'marks that will accommodate the largest value given as data.
  CALL FindNiceInterval(maxValue / 20)
END SUB

SUB GiveInstructions
  PRINT "Up to"; maxBars;
  PRINT "names and corresponding values may be given."
  PRINT "When all desired names and values have been entered,"
  PRINT "respond to the prompt for a name by pressing ENTER"
  PRINT "without giving a name."
END SUB
```

(continued)

Program 10-8. *(continued)*

```
SUB LabelBars
  SHARED barCount%, names$()
  FOR bar% = 1 TO barCount%
    FOR letter% = 1 TO 3
      LOCATE 22 + letter%, 7 + 2 * (bar% - 1)
      letter$ = MID$(names$(bar%), letter%, 1)
      IF letter$ = "" THEN letter$ = " "
      PRINT letter$;
    NEXT letter%
  NEXT bar%
END SUB

FUNCTION Pattern% (mode$, index%, bar%)
  SHARED values(), interval
  IF mode$ = "tick" THEN adjustment% = 4 ELSE adjustment% = 12
  extra% = values(bar%)/(interval/16) - 16*index%+adjustment%
  IF extra% < 0 THEN extra% = 0
  IF extra% >= 8 THEN
      Pattern% = 255
    ELSE
      Pattern% = 2 ^ (extra%) - 1
  END IF
END FUNCTION

SUB PrepareScreenAxisAndTickMarks
  SHARED interval, barCount%, format$
  SCREEN 2
  WINDOW (-40, -27)-(599, 172)
  LINE (0, 0)-(599, 0)
  LINE (0, 0)-(0, 164)
  FOR verticalPosition% = 8 TO 160 STEP 8
    LINE (0, verticalPosition%)-(-8, verticalPosition%)
  NEXT verticalPosition%
  FOR tick% = 1 TO 20
    LOCATE 22 - tick%, 1
    PRINT USING format$; interval * tick%;
  NEXT tick%
END SUB

SUB PrepareToPrint
  SHARED tick$, bar$, corner$
  WIDTH "LPT1:", 255
  'Set printer to graphic line spacing (8/72nds of an inch)
  'Both IBM and EPSON escape sequences given
```

Program 10-8. *(continued)*

```
      LPRINT CHR$(27); "@"; CHR$(27); "A"; CHR$(8); CHR$(2);
      LPRINT CHR$(27); "A"; CHR$(8);
      'Define 18-dot-wide characters used to form vertical axis
      tick$ = STRING$(10, CHR$(8)) + STRING$(2, CHR$(255)) +_
              STRING$(6, CHR$(0))
      bar$ = STRING$(10, CHR$(0)) + STRING$(2, CHR$(255)) +_
              STRING$(6, CHR$(0))
      corner$ = STRING$(10, CHR$(0)) + STRING$(2, CHR$(248)) +_
                STRING$(6, CHR$(8))
   END SUB

   SUB PrintBarLabels
      SHARED names$(), maxLength%, barCount%
      FOR letterCount% = 1 TO maxLength%
        LPRINT "        ";
        FOR bar% = 1 TO barCount%
          letter$ = MID$(names$(bar%), letterCount%, 1)
          IF letter$ = "" THEN letter$ = " "
          LPRINT letter$; " ";
        NEXT bar%
        LPRINT
      NEXT letterCount%
   END SUB

   SUB PrintChart
      SHARED title$
      CALL PrepareToPrint
      LPRINT title$
      LPRINT
      'Print two lines on printer for each row on screen
      FOR index% = 20 TO 1 STEP -1
        CALL PrintLine("tick", index%)
        CALL PrintLine("bar", index%)
      NEXT index%
      CALL PrintLastLine
      CALL PrintBarLabels
   END SUB

   SUB PrintGraphics (graphicsString$)
      'Graphics escape sequence for IBM, Epson, and clone printers
      low% = LEN(graphicsString$) MOD 256
      high% = LEN(graphicsString$) \ 256
      LPRINT CHR$(27);"L";CHR$(low%);CHR$(high%);graphicsString$;
   END SUB
```

(continued)

Program 10-8. *(continued)*

```
SUB PrintLastLine
  SHARED corner$, values(), barCount%, interval
  info$ = corner$
  FOR bar% = 1 TO barCount%
    extra% = values(bar%) / (interval / 16)
    IF extra% >= 4 THEN
        Ptn% = 248
      ELSE
        Ptn% = 2 ^ (extra% + 4) - 8
    END IF
    temp$ = STRING$(20, CHR$(Ptn%))
    info$ = info$ + CHR$(8) + CHR$(8) + temp$ + CHR$(8)+CHR$(8)
  NEXT bar%
  LPRINT "      ";
  CALL PrintGraphics(info$)
  LPRINT
END SUB

SUB PrintLine (mode$, index%)
  SHARED tick$, bar$, barCount%, interval, format$
  IF mode$ = "tick" THEN
      LPRINT USING format$; interval * index%;
      info$ = tick$
    ELSE
      LPRINT "      ";
      info$ = bar$
  END IF
  FOR bar% = 1 TO barCount%
    temp$ = STRING$(20, CHR$(Pattern%(mode$, index%, bar%)))
    info$ = info$ + CHR$(0) + CHR$(0) + temp$ + CHR$(0) + CHR$(0)
  NEXT bar%
  CALL PrintGraphics(info$)
  LPRINT
END SUB
```

Database Management

Hypothetically, you can call any collection of data a database. However, the term database usually refers to a collection of data that is stored on a disk, and that takes on a variety of appearances depending on the requirements at the time. Thus, a database can serve as the data source for a variety of applications.

A database management program is a program that can create and maintain a database.

Chapter 7 introduced random-access, sequential, and binary files. This section now uses the file-handling statements discussed there to create and maintain a database.

Opening a Generic Database

The primary data for the database will be stored in a random file. In order to create a random file, you must decide how many fields each record will have and how long each field will be. You need this in order to write the appropriate OPEN and FIELD statements for the random file. Also, knowing the type of information that each field will contain will help you give meaningful names to the field variables. For example, suppose that a database will hold names and phone numbers. Each record might consist of first name, last name, and phone fields that have lengths 10, 15, and 12, respectively. With this information, appropriate statements to open the database are

```
OPEN "PHONEDIR.DB" AS #1 LEN = 37
FIELD #1, 10 AS firstNamef$, 15 AS lastNamef$, 12 AS phonef$
```

To produce a general database management program, you should generalize these statements by removing specific values and replacing them with variables. The statements in Program Segment 10-9 carry out this generalization. Notice that the OPEN and FIELD statements no longer contain any constants that are specific to a particular database. These two statements can open any database with three fields. Since the generic field variables *item1f$*, *item2f$*, and *item3f$* no longer suggest the data they hold, this segment creates three additional variables — *item1Name$*, *item2Name$*, and *item3Name$* — to hold this information.

You can carry the above generalization one step further by introducing arrays to hold the field lengths and the field names, and to serve as field variables. In addition, you can place the information specific to PHONEDIR.DB in DATA statements. The generalized database opening statements are those used in Program Segment 10-10.

These statements are so general that you only need to make two small changes to apply them to a database with 4, 5, or more fields. You must change the

Program Segment 10-9.   A segment that produces generalized OPEN and FIELD statements

```
fileName$ = "PHONEDIR.DB"
item1Len = 10
item1Name$ = "First Name"
item2Len = 15
item2Name$ = "Last Name"
item3Len = 12
item3Name$ = "Phone"
recordLength% = item1Len + item2Len + item3Len
OPEN fileName$ AS #1 LEN = recordLength%
FIELD #1, item1Len AS item1f$, item2Len AS item2f$, _
          item3Len AS item3f$
```

DATA statements at the bottom of the main body, and you must add more fields to the FIELD statement. You can execute the proper FIELD statement for a given number of fields automatically — up to some predefined maximum number of fields — by replacing the FIELD statement in Program Segment 10-10 by a CALL to the procedure SetFields shown in Program Segment 10-11. The procedure SetFields uses a SELECT CASE structure to choose the correct FIELD statement for the given number of fields, which is *fieldCount%*.

Program Segment 10-10.   Opening a database using DATA statements

```
READ fileName$, fieldCount%
DIM itemName$(1 TO fieldCount%)   'description of field
DIM itemLen%(1 TO fieldCount%)    'length of field
DIM itemf$(1 TO fieldCount%)      'field variable for data
recordLength% = 0
FOR index% = 1 TO fieldCount%
  READ itemName$(index%), itemLen%(index%)
  recordLength% = recordLength% + itemLen%(index%)
NEXT index%
OPEN fileName$ FOR RANDOM AS #1 LEN = recordLength%
FIELD #1, itemLen%(1) AS itemf$(1), itemLen%(2) AS itemf$(2),_
          itemLen%(3) AS itemf$(3)
DATA "PHONEDIR.DB", 3
DATA "First Name", 10
DATA "Last Name", 15
DATA "Phone", 12
```

Program Segment 10-11. A segment that chooses a FIELD statement for a varying field count

```
SUB SetFields (fieldCount%)
  SELECT CASE fieldCount%
    CASE 1
      FIELD #1, itemLen%(1) AS itemf$(1)
    CASE 2
      FIELD #1, itemLen%(1) AS itemf$(1), itemLen%(2) AS itemf$(2)
    CASE 3
      FIELD #1,itemLen%(1)AS itemf$(1), itemLen%(2) AS itemf$(2),_
             itemLen%(3) AS itemf$(3)
    CASE 4
      FIELD #1,itemLen%(1)AS itemf$(1), itemLen%(2) AS itemf$(2),_
             itemLen%(3) AS itemf$(3), itemLen%(4) AS itemf$(4)
    'Continue until there are as many CASE statements as the
    ' maximum number of fields to be allowed in the database
  END SELECT
END SUB
```

The final generalization consists of removing the DATA statements from the program, and placing the information that describes the structure of a database in a sequential file. For a given database there then will be two files: a sequential file that holds the number, meanings, and lengths of the fields; and a random file that contains the actual records of the database. This section uses the conventions of placing the database structure in a file whose name has no extension and placing the database records in a file of the same name but with the extension ".DB."

Suppose that you have created a sequential file with the entries

    field count
    first field name
    first field length
    second field name
    second field length

and so on, in which delimiters separate the entries. This files describes a generic database. The statements in Program Segment 10-12 will open this database.

Program Segment 10-12. A segment that opens a database using a database description file

```
INPUT "Name of database"; dataFile$
OPEN dataFile$ FOR INPUT AS #1
INPUT #1, fieldCount%
DIM itemf$(1 TO fieldCount%), itemLen%(1 TO fieldCount%),_
    itemName$(1 TO fieldCount%)
recordLength% = 0
FOR index% = 1 TO fieldCount%
  INPUT #1, itemName$(index%), itemLen%(index%)
  recordLength% = recordLength% + itemLen%(index%)
NEXT index%
CLOSE #1
OPEN dataFile$ + ".DB" FOR RANDOM AS #1 LEN = recordLength%
CALL SetFields(fieldCount%)
```

After you open a generic database, you need a number of standard operations to maintain the database. Among these are the following:

- Creating a new database
- Appending a record to the end of a database
- Inserting a record in the middle of a database
- Deleting a record
- Listing the records
- Editing a record
- Sorting the records by one of the fields

The following sections discuss each of these operations in detail.

Creating a New Database

No records are required when you create a database — only the names and lengths of the fields. The interactive statements in Program Segment 10-13 request the name of the new database and the names and lengths of the fields and then produce a sequential file that contains the number of fields followed by the field names and lengths.

Program Segment 10-13.   A segment that creates a new database description file

```
CONST maxFields = 4
REDIM fieldName$(1 TO maxFields), fieldLen%(1 TO maxFields)
CLS
INPUT "Name for database (maximum of 8 letters)"; dataFile$
PRINT
PRINT "Enter one field name and field length per line."
PRINT "Separate field name and field length by a comma."
PRINT "End list by entering  ,0"
count% = 0      'Count of number of fields specified
INPUT nom$, length%
DO UNTIL nom$ = "" OR length% = 0
  count% = count% + 1
  fieldName$(count%) = nom$
  fieldLen%(count%) = length%
  IF count% = maxFields THEN EXIT DO
  INPUT nom$, length%
LOOP
OPEN dataFile$ FOR OUTPUT AS #1
WRITE #1, count%
FOR index% = 1 TO count%
  WRITE #1, fieldName$(index%), fieldLen%(index%)
NEXT index%
CLOSE #1
ERASE fieldName$, fieldLen%
```

NOTE   The statements in Program Segment 10-13 do not open the database.

The statements store the number of fields in the variable *count%*. Note the use of the named constant *maxFields*. This constant will appear at the beginning of the master database management program. The value of this constant should be the number appearing in the last CASE statement in the SELECT CASE block of the SetFields procedure of the master program.

Appending a Record to the End of a Database

Adding, or appending, a blank record to the end of a database is one of the simplest tasks of managing a database. First, you must determine the record

Program Segment 10-14.   A segment that appends a blank record to a database

```
lastRecord% = LOF(1) / recordLength%
FOR index% = 1 TO fieldCount%
  LSET itemf$(index%) = ""
NEXT index%
PUT #1, lastRecord% + 1
```

number of the last record currently in the database. You can do this by using the statement

```
lastRecord% = LOF(1) / recordLength%
```

The append process consists of assigning the null string to each field variable, and then placing this blank record after the last record. The statements in Program Segment 10-14 append a blank record to a generic database.

Inserting a Record into the Middle of a Database

Inserting a record is similar to appending a record but requires that you copy all records from a specified point on into the record having the next higher record number. You can accomplish this task by using a FOR loop that GETs records and PUTs them at the next higher record number. Since shifting record *r* overwrites record *r*+1, the FOR loop starts with the last record and steps backwards to the record that occupies the spot where you want to insert a new record. As in the append process, the final action is to PUT a blank record in the specified location. If a database has many records, an insertion near the beginning of the database may require a substantial amount of time to move the necessary records. The statements in Program Segment 10-15 insert a record into a generic database.

Deleting a Record from a Database

One method of deleting a record from a database is to attempt to reverse the process of inserting a record. If you want to delete record *n*%, you might try to use statements such as

```
lastRecord% = LOF(1) / recordLength%
FOR index% = n% + 1 TO lastRecord%
  GET #1, index%
  PUT #1, index% - 1
NEXT index%
```

Program Segment 10-15. A segment that inserts a record into a database

```
INPUT "Record number to insert before", n%
lastRecord% = LOF(1) / recordLength%
FOR index% = lastRecord% TO n% STEP -1
  GET #1, index%
  PUT #1, index% + 1
NEXT index%
FOR index% = 1 TO fieldCount%
  LSET itemf$(index%) = ""
NEXT index%
PUT #1, n%
```

However, these statements have two drawbacks. First, as with inserting, deleting a record near the beginning of a large database will be time-consuming. Second — and equally important from a programming point of view — moving all the records down by one record number does not remove the record with record number *lastRecord%*. In fact, this record now appears twice in the database. A possible solution to this problem is not to delete a record by moving records down, but to copy all records except the one to delete to a temporary file, erase the old database, and rename the temporary file with the name of the original database file. The statements in Program Segment 10-16 deletes record *n%* in this manner.

Notice that Program Segment 10-16 executes a new FIELD statement so that a single variable can reference an entire record. Notice also that, although Program Segment 10-16 assumes that the database is already open, the database will be closed after the segment executes.

Since deleting a record requires the long process of copying the entire file, it is common practice not to delete a record physically whenever you no longer need it, but rather to mark the record in a special way so that a program can ignore it. Later, after you mark many records for deletion, your program can copy the unmarked records to a new random file and erase the original file. This copying process is called packing. Marking records for deletion in anticipation of a later packing operation has the additional advantage that you can "undelete," or recover, a record at any time prior to the packing process.

To allow records to be marked as deleted, you should include an additional single-character field at the beginning of each database record. The database

Program Segment 10-16.   A segment that deletes a single record

```
lastRecord% = LOF(1) / recordLength%
FIELD #1, recordLength% AS file1f$
OPEN "temp" FOR RANDOM AS #2 LEN = recordLength%
FIELD #2, recordLength% AS file2f$
'Copy all records before n%
FOR index% = 1 TO n% - 1
  GET #1, index%
  LSET file2f$ = file1f$
  PUT #2, index%
NEXT index%
'Copy all records after n%
FOR index% = n% + 1 TO lastRecord%
  GET #1, index%
  LSET file2f$ = file1f$
  PUT #2, index% - 1
NEXT index%
CLOSE #1, #2
KILL dataFile$ + ".DB"
NAME "temp" AS dataFile$ + ".DB"
```

management program can produce this status field automatically when creating a database. A generic FIELD statement with the status field will have the form

```
FIELD #1, 1 AS statusf$, itemLen%(1) AS itemf$(1), itemLen%(2)
AS itemf$(2), etc.
```

The deletion process then becomes simply a matter of GETting the specified record, setting *statusf$* to some special value — perhaps an asterisk (*) — and then PUTting the record back. The statements in Program Segment 10-17 toggle the status field of a record back and forth between removed and restored.

The packing process consists of copying to another file all records that are not marked by an asterisk in their status field. The statements in Program Segment 10-18 will do the job. Note that, in the segment, *recordLength%* now includes the one-character length of *statusf$*. After the execution of this segment, the database will be closed.

Program Segment 10-17. A segment that marks records for removal

```
INPUT "Record Number to be removed/restored", n%
GET #1, n%
IF statusf$ = "*" THEN
    LSET statusf$ = " "
    PRINT "Record Restored"
  ELSE
    LSET statusf$ = "*"
    PRINT "Record Removed"
END IF
PUT #1, n%
```

Listing the Records of a Database

The volume of data listed from a database can vary from the entire database to only the records whose record numbers lie in a certain range. Also, the listings can consist of entire records or selected fields.

The statements in Program Segment 10-19 display the record number and the contents of each field for every record in a database. After displaying each

Program Segment 10-18. A segment that packs a database

```
lastRecord% = LOF(1) / recordLength%
FIELD #1, 1 AS statusf$, recordLength% - 1 AS file1f$
OPEN "temp" FOR RANDOM AS 2 LEN = recordLength%
FIELD #2, recordLength% AS file2f$
tempIndex% = 1
FOR index% = 1 TO lastRecord%
  GET #1, index%
  IF statusf$ = " " THEN
    LSET file2f$ = statusf$ + file1f$
    PUT #2, tempIndex%
    tempIndex% = tempIndex% + 1
  END IF
NEXT index%
CLOSE #1, #2
KILL dataFile$ + ".DB"
NAME "temp" AS dataFile$ + ".DB"
```

Program Segment 10-19. A segment that lists records from a database

```
lastRecord% = LOF(1) / recordLength%
FOR recordNumber% = 1 TO lastRecord%
  GET #1, recordNumber%
  PRINT USING "! #####"; statusf$, recordNumber%;
  FOR index% = 1 TO fieldCount%
    PRINT " "; itemf$(index%);
  NEXT index%
  PRINT
  IF (recordNumber% MOD 15=0)OR(recordNumber%=lastRecord%) THEN
      PRINT
      PRINT "Press any key to continue";
      a$ = INPUT$(1)
      PRINT
  END IF
NEXT recordNumber%
```

15th record, the program pauses to let the user examine the records. After the user presses a key, the program displays the next fifteen records.

Editing a Record

You can program the process of editing a record in a database in many ways. The simplest approach, which is illustrated by Program Segment 10-20, displays the field name and current value of each field of a specified record. After displaying the data for a specific field, the segment prompts the user for a replacement value. If the user presses <Enter> without giving a new value, the old value is retained.

More sophisticated editing routines display all of the field names and current values at one time, and allow you to the cursor to any of the old values. Then you can modify any value as if you were using a word processor in overwrite mode.

Sorting the Records by One Field

The technique for sorting a database is similar to the one used to sort a sequential file in Chapter 7. If your computer had sufficient memory available, you might read the entire database into *fieldCount*%+1 parallel arrays and

Program Segment 10-20. A segment that edits a database

```
INPUT "Record to be edited", n%
GET #1, n%
FOR index% = 1 TO fieldCount%
  PRINT itemName$(index%)
  PRINT itemf$(index%)
  INPUT "New Value", newItem$
  IF newItem$ <> "" THEN LSET itemf$(index%) = newItem$
NEXT index%
PUT #1, n%
```

then sort these arrays as described in Chapter 7. However, for sorts on a single field of a database, there is a faster and more memory-efficient approach that requires only two parallel arrays. You assign the values from the sort field of successive records to successive elements of the first array. You place the numbers 1 through *lastRecord%* in order into the second array. Therefore, each element of the second array holds the record number of the corresponding element of the first array. You then sort these parallel arrays based on the values in the first array. Finally, you copy the entire database to a temporary file in the order indicated by the now-shuffled record numbers held in the second array. You complete the sort by erasing the old database file and renaming the temporary file. This technique, known as sorting with pointers, is illustrated in Program Segment 10-21. After the segment sorts a database on a certain field, a binary search can be used to locate efficiently the record that contains a specified value in that field.

A Master Generic Database Management Program

The discussions above have covered many aspects of writing a program to create and manage a general-purpose database. You can easily add other features once you understand these fundamental tasks. The following master program employs the techniques presented earlier and embellishes them with data-validation statements.

As indicated by the named constant at the top of the program, you may specify a maximum of 10 fields in a database. (You can increase this number by adding more CASEs in the procedure SetFields.) Also, the program allows you to use a maximum of 15 characters in naming a field.

Program Segment 10-21. Sorting a database

```
lastRecord% = LOF(1) / recordLength%
INPUT "Number of field on which sort is to be made",
fieldNumber%
DIM recNum%(1 TO lastRecord%), value$(1 TO lastRecord%)
FOR index% = 1 TO lastRecord%
  GET #1, index%
  recNum%(index%) = index%
  value$(index%) = itemf$(fieldNumber%)
NEXT index%
CALL SortArrays(recNum%(), value$())
FIELD #1, 1 AS statusf$, recordLength% - 1 AS file1f$
OPEN "temp" FOR RANDOM AS #2 LEN = recordLength%
FIELD #2, recordLength% AS file2f$
FOR index% = 1 TO lastRecord%
  GET #1, recNum%(index%)
  LSET file2f$ = statusf$ + file1f$
  PUT #2, index%
NEXT index%
CLOSE #1, #2
KILL dataFile$ + ".DB"
NAME "temp" AS dataFile$ + ".DB"
```

The program displays a menu of supported operations. The user executes an operation by pressing the key enclosed in angle brackets, <>. All but two of the operations in the main menu were discussed previously. The two new operations are displaying the structure of a database — that is, field names and lengths — and displaying a listing of database files — that is, file names that end in .DB).

Many of the procedures share the variables *dataFile$*, *fieldCount%*, *itemf$( )*, *itemLen%( )*, *itemName$( )*, *statusf$*, *recordLength%*, and *lastRecord%*. These variables hold the following information about the database that is currently open:

- The *dataFile$* variable holds the name of the database. If *dataFile$* is the null string, then no database is open.

- The *fieldCount%* variable holds the number of fields in each record, and will be between 1 and *maxFields*.

- The array *itemf$*( ) holds the field variables.

- The array *itemLen %*( ) holds the length of each field.

- The array *itemName$*( ) holds the names of each field. These names must contain no more than *maxName* characters.

- The *statusf$* variable is the first field of each record. The character in this field is either a space or an asterisk. When the character is an asterisk, the current record is marked for deletion.

- The *recordLength %* variable is the length of the records in the database. The program calculates the length by adding up the values of *itemLen %*( ) and then adding 1 to account for *statusf$*.

- The *lastRecord %* variable is the record number of the last record in the database. Initially, the program computes *lastRecord %* by using the formula LOF(1) / *recordLength %*. At other times, such as during the append and insert procedures, the program computes a new value for *lastRecord %* by adding 1 to the old value.

The program could have listed these variables as procedure parameters and passed them as needed to the various procedures. This is generally the preferred programming technique. However, since these variables appear throughout the entire program, they are given global status and they are SHAREd where needed.

Program 10-22 illustrates many aspects of top-down design, data validation, and output formatting. An examination of the various procedures reveals a wide variety of programming techniques, not all of which have been discussed in detail.

There. We've gone from simple calculations with integer variables all the way to a full-scale database management program. If you've followed along carefully, you have not only a good grasp of QBasic, but a firm grounding in modern programming techniques and applications. From here, the sky's the limit.

Program 10-22. A master database management program

```
REM A general database management system         [10-22]
REDIM itemlen%(1)
REDIM itemf$(1), itemName$(1)
CONST true = -1, false = 0, maxName = 15, maxFields = 10
dataFile$ = ""
DO
  CALL DisplayMenu
  action$ = UCASE$(INPUT$(1))
  PRINT
  SELECT CASE action$
    CASE "A": CALL AppendRecord
    CASE "C": CALL CreateDatabase
    CASE "D": CALL DisplayStructure
    CASE "E": CALL GetRecordNumber("Record Number", n%)
              CALL EditRecord(n%)
    CASE "F": CALL DisplayDatabaseFiles
    CASE "I": CALL InsertRecord
    CASE "L": CALL ListRecords
    CASE "O": CALL GetDatabaseName
              CALL OpenDatabase
    CASE "P": CALL PackDatabase
    CASE "R": CALL RemoveOrRestoreRecord(n%)
    CASE "S": CALL SortDatabase
    CASE ELSE
  END SELECT
LOOP UNTIL action$ = "Q"
CLS
IF dataFile$ <> "" THEN CALL CloseDatabase
PRINT "Database closed"
END
noFiles:
  PRINT "No database files in "; dd$
  RESUME NEXT

SUB AppendRecord
  SHARED fieldCount%, itemf$(), statusf$, lastRecord%
  IF DatabaseIsOpen THEN
    lastRecord% = lastRecord% + 1
    LSET statusf$ = " "
    FOR index% = 1 TO fieldCount%
      LSET itemf$(index%) = ""
    NEXT index%
    PUT #1, lastRecord%
    CALL EditRecord(lastRecord%)
  END IF
END SUB
```

Program 10-22. *(continued)*

```
SUB CloseDatabase
  SHARED dataFile$, itemf$(), itemlen%(), itemName$()
  CLOSE #1
  ERASE itemf$, itemlen%, itemName$
  dataFile$ = ""
END SUB

SUB CreateDatabase
  SHARED dataFile$
  DIM fieldName$(1 TO maxFields), fieldLen%(1 TO maxFields)
  'If another database is open, close it before proceeding
  IF dataFile$ <> "" THEN CALL CloseDatabase
  CLS
  INPUT "Name for database (maximum of 8 letters)"; dataFile$
  IF dataFile$ = "" THEN EXIT SUB
  dataFile$ = LEFT$(dataFile$, 8)
  count% = 0        'Count of number of fields specified
  PRINT
  PRINT "Enter one field name and field length per line."
  PRINT "Separate field name and field length by a comma."
  PRINT "Field name limited to"; maxName; "characters. "
  PRINT "A Maximum of"; maxFields; "fields may be specified."
  PRINT
  PRINT "> ";
  LINE INPUT info$
  DO UNTIL (info$ = "") OR (count% = maxFields)
    comma = INSTR(info$, ",")
    IF comma <> 0 THEN
        count% = count% + 1
        fieldName$(count%)=LEFT$(LEFT$(info$,comma-1),maxName)
        fieldLen%(count%)=VAL(RIGHT$(info$,LEN(info$)-comma))
        IF fieldLen%(count%) = 0 THEN count% = count% - 1
      ELSE
        PRINT "Format error. Use name,length"
    END IF
    PRINT "> ";
    LINE INPUT info$
  LOOP

  IF count% > 0 THEN
      OPEN dataFile$ FOR OUTPUT AS #1
      WRITE #1, count%
      FOR index% = 1 TO count%
        WRITE #1, fieldName$(index%), fieldLen%(index%)
      NEXT index%
      CLOSE #1
```

(continued)

Program 10-22.   *(continued)*

```
        CALL OpenDatabase
      ELSE
        dataFile$ = ""
    END IF
END SUB

FUNCTION DatabaseIsOpen
  SHARED dataFile$
  IF dataFile$ = "" THEN
    PRINT "No database currently open"
    CALL GetDatabaseName
    CALL OpenDatabase
  END IF
  IF dataFile$ = "" THEN
      DatabaseIsOpen = false
    ELSE
      DatabaseIsOpen = true
  END IF
END FUNCTION

SUB DisplayDatabaseFiles
  SHARED dd$
  CLS
  INPUT "Drive/Directory to display"; dd$
  ch$ = RIGHT$(dd$, 1)
  IF (ch$<>"")AND(ch$ <> ":")AND(ch$ <> "\") THEN dd$ = dd$ + "\"
  dd$ = dd$ + "*.DB"
  ON ERROR GOTO noFiles
  PRINT
  FILES dd$
  PRINT
  PRINT "Press any key to continue"
  ON ERROR GOTO 0
  a$ = INPUT$(1)
END SUB

SUB DisplayFieldTitles
  SHARED fieldCount%, itemlen%(), itemName$()
  CLS
  PRINT "*  Rec#";
  FOR index% = 1 TO fieldCount%
    il% = itemlen%(index%)
    PRINT " "; LEFT$(itemName$(index%) + SPACE$(il%), il%);
  NEXT index%
```

Program 10-22. *(continued)*

```
    PRINT
    PRINT
END SUB

SUB DisplayMenu
  CLS
  PRINT "<A>ppend a record to database"
  PRINT "<C>reate a database"
  PRINT "<D>isplay structure of database"
  PRINT "<E>dit a specified record"
  PRINT "display list of database <F>iles"
  PRINT "<I>nsert blank record before specified record"
  PRINT "<L>ist records"
  PRINT "<O>pen an existing database"
  PRINT "<P>ack database"
  PRINT "<Q>uit"
  PRINT "<R>emove/recover a record"
  PRINT "<S>ort database on a given field"
  PRINT
  PRINT "Action?";
END SUB

SUB DisplayRecordForEdit (n%)
  SHARED fieldCount%, itemf$(), itemName$(), statusf$
  CLS
  PRINT "Record"; n%;
  IF statusf$ = "*" THEN PRINT "    REMOVED";
  PRINT
  FOR index% = 1 TO fieldCount%
    PRINT itemName$(index%);TAB(maxName+1);":";itemf$(index%)
    PRINT
  NEXT index%
END SUB

SUB DisplayStructure
  SHARED fieldCount%, itemlen%(), itemName$()
  IF DatabaseIsOpen THEN
    CLS
    PRINT "Field Name"; TAB(maxName + 2); "Field Length"
    FOR index% = 1 TO fieldCount%
      PRINT itemName$(index%); TAB(maxName+2); itemlen%(index%)
    NEXT index%
    PRINT
    PRINT "Press any key to continue."
```

(continued)

Program 10-22. *(continued)*

```
      a$ = INPUT$(1)
    END IF
END SUB

SUB EditRecord (n%)
  SHARED fieldCount%, itemf$()
  IF n% = 0 THEN EXIT SUB
  GET #1, n%
  CALL DisplayRecordForEdit(n%)
  FOR index% = 1 TO fieldCount%
    LOCATE 2 * index% + 1, maxName - 9, 1
    LINE INPUT "New value> ", newItem$
    IF newItem$ <> "" THEN LSET itemf$(index%) = newItem$
  NEXT index%
  PUT #1, n%
END SUB

SUB GetDatabaseName
  SHARED dataFile$
  IF dataFile$ <> "" THEN CALL CloseDatabase
  PRINT
  INPUT "Database to open"; dataFile$
END SUB

SUB GetFieldNumber (n%)
  SHARED fieldCount%, itemName$()
  CLS
  PRINT "Field   Field"
  PRINT "Number  Name"
  PRINT "------  ----------------"
  FOR index% = 1 TO fieldCount%
    PRINT USING " ##     &"; index%, itemName$(index%)
  NEXT index%
  PRINT
  DO
    INPUT "Number of field on which to perform sort"; n%
  LOOP UNTIL (n% >= 0) AND (n% <= fieldCount%)
END SUB

SUB GetRecordNumber (message$, n%)
  SHARED lastRecord%
  n% = 0
  IF DatabaseIsOpen AND (LastRecord% > 0) THEN
    PRINT
```

Program 10-22. *(continued)*

```
      DO
        PRINT message$;
        INPUT n%
      LOOP UNTIL (n% >= 0) AND (n% <= lastRecord%)
    END IF
END SUB

SUB InsertRecord
  SHARED fieldCount%, itemf$(), statusf$, lastRecord%
  IF DatabaseIsOpen THEN
    CALL GetRecordNumber("Record Number to insert before", n%)
    IF n% <> 0 THEN
      FOR index% = lastRecord% TO n% STEP -1
        GET #1, index%
        PUT #1, index% + 1
      NEXT index%
      lastRecord% = lastRecord% + 1
      LSET statusf$ = " "
      FOR index% = 1 TO fieldCount%
        LSET itemf$(index%) = ""
      NEXT index%
      PUT #1, n%
      CALL EditRecord(n%)
    END IF
  END IF
END SUB

SUB ListRecords   '15 records at a time
  SHARED fieldCount%, itemf$(), statusf$, lastRecord%
  IF DatabaseIsOpen THEN
    CALL GetRecordNumber("Record at which to start", sr%)
    IF sr%=0 THEN EXIT SUB
    CALL DisplayFieldTitles
    FOR recNum% = sr% TO lastRecord%
      GET #1, recNum%
      PRINT USING "! #####"; statusf$, recNum%;
      FOR index% = 1 TO fieldCount%
        PRINT " "; itemf$(index%);
      NEXT index%
      PRINT
      IF(recNum% MOD 15=0) OR (recNum%=lastRecord%) THEN
        PRINT
        PRINT "Press Q to quit, or any key to continue";
```

(continued)

Program 10-22.   *(continued)*

```
            a$ = UCASE$(INPUT$(1))
            IF A$="Q" THEN EXIT SUB
            IF recNum%<>lastRecord& THEN CALL DisplayFieldTitles
            PRINT
          END IF
        NEXT recNum%
    END IF
END SUB

SUB OpenAs2 (fileName$)
  SHARED recordLength%
  'any old version of fileName$ must be erased to insure that
  'the temporary file opened below is empty. However, KILLing a
  'file that doesn't exists is an error. So, before KILLing
  'fileName$, make sure that it exists by creating it.
  OPEN fileName$ FOR OUTPUT AS 2
  CLOSE 2
  KILL fileName$
  OPEN fileName$ FOR RANDOM AS 2 LEN = recordLength%
END SUB

SUB OpenDatabase
  SHARED dataFile$, fieldCount%, itemf$(), itemlen%(), itemName$()
  SHARED recordLength%, lastRecord%
  IF dataFile$ <> "" THEN
    OPEN dataFile$ FOR INPUT AS #1
    INPUT #1, fieldCount%
    REDIM itemf$(1 TO fieldCount%)
    REDIM itemlen%(1 TO fieldCount%)
    REDIM itemName$(1 TO fieldCount%)
    FOR index% = 1 TO fieldCount%
      INPUT #1, itemName$(index%), itemlen%(index%)
    NEXT index%
    CLOSE #1
    recordLength% = 1
    FOR index% = 1 TO fieldCount%
      recordLength% = recordLength% + itemlen%(index%)
    NEXT index%
    OPEN dataFile$ + ".DB" FOR RANDOM AS #1 LEN = recordLength%
    CALL SetFields
    lastRecord% = LOF(1) / recordLength%
  END IF
END SUB
```

Program 10-22. *(continued)*

```
SUB PackDatabase
   SHARED dataFile$, statusf$, recordLength%, lastRecord%
   IF DatabaseIsOpen THEN
     PRINT
     PRINT "Packing " + dataFile$ + ".DB"
     FIELD #1, 1 AS statusf$, recordLength% - 1 AS file1f$
     CALL OpenAs2("zzzzzzzz.tmp")
     FIELD #2, recordLength% AS file2f$
     zindex% = 1
     FOR rec% = 1 TO lastRecord%
       GET #1, rec%
       IF statusf$ = " " THEN
         LSET file2f$ = statusf$ + file1f$
         PUT #2, zindex%
         zindex% = zindex% + 1
       END IF
     NEXT rec%
     holdName$ = dataFile$
     CLOSE #2
     CALL CloseDatabase
     KILL holdName$ + ".DB"
     NAME "zzzzzzzz.tmp" AS holdName$ + ".DB"
     dataFile$ = holdName$
     CALL OpenDatabase
   END IF
END SUB


SUB RemoveOrRestoreRecord (n%)
   SHARED statusf$
   mesage$ = "Record number to be removed/restored"
   CALL GetRecordNumber(Message$, n%)
   IF n% <> 0 THEN
     GET #1, n%
     IF statusf$ = "*" THEN
         LSET statusf$ = " "
         PRINT "Record Restored"
       ELSE
         LSET statusf$ = "*"
         PRINT "Record Removed"
     END IF
     PUT #1, n%
     SLEEP 1
   END IF
END SUB
```

(continued)

Program 10-22.   *(continued)*

```
SUB SetFields
  SHARED fieldCount%, itemf$(), itemlen%(), statusf$
  SELECT CASE fieldCount%
    CASE 1: FIELD #1, 1 AS statusf$, itemlen%(1) AS itemf$(1)
    CASE 2: FIELD #1, 1 AS statusf$, itemlen%(1) AS itemf$(1), _
            itemlen%(2) AS itemf$(2)
    CASE 3: FIELD #1, 1 AS statusf$, itemlen%(1) AS itemf$(1), _
            itemlen%(2) AS itemf$(2), itemlen%(3) AS itemf$(3)
    CASE 4: FIELD #1, 1 AS statusf$, itemlen%(1) AS itemf$(1), _
            itemlen%(2) AS itemf$(2), itemlen%(3) AS itemf$(3), _
            itemlen%(4) AS itemf$(4)
    CASE 5: FIELD #1, 1 AS statusf$, itemlen%(1) AS itemf$(1), _
            itemlen%(2) AS itemf$(2), itemlen%(3) AS itemf$(3), _
            itemlen%(4) AS itemf$(4), itemlen%(5) AS itemf$(5)
    CASE 6: FIELD #1, 1 AS statusf$, itemlen%(1) AS itemf$(1), _
            itemlen%(2) AS itemf$(2), itemlen%(3) AS itemf$(3), _
            itemlen%(4) AS itemf$(4), itemlen%(5) AS itemf$(5), _
            itemlen%(6) AS itemf$(6)
    CASE 7: FIELD #1, 1 AS statusf$, itemlen%(1) AS itemf$(1), _
            itemlen%(2) AS itemf$(2), itemlen%(3) AS itemf$(3), _
            itemlen%(4) AS itemf$(4), itemlen%(5) AS itemf$(5), _
            itemlen%(6) AS itemf$(6), itemlen%(7) AS itemf$(7)
    CASE 8: FIELD #1, 1 AS statusf$, itemlen%(1) AS itemf$(1), _
            itemlen%(2) AS itemf$(2), itemlen%(3) AS itemf$(3), _
            itemlen%(4) AS itemf$(4), itemlen%(5) AS itemf$(5), _
            itemlen%(6) AS itemf$(6), itemlen%(7) AS itemf$(7), _
            itemlen%(8) AS itemf$(8)
    CASE 9: FIELD #1, 1 AS statusf$, itemlen%(1) AS itemf$(1), _
            itemlen%(2) AS itemf$(2), itemlen%(3) AS itemf$(3), _
            itemlen%(4) AS itemf$(4), itemlen%(5) AS itemf$(5), _
            itemlen%(6) AS itemf$(6), itemlen%(7) AS itemf$(7), _
            itemlen%(8) AS itemf$(8), itemlen%(9) AS itemf$(9)
    CASE 10:FIELD #1, 1 AS statusf$, itemlen%(1) AS itemf$(1), _
            itemlen%(2) AS itemf$(2), itemlen%(3) AS itemf$(3), _
            itemlen%(4) AS itemf$(4), itemlen%(5) AS itemf$(5), _
            itemlen%(6) AS itemf$(6), itemlen%(7) AS itemf$(7), _
            itemlen%(8) AS itemf$(8), itemlen%(9) AS itemf$(9), _
            itemlen%(10) AS itemf$(10)
  END SELECT
END SUB

SUB SortArrays(recNum%(), value$()) 'bubble sort implementation
  size% = UBOUND(recNum%, 1)
```

Program 10-22. *(continued)*

```
    FOR index1% = 1 TO size%
      exchanged% = false
      FOR index2% = 1 TO size% - index1%
        IF value$(index2%) > value$(index2% + 1) THEN
           'exchange index2% with index2%+1 in both arrays
           temp$ = value$(index2%)
           value$(index2%) = value$(index2% + 1)
           value$(index2% + 1) = temp$
           temp% = recNum%(index2%)
           recNum%(index2%) = recNum%(index2% + 1)
           recNum%(index2% + 1) = temp%
           exchanged% = true
        END IF
      NEXT index2%
      IF NOT exchanged% THEN EXIT SUB
    NEXT index1%
END SUB

SUB SortDatabase
  SHARED dataFile$, itemf$(), itemName$()
  SHARED statusf$, recordLength%, lastRecord%
  IF DatabaseIsOpen AND (lastRecord% >1) THEN
    CALL GetFieldNumber(fieldNumber%)
    IF fieldNumber% = 0 THEN EXIT SUB
    PRINT
    PRINT "Sorting "; dataFile$;
    PRINT ".DB on ";itemName$(fieldNumber%)
    DIM recNum%(1 TO lastRecord%), value$(1 TO lastRecord%)
    FOR index% = 1 TO lastRecord%
      GET #1, index%
      recNum%(index%) = index%
      value$(index%) = itemf$(fieldNumber%)
    NEXT index%
    CALL SortArrays(recNum%(), value$())
    FIELD #1, 1 AS statusf$, recordLength% - 1 AS file1f$
    CALL OpenAs2("zzzzzzzz.tmp")
    FIELD #2, recordLength% AS file2f$
    FOR index% = 1 TO lastRecord%
      GET #1, recNum%(index%)
      LSET file2f$ = statusf$ + file1f$
      PUT #2, index%
    NEXT index%
    holdName$ = dataFile$
    CLOSE #2
```

(continued)

Program 10-22. *(continued)*

```
       CALL CloseDatabase
       KILL holdName$ + ".DB"
       NAME "zzzzzzzz.tmp" AS holdName$ + ".DB"
       dataFile$ = holdName$
       CALL OpenDatabase
    END IF
END SUB
```

ASCII Table

Dec	Char	Dec	Char	Dec	Char
00	(null)	33	!	66	B
01	☺	34	"	67	C
02	●	35	#	68	D
03	♥	36	$	69	E
04	♦	37	%	70	F
05	♣	38	&	71	G
06	◄	39	'	72	H
07	(beep) •	40	(	73	I
08	▫ ○	41	)	74	J
09	(tab)	42	*	75	K
10	(line feed)	43	+	76	L
11	(home) ♂	44	,	77	M
12	(form feed) ♀	45	-	78	N
13	(carriage return) ♪	46	.	79	O
14	♫	47	/	80	P
15	☼	48	0	81	Q
16	▲	49	1	82	R
17	▼	50	2	83	S
18	↕	51	3	84	T
19	‼	52	4	85	U
20	¶	53	5	86	V
21	§	54	6	87	W
22	▬	55	7	88	X
23	↨	56	8	89	Y
24	↑	57	9	90	Z
25	↓	58	:	91	[
26	→	59	;	92	\
27	(cursor right) └	60	<	93	]
28	(cursor left) ↕	61	=	94	^
29	(cursor up) ◄	62	>	95	_
30	(cursor down) ►	63	?	96	`
31		64	@	97	a
32	(space)	65	A	98	b

Code	Char	Code	Char	Code	Char	Code	Char	Code	Char
99	c	132	ä	165	Ñ	198	╞	231	τ
100	d	133	à	166	ª	199	╟	232	Φ
101	e	134	å	167	º	200	╚	233	Θ
102	f	135	ç	168	¿	201	╔	234	Ω
103	g	136	ê	169	⌐	202	╩	235	δ
104	h	137	ë	170	¬	203	╦	236	∞
105	i	138	è	171	½	204	╠	237	φ
106	j	139	ï	172	¼	205	═	238	ε
107	k	140	î	173	¡	206	╬	239	∩
108	l	141	ì	174	«	207	╧	240	≡
109	m	142	Ä	175	»	208	╨	241	±
110	n	143	Å	176	░	209	╤	242	≥
111	o	144	É	177	▒	210	╥	243	≤
112	p	145	æ	178	▓	211	╙	244	⌠
113	q	146	Æ	179	│	212	╘	245	⌡
114	r	147	ô	180	┤	213	╒	246	÷
115	s	148	ö	181	╡	214	╓	247	≈
116	t	149	ò	182	╢	215	╫	248	°
117	u	150	û	183	╖	216	╪	249	∙
118	v	151	ù	184	╕	217	┘	250	·
119	w	152	ÿ	185	╣	218	┌	251	√
120	x	153	Ö	186	║	219	█	252	ⁿ
121	y	154	Ü	187	╗	220	▄	253	²
122	z	155	¢	188	╝	221	▌	254	■
123	{	156	£	189	╜	222	▐	255	(blank 'FF')
124	|	157	¥	190	╛	223	▀		
125	}	158	₧	191	┐	224	α		
126	~	159	ƒ	192	└	225	β		
127	⌂	160	á	193	┴	226	Γ		
128	Ç	161	í	194	┬	227	π		
129	ü	162	ó	195	├	228	Σ		
130	é	163	ú	196	─	229	σ		
131	â	164	ñ	197	┼	230	µ		

Built-In Functions

Note: *x* denotes values that typically have a fractional part. Values denoted by *n* and *m* are whole numbers, though values with fractional parts may be given and will be rounded automatically to whole numbers.

Array Functions

LBOUND(*arrayName*(*n*))	The smallest value allowed for the *n*th subscript.
UBOUND(*arrayName*(*n*))	The largest value allowed for the *n*th subscript.

Conversion Functions

CDBL(*x*)	The double-precision number determined by *x*.
CINT(*x*)	The integer determined by *x*.
CLNG(*x*)	The long integer determined by *x*.
CSNG(*x*)	The single-precision number determined by *x*.
CVD(*a$*)	The double-precision number encoded as *a$*.
CVI(*a$*)	The integer encoded as *a$*.
CVL(*a$*)	The long integer encoded as *a$*.
CVS(*a$*)	The single-precision number encoded as *a$*.
CVDMBF(*a$*)	The double-precision number encoded as *a$* by Microsoft Standard BASIC or a version of QuickBASIC preceding 4.0.

CVSMBF(*a$*)	The single-precision number encoded as *a$* by Microsoft Standard BASIC or a version of QuickBASIC preceding 4.0.
HEX$(*n*)	The string consisting of the hexadecimal representation of *n*.
MKD$(*x*)	The string encoding of the double-precision number *x*.
MKI$(*n*)	The string encoding of the integer *n*.
MKL$(*n*)	The string encoding of the long integer *n*.
MKS$(*x*)	The string encoding of the single-precision number *x*.
MKDMBF$(*x*)	The Microsoft Standard BASIC (and QuickBASIC versions preceding 4.0) string encoding of the double-precision number *x*.
MKSMBF$(*x*)	The Microsoft Standard BASIC (and QuickBASIC versions preceding 4.0) string encoding of the single-precision number *x*.
OCT$(*n*)	The string consisting of the octal representation of *n*.
STR$(*x*)	The string consisting of the decimal representation of *x*.
VAL(*a$*)	The numeric value of *a$*, where *a$* can be interpreted as a number.

Error-Control Functions

ERDEV	The error number from the device responsible for an error.
ERDEV$	The name of the device responsible for an error.
ERR	The error number of a run-time error.
ERL	The current or most recent line number when run-time error occurred.

File Functions

EOF(*n*)	-1 if the end of file *n* has been reached, 0 otherwise.
LOC(*n*)	Sequential file *n*: The number of 128-character blocks read or written. Random-access file *n*: The number of the current record. Binary file *n*: The number of bytes from the beginning of the file.
LOF(*n*)	The number of characters in file *n*.

Graphics Functions

PMAP(x, n)	The physical ($n = 0$) or natural ($n = 2$) coordinate for x.
PMAP(y, n)	The physical ($n = 1$) or natural ($n = 3$) coordinate for y.
POINT(x, y)	The color jar number of the point with coordinates (x,y).
POINT(n)	The "last point referenced" coordinate indicated by n.

Input Functions

INKEY$	The character(s), if any, waiting in the keyboard buffer.

Mathematical Functions

ABS(x)	The absolute value of x.
ATN(x)	The arctangent of the radian angle x.
COS(x)	The cosine of the angle of x radians.
EXP(x)	The natural log base e (2.71828...) raised to the x power: e^x
FIX(x)	The whole number obtained by discarding the decimal part of x.
INT(x)	The greatest whole number less than or equal to x.
LOG(x)	The natural logarithm of x.
RND	A pseudo-randomly selected number from 0 to 1, not including 1.
SIN(x)	The sine of the angle of x radians.
SGN(x)	The sign of x: +1 if $x > 0$, 0 if $x = 0$, or -1 if $x < 0$.
SQR(x)	The square root of x.
TAN(x)	The tangent of the angle of x radians.

Print Functions

LPOS(1)	The current "cursor position" in the print buffer.
SPC(n)	Print n spaces.
TAB(n)	Move to screen or print position n on the current line

Screen Functions

CSRLIN	The row of the screen that currently contains the cursor.
POS	The column number of the current text position of the cursor.

SCREEN(*r*,*c*)	The ASCII value of the character in row *r* column *c* of the screen.
SCREEN(*r*,*c*,1)	The color jar of the character at row *r* column *c* of the screen.

String Analysis/Manipulation Functions

ASC(*a$*)	The ASCII value of the first character of the string *a$*.
CHR$(*n*)	The character whose ASCII value is *n*.
INSTR(*a$*,*b$*)	The first position in *a$* at which the string *b$* occurs.
INSTR(*n*,*a$*,*b$*)	The first position at or after the *n*th character of *a$* at which the string *b$* occurs.
LCASE$(*a$*)	The string *a$* with all uppercase letters converted to lowercase.
LEFT$(*a$*,*n*)	The string consisting of the leftmost *n* characters of *a$*.
LEN(*a$*)	The number of characters (or length) in the string *a$*.
LTRIM$(*a$*)	The string *a$* with all leading spaces removed.
MID$(*a$*,*m*)	The string consisting of the characters of *a$* starting with character *m*.
MID$(*a$*,*m*,*n*)	The string consisting of the *n* characters of *a$* starting with character *m*.
RIGHT$(*a$*,*n*)	The string consisting of the rightmost *n* characters of *a$*.
RTRIM$(*a$*)	The string *a$* with all trailing spaces removed.
SPACE$(*n*)	The string consisting of *n* spaces.
STRING$(*n*,*a$*)	The string consisting of the first character of *a$* repeated *n* times.
STRING$(*n*,*m*)	The string consisting of the character with ASCII value *m* repeated *n* times.
UCASE$(*a$*)	The string *a$* with all lowercase letters converted to uppercase.

System-related Functions

ENVIRON$(*a$*)	The right side of the environment table entry named by *a$*.
ENVIRON$(*n*)	The *n*th equation in the environment table.
FRE("")	The number of memory locations available for storing new string data.

FRE(-1)	The number of memory locations available for new numeric arrays.
FRE(-2)	The smallest stack size that has occurred during the execution of the program.
INP(*n*)	The value of the byte read from port *n*.
IOCTL$(*n*)	The control string returned upon opening a device driver as *n*.
PEEK(*n*)	The value of the byte at offset *n* in the current memory segment.
SADD(*a$*)	The offset in the default data segment of the first byte of *a$*.
SETMEM(*n*)	The size of far memory after changing its size by *n*.
VARPTR(*var*)	The offset in VARSEG(*var*) of the value or descriptor for *var*.
VARSEG(*var*)	The memory segment containing the value or descriptor for *var*.
VARPTR$(*var*)	The five character string identifying *var*'s type and location.

Time Functions

DATE$	The current date in the form "mm-dd-yyyy."
TIME$	The current time expressed as a string of the form "hh:mm:ss."
TIMER	The number of seconds elapsed since midnight.

Miscellaneous Functions

PEN(*n*)	The light pen status indicated by *n*.
PLAY(0)	The number of notes remaining in the Music Background buffer.
STICK(*n*)	The joystick coordinate indicated by *n*.
STRIG(*n*)	The joystick button status indicated by *n*.

Converting Standard BASIC Programs to QBasic

Statements That Must Be Removed

Unsupported Statements

The following Standard BASIC statements are not supported in QBasic:

```
AUTO   RENUM
DELETE  EDIT  LIST  LLIST  LOAD  MERGE  NEW  SAVE
CONT
DEF USR   USR   MOTOR
```

The first three lines of commands are principally executed in "direct" mode (also known as "immediate" or "nonprogram" mode). The statements in the first line affect line numbers, which are optional and not recommended in QBasic. The commands in line 2 are easily accomplished from the Files menu or with the Editor.

When debugging a Standard BASIC program, the program can be stopped at some point and then continued with CONT from that point, after the values of variables have been examined in direct mode. After a QBasic program has been stopped it can be continued by pressing <F5>.

CALL, DEF USR, and USR are used in Standard BASIC to access a machine language program. These statements are not supported by QBasic. QBasic's CALL statement is used to access QBasic subprograms.

Certain computers (not including the IBM PC XT, PC AT, or PS/2) contain a cassette connector to which a cassette player can be attached. If so, the MOTOR statement can be used in Standard BASIC turn the cassette motor on and off. This feature is rarely used in Standard BASIC programs.

The following statements from Standard BASIC 2.1 that are valid only for the IBM PCjr are not supported in QBasic: PCOPY, NOISE, SOUND ON, SOUND OFF, and TERM. Also, in QBasic, CGA screen modes 3 through 6 are not available, the SOUND statement has no "voice" parameter, and the CLEAR statement has no "video memory" parameter.

Unsupported Variations of Supported Statements

```
CHAIN filespec,, ALL        Instead, list all of the variables in a
                            COMMON statement.

CHAIN MERGE filespec

CLEAR, n

VARPTR(#filenum)
```

Statements That Must Be Converted

In Standard BASIC, the CALL statement is used only to call a machine language subroutine. A statement of the form

```
CALL numvar (var1, var2, ...)
```

must be converted to the QBasic statement

```
CALL ABSOLUTE (var1, var2, ..., numvar)
```

In Standard BASIC, the statement

```
CHAIN filespec
```

can pass control to any program.

In Standard BASIC, when the statement

```
COMMON var1, var2, ...
```

appears in a program that chains to another program, the specified variables will be passed to the chained-to program. In QBasic, this COMMON statement must also be present in the program being chained to.

In Standard BASIC, the FRE function always returns the number of bytes in memory that are not being used. In QBasic, several different pieces of information can be returned depending on the type and value of the argument following FRE.

Other Concerns

There are many reserved words in QBasic that are not reserved words in Standard BASIC. Some of the ones that are most likely to occur as variable names in Standard BASIC programs are ABSOLUTE, AS, BINARY, CASE, CONST, DECLARE, DO, DOUBLE, EXIT, FREEFILE, FUNCTION, LBOUND, LOCAL, LOOP, PALETTE, SEEK, SELECT, SHARED, SLEEP, SUB, UBOUND, and UNTIL.

PEEK and POKE statements that access low memory (DEF SEG = 0) or ROM will serve the intended purpose in QBasic. However, PEEKs and POKEs in QBasic's data segment (called DGROUP) will usually fail to perform as expected.

Numbers with decimal part .5 are rounded up in Standard BASIC, but are rounded to the nearest even integer in QBasic. Actually, in QBasic, all functions and statements that expect an integer value round numbers with decimal part .5 to the nearest even integer. For instance, LOCATE 3.5,4.5 is the same as LOCATE 4,4.

If, when Standard BASIC terminates the execution of a program, the last PRINT statement suppressed a carriage return and line feed with a comma or a semicolon, then Standard BASIC performs a carriage return and line feed. Since QBasic does not do this, one program can begin displaying its contents where the other left off. Of course, this is easily avoided by beginning each program with a CLS statement.

In Standard BASIC, all arrays have memory allocated dynamically. Therefore, when they are erased, additional space in memory becomes available. In QBasic, memory is allocated statically to arrays whenever possible. Doing so speeds up access to arrays. However, this memory space cannot be recovered. If the size of available memory is a concern, then the metacommand $DYNAMIC can be used to create arrays that can be completely erased from memory.

In Standard BASIC, executing a program does not restore the screen mode to its default state SCREEN 0,0. However, in QBasic it does.

In Standard BASIC, you can save programs in three formats — compressed binary, ASCII, and protected. However, only programs saved in ASCII format (accomplished with the command SAVE *filespec*,A) can be executed in QBasic. If you see unexpected characters, such as the characters with ASCII values less than 32 or greater than 127, when you load a Standard BASIC program into QBasic's editor, then it has probably been saved in compressed binary or protected format. Programs in compressed binary format can be converted to ASCII format by LOADing them in Standard BASIC and then SAVEing them in ASCII format. Programs in protected format are more difficult to convert. The following steps will convert such a program in most versions of Standard BASIC.

1. Run the following program:

    ```
    10 OPEN "RECOVER.BAS" FOR OUTPUT AS #1
    20 PRINT #1, CHR$(255);
    30 CLOSE #1
    ```

2. LOAD the protected program into memory.

3. Enter LOAD "RECOVER.BAS"

4. SAVE the current program in ASCII format.

It is recommended that you remove all line numbers not referenced or needed in error-handling routines. They are not needed in QBasic and take up space in the compiler's symbol table. In addition, they slow down the compiler and might result in the message "Compiler out of memory."

The QBasic Run-Time Debugger

The QBasic run-time debugger is a useful tool for testing and debugging programs. The debugger allows the programmer to trace slowly through the lines of a program and to modify and view the values of variables as needed during execution. The QBasic run-time debugger is invoked by selecting the Debug option on the menu bar.

Stepping

The most valuable capability of the debugger is its ability to execute successive program statements while pausing in between. This is called stepping. Without stepping, the program would race to its conclusion, and many bugs would remain hidden from the programmer.

To step through a program, use the function keys <F8> and <F10>. When <F8> is pressed, the first line in the statement part of the program is highlighted. Pressing <F8> again executes the statement and moves the highlight to the statement immediately following that line. Each subsequent press of <F8> executes the highlighted statement and moves the highlighting to the following statement. Stepping provides an excellent way to follow the logical flow of a program through decision structures, subprograms and functions. When a procedure call is highlighted and <F8> is pressed, the highlight bar goes to the first line of the procedure. After stepping through all the statements in the procedure, the highlight bar returns to the statement immediately following the original calling statement. At any time, <F4> may be pressed to view the contents of the Output screen.

It may not always be desirable to step through each procedure. If a line containing a procedure call is highlighted and <F10> is pressed rather than <F8>, the entire procedure will be executed in a single step, and the statement following the procedure will be highlighted. It may help to remember that <F8> "traces through" a procedure, while <F10> "steps over" a procedure.

Viewing the Value of a Variable

While tracing through a program, it is usually desirable to know the value of a particular variable at some point in the program. To do this, move to the Immediate window by pressing <F6>. Then type CLS: PRINT followed by the name of the variable and press the <Enter> key. For instance, to view the value of *myWage*, type CLS: PRINT myWage and press <Enter>. The Output screen will appear and the value of the variable will be displayed. Press any key to return to the QBasic environment and then press <F6> to return to the current program line.

NOTE	Viewing the value of variables this way erases the program's current screen output.

Value Modification

It may be helpful in debugging to change the value of a variable while execution is suspended. Doing this can be used to escape an infinite loop when otherwise the exit condition for the loop would never be met. QBasic makes changing a variable's value in midstream easy. With the program suspended, press <F6> to move the cursor to the Immediate window. Then type in the name of the variable whose value is to be modified followed by an equal sign and the new value for the variable. For instance, to change the value of *r* to 3 enter: *r* = 3. After pressing the <Enter> key, the variable will have its new value. Pressing <F6> returns the cursor to the View window.

Breakpoints

A breakpoint causes program execution to be suspended when a certain line is reached. With the program suspended the values of variables can be displayed and modified as needed using the methods described in the preceding sections. After a program has been suspended at a breakpoint, it can be rerun from the beginning by pressing <Shift+F5> or continued from the breakpoint by pressing <F5> alone.

To establish a line as a breakpoint, move the cursor to that line and press <F9>. The selected line will appear highlighted. When the program is run, execution will be suspended when the highlighted line is reached, but before it is executed. Multiple breakpoints may be set in a program. Whenever any one of the specified breakpoints occurs, program execution is suspended. To remove a breakpoint line, move to that line and press <F9>.

A Debugging Walk-through

The following walk-through uses the debugging tools discussed above.

1. Enter the following program.

    ```
    CLS
    INPUT "Hourly wage: ", wage
    IF wage < 3.80 THEN
        PRINT "Below the minimum wage."
      ELSE
        PRINT "Ok"
        PRINT "Your approx. yearly income is ";
        PRINT USING "$##,###."; YrIncome(wage)
    END IF

    FUNCTION YrIncome (salary)
      YrIncome = 2000 * salary
    END FUNCTION
    ```

2. Return to the main program using <Shift+F2>. Move the cursor to the statement PRINT "Ok" and press <F9>. Notice that the line becomes highlighted. The line has been designated as a breakpoint.

3. Run the program by pressing <Shift+F5> and respond with an hourly wage of 6.50. Notice the program stops at the breakpoint.

4. Press <F4> to view the Output screen. Observe that the line PRINT "Ok" has not been executed. Press <F4> again to return to the View window.

5. Press <F5> to continue running the program to the end. (After viewing the output, press any key to return to the View window.)

6. Press <Shift+5> to rerun the program from the beginning, but this time respond with an hourly wage of 2.75. Notice that the program ran to the end since the breakpoint was never encountered during the execution of the program. Press any key to return to the View window.

7. Remove the breakpoint previously set by moving the cursor to that line and pressing <F9>. The line is no longer a breakpoint and is no longer highlighted.

8. Press <F8> several times to execute the program. Press any key to return to the View window.

9. Press <F10> several times to execute the program by stepping. Notice that the function is executed as a single statement. Pause between pushes.

10. Press <Shift+F2> to display the function YrIncome. Move the cursor to the line YrIncome = 2000 * salary. Make this a breakpoint by pressing <F9>.

11. Press <Shift+F5> to rerun the program. Enter an hourly wage of 5.00.

12. When program execution stops at the breakpoint, modify the value of *salary* by pressing <F6> and typing salary = 3.25. Press <F6> to return to the View window.

13. Press <F5> to continue execution of the program. Notice that the output shows an "Ok" because the initial input was above the minimum wage, but the annual figure computed (6,500.00) corresponds to the subminimum wage of 3.25. Press any key to return to the View window.

The QBasic Environment

This appendix discusses the eight Menu bar selections and their pull-down menus.

The File Menu Commands

Pressing <F> from the Menu bar (or <Alt+F> from the View or Immediate windows) pulls down the File menu, which contains the following six command options.

New

The New command clears any current program from the editor's memory, allowing a new program to be written. The new program is given the default name of Untitled.BAS. If the New command is given when a recently edited program is in memory, QBasic provides an opportunity to save this edited program before the editor's memory is cleared.

Open

The Open command copies a program from a disk into the View window so that the program can be edited or run. If the New command is given when a recently edited program is in memory, QBasic provides an opportunity to save this edited program before the editor's memory is cleared.

The command exhibits a box with the cursor in a rectangle entitled "File Name." To load a file, type the filename (including the drive and path if warranted) into the rectangle and press the <Enter> key. If the file name has the standard extension of BAS, you need not include the extension. (To specify a file whose name has no extension, include the period at the end of the file name.) If the file you request is not present, QBasic assumes you want to start working on a new program that will later be saved in a file with this new name.

An alternate way of loading a file is provided by the Files rectangle which displays the names of all the files with extension BAS in the current directory of the current drive. A program can be loaded by pressing the <Tab> key until the Files rectangle is active, moving to the desired name with the direction keys, and pressing the <Enter> key. The drive can be changed by making a selection from the Dir/Drives rectangle.

The drive and/or directory of the programs displayed in the Files rectangle can be changed by typing and Entering the identifying path in the File Name rectangle. Wild card characters — the asterisk and question mark — can be used to request a class of file names from the directory. A question mark in a file name indicates that any character can occupy that position. An asterisk in either part of the file name, the first eight positions, or the extension indicates that any character can occupy that position and all the remaining positions in the part. For instance, typing and entering A:\TOM\?R*.BAS displays all files on the A drive in the directory TOM having R as the second letter and having the extension BAS.

Save

The Save command copies the program currently in memory onto a disk. If the program has not been named (that is, if its current name appears as Untitled in the Title bar), QBasic exhibits an input box titled File Name that provides the opportunity to give the file a meaningful name. If the file name ends with a period, then it will be saved with no extension. Otherwise, if the file name has no extension, the extension BAS will automatically be added. The file is saved in the current directory of the current drive unless instructed otherwise by preceding the file name with a drive and/or path. The drive also can be selected from the Dir/Files rectangle.

Save As

The Save As command copies the program currently in memory onto a disk after providing an opportunity to save the program under a name other than the current name. The dialog box is identical to the one for Save.

Print

The Print command prints a hard copy the currently selected text, the current window, or the complete program currently in memory depending on which option is selected.

Exit

The Exit command abandons QBasic and returns to DOS. If the Exit command is given when the program in the View window has not been saved in its current form, the user is given the opportunity to do so before QBasic is abandoned.

The Edit Menu Commands

Pressing <E> from the Menu bar (or <Alt+E> from the View or Immediate windows) pulls down the Edit menu, which contains the following four command options.

Cut

The Cut command removes the selected block of text from the View window and places it in the clipboard.

Copy

The Copy command places a copy of the selected block of text into the clipboard. The copied text will still be in the View window.

Paste

The paste command inserts, at the cursor, a copy of the contents of the clipboard.

Clear

The Clear command removes the selected text without saving it in the clipboard. (Clipboard contents remain unaltered.)

The View Menu Commands

Pressing <V> from the Menu bar (or <Alt+V> from the View or Immediate windows) pulls down the View menu, which contains the following three command options.

SUBs

The SUBs command displays a dialog box used to select a procedure to view or delete.

Split

The Split command divides the View window horizontally so two parts of a program can be accessed at the same time. The <F6> and <Shift+F6> keys move between the windows. The size of the active window can be expanded one line at a time with <Alt+Plus> and shrunk with <Alt+Minus>. <Ctrl+F10> toggles between expanding the active window to fill the screen or returning it to its former size.

Output Screen

The Output Screen command toggles to and from the display of the output screen. The same function is performed by the <F4> key.

The Search Menu Commands

Pressing <S> from the Menu bar (or <Alt+S> from the View or Immediate windows) pulls down the Search menu, which contains the following three command options.

Find

The Find command begins at the cursor, and searches for the first occurrence of a specified symbol, word, or phrase.

Repeat Last Find

The Repeat Last Find command looks for the next occurrence of the text most recently searched for by the Find command.

Change

The Change command begins at the cursor, finds the first occurrence of specified symbol, word, or phrase, and replaces it with new text.

The Run Menu Commands

Pressing <R> from the Menu bar (or <Alt+R> from the View or Immediate windows) pulls down the Run menu, which contains the following three command options.

Start

The Start command executes the program currently in memory, beginning with the first line. Pressing <Shift+F5> performs the same function.

Restart

When a program has been suspended before completion, the Restart command specifies that the next call for execution of the program should restart the program from the beginning.

Continue

When a program has been suspended before completion, the Continue command resumes execution at the suspension point.

The Debug Menu Commands

Pressing <D> from the Menu bar (or <Alt+D> from the View or Immediate windows) pulls down the Debug menu, presenting the following six command options.

Step

The Step command executes the program one statement at a time. Each invocation of the command executes the next statement.

Procedure Step

The Procedure Step command executes the program one statement at a time without stepping through the statements inside procedures one at a time. Entire procedures are executed as if they were a single statement.

Trace On

The Trace On line shows the current status of the Trace toggle. When Trace On is preceded by a dot, each statement will be highlighted as it is executed. This feature lets you observe the general flow of the program.

Toggle Breakpoint

A breakpoint is a line of the program at which program execution is automatically suspended by QBasic. The Toggle Breakpoint command toggles (that is, sets or clears) the line containing the cursor as a breakpoint.

Clear all Breakpoints

The Clear all Breakpoints commands removes all breakpoint indicators that have been set with the toggle breakpoint command.

Set Next Statement

The Set Next Statement specifies that the line containing the cursor be the next line executed.

The Options Menu Commands

Pressing <O> from the Main Menu (or <Alt+O> from the View or Immediate windows) pulls down the Options command menu, presenting the following three command options.

Display

The Display command generates a dialog box that can be used to custom-color the foreground and background text typed into the View windows and statements highlighted during debugging, to select or deselect the scroll bars used by a mouse, and to specify the number of spaces tabbed by the <Tab> key.

Help Path

The Help Path command is used to tell QBasic where to look for the file QBasic.HLP, the file containing the Help information. Normally, the file is in the same directory as QBasic.EXE. If not, the path specifying the directory containing QBasic.HLP should be entered in the rectangle invoked by the Help Path command. A complete path consists of a disk drive followed by a sequence of subdirectories.

Syntax Checking

Normally, when a line of text is Entered, QBasic's smart editor automatically checks the correctness of the line, capitalizes key words, and adds extra spaces to improve readability. This feature is enabled when Syntax Checking is preceded with a dot. The Syntax Checking command toggles this state.

The Help Menu Commands

Pressing <H> from the Menu bar (or <Alt+H> from the View or Immediate windows) pulls down the Help menu, which contains the following five command options.

Index

The Index command displays an alphabetical list of keywords. Information on a keyword can be obtained by placing the cursor on the keyword and pressing the <Enter> key or <F1>. Pressing a letter key moves the cursor to the first keyword beginning with that letter.

Contents

The Contents command displays a menu of topics on which information is available. After the <Tab> or direction keys are used to move the cursor to a topic, pressing <Enter> or <F1> displays the information.

Topic

When the cursor is located at a keyword in the View window, you can invoke the Topic command to obtain information about that word.

Using Help

The Using Help command displays information about how to obtain on-line help.

About

The About command displays the number and copyright dates of the version of QBasic currently in use.

Reserved Words

These words may not be used as labels or as names for variables or procedures.

ABS	CASE	CSRLIN
ABSOLUTE	CDBL	CVD
ACCESS	CHAIN	CVDMBF
ALIAS	CHDIR	CVI
AND	CHR$	CVL
ANY	CINT	CVS
APPEND	CIRCLE	CVSMBF
AS	CLEAR	DATA
ASC	CLNG	DATE$
ATN	CLOSE	DECLARE
BASE	CLS	DEF
BEEP	COLOR	DEFDBL
BINARY	COM	DEFINT
BLOAD	COMMAND$	DEFLNG
BSAVE	COMMON	DEFSNG
BYVAL	CONST	DEFSTR
CALL	COS	DIM
CALLS	CSNG	DO

DOUBLE	INTEGER	OPTION
DRAW	IOCTL	OR
ELSE	IOCTL$	OUT
ELSEIF	IS	OUTPUT
END	KEY	PAINT
ENDIF	KILL	PALETTE
ENVIRON	LBOUND	PCOPY
ENVIRON$	LCASE$	PEEK
EOF	LEFT$	PEN
EQV	LEN	PLAY
ERASE	LET	PMAP
ERDEV	LINE	POINT
ERDEV$	LIST	POKE
ERL	LOC	POS
ERR	LOCATE	PRESET
ERROR	LOCK	PRINT
EVENT	LOF	PSET
EXIT	LOG	PUT
EXP	LONG	RANDOM
FIELD	LOOP	RANDOMIZE
FILEATTR	LPOS	READ
FILES	LPRINT	REDIM
FIX	LSET	REM
FN	LTRIM$	RESET
FOR	MID$	RESTORE
FRE	MKD$	RESUME
FREEFILE	MKDIR	RETURN
FUNCTION	MKDMBF$	RIGHT$
GET	MKI$	RMDIR
GOSUB	MKL$	RND
GOTO	MKS$	RSET
HEX$	MKSMBF$	RTRIM$
IF	MOD	RUN
IMP	NAME	SADD
INKEY$	NEXT	SCREEN
INP	NOT	SEEK
INPUT	OCT$	SEG
INPUT$	OFF	SELECT
INSTR	ON	SETMEM
INT	OPEN	SGN

SHARED	STRING$	UNLOCK
SHELL	SUB	UNTIL
SIN	SWAP	USING
SINGLE	SYSTEM	VAL
SLEEP	TAB	VARPTR
SOUND	TAN	VARPTR$
SPACE$	THEN	VARSEG
SPC	TIME$	VIEW
SQR	TIMER	WAIT
STATIC	TO	WEND
STEP	TROFF	WHILE
STICK	TRON	WIDTH
STOP	TYPE	WINDOW
STR$	UBOUND	WRITE
STRIG	UCASE$	XOR
STRING	UEVENT	

QBasic Statements, Functions, and Metacommands

The superscript numbers following some of these sections refer to supporting topics presented at the end of this appendix.

ABS   The function ABS strips the minus signs from negative numbers while leaving other numbers unchanged. If x is any number, then the value of $ABS(x)$ is the absolute value of x.

ASC   The extended ASCII table associates a number (from 0 to 255) with each of the characters available to the computer. The value of $ASC(a\$)$ is the ASCII value of the first character of the string $a\$$.

ATN   The trigonometric function ATN, or arctangent, is the inverse of the tangent function. For any number x, $ATN(x)$ is an angle in radians between $-\pi/2$ and $\pi/2$ whose tangent is x.[2]

BEEP   The statement BEEP produces a sound of frequency 800 Hz that lasts a fraction of a second.

BLOAD   The statement BLOAD *filespec, m* places the bytes contained in the file *filespec* into successive memory locations beginning at offset m in the current segment of memory. If the contents of successive memory locations are saved in a file with the BSAVE statement, then they can later be restored with the statement BLOAD *filespec*. (This process is commonly used to save and later restore the contents of the screen.)[9, 4]

BSAVE   The statement BSAVE filespec, *n, m* stores in the file *filespec* the contents of the *m* consecutive memory locations beginning at offset *n* in the current segment or memory.[9, 4]

CALL   A statement of the form CALL *SubprogramName(argList)* is used to execute the named subprogram, passing to it the variables and values in the list of arguments. Arrays appearing in the list of arguments should be specified by the array name followed by empty parentheses. The value of a variable argument may be altered by the subprogram unless the variable is surrounded by parentheses. After the statements in the subprogram have been executed, program execution continues with the statement following CALL.

NOTE   The keyword CALL may be omitted. In this case, the parentheses are omitted and the statement is written *SubprogramName argList*.

CALL ABSOLUTE   The CALL ABSOLUTE statement passes control to a machine language subprogram in much the same way that CALL passes control to a procedure. The statement CALL ABSOLUTE (*argList, offvar*) passes control to the machine language program beginning at the memory location whose offset in the current segment of memory is the value of the numeric variable *offvar*. The arguments are used by the machine language subprogram. The statement CALLS ABSOLUTE works like CALL ABSOLUTE except that both segment and offset are passed for each of the arguments.[9]

CDBL   The function CDBL converts integer, long integer, and single-precision numbers to double-precision numbers. If x is any number, then the value of $CDBL(x)$ is the double-precision number determined by x.

CHAIN   The CHAIN statement passes control from the current program to another program contained on disk. The CHAIN *filespec* statement will load and execute the source code program contained in *filespec* (appending the .BAS extension if none was specified). Placing COMMON statements in the two programs allows the first program to pass the values of the variables appearing in its COMMON statement to corresponding variables in the second program's COMMON statement.

CHDIR   The statement CHDIR *path* changes the current directory on the specified disk drive to the subdirectory specified by *path*. For example, CHDIR "C:\" specifies the root directory of the *c* drive as the current directory. Omitting a drive letter in *path* causes the default drive to be used.[3]

CHR$ If *n* is a number from 0 to 255, then CHR$(*n*) is the character in the ASCII table associated with *n*.

CINT   The function CINT converts long integer, single-precision, and double-precision numbers to integer numbers. If *x* is any number from -32,768 to 32,767, then the value of CINT(*x*) is the (possibly rounded) integer constant that *x* determines.

CIRCLE   The statement CIRCLE (*x,y*),*r,c,r1,r2,a* draws a portion, or all, of an ellipse. The center of the ellipse is the point (*x,y*) and the longer radius is *r*. The color of the ellipse is determined by *c*. If *r1* and *r2* are present, then the computer draws only the portion of the ellipse that extends from the radius line at an angle of ABS(*r1*) radians with the horizontal radius to the radius line at an angle of ABS(*r2*) radians with the horizontal radius line in a counterclockwise direction. If either *r1* or *r2* is negative, then the computer also draws its radius line. The ratio of the length of the vertical diameter to the length of the horizontal diameter will be *a*. (If *a* is missing, the figure drawn will be a circle.)[2, 5, 6]

CLEAR   The statement CLEAR resets all variables and elements of static arrays to their default values, closes all files, deletes all dynamic arrays from memory, and reinitializes the stack. Also, if ,,*s* is added after the CLEAR statement, the stack size is set to *s*.[17, 1]

CLNG   The function CLNG converts integer, single-precision, and double-precision numbers to long integer numbers. If x is any number from -2,147,483,648 to 2,147,483,647, then the value of CLNG(*x*) is the (possibly rounded) long integer constant that *x* determines.

CLOSE   The statement CLOSE #*n* closes the file that has been opened with reference number *n*. By itself, CLOSE closes all open files.

CLS   The statement CLS clears the screen and positions the cursor at the upper-left of the screen. If a graphics viewport is active (see *VIEW*), then the statement CLS clears the viewport. The statement CLS 0 clears the entire screen. The statement CLS 1 clears the active graphics viewport if one exists;

otherwise, it clears the entire screen. The statement CLS 2 clears only the text viewport (see *VIEW PRINT*).

COLOR   In text-only mode (SCREEN 0), the COLOR statement produces either special effects (such as underlined text) or colors, depending on the type of monitor. The statement COLOR *f, b, bd* sets the foreground color to *f*, the background color to *b*, and the border color to *bd*, where *f* ranges from 0 to 15 and *b* from 0 to 7. The statement COLOR *f*+16, *b, bd* selects the same colors as the statement just given, but with a blinking foreground.

In screen mode 1, two palettes of four colors each are available. The statement COLOR *b, p* specifies *b* as the background color and *p* as the palette. Text will appear in color 3 of the selected palette and graphics may be displayed in any color of that palette.

In EGA and VGA modes 7, 8, and 9, a palette of 16 colors is available for text and graphics. The statement COLOR *f, b* sets the foreground color to the color assigned to palette entry *f* and the background color to the color assigned to palette entry *b*, where *f* and *b* range from 0 to 15.

In the VGA and MCGA modes 12 and 13, the statement COLOR *f* sets the foreground color to the color assigned to palette entry *f*. (The background is set to color *c* with the statement PALETTE 0, *c*.)[5, 6]

COM(*n*)   The statement COM(*n*) enables, disables, or defers trapping of the *n*th communications port depending on whether it is followed by ON, OFF, or STOP, respectively.[15, 10]

COMMON   If a statement of the form COMMON *fromvar1, fromvar2, ..., fromVarN* precedes a CHAIN statement, and a statement of the form COMMON *tovar1, tovar2, ..., toVarN* appears in the chained-to program, then the value of *fromvar1* is assigned to *tovar1*, the value of *fromvar2* is assigned to *tovar2*, and so on. Although the names of corresponding COMMON variables need not be the same, corresponding variables must be of the same type: string, integer, long integer, single-precision, double-precision, or user-defined record type. The type of each variable is either determined by a type-declaration tag or by inserting words of the form AS type. When the statement COMMON SHARED *var1, var2, ...,* appears in a program, then the specified variables will be shared with all procedures in the program. COMMON statements must appear before any executable statements in a program. COMMON statements may not appear inside a procedure.

CONST   The statement CONST *constantName = expression* causes QBasic to replace every occurrence of *constantName* with the value of the expression. This replacement takes place before any lines of the program are executed. Unlike LET, CONST does not set up a location in the program's memory for a variable. A constantName may appear in only one CONST statement and may not appear on the left side of a LET statement. We call constantName a *symbolic constant* or *named constant.*

COS   The value of the trigonometric function COS(*x*) is the cosine of an angle of *x* radians.[2]

CSNG   The function CSNG converts integer, long integer, and double-precision numbers to single-precision numbers. If *x* is any number, then the value of CSNG(*x*) is the single-precision number that *x* determines.

CSRLIN   At any time, the value of the function CSRLIN is the number (1, 2, 3, ...) of the line of the screen on which the cursor is located.[8]

CVI, CVL, CVS, CVD   With the buffer method of working with random-access files, numbers to be recorded in files by QBasic's LSET and PUT statements must first be transformed into strings. They are transferred back by these four functions. If an integer was transformed into the string *a$* of length 2, then the value of CVI(*a$*) will be the original number. Similarly, CVL(*a$*), CVS(*a$*) or CVD(*a$*) will be the long integer, single-precision or double-precision numbers that were transformed by QBasic into *a$*, a string of length 4, 4, or 8.[11]

CVSMBF, CVDMBF   Random-access files created in Microsoft BASIC, GW-BASIC, BASICA, or early versions of QuickBASIC, use a method different from QBasic's for storing numbers as strings. Single- and double-precision numbers that have been converted to strings by one of these earlier versions of BASIC and entered into random-access files can be converted to QBasic's numeric format by these two functions.[11]

DATA   The statement DATA *const1, const2,* ... holds constants. READ statements read these constants and assign them to variables.

**DATE$**   The value of the function DATE$ is the current date returned as a string of the form mm-dd-yyyy. If *d$* is a string of this form, then the statement DATE$ = *d$* resets the date as specified by *d$*.

DECLARE   The optional statement DECLARE SUB *SubprogramName* (*par1,* *par2,...*) or the statement DECLARE FUNCTION *FunctionName* (*par1, par2,...*) indicates that the specified procedure is called by the program. The type of each parameter is either determined by a type-declaration tag or words of the form AS type. The parameters must match the types of the corresponding parameters in the procedure definition. A parameterless procedure should appear in a DECLARE statement with an empty pair of parentheses. QBasic uses the DECLARE statements to check that subprogram calls use the proper number and types of arguments. DECLARE statements for each procedure are automatically inserted at the top of the program when it is saved. DE-CLARE statements may not appear inside procedures.

DEF FN/END DEF   DEF FN user-defined functions are created in one of two ways: by a single-line definition of the form DEF FN*name*(*parList*) = *expression*; or by a multi-line block that begins with a statement of the form DEF FN*name*(*parList*), which is followed by one or more statements that calculate the value of the function, and ends with the statement END DEF. The items appearing in the list of variables *parList* constitute the input for the function. If one of the statements in the block has the form *FNname* = *expression*, then the output of the function is expression.

DEF FN functions must be defined before they may be used. That is, they must be physically positioned earlier in the source text. Variables inside a multi-line block are global (that is, shared throughout the program) unless they are declared early in the block to be static by a statement of the form STATIC *var1, var2, ...* Static variables are not accessible outside of the block; however, they retain their values between subsequent calls to the function. This method of creating user-defined functions is perhaps obsolete with the introduction of the FUNCTION statement which supports recursion and may take arrays and records as arguments.

DEFINT, DEFLNG, DEFSNG, DEFDBL, DEFSTR   A variable can be as-signed a type by either a type-declaration tag or an AS clause. A statement of the form DEFINT letter specifies that any "untyped" variable whose name begins with the specified letter will have integer type. A statement of the form DEFINT *letter1-letter2* specifies that all "untyped" variables whose names begin with a letter in the range *letter1* through *letter2* will have integer type. The statements DEFLNG, DEFSNG, DEFDBL, and DEFSTR specify the corre-sponding types for long integer, single-precision, double-precision, and string variables, respectively. A DEFtype statement is automatically displayed above procedures created after the DEFtype statement is placed in the main body of the program.

DEF SEG   The statement DEF SEG = *n* specifies that the *current segment* of memory consist of memory locations 16**n through 16**n + 65,535. Subsequently, all statements that access memory directly — like PEEK, POKE, BLOAD, and BSAVE — will refer to memory locations in this range.[9]

DIM   The statement DIM *arrayName*(*m* TO *n*) declares an array with subscripts ranging from *m* to *n*, inclusive, where *m* and *n* are in the normal integer range of -32,768 to 32,767. A statement of the form DIM *arrayName*(*m* TO *n,p* TO *q*) declares a doubly subscripted, or two-dimensional, array. Three and higher dimensional arrays are declared similarly. If *m* and *p* are zero, the DIM statements above may be changed to DIM *arrayName*(*n*) and DIM *arrayName*(*n,q*). The statement DIM *variableName* AS *variableType*, where *variableType* is INTEGER, LONG, SINGLE, DOUBLE, STRING, STRING**n, or a user-defined type, specifies the type of the variable. Inserting SHARED after the word DIM in the main body of a program allows all procedures to access the array or variable.[17]

DO/LOOP   A statement of the form DO, DO WHILE *cond*, or DO UNTIL *cond*, is used to mark the beginning of a block of statements that will be repeated. A statement of the form LOOP, LOOP WHILE *cond*, or LOOP UNTIL *cond* is used to mark the end of the block. Each time a statement containing WHILE or UNTIL followed by a condition is encountered, the truth value of the condition determines whether the block should be repeated or whether the program should jump to the statement immediately following the block. A DO loop may also be exited at any point with an EXIT DO statement.

DRAW   The graphics statement DRAW *a$*, where *a$* is a string of directions and arguments, is used to draw figures on the screen in much the same way figures are drawn with pencil and paper. The rich and varied command strings constitute a miniature graphics language. The DRAW statement can be used to produce straight lines beginning at the last point referenced and extending in several directions. After each line is drawn, the end point of that line becomes the "last point referenced" for the next DRAW statement. The possible directions are: U (up), D (down), L (left), R (right), E (northeast), F (southeast), G (southwest), H (northwest). If *Y* is one of these directions and *n* is a number, then the statement DRAW "*Yn*" draws a line of *n* units in the specified direction. If a direction is preceded by N, the last point referenced will not change after the line is drawn. If a direction is preceded by B, an invisible line will be drawn and the last point referenced will change to the endpoint of that line. Several such statements may be combined into a statement of the form DRAW "*Yn Zm* ...." Some other variations of the DRAW statement are:

DRAW "An"	draw subsequent lines rotated by $n*90$ degrees
DRAW "Cn"	draw subsequent lines in color n of the current palette
DRAW "M x,y"	draw a line from the last point referenced to (x,y) (Preceding x or y with a plus sign or minus sign causes relative coordinates to be used.)
DRAW "P c, b"	fill in the closed region of boundary color b containing the last point referenced with the color c of the current palette
DRAW "Sn"	change the unit scale to $n/4$ of the the original scale
DRAW "TAn"	draw subsequent lines rotated by n degrees

DRAW statements can use numeric variables to provide the numeric arguments of commands by employing the STR$ function. For instance, the statement DRAW "M 100,25" may be written as x=100: y=25: DRAW "M" + STR$($x$) + "," + STR$(y).[7, 8, 6]

$DYNAMIC   The metacommand REM $DYNAMIC specifies that any array dimensioned after this point in the program should have its memory allocated dynamically at run-time. Dynamic arrays have the advantage that you may ERASE them to free up memory or REDIMension them to change their size. Array memory allocation is automatically dynamic if the array is local to a non-STATIC procedure, the array is DIMensioned using a variable, or the array is declared in a COMMON or REDIM statement.[16, 17]

END   The statement END terminates the execution of the program and closes all files. Also, the statements END DEF, END FUNCTION, END IF, END SELECT, END SUB, and END TYPE are used to denote the conclusion of multiline function definitions, function blocks, IF blocks, SELECT CASE blocks, subprograms, and user-defined record type declarations.

ENVIRON   QBasic has an environment table consisting of equations of the form "*name=value*" that is inherited from DOS when QBasic is invoked. The ENVIRON statement is used to alter this table. The statement ENVIRON "*name=;*" removes any equation whose left side is *name*. The statement ENVI-RON "*name=value*" places the equation in quotes in the table.

ENVIRON$ If *name* is the left side of an equation in QBasic's environment table, then the value of the function ENVIRON$("*name*") will be the string consisting of the right side of the equation. The value of ENVIRON$(*n*) is the *n*th equation in QBasic's environment table.

EOF   Suppose a file has been opened for input with reference number *n*. The value of the function EOF(*n*) will be -1 (true) if the end of the file has been reached and 0 (false) otherwise.

NOTE   The logical condition NOT EOF(*n*) is true until the end of the file is reached.

When used with a communications file, EOF(*n*) will be true if the communications buffer is empty and false if the buffer contains data.

ERASE   For static arrays, the statement ERASE *arrayName* resets each array element to its default value. For dynamic arrays, the statement ERASE *arrayName* deletes the array from memory.[17, 1]

NOTE   After a dynamic array has been ERASEd, it may be dimensioned again. However, the number of dimensions must be the same as before.

**ERDEV and ERDEV$**   After a device error occurs, the value of ERDEV provides information about the type of error and gives certain attributes of the device. The value of ERDEV$ is the name of the device. These functions are used in error-handling routines.[15, 10]

ERR and ERL   After an error occurs during the execution of a program, the value of the function ERR will be a number identifying the type of error, and the value of the function ERL will be the line number of the program statement in which the error occurred. (If the statement containing the error has no line number, then nearest line number preceding it is returned. If no line number precedes it, a value of 0 is returned.) These functions are used in error-trapping routines.[15]

ERROR   The statement ERROR *n* simulates the occurrence of the run-time error identified by the number *n*, where *n* may range from 0 to 255. It is a useful debugging tool.

EXIT   The EXIT statement may be used in any of the five forms EXIT FOR, EXIT SUB, EXIT FUNCTION, EXIT DEF, and EXIT DO. The EXIT statement causes program execution to jump out of the specified structure prematurely: EXIT FOR jumps out of a FOR/NEXT loop to the statement following NEXT, EXIT SUB jumps out of a subprogram to the statement following the CALL statement, and so on.

EXP   The value of the function EXP(x) is e^x, where e (about 2.71828) is the base of the natural logarithm function.

FIELD   With the buffer method of handling random-access files, a statement of the form FIELD #*n*, *w1* AS *strvar1*, *w2* AS *strvar2*, ... partitions each record of the file with reference number *n* into fields of widths *w1*, *w2*,... and names *strvar1*, *strvar2*, ... The sum *w1* + *w2* + ... usually equals (but must not exceed) the record length specified when the file was opened. The GET statement assigns values directly to the string variables *strvar1*, *strvar2*, ...

FILEATTR   After a file has been opened with reference number *n*, the value of the function FILEATTR (n,1) is 1, 2, 4, 8, or 32 depending upon whether the file was opened for INPUT, OUTPUT, APPEND, RANDOM, or BINARY, respectively. The value of the function FILEATTR (n,2) is the file's DOS file handle, a number that uniquely identifies the file and is used in assembly language programming.

FILES   The statement FILES *path* produces a listing of the files in the directory specified by *path*. Variations of the statement produce selected sublistings. If *path* is not included, FILES produces a listing of all the files in the current directory of the default drive.[3]

FIX   The value of the function FIX(x) is the whole number obtained by discarding the decimal part of the number *x*.

FOR/NEXT   The statement FOR *index* = *a* TO *b* STEP *s* sets the value of the variable *index* to *a* and repeatedly executes the statements between itself and the statement NEXT *index*. Each time the NEXT statement is reached, *s* is added to the value of *index*. This process continues until the value of *index* passes *b*. Although the numbers *a*, *b*, and *s* may have any numeric type, the lower the precision of the type, the faster the loop executes. The statement FOR *index* = *a* TO *b* is equivalent to the statement FOR *index* = *a* TO *b* STEP 1. The index following the word NEXT is optional.

FRE   At any time, the value of the function FRE(" ") or FRE(0) is the amount of memory available for storing new string data. The value of the function FRE(-1) is the number of memory locations available for new numeric arrays. This function is useful in determining whether or not sufficient memory remains to declare a new numeric array. The value of FRE(-2) is the smallest amount of space on the stack that has existed at any time during the execution of the program. For *n* different than -1 or -2, the value of FRE(*n*) is the same as the value of FRE(0).

FREEFILE   When files are opened, they are assigned a reference number from 1 to 255. At any time, the value of the function FREEFILE is the next available reference number.

FUNCTION   A function is a multi-statement block beginning with a statement of the form FUNCTION *FunctionName*(*parList*), followed on subsequent lines by one or more statements for carrying out the task of the function, and ending with the statement END FUNCTION. The parameter list, *parList*, is a list of variables through which values will be passed to the function when the function is called. Parameter types may be numeric, (variable-length) string, user-defined record type, or array. The types of the parameters may be specified with type-declaration tags, DEFtype statements, or AS clauses. Array names appearing in the parameter list should be followed by an empty pair of parentheses. Functions are named with the same conventions as variables, except that the name may not begin with FN. The value of a variable argument used in calling a function may be altered by the function unless the variable is surrounded by parentheses. Variables are local to the function unless declared as STATIC or SHARED. A statement of the form FUNCTION *FunctionName*(*parList*) STATIC specifies that all variables local to the function be treated as static by default; that is, they are invisible outside of the function but retain their values between function calls. Functions may invoke themselves (called *recursion*) or other procedures. However, no procedure may be defined inside of a function.

GET (Files)   User-defined record types provide an efficient means of working with random-access files. After a user-defined record type is defined and a variable of that type, call it *recVar*, is declared, the file is opened with a length equal to LEN (*recVar*). The *r*th record of the random-access file is retrieved and assigned to *recVar* with the statement GET #*n,r,recVar*.

The GET statement is also used to retrieve data from a binary file and assign it to any type of variable. Suppose *var* is a variable that holds a value consisting of *b* bytes. (For instance, if *var* is an integer variable, then *b* is 2. If *var* is an ordinary string variable, then *b* will equal the length of the string currently assigned to it.) The statement GET #*n,p,var* assigns to the variable *var*, the *b* consecutive bytes beginning with the byte in position *p* of the binary file having reference number *n*.

NOTE   The positions are numbered 1, 2, 3, ...

If *p* is omitted, then the current file position is used as the beginning position.

With the buffer method of working with random-access files, the statement GET #*n,r* retrieves record number *r* from the random-access file having reference number *n* and assigns the record's values to the variables appearing in FIELD statements. (If *r* is omitted, the record after the one most recently accessed by a GET or PUT statement is retrieved.)[11, 12]

GET (Graphics)   A graphics statement of the form GET (*x1,y1*)-(*x2,y2*), *arrayName* stores a description of the rectangular portion of the screen having upper left-hand corner (*x1,y1*) and lower-right corner (*x2,y2*) in the array *arrayName*. The rectangular region can then be duplicated at another location of the screen with a PUT statement. GET and PUT statements are the key tools for animation.[8]

GOSUB   A statement of the form GOSUB label causes a jump to the statement beginning at label. When the statement RETURN is reached, the program jumps back to the statement following the GOSUB statement.[13, 14]

NOTE   Both the GOSUB statement and its target must be in the same part of the program, either both in the main body or both in a single procedure.

GOTO   The statement GOTO *label* causes an unconditional jump to the first statement after the specified label.[13]

NOTE The GOTO statement and its target must be in the same part of the program.

HEX$ If *n* is a whole number from 0 to 2,147,483,647, then the value of the function HEX$(*n*) is the string consisting of the hexadecimal representation of *n*.

IF (single line) A statement of the form IF *condition* THEN *action* causes the program to take the specified action if *condition* is true. Otherwise, execution continues at the next line. A statement of the form IF *condition* THEN *action1* ELSE *action2* causes the program to take *action1* if *condition* is true and *action2* if *condition* is false.

IF (block) A block of statements beginning with a statement of the form IF *condition* THEN and ending with the statement END IF, indicates that the group of statements between IF and END IF are to be executed only when *condition* is true. If the group of statements is separated into two parts by an ELSE statement, then the first part will be executed when *condition* is true and the second part when *condition* is false. Statements of the form ELSEIF *condition* may also appear and define groups of statements to be executed when alternate conditions are true.

**INKEY$** The statement *a$* = INKEY$ assigns to the variable *a$* the one or two character string that identifies the next keystroke waiting in the keyboard buffer. Number, letters, and symbols are identified by a single character. Keys such as F1, Home, and Ins, are identified by two characters, CHR$(0) followed by CHR$(*n*), where *n* is the "scan code" for the key. If no keystroke is waiting, the null string, " ", is assigned to *a$*.

INP The value of the function INP(*n*) is the value of the byte read from port *n*.[10]

INPUT A statement of the form INPUT *var* causes the computer to display a question mark and to pause until the user enters a response. This response is then assigned to the variable *var*. Statements of the form INPUT "*prompt*"; *var* insert a prompting message before the question mark, statements of the form INPUT "*prompt*", *var* display the prompt without the question mark, and statements of the form INPUT; *var* suppress a carriage return following the entering of the response. In each of the above statements, *var* may be replaced by a number of variables separated by commas. After the user responds with the proper number of values (separated by commas) and presses <Enter>, each of the values is assigned to the corresponding variable.

INPUT# The statement INPUT #*n*, *var* reads the next item of data from a sequential file that has been opened for INPUT with reference number *n* and assigns the item to the variable *var*. The statement INPUT #*n*, *var1*, *var2*, ... reads a sequence of values and assigns them to the variables.

**INPUT$** A statement of the form *a$* = INPUT$(*n*) causes the program to pause until the user types *n* characters. The string consisting of these *n* characters is then assigned to *a$*. The statement *a$* = INPUT$(*n,m*) assigns the next *n* characters from the file with reference number *m* to *a$*.

INSTR The value of the function INSTR(*a$,b$*) is the position of the string *b$* in the string *a$*. The value of INSTR(*n,a$,b$*) is the first position at or after the *n*th character of *a$* that the string *b$* occurs. If *b$* does not appear as a substring of *a$* then the value is 0.

INT The value of the function INT(*x*) is the greatest whole number that is less than or equal to *x*.

IOCTL and IOCTL$ After a device has been opened with reference number *n*, the value of the function IOCTL$(*n*) is a control string read from the device driver, and a statement of the form IOCTL #*n*, *a$* sends the string *a$* to the driver.[10]

KEY The statement KEY *n*, *a$* assigns the string *a$* to function key F*n*. The string *a$* must have length 15 or less and *n* may be any number from 1 to 10 (and also 30 and 31 for function keys F11 and F12 on the 101-key keyboards). After KEY *n*, *a$* is executed, pressing the key F*n* has the same effect as typing the characters in *a$*. The statement KEY ON may be used to display the first six characters of the assigned strings on the last row of the Output window. The statement KEY OFF turns this display off. The statement KEY LIST displays all the assigned strings in their entirety.

KEY(*n*) The statement ON KEY(*n*) GOSUB label sets up the trapping of function key *n*. After KEY(*n*) ON is executed, pressing F*n* at any time causes program control to transfer to the subroutine beginning at label. Trapping is disabled with KEY(*n*) OFF and deferred with KEY(*n*) STOP. The subroutine at label must be in the main body of the program (or after its END statement).[15, 13, 14]

KILL The statement KILL *filespec* erases the specified disk file.[4]

LBOUND For a one-dimensional array *arrayName*, the value of the function LBOUND(*arrayName*) is the smallest subscript value that may be used. For any array *arrayName*, the value of the function LBOUND(*arrayName*, *n*) is the smallest subscript value that may be used for the *n*th subscript of the array. For example, after the statement DIM example(1 TO 31,1 TO 12,1990 TO 1999) is executed, the value of LBOUND(example, 3) is the smallest value allowed for the third subscript of example( ), which is 1990.

**LCASE$** The value of the string function LCASE$(*a$*) is a string identical to *a$* except that all uppercase letters are changed to lowercase.

**LEFT$** The value of the function LEFT$(*a$,n*) is the string consisting of the leftmost *n* characters of *a$*. If *n* is greater than the number of characters in *a$*, then the value of the function will be *a$*.

LEN The value of LEN(*a$*) is the number of characters in the string *a$*. If *var* is not a variable-length string variable, then the value of LEN(*var*) is the number of bytes needed to hold the value of the variable in memory. That is, LEN(*var*) is 2, 4, 4, or 8 for integer, long integer, single-precision, and double-precision variables. LEN(*var*), when *var* is a variable with a user- defined record type, is the number of bytes of memory needed to store the value of the variable.

LET The statement LET *var* = *expr* assigns the value of the expression to the variable. If *var* is a fixed-length string variable with length *n* and LEN(*expr*) is greater than *n*, then just the first *n* characters of *expr* are assigned to *var*. If LEN(*expr*) < *n*, then *expr* is padded on the right with spaces and assigned to *var*. If *var* has a user-defined type, then *expr* must be of the same type. The statement *var* = *expr* is equivalent to LET *var* = *expr*.

LINE The graphics statement LINE (*x1,y1*)-(*x2,y2*) draws a line connecting the two points. (If the first point is omitted, then the line is drawn from the last point referenced to the specified point.) The line is in color *c* of the current palette if LINE (*x1,y1*)-(*x2,y2*),*c* is executed. The statement LINE (*x1,y1*)-(*x2,y2*),,B draws a rectangle with the two points as opposite vertices. (If *B* is replaced by *BF*, a solid rectangle is drawn.) If *s* is a number in hexadecimal notation from 0 to &HFFFF, then LINE (*x1,y1*)-(*x2,y2*),,,*s* draws a styled line (with the pattern determined by *s*) connecting the two points.[7, 8, 6]

LINE INPUT   The statements LINE INPUT *a$*, LINE INPUT "*prompt*"; *a$*, and LINE INPUT "*prompt*", *a$* are similar to the corresponding INPUT statements. However, the user may respond with any string, even one containing commas, leading spaces, and quotation marks. The entire string is assigned to the string variable *a$*.

LINE INPUT#   After a file has been opened as a sequential file for INPUT with reference number *n*, the statement LINE INPUT #*n*, *a$* assigns to the string variable *a$* the string of characters from the current location in the file up to the next pair of carriage return/line feed characters.

LOC   This function gives the current location in a sequential, random-access, or binary file. For a sequential file with reference number *n*, LOC(*n*) is the number of blocks of 128 characters read from or written to the file since it was opened. For a random-access file, LOC(*n*) is the current record (either the last record read or written, or the record identified in a SEEK statement). For a binary file, LOC(*n*) is the number of bytes from the beginning of the file to the last byte read or written. For communications, the value of LOC(*n*) is the number of bytes waiting in the communications buffer with reference number *n*.[12]

LOCATE   The statement LOCATE *r,c* positions the cursor at row *r*, column *c* of the screen. The statement LOCATE,,0 turns the display of the cursor off, while the statement LOCATE,,1 turns the display back on. If *m* and *n* are whole numbers between 0 and 31, then the statement LOCATE,,,*m,n* will change the size of the cursor.

LOCK   The LOCK command is intended for use in programs that operate on a network. The DOS command SHARE enables file sharing and should be executed from DOS prior to using the LOCK statement. After a file has been opened with reference number *n*, the statement LOCK #*n* denies access to the file by any other process. For a random-access file, the statement LOCK #*n*, *r1* TO *r2* denies access to records *r1* through *r2* by any other process. For a binary file, this statement denies access to bytes *r1* through *r2*. The statement LOCK #*n*, *r1* locks only record (or byte) *r1*. For a sequential file, all forms of the LOCK statement have the same effect as LOCK #*n*. The UNLOCK statement is used to remove locks from files. All locks should be removed before a file is closed or the program is terminated.[12]

LOF   After a file has been opened with reference number *n*, the number of characters in the file (that is, the length of the file) is given by LOF(*n*). For communications, the value of LOF(n) equals the number of bytes waiting in the communications buffer with reference number n.

LOG   If x is a positive number, then the value of LOG(x) is the natural logarithm (base e) of x.

LPOS   Printers have buffers that hold characters until they are ready to be printed. The value of LPOS(1) is the current position in the buffer of the first printer (LPT1) and LPOS(2) is the current position for the second printer (LPT2).

LPRINT and LPRINT USING   These statements print data on the printer in the same way PRINT and PRINT USING display data on the screen. In addition, LPRINT may be used to set various print modes, such as the width of the characters and the vertical spacing.

LSET   If *af$* is a field variable of a random-access file, then the statement LSET *af$* = *b$* assigns the string *b$*, possibly truncated or padded on the right with spaces, to *af$*. If *a$* is an ordinary variable, then the statement LSET *a$* = *b$* replaces the value of *a$* with a string of the same length consisting of *b$* truncated or padded on the right with spaces. LSET also can be used to assign a record of one user-defined type to a record of a different user-defined type.[11]

**LTRIM$**   The value of the function LTRIM$(*a$*) is the string obtained by removing all the spaces from the beginning of the string *a$*. The string *a$* may be either of fixed or variable length.

**MID$**   The value of the function MID$(*a$,m,n*) is the substring of *a$* beginning with the *m*th character of *a$* and containing up to *n* characters. If the parameter *n* is omitted, MID$(*a$,m*) is all the characters of *a$* from the *m*th character on. The statement MID$(*a$,m,n*) = *b$* replaces the characters of *a$*, beginning with the *m*th character, by the first *n* characters of the string *b$*.

MKDIR   The statement MKDIR *path\dirName* creates a subdirectory named *dirName* in the directory specified by *path*.[3]

MKI$, MKL$, MKS$, MKD$ These functions convert integer, long integer, single- precision, and double-precision numbers into strings of lengths 2, 4, 4, and 8, respectively. This conversion is needed with the buffer method of working with random-access files.[11]

MKSMBF\$, MKDMBF\$ With the buffer method of working with random-access files, these functions convert single-precision, and double-precision numbers into strings of lengths 4 and 8, respectively, in the Microsoft Binary Format. This conversion is necessary before placing these numbers into random-access files that will be read with Microsoft BASIC, GW-BASIC, BASICA, or early versions of QuickBASIC.[11]

NAME   The statement NAME *filespec1* AS *filespec2* is used to change the name and/or the directory of *filespec1* to the name and/or directory specified by *filespec2*. The two filespecs must refer to the same drive.[4]

OCT\$ If n is a whole number between 0 and 2,147,483,647, then OCT\$(n) is the octal (that is, base 8) representation of n.

ON COM(n)   If n is the number 1 or 2, then the statement ON COM(n) GOSUB *label* sets up the trapping of the nth communications port. After COM(n) ON is executed, information coming into the port causes a GOSUB to *label*. The subroutine at *label* must be in the main body of the program (or after its END statement).[15, 10, 13, 14]

ON ERROR   The statement ON ERROR GOTO *label* sets up error trapping. An error then causes a jump to an error-handling routine beginning at *label*. The label must be in the main body of the program. See the discussion of RESUME for further details.[15, 13]

ON...GOSUB and ON...GOTO   The statement ON expression GOSUB *label1*, *label2*, ... causes a GOSUB to *label1*, *label2*, ... depending upon whether the value of the expression is 1, 2, ... Similarly, the GOTO variation causes an unconditional jump to the appropriate label. The GOSUB or GOTO statement and its target must be in the same part of the program, either both in the main body or both in the same procedure.[13]

ON KEY(n)   The statement ON KEY(n) GOSUB *label* sets up trapping of the function key Fn. After KEY(n) ON is executed, pressing Fn causes a GOSUB to *label*. The subroutine at *label* must be in the main body of the program (or after its END statement).[15, 13, 14]

ON PEN   The statement ON PEN GOSUB *label* sets up trapping of a light pen. After PEN ON is executed, pressing the metal clip on the light pen or pressing the light pen to the screen as appropriate, causes a GOSUB to *label*.

The subroutine at *label* must be in the main body of the program (or after its END statement).[15, 13, 14]

ON PLAY(*n*)   The music background buffer holds notes that have been specified by PLAY statements and are waiting to be played. If *n* is a whole number, then the statement ON PLAY(*n*) GOSUB *label* sets up trapping of the music buffer. After PLAY ON is executed, as soon as the number of notes in the buffer falls below *n*, the program GOSUBs to *label*. The capacity of the music background buffer is 32 notes, counting pauses between notes as notes. The subroutine at *label* must be in the main body of the program (or after its END statement).[15, 13, 14]

ON STRIG(*n*)   If *n* is 0, 2, 4, or 6, the statement ON STRIG(*n*) GOSUB *label* sets up trapping of one of the joystick buttons. The numbers 0 and 4 are associated with the lower and upper buttons of the first joystick and the numbers 2 and 6 are associated with the lower and upper buttons of the second joystick. After STRIG(*n*) ON is executed, pressing the button associated with *n* causes a GOSUB to *label*. The subroutine at *label* must be in the main body of the program (or after its END statement).[15, 13, 14]

ON TIMER   If *n* is an integer from 1 to 86400 (1 second to 24 hours), the statement ON TIMER(*n*) GOSUB *label* sets up trapping of the computer's internal clock. After TIMER ON is executed, every *n* seconds the program GOSUBs to the subroutine beginning at *label*. The subroutine at *label* must be in the main body of the program (or after its END statement).[15, 13, 14]

OPEN   The statement OPEN *filespec* FOR *mode* AS #*n* allows access to the file *filespec* in one of the following modes: INPUT (information can be read sequentially from the file), OUTPUT (a new file is created and information can be written sequentially to it), APPEND (information can be added sequentially to the end of a file), or BINARY (information can be read or written in an arbitrary fashion). The statement OPEN *filespec* FOR RANDOM AS #*n* LEN = *g* allows random-access to the file *filespec* in which each record has length *g*. Throughout the program, the file is referred to by the reference number *n* (from 1 through 255). Some other variations of the OPEN statement are OPEN "SCRN" FOR OUTPUT AS #*n*, OPEN "LPT1" FOR OUTPUT AS #*n*, and OPEN "KYBD" FOR INPUT AS #*n*, which allow access to the screen, printer, and keyboard as if they were sequential files.[4, 12]

DOS 3.0 and later versions support networking and make possible two enhancements to the OPEN statement. (The DOS command SHARE enables file sharing and should be executed from DOS prior to the use of the enhanced variations of the OPEN statement.) QBasic accesses data files in two ways; it reads from them or writes to them. When several processes may utilize a file at the same time, accurate file handling requires that certain types of access be denied to anyone but the person who has opened the file. The statement OPEN *filespec* FOR *mode* LOCK READ AS #*n* or OPEN *filespec* FOR RANDOM LOCK READ AS #*n* LEN = *g* opens the specified file and forbids any other process from reading the file as long as the file is open. LOCK WRITE forbids any other process from writing to the file as long as the file is open. LOCK READ WRITE forbids any other process from reading or writing to the file as long as the file is open. LOCK SHARED grants full access to any other process. Except with LOCK SHARED, if a file is currently opened and locked by a process for a certain access mode, then another process attempting to open the file for the same mode will receive the message "Permission denied" and be denied access.

OPEN "COM... If *n* is 1 or 2, then the statement OPEN "COM*n*:*b*,*p*,*d*,*s*,*L*" AS #*m* LEN=*g* provides access to the *n*th serial port using reference number *m* and specifies the block size (*g*), the speed of transmission (*b*), the parity (*p*), the number of data bits to be used in transmitting each character (*d*), the number of stop bits (*s*), and the line parameters (*L*).

OPTION BASE After the statement OPTION BASE *m* is executed, where *m* is 0 or 1, a statement of the form DIM *arrayName*(*n*) defines an array with subscripts ranging from *m* to *n*. QBasic's extended DIM statement, which permits both lower and upper subscript bounds to be specified for each array, achieves a wider range of results, making its use preferable to OPTION BASE.

OUT The statement OUT *n*,*m* sends the byte *m* to port *n*.[10]

PAINT If (*x*,*y*) is an unlit interior point of a region of the screen, then the statement PAINT (*x*,*y*) fills the region. In medium-resolution graphics mode, if the boundary has color *b* of the current palette and *c* is one of the colors of the current palette, then the statement PAINT (*x*,*y*),*c*,*b* fills the bounded region with the color *c*. If *t$* is a string of length at most 64 characters, then the statement PAINT (*x*,*y*), *t$* fills the region with a repeating pattern based on a tile determined by *t$*.[8, 6]

PALETTE and PALETTE USING When a graphics monitor is attached to an EGA, VGA, or MCGA display card, the PALETTE statement loads colors into the palette "jars" whose numbers range from 0 to 3, 0 to 15, 0 to 63, or 0 to 255. The statement PALETTE *m, n* assigns the *n*th color to the *m*th palette jar. The statement PALETTE USING array(0) specifies that each palette jar be filled with the corresponding color number stored in the array element: *array*(0) in jar 0, *array*(1) in jar 1, and so on.[5, 6]

PCOPY   Depending upon the screen mode in use, the video adapter card may have extra memory locations that give it the capability of working with several screens, called *pages*. (See the discussion of the SCREEN statement for details.) For instance, with an 80 characters per line text mode screen, the Color Graphics Adapter has four pages. The statement PCOPY *m,n* copies the contents of page *m* onto page *n*.

PEEK   Each memory location contains a number from 0 to 255. If *n* is a number from 0 to 65,535, then the value of PEEK(*n*) is the number stored at offset *n* in the current segment of memory.[9]

PEN   The statements PEN ON, PEN OFF, and PEN STOP respectively enable, disable, and defer the reading of the status of the light pen. For each *n* from 0 to 9, the value of the function PEN(*n*) gives information about the status of the light pen.

PLAY (function)   The music background buffer holds notes that have been specified by PLAY statements and are waiting to be played. The value of the function PLAY(0) is the number of notes currently in the music background buffer waiting to be played.

PLAY (statement)   The statement PLAY *a$*, where *a$* is a string of notes and parameters, produces musical notes with most of the embellishments indicated by sheet music. The rich and varied strings constitute a miniature music language. A note can be identified by one of the letters A through G, possibly followed by a plus or minus sign to indicate a sharp or a flat. A 1/*n*th note pause is specified by P *n*. The parameters O, L, T, MF, MB, ML, MS, and MN specify attributes of subsequent notes and are sometimes combined with a number giving a magnitude for the attribute. The parameter O *n*, where *n* ranges from 0 through 6, specifies the octave of subsequent notes. The parameter L *n*, where *n* ranges from 1 to 64, causes subsequent notes to be 1/*n*th notes. (For instance, *n* = 4 produces quarter notes.) The parameter T *n*, where *n* ranges from 32 to 255, sets the tempo of subsequent notes to *n* quarter notes per minute. The default values for the parameters O, L, and T are 4, 4, and 120, respectively. The parameter MF (music foreground) causes all notes to be played before the computer executes additional statements, while MB

n	*c*	*value of PMAP(c,n)*
0	natural x coordinate	physical x coordinate
1	natural y coordinate	physical y coordinate
2	physical x coordinate	natural x coordinate
3	physical y coordinate	natural y coordinate

Table G.1. The PMAP Function

(music background) places up to 32 notes in a buffer that plays the notes while the program continues to execute. The parameters ML (music legato) and MS (music staccato), respectively decrease and increase the durations of notes; MN returns the durations to normal articulation. PLAY statements can give the numeric argument of a command as the value of a numeric variable by using the STR$ function. For instance, the statement PLAY "D8" may be written as n = 8: PLAY "D" + STR$(n).

PMAP The graphics function PMAP converts the natural coordinates of a point to the physical coordinates and vice versa as shown in Table G.1.[8]

POINT In graphics mode, the value of the function POINT(x,y) is the number of the color of the point with coordinates (x,y). (With an EGA or VGA graphics card, POINT(x,y) gives the palette number assigned to the point.) The values of the functions POINT(0) and POINT(1) are the first and second physical coordinates of the last point referenced, and the values of POINT(2) and POINT(3) are the first and second natural coordinates of the last point referenced.[7, 5, 8, 6]

POKE Each memory location contains a number from 0 to 255. If *n* is a number from 0 to 65,535, then the statement POKE *n,m* stores the number *m* at offset *n* in the current segment of memory.[9]

POS The value of the function POS(0) is the column number of the current position of the cursor.

PRESET (See *PSET.*)

PRINT The PRINT statement is used to display data on the screen. The statement PRINT *expression* displays the value of the expression at the current position of the cursor and moves the cursor to the beginning of the next row of the screen. (Numbers are displayed with a trailing space and positive numbers with a leading space.) If the statement is followed by a semicolon or comma, then the cursor will not move to the next row after the display, but rather will move to the next position or print zone, respectively. Several expressions may be placed in the same PRINT statement if separated by semicolons (to display them adjacent to one another) or by commas (to display them in successive zones).

PRINT USING   The statement PRINT USING *a$*; *list of expressions* displays the values of the expressions (possibly interspersed with text from *a$*) in formats specified by *a$*. The statement can be used to align and display financial quantities with dollar signs, commas, asterisks, two decimal places, and preceding or trailing signs (+ or -). Numbers are formatted with the symbols #, +, $, $$, *, **, ^^^^, comma, and period. Strings are formatted via the symbols &, !, and \\. See Tables G.2 and G.3.

NOTE   If you wish to use one of the above special symbols for text in a format string, you must precede it with an underscore (_).

PRINT# and PRINT# USING   After a file has been opened as a sequential file for output or append with reference number *n*, the statements PRINT #*n,expression* and PRINT #*n*,USING *a$;expression* place the value of the expression into the file in the same way PRINT and PRINT USING display it on the screen.

PSET and PRESET   In graphics modes, the statement PSET (*x,y*) displays the point with coordinates (*x,y*) in the foreground color and the statement PRESET (*x,y*) displays it in the background color. The statement PSET (*x,y*),*c* or the statement PRESET(*x,y*),*c* causes the point (*x,y*) to be displayed in color *c* of the current palette.[7, 5, 8, 6]

PUT (Files)   With the buffer method of working with random-access files, after the file has been opened with reference number *n* and values have been assigned to the field variables, the statement PUT #*n,r* places these values in the *r*th record of the file. (If *r* is omitted, the record after the one most recently accessed by a GET or PUT statement will be filled.)

Suppose *recVar* is a variable of a user-defined record type and that a file has been opened with a statement of the form OPEN *fileName* FOR RANDOM AS

Symbol	Meaning	n	a$	Result
#	Each sharp symbol stands for one digit in a numeric field	1234.6	"########"	1235
		123	"########"	123
		123.4	"########"	123
		12345	"####"	%12345
.	Denotes the placement of the decimal point	123.4	"######.#"	123.4
,	Causes commas to be displayed to the left of every third digit to the left of the decimal point, as appropriate	12345	"#######,"	12,345
$	Displays a $ sign as the first character of the field	23.45	"$####.##"	$ 23.45
$$	Displays a $ sign immediately before the first digit displayed	23.45	"$$###.##"	$23.45
**	Inserts asterisks in place of leading blanks	23.45	"**######"	*****23
*	Displays an asterisk as the first character of the field	23.45	"*#######"	*
^^^^	(at end) Displays the number in exponential notation	-12	"##.#^^^^"	1.2E+04
		12345	"#.##^^^^"	-.12E+01
^^^^^	(at end) Displays the number in expanded exponential notation	12345	"#.#^^^^^"	1.2E+004
+	Reserves a space for the sign of the variable	12	"+#######"	+12
		-12	"######+"	12-

Table G-2.   Results Obtained from Executing PRINT USING a$; n

#n LEN = LEN(*recVar*). The statement PUT #*n,r,recVar* places the value of *recVar* in the *r*th record of the file.

The PUT statement is also used to place data into a file opened as a binary file. Suppose *var* is a variable that holds a value consisting of *b* bytes. (For instance, if *var* is an integer variable, then *b* is 2. If *var* is an ordinary string variable, then *b* will equal the length of the string currently assigned to it.) The statement PUT #*n,p,var* writes the successive bytes of *var* into the *b* consecutive locations beginning with position *p* in the binary file with reference number *n*.

a$	Meaning	x$	Result
&	Display entire string	"Nebraska"	Nebraska
!	Display first letter of string	"Nebraska"	N
\ \	Display first *n* letters of string (where there are *n*-2 spaces between the slashes). Here demonstrated with *n*=4.	"Nebraska"	Nebr

Table G-3. Results Obtained by Executing PRINT USING a$; x$

NOTE   The positions are numbered 1, 2, 3, ...

If *p* is omitted, then the current file position is used as the beginning position.[11, 12]

PUT (Graphics)   After a rectangular region of the screen has been stored in the array *arrayName* by a GET statement, the statement PUT (*x,y*),*arrayName*,PSET places an exact image of the rectangular region on the screen positioned with its upper-left corner at the point (*x,y*). The following list shows the possible alternatives to PSET in the statement and the conditions in which points on the high resolution graphics screen will be white after PUT is executed for each alternative.[7, 8]

The point in the resulting graphic image will be white when using:

> XOR   if the corresponding point is white in either the stored image or the original screen image, but not both (default).
>
> AND   if the corresponding point is white in the stored image and also in the original screen image.
>
> OR   if the corresponding point is white in either the stored image or the original screen image or both.
>
> PRESET   if the corresponding point is black in the stored image.

RANDOMIZE   The statement RANDOMIZE TIMER automatically uses the computer's clock to seed the random number generator. RANDOMIZE by itself requests a seed, and RANDOMIZE *n* seeds the generator with a number determined by *n*. If the random number generator is not seeded, the same list of numbers will be generated by RND each time a program is executed.

READ   The statement READ *var1, var2, ...* assigns to *var1* the first unused constant stored in a DATA statement, to *var2* the next unused constant, and so on.

REDIM   The statement REDIM *arrayName(...)* erases the array from memory and recreates it. The information inside the parentheses has the same form and produces the same result as that in a DIM statement. After the REDIMensioning, all elements have their default values. Although the ranges of the subscripts may be changed, the number of dimensions must be the same as in the original DIMensioning of the array. Inserting SHARED right after REDIM in a REDIM statement in the main body of a program, allows all procedures in the program to share the array. Only dynamic arrays may be redimensioned.[17, 1]

REM   The statement REM allows documentation to be placed in a program. A line of the form REM *comment* is ignored during execution. The REM statement is also used to place metacommands into the program. The REM statement may be abbreviated as an apostrophe.

RESET   The statement RESET closes all open files. Using RESET is equivalent to using CLOSE with no file reference numbers.

RESTORE   The statement RESTORE *label* causes the next request to READ an item of data to take the first item in the DATA statement following the indicated label. If the *label* parameter is omitted, the first DATA statement in the program will be accessed. Subsequent READ statements will continue selecting data from that point on.[13]

RESUME   When the statement RESUME is encountered at the end of an error-handling routine, the program branches back to the statement in which the error was encountered. The variations RESUME *label* and RESUME NEXT cause the program to branch to the statement at the indicated label or to the statement following the statement in which the error occurred, respectively. (The combination of ON ERROR and RESUME NEXT is similar to the combination GOSUB and RETURN.)[13]

RETURN   When the statement RETURN is encountered at the end of a subroutine, the program branches back to the statement following the one containing the most recently executed GOSUB. The variation RETURN *label* causes the program to branch back to the statement following the indicated label.[13, 14]

RIGHT\$ The value of the function RIGHT\$(*a\$,n*) is the string consisting of the rightmost *n* characters of *a\$*. If *n* is greater than the number of characters of *a\$*, then the value of the function is *a\$*.

RMDIR   If *path* specifies a directory containing no files or subdirectories, then the statement RMDIR *path* removes the directory.[3]

RND   The value of the function RND is a randomly selected number from 0 to 1, not including 1. The value of INT(*n**RND)+1 is a random whole number from 1 to *n*.

RSET   If *af\$* is a field variable of a random-access file, then the statement RSET *af\$*= *b\$* assigns the string *b\$* to *af\$*, possibly truncated or padded on the left with spaces. If *a\$* is an ordinary variable, then the statement RSET *a\$* = *b\$* replaces the value of *a\$* with a string of the same length consisting of *b\$* truncated or padded on the left with spaces.[11]

RTRIM\$ The value of the function RTRIM\$(*a\$*) is the string obtained by removing all the spaces from the end of the string *a\$*. The string *a\$* may be either fixed-length or variable-length.

RUN   The statement RUN restarts the currently executing program. All values previously assigned to variables are deleted. The variation RUN *filespec* loads the specified program from a disk and executes it. The specified program must be a QBasic program. The statement RUN *label* restarts the current program at the point referenced.[4, 13]

SADD   The value of the function SADD(*a\$*) is the offset of the variable-length string *a\$* in DGROUP, the default data segment.[9]

SCREEN (Function)   The value of the function SCREEN(*r,c*) is the ASCII value of the character in the *r*th row, *c*th column of the screen. The value of SCREEN(*r,c*,1) is the number of the palette jar used to color the character.[6]

SCREEN (Statement)   A monitor can be placed in the desired screen mode by one of the statements in Table G.4.

Statement	Mode
SCREEN 0	text mode
SCREEN 1	medium-resolution graphics mode
SCREEN 2	high-resolution graphics mode
SCREEN 3	720×348 Hercules graphics mode, two colors
SCREEN 7	320×200 16 color EGA, VGA adapters
SCREEN 8	640×200 16 color EGA, VGA adapters
SCREEN 9	640×350 4 to 16 color EGA, VGA adapters
SCREEN 10	640×350 monochrome EGA adapters
SCREEN 11	640×480 2-color MCGA, VGA adapters
SCREEN 12	640×480 16-color VGA only
SCREEN 13	320×200 256-color MCGA, VGA adapters

Table G-4.   The SCREEN Statement

When a graphics adapter is used in text mode, the computer can store the contents of several different screens, called *pages*. The number of pages allowed, call it *n*, depends on the graphics adapter and selected mode. At any time, the page currently displayed is called the *visual* page and the page currently being written to is called the *active* page. If *a* and *v* are numbers from 0 to *n*-1 then the statement SCREEN ,,*a,v* designates page *a* as the active page and page *v* as the visual page.[5]

SEEK   The statement SEEK #*n,p* sets the current file position in the binary or random-access file referenced by *n* to the *p*th byte or record of the file, respectively. After the statement is executed, the next GET or PUT statement will read or write bytes, respectively, beginning with the *p*th byte or record. The value of the function SEEK(*n*) is the current file position either in bytes or by record number. After a PUT or GET statement is executed, the value of SEEK(*n*) is the number of the next byte or record.[11, 12]

SELECT CASE   The SELECT CASE statement provides a compact method of selecting for execution one of several blocks of statements based on the value of an expression. The SELECT CASE block begins with a line of the form SELECT CASE *expression* and ends with the statement END SELECT. In between are statements of the form CASE *valueList* and perhaps the statement CASE ELSE. The items in the *valueList* may be individual values, or ranges of values such as "*a* TO *b*" or "IS < *a*." Each of these CASE statements is followed by a block of one or more statements. The block of statements following the first CASE *valueList* statement for which *valueList* includes the value of *expression* is the only block of statements executed. If none of the value lists include the value of *expression* and a CASE ELSE statement is present, then the block of statements following the CASE ELSE statement is executed.

SETMEM The far heap is the area of memory where variables outside the default data segment are stored. The SETMEM function both alters and returns the size of the far heap. The numeric expression *n* specifies the number of bytes by which to increase or decrease the far heap; the heap size is increased if *n* is positive or decreased if *n* is negative. The value of the function SETMEM(n) is the amount of memory in the far heap after the change.

SGN The value of the function SGN(x) is 1, 0, or -1, depending upon whether x is positive, zero, or negative, respectively.

SHARED A statement of the form SHARED *var1,var2,* ... can be used at the beginning of a procedure to specify that variables *var1, var2,* ..., are shared with the main body. The type of each variable is either determined by a type-declaration tag, a DEFtype statement, or an AS clause. If an AS clause is used in the SHARED statement, then an AS clause must be used to declare the type of the variable in the main body of the program. Any change made to a shared variable by the procedure will change the variable of the same name in the main body, and vice versa. Declaring a variable as SHARED in a procedure allows the variable to be used by both the main body and the procedure without passing it as an argument. Arrays dimensioned in the main body of the program may be shared with procedures by listing their names followed by empty parentheses in a SHARED statement.

SHELL If *c$* is a DOS command, then the statement SHELL *c$* suspends execution of the QBasic program, executes the DOS command specified by *c$*, and then resumes execution of the QBasic program. The statement SHELL by itself suspends program execution and invokes a copy of DOS. Entering the command EXIT resumes execution of the QBasic program after the SHELL statement.

SIN For any number x, the value of the trigonometric function SIN(x) is the sine of the angle of x radians.[2]

SOUND The statement SOUND *f,d* generates a sound of pitch *f* hz for a duration of *d**.055 seconds. The value of *f* must be at least 37.

NOTE The keys of the piano have frequencies ranging from 55 to 8,372 hz.

SPACE$ If *n* is an integer from 0 to 32,767, then the value of the function SPACE$(*n*) is the string consisting of *n* spaces.

SPC The function SPC is used in PRINT, LPRINT, and PRINT# statements to generate spaces. For instance, the statement PRINT *a$*; SPC(*n*); *b$* skips *n* spaces between the displays of the two strings.

SQR For any nonnegative number *x*, the value of the square root function SQR(*x*) is the nonnegative number whose square is *x*.

STATIC A statement of the form STATIC *var1,var2,* ... can be used at the beginning of the definition of a procedure to specify that the variables *var1, var2,* ... are static local variables in the procedure. Memory for static variables is permanently set aside by QBasic, allowing static variables to retain their values between successive calls of the procedure. The type of each variable is either determined by a DEF*type* statement, a type-declaration tag, or an AS clause. Static variables have no connection to variables of the same name outside the procedure, and so may be named without regard to "outside" variables. Arrays may be declared static by listing their names followed by empty parentheses in a STATIC statement, and then dimensioning them in a subsequent DIM statement.

$STATIC The metacommand REM $STATIC tells QBasic to use a static, or permanent, allocation of memory for arrays appearing in subsequent DIM statements, if possible. Effectively, the $STATIC metacommand reverses the effect of any previous $DYNAMIC metacommand by allowing arrays that are normally static by default to be allocated as static. An array is static by default if it is DIMensioned with constant upper and lower bounds, implicitly dimensioned by appearing in a statement without first being declared in a DIM statement, or if it is DIMensioned within a STATIC procedure.[16, 17]

STICK For *n* = 0 or 1, the value of the function STICK(*n*) is the *x*- or *y*-coordinate, respectively, of the first joystick lever. For *n* = 2 or 3, the function gives the corresponding information for the second joystick.

STOP The statement STOP suspends the execution of a program. Execution can be resumed beginning with the first statement after the STOP statement by pressing <F5>.

**STR$**   The STR$ function converts numbers to strings. The value of the function STR$($n$) is the string consisting of the number n in the form normally displayed by a print statement.

STRIG   The statements STRIG ON and STRIG OFF respectively enable and disable the reading of the status of the joystick buttons. For each n from 0 to 7, the value of the function STRIG(n) gives information about the status of the joystick button.

STRIG(n)   The statement ON STRIG(n) GOSUB *label* sets up the trapping of one of the joystick buttons. The numbers $n = 0$ and $n = 4$ are associated with the lower and upper buttons of the first joystick respectively, and the numbers $n = 2$ and $n = 6$ are associated with the lower and upper buttons of the second joystick. The pressing of the corresponding button anytime after STRIG(n) ON is executed causes a GOSUB to the subroutine at *label*.[15, 13, 14]

STRING$ If n is a whole number from 0 to 32,767, then the value of STRING$($n,a\$$) is the string consisting of the first character of $a\$$ repeated n times. If m is a whole number from 0 to 255, then the value of the function STRING$($n,m$) is the string consisting of the character with ASCII value m repeated n times.

SUB/END SUB   A subprogram is a multistatement block beginning with a statement of the form SUB *SubprogramName(parList)*, followed on subsequent lines by one or more statements for carrying out the task of the subprogram, and ending with the statement END SUB. The parameter list *parList* is a list of variables through which values will be passed to the subprogram whenever the subprogram is called. (See the discussion of CALL.) Parameters may be numeric or (variable- length) string variables as well as arrays.

SWAP   If *var1* and *var2* are two variables of the same type then the statement SWAP *var1, var2* exchanges the values of the two variables.

SYSTEM   The statement SYSTEM terminates program execution, closes all files, and returns control to the QBasic environment.

TAB   The function TAB(n) is used in PRINT, LPRINT, and PRINT# statements to move the cursor to position n and place spaces in all skipped-over positions. If n is less than the cursor position, then the cursor is moved to the nth position of the next line.

TAN   For any number x (except for $x=\pi/2$, $-\pi/2$, $3*\pi/2$, $-3*\pi/2$, and so on), the value of the trigonometric function TAN(x) is the tangent of the angle of x radians.[2]

**TIME$**   The value of the function TIME$ is the current time expressed as a string of the form hh:mm:ss. (The hours range from 0 to 23, as in military time.) If $t\$$ is such a string, then the statement TIME$ = $t\$$ sets the computer's internal clock to the corresponding time.

TIMER   The value of the function TIMER is the number of seconds from midnight to the time currently stored in the computer's internal clock.

TRON and TROFF   These statements, which are abbreviations of "trace on" and "trace off," are used to debug programs. The statement TRON causes the program to execute slower than normal and for each statement to be highlighted on the screen as it executes. The statement TROFF terminates this tracing.

TYPE/END TYPE   A multi-statement block beginning with TYPE *typeName* and ending with END TYPE creates a user-defined record type. Each statement inside the block has the form *elt* AS *type*, where *elt* is a variable (without a type-declaration tag) and *type* is either INTEGER, LONG, SINGLE, DOUBLE, STRING*n (that is, fixed-length string), or another user-defined record type. After a statement of the form DIM *var* AS *typeName* appears, the element corresponding to the statement *elt* AS *type* is referred to as *var.elt*. TYPE statements may not appear inside procedures.

UBOUND   For a one-dimensional array *arrayName*, the value of the function UBOUND(*arrayName*) is the largest subscript value that may be used. For any array *arrayName*, the value of the function UBOUND(*arrayName*, n) is the largest subscript value that may be used for the nth subscript of the array. For example, after the statement DIM example(1 TO 31,1 TO 12,1990 TO 1,999) is executed, the value of UBOUND(example, 3) is the largest value allowed for the third subscript of example( ), which is 1,999.

**UCASE$**   The value of the string function UCASE$($a\$$) is a string identical to $a\$$ except that all lowercase letters are changed to uppercase.

UNLOCK   The UNLOCK command is intended for use in programs that operate on a network. The DOS command SHARE enables file sharing and should be executed from DOS prior to using the LOCK and UNLOCK statements. After a LOCK statement has been used to deny access to all or part of a file (see the discussion of LOCK for details), a corresponding UNLOCK statement can be used to restore access. Suppose a data file has been opened as reference number *n*. The locks established by the statements LOCK #*n*; LOCK #*n*, *r1*; and LOCK #*n*, *r1* TO *r2* are undone by the statements UNLOCK #*n*; UNLOCK #*n*, *r1*; and UNLOCK #*n*, *r1* TO *r2*, respectively. There must be an exact correspondence between the locking and the unlocking statements used in a program, that is, each set of paired statements must refer to the same range of record numbers or bytes.

VAL   The VAL function is used to convert strings to numbers. If the leading characters of the string *a$* corresponds to a number, then VAL(*a$*) will be the number represented by these characters. For any number *n*, VAL(STR$(*n*)) is *n*.

VARPTR and VARSEG   The values of the functions VARSEG(*var*) and VARPTR(*var*) are the segment of memory and the offset in that segment where the value of *var* (if it is a numeric or fixed-length string) or of the descriptor of *var* (if it is a variable-length string or an array variable) is located.[9]

**VARPTR$**   The value of the function VARPTR$(*var*) is a five-character string whose first character identifies the type of the variable and whose last four characters specify the location of the variable in memory. This function can be used in conjunction with DRAW and PLAY.

VIEW   The graphics statement VIEW establishes a rectangular portion of the screen as a *graphics viewport* which will contain all subsequent figures drawn by graphics statements. There are three variations of the VIEW statement.

In medium resolution graphics mode, the pair of statements WINDOW SCREEN (0,0)-(319,199): VIEW (*x1,y1*)-(*x2,y2*),*c,b* establish a viewport with upper left-hand corner at physical coordinates (*x1,y1*) and lower right-hand corner at physical coordinates (*x2,y2*). The rectangle will have background color *c* and a boundary of color *b*, where *b* and *c* are two colors of the current palette. Subsequent graphics statements will scale their displays and place them into the viewport as if it were the entire screen. For the other graphics modes, the numbers 319 and 199 should be replaced by the physical *x*- and *y*-coordinates of the point in the lower right-hand corner of the screen.

If no WINDOW statement is active, the statement VIEW (*x1,y1*)-(*x2,y2*),*c,b* establishes a viewport at the same location and with the same colors as above.

However, instead of forcing a future drawing to fit inside the viewport, subsequent graphics statements do no scaling, but simply translate the drawing $x1$ points to the right and $y1$ points down, and clip the drawing at the edge of the view port; only that portion of the translated drawing which falls inside the viewport are displayed.

If no WINDOW statement is active, the statement VIEW SCREEN $(x1,y1)$-$(x2,y2),c,b$ establishes a viewport at the same location and with the same colors as in the first discussion. However, instead of scaling down or translating a future drawing, subsequent graphics statements simply clip the drawing at the edge of the viewport; only that portion of the drawing which falls within the viewport are displayed.[5, 8, 6]

VIEW PRINT   Normally, the screen holds 25 lines of text numbered 1 through 25. However, only lines 1 through 24 scroll. These lines are called the "text viewport." The statement VIEW PRINT *lineA* TO *lineB* causes the text viewport to consist of lines *lineA* through *lineB*. After its execution, all text displayed with PRINT statements will appear in the viewport and only the lines in the viewport will scroll. The LOCATE statement is only valid if the line number specified is within the current text viewport, and the CLS statement affects only the viewport. Text lying outside of the text viewport stays fixed. The statement VIEW PRINT by itself causes the entire screen to scroll. It has the same effect as VIEW PRINT 1 TO *h*, where *h* is the number of text lines on the screen.

WAIT   If p is a port number, q is the value of a byte to be received at port p, and n and m are integers from 0 to 255, then the statement WAIT p, n, m suspends the execution of the program until the condition $((q\,\text{XOR}\,m)\,\text{AND}\,n) <> 0$ is true for the byte with value q received at port p.[10]

WHILE/WEND   A WHILE ... WEND loop is a sequence of statements beginning with a statement of the form WHILE *condition* and ending with the statement WEND. After the WHILE statement is executed, the computer repeatedly executes the entire sequence of statements inside the loop as long as the condition is true.

WIDTH   When used with a monitor other than a Monochrome Display, the statement WIDTH 40 causes text to be displayed in wide characters with 40 characters per line. (The first PRINT zone contains 14 positions and the second 26 positions.) The standard 80 character per line format is restored with the statement WIDTH 80. (The first four PRINT zones consist of 14 positions and the fifth consists of 24 positions.) In graphics modes, the WIDTH statement either has no effect or alters the mode to one that features the indicated number of characters per line.

The EGA, VGA, and the MCGA video adapter cards are capable of displaying 25, 30, 43, 50, or 60 lines of text depending on the type of adapter, the type of monitor, and the screen mode. When *t* is a valid length for the video adapter, the statement WIDTH ,*t* sets the number of lines of text to *t*.

If *s* is an integer less than 255, the statement WIDTH "LPT1",*s* causes QBasic to permit at most *s* characters to be printed on a single line by LPRINT statements. QBasic will send a carriage return/line feed pair to the printer after *s* characters have been printed on a line, even if LPRINT would not otherwise start a new line at that point. The statement WIDTH "LPT1",255 specifies infinite width; that is, a carriage return/line feed pair will be sent to the printer only when requested by LPRINT. The same effects can be obtained with the statement WIDTH LPRINT *s*.

WINDOW   The graphics statement WINDOW (*x1*,*y1*)-(*x2*,*y2*) imposes a standard (right-hand) coordinate system on the screen with the x-coordinates of points ranging from *x1* to *x2* and y-coordinates ranging from *y1* to *y2*. Subsequent graphics statements place figures on the screen scaled in accordance with this coordinate system. If the statement WINDOW is replaced by WINDOW SCREEN, then a left-hand coordinate system is imposed. That is, the y-coordinates of points are lower in the higher areas on the screen.[8]

WRITE   The statement WRITE *exp1*,*exp2*, ... displays the values of the expressions one after the other on the screen. Strings appear surrounded by quotation marks and numbers do not have leading or trailing spaces. All commas are displayed and do not induce jumps to successive print zones. After all the values are displayed, the cursor moves to the beginning of the next line.

WRITE#   After a sequential file is opened for output or append with reference number *n*, the statement WRITE #*n*, *exp1*,*exp2*, ... records the values of the expressions one after the other into the file. Strings appear surrounded by quotation marks, numbers do not have leading or trailing spaces, all commas in the expressions are recorded, and the characters for carriage return and line feed are placed following the data.

Supporting Topics

1. Default values: Before a numeric, variable-length string, or fixed-length string variable of length *n* has been assigned a value by the program, its value is 0, the null string (" "), or a string of *n* CHR$(0) characters respectively.

2. Radian measure: The radian system of measurement measures angles in terms of a distance around the circumference of the circle of radius 1. If the vertex of an angle between 0 and 360 degrees is placed at the center of the circle, then the length of the arc of the circle contained between the two sides of the angle is the radian measure of the angle. An angle of d degrees has a radian measure of $(\pi/180)*d$ radians.

3. Directories: Think of a disk as a master folder holding other folders, each of which might hold yet other folders. Each folder, other than the master folder, has a name. Each folder is identified by a *path*: a string beginning with a drive letter, a colon, and a backslash character, ending with the name of the folder to be identified, and listing the names of the intermediate folders (in order) separated by backslashes. For instance the path "C:\DAVID\GAMES" identifies the folder GAMES which is contained in the folder DAVID, which in turn is contained in the master folder of drive C.

    Each folder is called a *directory* and the master folder is called the *root directory*. When a folder is opened, the revealed folders are referred to as its *subdirectories*. Think of a file as a piece of paper inside one of the folders. Thus, each directory contains files and subdirectories.

    At any time, one of the directories is said to be the *current directory*. Initially the root directory is the current directory. The currect directory can be changed from DOS with the CD command or from QBasic with the CHDIR command. DOS and QBasic statements that access files, such as DIR and FILES, act on the files in the current directory unless otherwise directed.

    The *default drive* is the drive whose letter appeared in the DOS prompt when QBasic was invoked. If a drive is missing from a path, then the drive is assumed to be the default drive.

4. Filespec: The filespec of a file on disk is a string consisting of the letter of the drive, a colon, and the name of the file. If directories are being used, then the file name is preceded by the identifying path.

5. Colors for CGA monitors: 16 different colors, identified by the numbers 0 through 15, are available on standard color monitors (that is, monitors that can be attached to the Color Graphics Adapter card).

0 Black	4 Red	8 Gray	12 Light Red
1 Blue	5 Magenta	9 Light Blue	13 Light Magenta
2 Green	6 Brown	10 Light Green	14 Yellow
3 Cyan	7 White	11 Light Cyan	15 Intense White

In text mode, which is invoked with the statement SCREEN 0, any of the colors are available as foreground colors and the first eight are also available as background colors. In medium resolution graphics mode, which is invoked with the statement SCREEN 1, two palettes of four colors each are available.

Palette 0:	0. Background color	1. Green	2. Red	3. Brown
Palette 1:	0. Background color	1. Cyan	2. Magenta	3. White

In high resolution graphics mode, invoked with the statement SCREEN 2, only two colors, black (0) and white (1) are available. See the discussion of SCREEN for the ranges of colors available in the higher graphics modes.

6. Palettes: A palette can be thought of as a collection of numbered jars that can hold paint. The number of jars available varies with the screen mode. Although the jars hold specified default colors, EGA, MCGA, and VGA adapters allow the colors to be changed with the PALETTE statement. Statements of the form PSET $(x,y),c$ and CIRCLE $(x,y),r,c$ use the color in the cth paint jar. In the absence of a COLOR statement, the PRINT statement displays characters with the color in jar 0 as the background color and the color in the highest numbered jar as the foreground color.

7. Last point referenced: At any time, one point on the screen is designated as the "last point referenced." Initially it is the point in the center of the graphics screen. After a graphics statement is executed, the point changes to one of the points used in the statement. For instance, after a circle is drawn, the center of the circle becomes the last point referenced. After a line is drawn, the right point named in the LINE statement becomes the last point referenced.

8. Graphics coordinate systems: The standard graphics coordinate system is called the *physical* coordinate system. For the CGA screen modes (SCREEN 1 or SCREEN 2), the *y* coordinates range from 0 to 199 moving from the top to the bottom of the screen, and the *x* coordinates range from 0 to 319 in medium- resolution graphics mode and from 0 to 639 in high-resolution graphics mode, moving from the left to the right side of the screen. See the discussion of SCREEN for the ranges in the higher graphics screen modes. The WINDOW statement can be used to specify a different coordinate system, called a *natural* or *logical* coordinate system. Points can also be specified in terms of *relative coordinates.* The phrase STEP (*x,y*) refers to the point obtained by starting at the last point referenced and moving *x* units in the horizontal direction and *y* units in the vertical direction. Relative coordinates can be used in all statements that produce graphics.

9. Memory: Each memory location holds an integer from 0 to 255. This unit of data or memory is called a byte. The computer's memory is divided into blocks of memory locations called *segments.* Each segment is 65,536 bytes in size. Within a segment, a particular memory location can be specified by giving its *offset* (a number from 0 to 65,535) from the beginning of the segment. Thus, to locate an item in memory, both its segment and offset within that segment must be known, although in many cases just the offset is sufficient. Segments overlap; that is, the same portion of memory may be considered to be within different segments. Segment 0 extends from location 0 to location 65,535. Segment 1 extends from location 16 to location 65,551. Segment 2 extends from location 32 to 65,567, and so on. For instance, the 34th memory location can be identified as segment 0: offset 34, segment 1: offset 18, or segment 2: offset 2. QBasic reserves a special segment, called the *Default Data Segment* or DGROUP, where it stores variables, special values such as the current row and column of the cursor, and the value of the random seed. The *current segment of memory* is used in conjunction with the offsets given in BLOAD, BSAVE, PEEK, and POKE statements. At the start of program execution, the current segment of memory is the Default Data Segment. It can be changed at any time by the DEF SEG statement.

10. Device: Some examples of devices are the video screen, keyboard, printer, modem, and diskette drives. The computer's microprocessor receives data from and sends data to the various devices of the computer through what are called ports. Each port is identified by a number from 0 to 65,535. A byte of data consists of a number from 0 to 255.

11. Random-access files: The two methods for writing records to and reading records from random-access files are the record variable method and the buffer method. The record variable method is discussed in Chapter 9. With the buffer method, a portion of memory referred to as a buffer is set aside for the file. A FIELD statement specifies fixed-length string field variables whose values are held in the buffer. LSET and RSET statements assign values to the field variables, and PUT and GET statements move the contents of the buffer into a record of the file, and vice versa, respectively. The functions CKI, CKL, CKS, and CKD are used to convert numbers to fixed-length strings prior to being placed into the buffer by LSET and RSET statements. After a GET statement places a record in the buffer, the functions MKI, MKL, MKS, and MKD are used to convert the these strings back into numbers of the appropriate type.

12. Binary file: A file that has been opened with a statement of the form OPEN *filespec* FOR BINARY AS #*n* is regarded simply as a sequence of characters occupying positions 1, 2, 3, ... At any time, a specific location in the file is designated as the "current position." The SEEK statement can be is used to set the current position. Collections of consecutive characters are written to and read from the file beginning at the current position with PUT and GET statements, respectively. After a PUT or GET statement is executed, the position following the last position accessed becomes the new current position.

13. Label: QBasic supports two mechanisms for identifying program lines that are the destinations of statements such as GOTO and GOSUB: line numbers and descriptive labels. Descriptive labels are named using the same rules as variables, and are followed by a colon. When a label appears in a GOTO or GOSUB statement, execution jumps to the statement following the line containing the label. We use the word *label* to refer to either a descriptive label or a line number.

14. Subroutines: A subroutine is a sequence of statements beginning with a label and ending with a RETURN statement. A subroutine is meant to be branched to by a GOSUB statement and is usually placed so that it cannot be entered inadvertently. For instance, in the main body of a program, subroutines might appear after an END statement.

15. Event trapping: Special events, such as the pressing of a function key or the occurrence of an error, can be set to trigger a jump to a subroutine. These events are specified by statements of the general form *Event* ON and ON *Event* GOSUB *label* that cause the computer to check for the event after the execution of each statement. If the event has occurred,

the computer then performs a GOSUB to the subroutine at *label*. Trapping is disabled with *Event* OFF and deferred with *Event* STOP.

16. Metacommand: The statements $STATIC, and $DYNAMIC are called metacommands. Metacommands instruct the interpreter to insert certain code into the program or to treat certain QBasic statements in a particular way. Because metacommands are not executed, they are preceded by the reserved word REM (or an apostrophe). For instance, the statement REM $STATIC or '$STATIC tells the interpreter to store arrays in a special way.

17. Static versus dynamic: QBasic uses two methods of storing arrays, dynamic and static. The memory locations for a static array are set aside at compile time and this portion of memory may not be freed for any other purpose. The memory locations for a dynamic array are assigned at run-time and can be freed for other purposes. Although dynamic arrays are more flexible, static arrays can be accessed faster. QBasic uses the dynamic allocation of arrays if either the range in a DIM statement is specified by a variable or the programmer insists on dynamic allocation with a $DYNAMIC metacommand.

How To

Invoke and Exit QBasic

A. Invoke QBasic on a computer that requires a floppy boot diskette (that is, has no hard disk drive).

1. Place a DOS boot diskette into the A diskette drive.
2. Turn on the computer and monitor and wait for the DOS prompt to be displayed. (If prompted for the date and time, respond appropriately.)
3. Remove the DOS boot diskette from the A drive and replace it with the diskette containing QBASIC.EXE.
4. Type QBASIC and press the <Enter> key.
5. When the screen querying about the Survival Guide appears, replace the diskette in the A drive with the diskette containing QBASIC.HLP.

B. Invoke QBasic from diskettes on a computer that boots from a hard disk.

1. Turn on the computer and monitor and wait for the DOS prompt to be displayed. (If prompted for the date and time, respond appropriately.)

2. Place the diskette containing QBASIC.EXE into the A diskette drive.

3. Make the A drive the current drive by typing A: and pressing the <Enter> key.

4. Type QBASIC and press the <Enter> key.

5. When the screen querying about the Survival Guide appears, replace the diskette in the A drive with the diskette containing QBASIC.HLP.

C. Invoke QBasic after installation onto a hard disk.

1. Turn on the computer and monitor, and wait for the DOS prompt to be displayed. (If prompted for the date and time, respond appropriately.)

2. Type CD \DOS and press the <Enter> key.

3. Type QBASIC and press the <Enter> key.

D. Allow graphics when the monitor is a monochrome display that is attached to a Hercules card.

1. Before invoking QBasic, run MSHERC.COM from DOS.

NOTE The statement SCREEN 3 must appear in any program prior to the use of graphics statements.

E. Allow the use of a mouse.

1. Before invoking QBasic, run MOUSE.COM from DOS.

F. Exit QBasic.

1. Press the <Esc> key.

2. Press <Alt/F/X>.

3. If the program in the View window has not been saved, QBasic will prompt you about saving it.

NOTE In many situations, step 1 is not needed.

Manage Programs

    A. Run a program from QBasic.

        1. Press <Alt/R/S>.

        Or,

        1. Press <Shift+F5>. (Normally, <F5> alone will run the program. However, if the program has been stopped before its end, <F5> continues execution from the stopping point, whereas <Shift+F5> executes the program from the beginning.)

    B. Save the current program on a disk.

        1. Press <Alt/F/S> or <Alt/F/A>.

        2. Type the name of the program, if requested, and press the <Enter> key.

NOTE   After a program has been saved once, updated versions can be saved under the same name by pressing <Alt/F/S>. <Alt/F/A> is used to save the program under a new name.

    C. Begin a new program in the View window.

        1. Press <Alt/F/N>.

        2. If an unsaved program is in the View window, QBasic will prompt you about saving it.

    D. Open a program stored on a disk.

        1. Press <Alt/F/O>.

        2. Type a filespec into the top rectangle of the dialog box and press the <Enter> key. Alternately, press the <Tab> key to penetrate the region containing the names of the files on the disk, and then use the cursor-moving keys and the <Enter> key to select one of the listed files.

        3. If the program in the View window has not been saved, QBasic will prompt you about saving it.

E. Name a program.

1. Save it with <Alt/F/A>.

Use the Editor

A. Determine the row and column position of the cursor.

1. Look at the pair of numbers at the bottom right of the screen separated by a colon on the status bar.
2. The first number gives the row, and the second number gives the column.

B. Mark a section of text as a block.

1. Move the cursor to the beginning or end of the block.
2. Hold down a <Shift> key and use the direction keys to highlight a block of text.
3. To unblock text, release the <Shift> key and press a cursor key.

C. Delete a line of a program.

1. Move the cursor to the line.
2. Press <Ctrl+Y>.

Or,

1. Mark the line as a block. (See item B of this section.)
2. Press <Shift+Del>.

NOTE In the maneuvers above, the line is placed in the clipboard and can be retrieved by pressing <Shift+Ins>. To delete the line without placing it in the clipboard, mark it as a block and press <Del>.

D. Move a line within the View window.

1. Move the cursor to the line and press <Ctrl+Y>.
2. Move the cursor to the target location.
3. Press <Shift+Ins>.

E. Use the clipboard to move or duplicate statements.

    1. Place the cursor on the first character of the statement (or group of statements).

    2. Hold down a <Shift key> and move the cursor to the right (and/or down) to highlight the selected block of text.

    3. Press <Shift+Del> to delete the block and place it into the clipboard. Or, press <Ctrl+Del> to place a copy of the block into the clipboard.

    4. Move the cursor to the location where you desire to place the block.

    5. Press <Shift+Ins> to place a copy of the text in the clipboard at the cursor.

F. Search for specific text in program.

    1. Press <Alt/S/F>.

    2. Type sought-after text into rectangle.

    3. Select desired options if different from the defaults.

    4. Press the <Enter> key.

    5. To repeat the search, press <F3>.

G. Search and change.

    1. Press <Alt/S/C>.

    2. Type sought-after text into first rectangle.

    3. Press <Tab>.

    4. Type replacement text into second rectangle.

    5. Select desired options if different from the defaults.

    6. Press the <Enter> key.

H. Change from "Syntax Checking On" to "Syntax Checking Off" or vice versa.

    1. Press <Alt/O>.

    2. "Syntax checking" is preceded by a dot if the feature is active. Press <S> if you want to change the selection or press the <Esc> key to exit.

I.   Check the syntax of a line (assuming "Syntax checking" is enabled).

   1.   Move the cursor to the line.

   2.   Edit the line in some way. For example, type = and then press <Back-space>.

   3.   Press the <Down Arrow> key.

NOTE   The syntax of a line is automatically checked whenever the cursor is moved off an edited line, either by pressing the <Enter> key or a cursor moving key.

J.   Cancel changes made to a line.

   1.   Do not move the cursor from the line.

   2.   Press <Ctrl+Q/L> to restore line to the form it had when the cursor was last moved from the line.

Get Help

A.   View the syntax and purpose of a QBasic keyword.

   1.   Type the word into the View window.

   2.   Place the cursor on, or just following, the keyword.

   3.   Press <F1>.

   Or,

   1.   Press <Alt/H/I/[first letter of keyword]>.

   2.   Use the direction keys to highlight the keyword.

   3.   Press the <Enter> key.

B.   Display an ASCII table.

   1.   Press <Alt/H/C>.

   2.   Press <Tab> to move the cursor to "ASCII Characters" and press the <Enter> key.

   3.   Use <PgDn> and <PgUp> to move between the extended and standard ASCII character sets.

C. Obtain a list of common editing and debugging commands.

    1. Press <Alt/H/C/S/Enter>.

D. Obtain other useful reference information.

    1. Press <Alt/H/C>.

    2. Use <Tab> and <Shift+Tab> to highlight a topic.

    3. Press the <Enter> key.

E. Obtain general information about using the help menu.

    1. Press <Shift+F1>.

F. Obtain information about the selections in a pull-down menu.

    1. See item D in *Manage Menus.*

G. Obtain a list of QBasic's reserved words.

    1. Press <Alt/H/I> and use the <Down Arrow> key to scroll through the list.

NOTE   To obtain information about a word, move the cursor to the word and press the <Enter> key.

Manipulate a Dialog Box

A. Use a dialog box.

A dialog box contains three types of items: rectangles, option lists, and command buttons. An option list is a sequence of option buttons of the form ( ) option or [ ] option, and a command button has the form < command >.

    1. Move from item to item with the <Tab> key. (The movement is from left to right and top to bottom. Use <Shift+Tab> instead of <Tab> to reverse the direction.)

    2. Inside a rectangle, either type in the requested information or use the direction keys to make a selection.

3. In an option list, an option button of the form ( ) option can be activated with the direction keys. A dot inside the parentheses indicates that the option has been activated.

4. In an option list, an option button of the form [ ] option can be activated or deactivated by pressing the space bar. An X inside the brackets indicates that the option has been activated.

5. A highlighted command button is invoked by pressing the <Enter> key.

B. Cancel a dialog box.

1. Press the <Esc> key.

Or,

1. Press the <Tab> key until the command button < Cancel > is highlighted and then press the <Enter> key.

Manage Menus

A. Close a pull-down menu.

1. Press the <Esc> key.

B. Open a pull-down menu.

1. Press <Alt>.
2. Press the first letter of the name of the menu. Alternately, press the <Down Arrow> key, use the direction keys to move the highlighted cursor bar to the menu name, and press the <Enter> key.

C. Make a selection from a pull-down menu.

1. Open the pull-down menu. One letter in each item that is eligible to be used will be emphasized by being highlighted or having a different color than the other letters.
2. Press the emphasized letter. Alternately, use the <Down Arrow> key to move the cursor bar to the desired item and then press the <Enter> key.

D. Obtain information about the selections in a pull-down menu.

1. Open the pull-down menu.

2. Use the <Down Arrow> key to move the highlighted cursor bar to the desired item.

3. The status bar at the bottom of the screen will give a brief description of the item.

4. Pressing <F1> gives additional information.

E. Look at all the menus in the menu bar.

1. Press <Alt/F>.

2. Press the <Right Arrow> key each time you want to see a new menu.

Manage Procedures

A. Look at an existing procedure.

1. Press <Shift+F2> repeatedly to cycle through all the procedures.

Or,

1. Press <F2>. The top entry is the main body of the program and the remaining entries are procedures.

2. Use the direction keys and the <Enter> key to select the desired procedure.

B. Create a procedure.

1. Move to a blank line.

2. Type SUB (for a subprogram) or FUNCTION (for a function) followed by the name of the procedure and any parameters.

3. Press the <Enter> key. (A new window will appear containing the procedure heading and an END statement.)

4. Type the procedure into the new window.

Or,

1. Press <Alt/E/S> (for a subprogram) or< Alt/E/F> (for a function). (A dialog box will appear.)
2. Type the name of the procedure and any parameters into the Name rectangle.
3. Press the <Enter> key. (A new window will appear containing the procedure heading and an END statement.)
4. Type the procedure into the new window.

NOTE To return to the main body of the program, press <F2/Enter>.

C. Alter a procedure.

1. Press <Shift+F2> until the desired procedure is displayed.
2. Make changes as needed.

Or,

1. Press <F2>.
2. Move the cursor bar to the desired procedure.
3. Press the <Enter> key.

D. Remove a procedure.

1. Press <F2>.
2. Move the cursor bar to the desired procedure.
3. Press <Tab/D/Enter>.

E. Insert an existing procedure into a program.

1. Open the program containing the procedure and press <Shift+F2> until the procedure appears on the screen.
2. Mark the procedure as a block. That is, move the cursor to the first statement of the procedure, hold down a <Shift> key, and move the cursor to the last statement of the procedure.
3. Press <Ctrl+Ins> to place the procedure into the clipboard.
4. Open the program in which the procedure is to be inserted.

5. Move the cursor to a blank line.

6. Press <Shift+In>s to place the contents of the clipboard into the program.

Manage Windows

A. Change the active window, that is, the window which contains the cursor and has its title highlighted.

    1. Press <F6> until desired window becomes active.

B. Split a screen to obtain multiple View windows.

Option 1: Both parts will contain same text.

    1. Press <Alt/V/P>.

Option 2: Second part will contain any procedure.

    1. Press <Alt/V/P>.
    2. Press <F6>.
    3. Press <F2>.
    4. Move cursor bar to desired procedure.
    5. Press <Enter>.

C. Unsplit a screen.

    1. Use <F6> to select window to be retained.
    2. Press <Alt/V/P>.

D. Zoom the active window to fill the entire screen.

    1. Press <Ctrl+F10>.
    2. To return window to original size, press <Ctrl+F10> again.

E. Make a small change in the size of the active window.

    1. Press <Alt+Plus> to enlarge by one line.
    2. Press <Alt+Minus> to contract by one line.

Alter the Appearance of the View Window

A. Remove the scroll bars from or add them to the View window. (The scroll bars are needed when a mouse is used.)

   1. Press <Alt/O/D/Tab/Tab/Tab>.
   2. The space bar can be pressed to alternate between having and not having an X at the cursor. The presence of an X produces scroll bars.
   3. Press the <Enter> key.

B. Change certain colors used by QBasic.

   1. Press <Alt/O/D>.
   2. Press <Tab> or <Shift+Tab> to move around the dialog box.
   3. Use the direction keys to make a selection within each region of the dialog box.
   4. To change a toggled selection, such as "Scroll bars," press the space bar.
   5. When all selections have been made, press the <Enter> key.

NOTE   When QBasic is exited, these selections will be saved in a file named QB.INI. If this file is present on the same disk and directory as QBASIC.EXE when QBasic is next invoked, it will determine QBasic's display settings.

C. Invoke QBasic in black & white.

   1. Type QBASIC /B and press the <Enter> key when invoking QBasic from DOS.

D. Invoke QBasic with the maximum number of lines supported by the adapter.

   1. Type QBASIC /H and press the <Enter> key when invoking QBasic from DOS.

Use the Printer

A. Obtain a printout of a program.

1. Press <Alt/F/P>.
2. Press the <Enter> key.

NOTE To print just the text selected as a block or the active (current) window, use the direction keys to select the desired option.

B. Obtain a printout of a text Output window.

1. Press <F4> to switch to the Output window if necessary.
2. Press <Shift+PrtSc>.

TIP After the program terminates, the phrase "Press any key to continue" can be removed by pressing <F4> twice.

C. Obtain a printout of a graphics Output window.

1. With DOS Versions 3.0 or later, run the DOS memory-resident program GRAPHICS.COM before invoking QBasic. Then, proceed as in item B above. The adapter cards and printers supported by GRAPHICS.COM are limited. All versions of DOS support the CGA adapter and dot-matrix printers.

NOTE Alternately, this task can be accomplished by adding special code to the program that reads each memory location of the adapter card and sends this information to the printer opened as a binary file. This method requires patience and detailed knowledge of the specific adapter card and printer.

Use the Debugger

A. Stop a program at a specified line.

1. Place the cursor at the beginning of the desired line.
2. Press <F9>. (This highlighted line is called a *breakpoint*. When the program is run it will stop at the breakpoint before executing the statement.)

NOTE   To remove this breakpoint, repeat steps 1 and 2.

B. Remove all breakpoints.

1. Press <Alt/D/C>.

C. Run a program with each statement highlighted as it is executed.

1. Press <Alt/D>.
2. If the "Trace On" selection is preceded by a mark, press <F5>. Otherwise, press <T/F5>.

NOTE   To turn off tracing, press <Alt/D/T>.

D. Run a program one statement at a time.

1. Press <F8>. The first executable statement will be highlighted.
2. Press <F8> each time you want to execute the currently highlighted statement.

NOTE   At any time you can view the Output screen by pressing <F4>.

E. Run the program one statement at a time, but execute each procedure call without stepping through the statements in the procedure one at a time.

1. Press <F10>. The first executable statement will be highlighted.
2. Press <F10> each time you want to execute the currently highlighted statement.

NOTE At any time you can view the Output screen by pressing <F4>.

F. Continue execution of a program that has been suspended.

   1. Press <F5>.

NOTE Each time a change is made in a suspended program that prevents the program from continuing, QBasic displays a dialog box with two options to choose from: Continue without the change, or restart the program from the beginning.

G. Execute a program up to the line containing the cursor.

   1. Press <F7>.

H. Have further stepping begin from the top of the program with all variables cleared.

   1. Press <Alt/R/R>.

I. Have further stepping begin at the line containing the cursor (no variables are cleared).

   1. Press <Alt/D/N>.

J. Execute a statement from the immediate window.

   1. Press <F6> to move the cursor to the immediate window.
   2. Type the statement into the immediate window.
   3. Press the <Enter> key with the cursor on the statement.

Using a Mouse

Preliminaries

To use a mouse with QBasic, the program MOUSE.COM must be executed to load the mouse driver. After executing it, the message "Mouse is enabled" will appear. In addition, a compatible mouse must be properly installed. The specifics of the mouse and mouse driver may vary. Consult the documentation included with your mouse for details.

If the mouse driver is loaded, the mouse is installed properly, and QBasic is invoked, then a small rectangle should appear near the middle of the screen. This is the mouse cursor and its position on the screen should correspond to the motion of the mouse on the desktop. The mouse cursor is usually referred to simply as "the mouse." No confusion should result since the actual mouse and the mouse cursor on the screen move together.

If the mouse is visible, move it to a menu option and press the left button. Pressing the button in this way is called "clicking on the option." The menu should pull-down and its options should appear. These in turn can be selected by moving the mouse to click on the desired option. To remove a pull-down menu, move the mouse cursor to a blank area of the screen and click on nothing.

If the mouse is not visible when QBasic is first invoked, then it possibly is the same color as the screen background. Try moving the mouse around the screen. If the mouse becomes visible in nonbackground regions of the screen, move the mouse to the Options menu, click the (left) button to get a pull-down menu, and then click the (left) button on display. Select a background region that makes the mouse visible by pressing the down cursor and up cursor keys to change the color selection until the mouse becomes visible in the background region.

Another way to select an item is by "dragging." Dragging refers to holding down the mouse button while moving the cursor. Dragging can be used with menus to produce a highlight in the menu rather than a mouse cursor. A menu option is selected by dragging until the option is highlighted and then releasing the button.

Using the Mouse

Refer to Figure I-1.

Select a Menu Item

Click on the menu name, and then click on the desired item in the pull-down menu that appears. Or, move to the menu name and drag downward until the selection bar reaches the item of choice. Then release the button to select the item.

Cancel a Selected Menu

Click anywhere outside the menu.

Select an Action from the Reference Bar

Click on the action name. For example, to run the program in the Edit window, click on <F5-Run>.

Size a Window

Move the mouse to the title bar, and then drag the phantom window to the desired size.

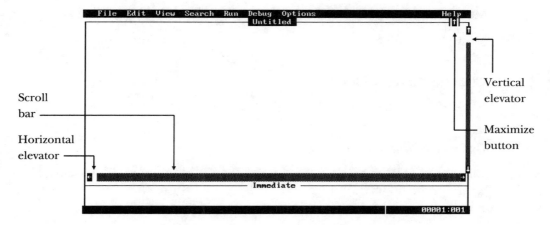

Figure I-1. Buttons used with a mouse

Open an Existing File

Click on File and then on Open in the pull-down menu. In the resulting dialog box, click once on the desired file name, and once on OK. Or, double-click on the file name; that is, click twice in rapid succession.

Select an Edit Block

Move the mouse to one end of the block and then drag to the other end of the block.

Scroll Vertically

Move the mouse to the vertical elevator and then drag the mouse in the appropriate direction. Or, move the mouse to the appropriate arrow at the end of the scroll bar at the right of the screen and then hold down the button.

Scroll Horizontally (Pan)

Move the mouse to the horizontal elevator and then drag the mouse in the appropriate direction. Or, move the mouse to the appropriate arrow at the end of the scroll bar at the bottom of the screen and then hold down the button.

Move Text Cursor in Edit Window

Move the mouse to where you want the text cursor and then click.

Change Active Windows

Click in any visible part of the window to be activated.

Fill Screen with Current Window

Click once in the maximize (upper right-hand) button. Or, double-click anywhere in the title bar.

Return Current Window to Normal Size

Click once in the maximize (upper right-hand) button. Or, double-click anywhere in the title bar.

Index

QBasic Programming
Disk Offer

A companion disk is available for this book. This diskette contains all of the programs in the book plus 15 bonus utilities, including the time-saving BASTOQB.EXE utility, which converts a GW-BASIC or BASICA program to a correct and efficient QBasic program. This utility finds all statements not supported by QBasic and, if possible, replaces them with the equivalent QBasic statements.

The other utilites are source code procedures (each procedure is fully documented):

BANNER.BAS	Create a banner on a dot-matrix printer
BLOAD.BAS	Restore the contents of the screen saved with BSAVE.BAS
BSAVE.BAS	Save the contents of the screen (any monitor or mode) on disk
CALENDAR.BAS	Pop-up calendar for text mode
DBD.BAS	Actual number of days between two dates
DBD360.BAS	The number of days between two dates with the 30/360 method
DEPREC.BAS	Straight-line, sum-of-the-digits, or double-declining depreciation
GETFILES.BAS	Create ordered arrays holding the names, dates, and times of files in a directory
GR2DOT.BAS	Graphics mode screen dump to dot-matrix printer
GR2HP.BAS	Graphics mode screen dump to HP LaserJet printer
HARDWARE.BAS	Report the hardware configuration of the computer
INTERNAL.BAS	Internal rate of return for a sequence of payments
KEYCTRL.BAS	Set and read the status of <Caps Lock>, <Num Lock>, and <Scroll Lock> keys
MENU.BAS	Pop-up menu generator

To order your diskette, send your name, address, and diskette size (5 1/4" or 3 1/2"), along with a check or money order for $20.00 (MD residents add 5% sales tax), to:

David's Utilities
P.O. Box 728
College Park, MD 20740

Make check payable to *David's Utilities*.